The Constitutional Presidency

THE JOHNS HOPKINS SERIES IN CONSTITUTIONAL THOUGHT

Sanford Levinson and Jeffrey K. Tulis, *Series Editors*

The Constitutional Presidency

Edited by
JOSEPH M. BESSETTE
JEFFREY K. TULIS

The Johns Hopkins University Press
Baltimore

© 2009 The Johns Hopkins University Press
All rights reserved. Published 2009
Printed in the United States of America on acid-free paper
9 8 7 6 5 4 3 2 1

The Johns Hopkins University Press
2715 North Charles Street
Baltimore, Maryland 21218-4363
www.press.jhu.edu

Library of Congress Cataloging-in-Publication Data

The constitutional presidency / edited by Joseph M. Bessette, Jeffrey K. Tulis.
    p. cm. — (The Johns Hopkins series in constitutional thought)
  Includes bibliographical references and index.
  ISBN-13: 978-0-8018-9295-0 (hardcover : alk. paper)
  ISBN-10: 0-8018-9295-3 (hardcover : alk. paper)
  ISBN-13: 978-0-8018-9296-7 (pbk. : alk. paper)
  ISBN-10: 0-8018-9296-1 (pbk. : alk. paper)
  1. Presidents—United States. 2. Executive power—United States. I. Bessette,
Joseph M. II. Tulis, Jeffrey.
  JK516.C58 2009
  352.230973–dc22   2008043994

A catalog record for this book is available from the British Library.

*Special discounts are available for bulk purchases of this book. For more information,
please contact Special Sales at 410-516-6936 or specialsales@press.jhu.edu.*

The Johns Hopkins University Press uses environmentally friendly book materials,
including recycled text paper that is composed of at least 30 percent post-consumer
waste, whenever possible. All of our book papers are acid-free, and our Jackets and
covers are printed on paper with recycled content.

CONTENTS

When George W. Bush left office in January 2009, he became only the sixth president in a century, and the thirteenth in the history of the Republic, to serve two full terms. Of the dozens of important political leaders who have shaped the fate of the nation, only a rare few have had the opportunity afforded by eight years in our highest office. In the last year of his administration, President Bush's approval ratings were among the lowest for any president since Harry S Truman, who still holds the record for lowest approval since Gallup began asking the question in the late 1930s. It will be some years before we can fully and fairly assess Bush's political legacy, including the successes and failures of his policy choices. Will he go down as a failed president; or will his stature, like Truman's, grow as the years pass? One thing is clear now: Bush's actions generated a robust and wide-ranging debate about the place of the presidency in the constitutional order.

Constitutional controversy began even before Bush took office, when the election of 2000 produced the most serious legal dispute regarding presidential selection since the nineteenth century. Once in office, the new president embraced a theory of the "unitary executive," used signing statements as instruments to amend legislation through partial enforcement, and adopted vigorous policies to fight a "war on terror." These actions dramatically exposed fundamental tensions between an energetic executive and the constraints of law and legislative accountability. Consequently, the place of the presidency in our constitutional order is again a central issue in American politics.

This debate resembles the intellectual and political ferment caused by the Vietnam War and the Watergate scandal, which culminated just over three decades ago. Around the time of this earlier debate, as we noted in our previous book, *The Presidency in the Constitutional Order*, there were two intellectual communities that had little to say to one another. There were legalists (mainly law professors) who attended to questions of textual meaning and Supreme Court doctrine and political scientists who studied the nature of presidential behavior and the forces that shaped it.

We urged that scholars and citizens concerned about the presidency in the constitutional order recover, renew, and reinvent an older, more capacious kind of political science—one that combined the legalist's concern for constitutional standards with the political scientist's interest in the sources, causes, and consequences of presidential behavior.

Our earlier book brought together scholars who shared this aspiration and who, like us, wished to encourage a broader constitutional scholarship on the American presidency. We were gratified at its reception within the discipline and by the subsequent flourishing of public law studies of executive power within political science. Given the renewed interest in the theme of our earlier book, we were asked to consider a second edition. We decided that so much had changed since 1981, both in the American constitutional order and in scholarship on the presidency, that we could not simply revise or update the book. A whole new volume was needed to take account of changes in American politics and in political science.

To underline the originality of the present book, we changed the title. *The Constitutional Presidency* offers entirely new and original research, except for the opening chapter by us, which is substantially revised from our earlier book. Although this new volume offers the same general approach as our 1981 book, it is distinct in two important ways. Our earlier book, written toward the end of the Jimmy Carter administration, when the president's place in the constitutional order was diminished due to a Watergate and Vietnam "syndrome," made a constitutional case for a strong presidency. It was also composed to honor the work of Herbert J. Storing, who had recently and unexpectedly died. The contributors were all students or colleagues who shared and embraced Storing's distinctive approach to the study of American politics as well as his conclusion that the Constitution established a very energetic executive. By contrast, the present book, written in the midst of a controversial war, offers a greater range of views on the constitutional propriety of a strong presidency. In addition to those who carry on Storing's perspective, we have included a number of distinguished scholars who share our original aspiration to develop a distinctly political (and not merely legalistic) understanding of the constitutional presidency but who have developed theories that differ from Storing's in important ways.

Like our earlier effort, this book is not a textbook, although we expect that it will be just as useful in courses. Like the first book, this one seeks to gather the best new scholarship on important constitutional topics produced by scholars who have genuinely new and significant things to say that cannot be found elsewhere. Although prompted by the controversies of the day, our topics are not limited to issues that arose in the Bush administration; nor do we include chapters on every current constitutional issue. Represented here is important work on the most significant issues regarding the place of the presidency in the constitutional order that have emerged over the last quarter century. We have also included new scholarship on some of the enduring issues that we treated in our earlier book. All of the chapters examine the presidency from the vantage point of the political system as a whole and probe the principles that animate the American constitutional order.

In our introductory chapter, we identify the predominant approaches to the study of the presidency. Illustrating how the gap between the "legal" and "political" modes of analysis can be bridged, we suggest that constitutional analysis may be indispensable to an adequate description of political behavior while also serving as the source of standards for evaluating presidential conduct. In the second chapter, Joseph M. Bessette and Gary J. Schmitt offer a theory of the structure and meaning of Article II, the section of the Constitution that establishes the presidency. By comparing the clauses of this article with executive articles in the states under the Articles of Confederation, Bessette and Schmitt uncover a constitutional architecture of powers and duties missed by previous commentators.

Schmitt follows with a chapter that offers an interpretation of the president's foreign affairs powers based on a new look of the famous debate in 1793 between Alexander Hamilton and James Madison (also known as the Pacificus-Helvidius debate) over President George Washington's Proclamation of Neutrality and of the relationship of the constitutional arguments to the politics that produced the proclamation and that resulted from it. Schmitt is the first to connect the legal arguments with the politics surrounding American neutrality in the European war and to show the relevance to present circumstances.

It has long been a commonplace understanding that Theodore Roosevelt and William Howard Taft embraced contrasting understandings of presidential power, with Roosevelt favoring a strong presidency and Taft a more restrained one bound tightly to the law. In his chapter, Lance Robinson shows how Taft's view supports a more robust presidency than had previously been noticed, while Roosevelt's view, ostensibly Hamiltonian, dangerously severs presidential power from its constitutional sources.

Turning to contemporary controversies, David K. Nichols shows how the disputed presidential election in 2000, which resulted in the Supreme Court case *Bush v. Gore*, reveals much more than partisan conflict. Nichols details the deeper constitutional principles at issue in *Bush v. Gore*, including federalism, the rule of law versus personal discretion, Judicial deference to political institutions, and, finally, the republican and democratic foundations of American constitutionalism. *Bush v. Gore* offers students of the presidency a fascinating window on the constitutional architecture of presidential selection.

We next turn to Richard M. Pious's assessment of the arguments advanced on behalf of military tribunals in light of his well-known theory of presidential prerogatives. In his chapter, Pious shows how the legitimacy of prerogative powers depends on how Congress and the Court respond to them. He distinguishes between uses of power that produce "frontlash" effects, whereby the president succeeds by dividing his institutional opponents; "backlash" effects, whereby the president succeeds but at a very high political cost; and "overshoot" effects, whereby presidents are brought down by investigation.

In our previous book, we stressed that the formal Constitution was more important in shaping presidential behavior than political scientists generally realized. In his chapter that demonstrates this, Kenneth R. Mayer synthesizes a large body of research on executive orders produced over the past twenty years. Mayer shows how important, effective, and significant the president's use of unilateral power is, despite Richard Neustadt's influential argument to the contrary.

Jasmine Farrier diagnoses the puzzle that since World War II, Congress has alternated between delegating and expanding its budget-making authority, while the executive branch has consistently advanced its institutional ambition to control this process. The result is a messy hybrid that is not easily rationalized in constitutional terms. Despite the idea that budget-making lies at the very heart of the legislative function, Farrier shows how the president's structural advantages in the constitutional order complicate the systemic picture.

President George W. Bush and Vice President Richard B. Cheney's repeated conflicts with Congress over requests for documents and testimony has refocused attention and concern on executive privilege. David A. Crockett shows how the right to keep confidences and secrets in the executive branch is at once a vital constitutional power and in tension with legitimate and competing congressional responsibilities. He argues that these disputes are usually resolved, as they should be, through institutional conflict, not litigation.

Jeffrey K. Tulis offers a new theory of Congress's impeachment power. He shows how a robust political understanding of impeachment is required by the nature and structure of a separation of powers regime. Thus, the modern tendency to reduce impeachment to a legal process reveals a general pathology, characteristic of the whole constitutional order.

Finally, James W. Ceaser shows how constitutional thinking necessarily comprehends topics beyond those familiar to lawyers and courts, such as the meaning of leadership itself. Ceaser traces the meaning and origins of demagoguery and shows how the Constitution was constructed to contend with this problem. In his view, the Constitution has largely been successful in preventing the worst form of leadership from infecting the office of the president of the United States.

This volume was made possible through the support of Claremont McKenna College's Henry Salvatori Center for the Study of Individual Freedom in the Modern World. We thank its former director, Charles R.Kesler, and its current director, Mark Blitz, for their enthusiastic support and for providing the funds necessary to bring this project to completion. All of the authors in this volume attended one of two workshops on "The Presidency and the Constitution" held at Claremont McKenna College in April and May 2006 to discuss their drafts. All seemed to agree that these meetings helped to sharpen the arguments and to promote the coherence of the volume as a whole. We thank Elvia Huerta, administrative assistant of the Salvatori Center, for ably handling all the logistical arrangements necessary to make these workshops a success. We also thank Curt Nichols for composing the index with support from the Public Policy Institute in the Department of Government, University of Texas at Austin. The idea for this book was born thirty years ago at the White Burkett Miller Center for Public Affairs at the University of Virginia, and the initial articulation of that idea became the Miller Center's first university press book. We are very pleased that both the idea and the Miller Center have grown and prospered over the past three decades.

Portions of Chapter 1 originally appeared in Joseph M. Bessette and Jeffrey Tulis, *The Presidency in the Constitutional Order* (Louisiana State University Press, 1981). An earlier version of Chapter 3 by Gary J. Schmitt was published in the *Political Science Reviewer* 29 (2000). A shorter version of Chapter 11 by James W. Ceaser appeared in *Critical Review* 19 (Spring 2008). We gratefully acknowledge permission to incorporate material from these three essays.

Joseph M. Bessette, Claremont, California
Jeffrey K. Tulis, Austin, Texas

The Constitutional Presidency

CHAPTER ONE

On the Constitution, Politics, and the Presidency

JOSEPH M. BESSETTE *and* JEFFREY K. TULIS

S INCE THE EARLY Republic, Americans have debated, sometimes passionately, the place of the presidency in the American constitutional order. Alexander Hamilton and his followers looked to the presidency to bring the necessary power and energy to constitutional government, while Thomas Jefferson and his partisans feared that too much presidential power verged on monarchy and compromised the republican character of the regime. Hamiltonian and Jeffersonian views have competed for public legitimacy throughout American history in a cyclical pattern of ideological dominance. What is not so well known is that, in a muted and somewhat distorted form, these classic perspectives and this alternating pattern can also be seen in the history of scholarship on the presidency.

Although the nation's highest office has been a focus of political, journalistic, and intellectual fascination throughout American history, it was only in the middle part of the twentieth century that it became a specialized subject within the discipline of political science. Indeed, political science itself did not become a recognized discipline until the beginning of the twentieth century. By midcentury several now-classic writings set the terms of debate in political science, and in the world of letters more generally, on the topic of the place of the presidency in the constitutional order. For example, much of the impassioned political debate and growing scholarly literature on the alleged excesses of executive power under President George W. Bush is a manifestation of a mode of analysis that was given classic expression more than six decades ago in what was for many years the standard text on the presidency: Edward Corwin's *The President: Office and Powers.*

Corwin described his work as "primarily a study in American public law." Its central theme was "the development and contemporary status of presidential power and of the presidential office under the Constitution." The study began with an analysis of the executive office as established by the Constitutional Convention in 1787, went on to examine the legal and constitutional development of the office, and ended with a call for institutional reforms to check "a history of presidential aggrandizement." Not surprisingly, much of the study was an examination of the legal doctrines promulgated by the federal courts. In the last edition that appeared during his lifetime, Corwin cited more than 250 judicial decisions. The clear import of his analysis was that the modern presidency threatens to break free from constitutional restraints, that this poses a serious danger for American democracy, and that this calls for a regeneration of respect for constitutional norms. However beneficial presidential leadership might be in specific instances, Corwin suggested, an unfettered executive power is the antithesis of constitutionalism.[1]

Around the time that Corwin published his last edition (1957), his text was both substantively and methodologically at odds with far-reaching developments in scholarship on American politics.[2] One of these was the increasing extent to which political scientists were turning their attention away from formal rules and procedures to focus instead on actual political behavior, which, it was argued, was little influenced by laws and constitutions. In the field of presidential studies, this new orientation was given its most articulate and influential expression in Richard Neustadt's *Presidential Power: The Politics of Leadership*, which was first published in 1960. Neustadt's subject was the "power problem" faced by every president: "From the moment he is sworn the man confronts a personal problem: how to make those powers work for *him*. That problem is the subject of this book. My theme is personal power and its politics: what it is, how to get it, how to keep it, how to use it." Neustadt emphasized that the formal authorities vested by the Constitution were not the main determinants of effectual presidential power: *"The probabilities of power do not derive from the literary theory of the Constitution."* Rather, a president's power "is the product of his vantage points in government, together with his reputation in the Washington community and his prestige outside." According to Neustadt some of these "vantage points" derive from the formal authorities vested by the Constitution; thus "formal power" is indispensable to a president's "personal influence." Although Neustadt conceded this much, what was truly distinctive about his approach was how little it had to say about specific constitutional provisions. The whole thrust of his analysis was to move us away from formal authority in explaining actual presidential power; for distinctions of the sort employed in constitutional analysis seemed to him to have no effect on presidents: "The things [the president] personally has to do are no respecters of the lines between 'civil' and 'military,' or 'foreign' and 'domestic,' or 'legislative' and 'executive' or 'administrative' and 'political.' At his desk—and there alone—distinctions of these sorts lose their last shred of meaning."[3]

While Neustadt was rejecting the Constitution as the most important source for understanding the actual exercise of presidential power, other students of American politics were rejecting constitutional analysis for a related but distinct reason: because, in their view, the principles of separation of powers and checks and balances, which lay at the heart of the American constitutional order, made it virtually impossible for American institutions to generate the political leadership necessary to meet contemporary national needs. The foremost proponent of this view was James MacGregor Burns, whose *Deadlock on Democracy* appeared in 1963.

Reflecting a theme that dates back at least to the writings of Woodrow Wilson and the beginning of professional political science, Burns argued that the fear of arbitrary power and of majority tyranny so dominated the minds of the framers that they devised a political system that made any kind of effective political action extremely difficult, if not impossible, at least while constitutional forms were observed. To a large extent, "our system was designed for deadlock and inaction."[4]

For Burns and a host of other political scientists, the way to get around the inherent limitations of the American constitutional system was twofold: to reform the American two-party system in the direction of more programmatic and more highly structured nationally based organizations and to strengthen the institution of the presidency at the head of the majority party. Consequently, these political scientists recommended a variety of political reforms, some simply requiring voluntary changes on minor matters, some requiring new legislation at the state or national levels, and some mandating amendments to the Constitution. In the last category were proposals for a four-year term for members of the House of Representatives (and perhaps also for senators) synchronized with the presidential term, reform of the electoral college in favor of a more direct popular election, and a reduction in the numbers of senators necessary to ratify a treaty from two-thirds to a simple majority. Those who advanced these and similar reforms implicitly rejected several principles of the American constitutional order as the proper standard for guiding politics in the middle of the twentieth century.[5]

As a result of the developments reflected in the works of Neustadt, Burns, and others, by the middle of the 1960s the constitutional, or public law, approach was well out of the mainstream of presidential studies. This began to change when Vietnam, Watergate, and other perceived abuses of presidential power led some scholars to reject the predominant political approaches to the study of the presidency because of their apparent lack of standards to limit presidential conduct and their implicit encouragement of executive branch aggrandizement. One result of this reaction was the resurgence of the public law approach in a variety of studies that attempted to judge presidential action against the traditional standard of constitutionality.[6] In varying degrees the authors of these studies turned to the document written in 1787, to the original intentions of its framers, and to the development of constitutional doctrine throughout American history for a set of standards against which to judge presidential actions and on the basis of which to curb future abuses.

Although these studies are still valuable in reminding us that executive power unconstrained by law is a danger to republican government, they suffered from the same kinds of limitations that characterized the earlier constitutional approach to the study of American politics. First, they were of little help in explaining why political leaders behave the way they do: the connection between constitutional forms and political practice was largely undeveloped. Second, they were particularly weak at demonstrating why the constitutional standards that derive from the document drafted in 1787 should be embraced as a guide for contemporary politics.

It should be noted that most of the contributors to the Watergate-era public law studies were law professors rather than political scientists.[7] This is one reason why these studies were not centrally concerned with explaining political behavior. Moreover, a mode of analysis that focuses on questions of legality cannot in itself determine whether greater political benefits will derive from strict adherence to the existing fundamental law or perhaps from its alteration or even rejection. In the post-

Watergate period legalists forcefully argued that our national well-being would be enhanced if we reinvigorated the principles of the American Constitution. Such prescriptions, however, were derived not from legal analysis per se but from political reasoning and political judgment.

Political scientists also contributed to the post-Watergate reconsideration of presidential power. Several works appeared that, like the public law studies, were highly critical of the earlier "textbooks" on the presidency for emphasizing political effectiveness over public responsibility.[8] They differed from these earlier political studies not so much in method or approach as in their call for a more accountable or democratic presidency. As with the constitutional studies at the time, the purpose of these texts was to establish a set of principles or guidelines that would bring executive power under control. These principles, however, were not sought primarily through a reconsideration of the American constitutional design but largely from political assessments of the performance of the Kennedy, Johnson, and Nixon administrations.

As a result, by the late 1970s the constitutional and political approaches were effectively divorced. The legalists seemed unable or unwilling to show how constitutional interpretation was relevant to understanding and guiding contemporary political behavior. The political scientists seemed susceptible to the charge that the emancipation of presidential studies from a concern with legal and constitutional restraints had implicitly encouraged the abuses of executive power they had recently witnessed and that the newly devised standards for restraining presidents had an unsatisfactory ad hoc quality to them that could not match the long-term effectiveness of constitutional safeguards.

Over the last quarter of the twentieth century, presidential scholars have produced a series of increasingly sophisticated books that have brought constitutional analysis back into the mainstream of political science. In the public law tradition, Louis Fisher's prodigious work resulted in a series of singular books that touched on every major separation of powers controversy. Fisher has shown how, over the course of American history, the articulation of constitutional meaning often resulted more from conflict between the president and Congress than from Supreme Court decisions.[9] He has argued that recent presidents of both parties have overstepped constitutional limitations and that Congress has abdicated many of its most basic constitutional responsibilities.[10]

Students of presidential strategy have also taken the Constitution more seriously than previously. Two communities of scholars have been particularly influential—both labeling themselves "institutionalists." One group, the "rational choice institutionalists," takes its theoretical orientation from economics and has explored the ways a president's interests are advantaged, as well as constrained, by institutional arrangements, especially constitutionally constructed arrangements.[11] William Howell, for example, shows how Neustadt greatly underestimated the president's ability to command because Neustadt misunderstood the significance of the president's structural place in the constitutional order.

The other community, "historical institutionalists," seeks to uncover patterns of presidential behavior over time, and has given explicit attention to the ways the Constitution structures or constrains those patterns. The best example of this kind of work, and perhaps the most influential book on the presidency since Neustadt's *Presidential Power*, is Stephen Skowronek's, *The Politics Presidents Make*.[12] Skowronek refutes Neustadt in three important ways. As we indicated above, Neustadt viewed the Constitution as largely irrelevant to the strategic concerns of modern presidents. Skowronek shows how the Constitution is of continuing relevance as an important and enduring structure. He also shows how nineteenth-century presidents faced the same central leadership problems as do modern presidents; whereas Neustadt regarded modern (mid-twentieth century) circumstances as fundamentally different from those anticipated by the founders. Finally, Skowronek shows how presidents face different leadership challenges, indeed different conceptions of leadership itself, depending on where they fall in the life history of the partisan regime with which they are affiliated. Neustadt, by contrast, viewed the leadership task as essentially identical for all modern presidents.

Despite these important correctives of Neustadt, criticisms that resonate well with the perspective we articulate here, it is important to note that Skowronek (and indeed the "rational choice" institutionalists as well) continue to adopt the basic strategic and institutional perspective that Neustadt inaugurated. For both Neustadt and Skowronek, the polity is understood from the perspective of the presidency. Although Skowronek has complicated the picture of how presidents can be successful, he, like Neustadt, understands presidential success as equivalent to achieving the polity's goals.[13] Louis Fisher and others also understand the polity from a similar "institutionally partisan" perspective, except that for them Congress holds the privileged position rather than the presidency, almost as if ours were a parliamentary system in which the legislature is the first or "supreme" branch.[14]

A final category of presidential studies published over the past twenty-five years adopts a self-consciously systemic approach. Rather than view the polity from the perspective of the presidency (or Congress), these studies analyze the presidency in light of the multiple contending and at times conflicting principles of the polity as a whole. We contributed to this enterprise with the publication of the predecessor to our present book, *The Presidency in the Constitutional Order*, as well as with books on leadership in an altered constitutional order (*The Rhetorical Presidency*) and on the neglected role of deliberation in Congress and national politics more generally (*The Mild Voice of Reason*).[15] A superb example of this approach, and perhaps the most profound book in more recent times on the presidency and executive power more generally, is Harvey Mansfield's *Taming the Prince: The Ambivalence of Executive Power*, published in 1991. One of Mansfield's key insights was that executive power not only competes with other legitimate powers in a well-constituted political order but that it is also itself a combination of competing needs or principles, one pointing to subservience to a legislature and another to discretion and independence.

In general, all of these self-consciously "systemic" studies examine the ways in which forms and formalities influence the actual behavior of politicians and citizens and how these behaviors are both constrained and informed by a complex constitutional order composed of principles often in tension with one another. This chapter serves as a background and introduction to the studies of particular issues or controversies addressed in subsequent chapters of this book. Here we describe and defend the various ways in which political forms may influence practice and articulate the core problem of competing principles that lies at the heart of the American constitutional order.

The Constitution and Political Behavior

Despite the revived interest in constitutional politics in recent decades, conventional wisdom in political science and the legal academy remains skeptical of, if not simply hostile to, the idea that the Constitution really matters to the conduct of day-to-day political life. As one prominent law professor has written: "The historical Constitution remains an honored relic, preserved intact in the National Archives. It is a symbol of the nation, much like the flag. In a secular society such as the United States, it is a substitute for God. The ancient Document is worshipped, and vested with mystery and authority and seeming power that no parchment could ever have."[16]

Political scientists in particular tend not to attach much explanatory weight to the Constitution in their accounts of American politics—either because they believe that more than two centuries of social, economic, and technological change have rendered the original arrangements obsolete or because in their view constitutional forms never have much more than a tenuous relationship to practice. Nonetheless, most students of contemporary politics would at least concede that the Constitution establishes the parameters for political conflict or serves as the arena in which that conflict works itself out. In effect, the Constitution sets forth the "rules of the game" for the players in American politics—rules that are not comprehensive, unambiguous, or universally adhered to but on which there is such widespread consensus among the American people that their flagrant violation is not readily tolerated (at least outside of national emergency situations).

The Watergate controversy illustrates the point well. It is a constitutional rule that a president may be removed from office when a majority of the House of Representatives accuses him of, and two-thirds of the Senate convicts him of, "Treason, Bribery, or other high Crimes and Misdemeanors." This rule had lain dormant for a century, and serious constitutional scholars had come to judge it a dead letter. Yet Congress resuscitated the relevant twenty-one words of the founding document when circumstances seemed to call for it.

A mark of the force of the rule is that there was no serious issue whether Richard M. Nixon would peaceably step down after possible conviction by the Senate. This seems to have been assumed by all. And certainly this attachment to constitutional principle extended to the civilian and military employees of the executive branch, few of whom, it seems safe to speculate, would have taken orders from the "president" after a conviction vote by the Senate. There *was* some thought that Nixon would refuse to comply with an order of the U.S. Supreme Court to turn over incriminating tapes. Yet, even a constitutional rule not explicitly set forth in the document itself and that had been the subject of some controversy earlier in our history—namely, that the president must comply with the directives of the Supreme Court respecting the interpretation of his own powers—even this rule was so widely accepted during the Watergate period that many believed that Nixon's refusal to comply would itself have led to conviction and removal from office. Similarly, although President Bill Clinton did not come close to removal in his Senate trial in 1999, no one doubted that had two-thirds of the Senate voted to convict, the president would have voluntarily relinquished power and position.

Extraordinary times have a way of bringing constitutional issues to the fore; ordinary times are as much influenced by constitutional rules and procedures, but because that influence is regular and pervasive it is less noticed. For example, the constitutional mandate that members of the House must run for reelection every two years and senators every six years, that membership in the two branches be based on different principles of representation, that the Senate must consent to treaties and appointments, or that every bill passed by Congress must go to the president for a possible veto—these are all "rules of the game" that affect everyday politics. In a wide variety of ways, political actors are forced to accommodate their behavior to generally accepted constitutional requirements.

It often happens, however, that the constitutional status of a proposed action, especially one to be taken by the president, is ambiguous. May a president constitutionally refuse to spend all the money appropriated by Congress if massive budget deficits pose an inflationary threat? May he constitutionally refuse to fulfill a congressional request for information related to White House deliberations or sensitive national security matters? May he constitutionally employ the armed forces without statutory authorization to protect Americans overseas? In cases like these presidents are invariably led to defend their actions as consistent with the principles of the constitutional system. Scholars often dismiss these public explanations as mere rhetoric, attempts to give a cover of legitimacy to actions that emanate from political and policy judgments rather than constitutional analysis. What is often overlooked, however, is that the necessity to find some constitutional grounds for questionable political acts may itself influence the selection or character of the actions. The written document may mold political behavior by forcing presidents and members of Congress to give serious thought to the constitutional propriety of anticipated actions, even if they have no personal constitutional scruples per se.

Of course, political actors may in fact believe their constitutional rhetoric. We would not be surprised if a president, facing a possible constitutional confrontation with Congress, came genuinely to accept the arguments of attorneys in the White House and the Department of Justice articulating and defending presidential prerogatives. Nor would we be surprised if representatives and senators came to accept the logic of different arguments defending congressional rights in such a conflict. Here we see the joining of personal interest and constitutional principle. "The interest of the man," Madison wrote in *The Federalist*, "must be connected with the constitutional rights of the place."[17] Those who serve in the executive and legislative branches have a personal interest in defending the constitutional prerogatives of their institution. How else to understand, for example, Congress's determined efforts in the 1970s to recapture its proper constitutional role in the areas of war powers (War Powers Resolution of 1973) and spending (Congressional Budget and Impoundment Control Act of 1974). Indeed, the Constitution itself requires that all those who serve under it "shall be bound by Oath or Affirmation, to support this Constitution"; and it imposes on the president the special obligation "faithfully [to] execute the office of President of the United States, and . . . [to] preserve, protect and defend the Constitution of the United States." Although these injunctions alone are not sufficient to guarantee fidelity to the Constitution, they do reflect the framers' beliefs that (1) officeholders have an obligation to abide by the Constitution, (2) a solemn and public promise to do so can usefully reinforce that obligation, and (3) the success of American government depends on the firm attachment of officeholders to the principles of the fundamental law.

It is hard to overstate the extent to which the architects of the American constitutional order designed their institutions to mold behavior in beneficial directions. For example, one of the principal fears when the Constitution was drafted was that the nonlegislative institutions would lack the independence necessary to resist encroachments from the body of the people's representatives (a lesson learned from the state experience during the Confederation period). For the presidency the solution was to construct the office so that the occupant would have both the personal incentive and the means to stand up to Congress when the constitutional balance was threatened. This meant making the office institutionally independent of Congress (by a nonlegislative mode of election and a salary that could not be raised or lowered during the president's term), giving the president the means to block legislation that encroached on his office (qualified veto), and making the office weighty enough to generate personal efforts by its occupant to protect its constitutional status (four-year term, indefinite reeligibility, and significant powers).

The extraordinary success of this element of the original design has been largely overlooked; yet the historical record demonstrates that even the so-called weak presidents, presidents who were unwilling or unable to compete with Congress for the direction of national policy, have vigorously defended the prerogatives of the executive office when these were thought to be threatened by congressional action. Perhaps the most striking case was the adamant opposition of James Buchanan (usually regarded as among the weakest of the weak presidents and cited by Teddy Roosevelt as the ministerial or messenger-boy president par excellence) to what he took to be an improper investigation into the conduct of the executive branch by the House of Representatives in 1860: "Except in [cases of impeachment]," he protested to the House, "the Constitution has invested the House of Representatives with no power, no jurisdiction, no supremacy whatever over the President. In all other respects he is quite as independent of them as they are of him. As a coordinate branch of the Government he is their equal. . . . He will defend [the people] . . . to the last extremity against any unconstitutional attempt, come from what quarter it may, to abridge the constitutional rights of the Executive and render him subservient to any human power except themselves."[18] This hardly reflects the accepted historical assessment, derived from the first Roosevelt, that Buchanan held "the narrowly legalistic view that the President is the servant of Congress rather than of the people."[19]

This is not to say that presidents (or legislators) always fight hard to protect their constitutional prerogatives. President Ronald Reagan, for example, twice signed extensions of the Ethics in Government Act of 1978 even though he believed that its provisions insulating independent counsels from presidential control were unconstitutional. In signing the 1987 extension, he asserted that the law "raises constitutional issues of the most fundamental and enduring importance" by "divest[ing] the President of his fundamental constitutional authority to enforce our nation's laws." It violated the constitutional principle that those who exercise core executive functions "must be subject to executive branch appointment, review, and removal." Yet Reagan signed this arguably unconstitutional bill. He himself called this an "extraordinary step," given his "very strong doubts about its constitutionality." In so doing, Reagan made no mention of political pressures to sign the bill, especially strong in the wake of the Iran-Contra scandal that broke a year before. Rather, he noted that the constitutional issues were "now squarely before the United States Court of Appeals for the District of Columbia Circuit. . . . The courts are in the process of deciding these questions."[20] A year later in *Morrison v. Olson* the Supreme Court handed the administration a decisive defeat by upholding the independent counsel provisions by a 7–1 vote.

As this example shows, political pressures can sometimes overwhelm the natural tendency of elected officials to fight to protect the constitutional prerogatives of their office. This failure to defend "the constitutional rights of the place" is made more likely when everyone simply defers to the courts to determine constitutionality. It is a risky business, as Reagan learned in this case and Congress has in some executive privilege controversies, for elected officials to expect the courts to protect their prerogatives. Had Reagan vetoed the independent counsel statute on constitutional grounds and had his veto been upheld by Congress, his constitutional understanding would have prevailed, despite the fact that nearly the entire Supreme Court held a different view. In some cases the Court may not have the final say on what the Constitution means.

Earlier in our history, political leaders were less inclined to defer to the Court on large constitutional questions. Thomas Jefferson, Andrew Jackson, and Abraham Lincoln all shared the belief that presidents and legislators had an obligation to consider the constitutional dimensions of their actions, that they were not free simply to pass the buck to the Supreme Court. Jackson put the point clearly in his veto of the bill to recharter the Bank of the United States: "The Congress, the Executive, and the Court must each for itself be guided by its own opinion of the Constitution. Each public officer who takes an oath to support the Constitution swears that he will support it as he understands it, and not as it is understood by others. It is as much the duty of the House of Representatives, of the Senate, and of the President to decide upon the constitutionality of any bill or resolution which may be presented to them for passage or approval as it is of the supreme judges when it may be brought before them for judicial decision."[21] Although Jackson went further than Jefferson and Lincoln in suggesting that the president was not obligated to follow the Supreme Court's interpretation of the Constitution, all three agreed that the members of the political branches must engage in constitutional analysis.

Despite some important exceptions, on the whole both the "weak" and "strong" presidents have fought to protect the constitutional prerogatives of the office. Nonetheless, they differ unmistakably in their impact on public policy, a difference that is at least partly attributable to personal inclinations. Some presidents seem clearly to have conceded congressional supremacy in policy-making; others have spared little effort to move the country and Congress in the direction they have thought wise. American political history has been punctuated in an irregular way by presidents of the latter type. The emergence of such activist presidents appears more the result of accident or chance than the manifestation of systemic factors. Yet a reconsideration of the constitutional design indicates that two particular provisions play a large role in inclining presidents to exercise their powers in a positive way to promote their policy aims.

In *The Federalist* Alexander Hamilton identified these as the substantial, four-year, term of office and the opportunity a president has to succeed himself. Together these would give the president "the inclination and the resolution to act his part well" and would provide "the community time and leisure to observe the tendency of his measures and thence to form an experimental estimate of their merits." The prospect of reelection would encourage the president to undertake projects in the public interest and the four years between elections would ensure that he had "time enough . . . to make the community sensible of the propriety of the measures he might incline to pursue."

Further discussion in *The Federalist* shows that the reelection provision was also intended to encourage even those occupants of the executive office who might lack the wisdom and virtue of the ideal type to act in ways conducive to the public good. "An avaricious man," for example, "who might happen to fill the office" will want to do a creditable enough job to be reelected, even if only to continue to satisfy his avarice. Similarly, an "ambitious man . . . seated on the summit of his country's honors" will want to act in ways to merit reelection in order "to prolong his honors." At the peak of the hierarchy of passions is "the love of fame, the ruling passion of the noblest minds." The institution of the presidency accommodates even this passion by making it possible for the president "to plan and undertake extensive and arduous enterprises for the public benefit, requiring considerable time to mature and perfect." If these projects are successful, the president earns enduring fame from future generations.[22]

Of course, not all presidents have striven to promote "extensive and arduous [public] enterprises." If, as we have argued, the Constitution has a real molding effect on presidential behavior, how can we explain the obvious differences between a Buchanan and a Lincoln, the first Roosevelt and his successor Taft, or a Hoover and an FDR? One reason for these contrasts is suggested by the above quotations from *The Federalist*. The presidency is by constitutional arrangement such a highly personalized office that it will necessarily reflect the particular virtues (and vices), talents, passions, and goals of its occupant. Consequently, we would expect the functioning of the executive office throughout American history to manifest some of the variety in human types characteristic of those who have served in high political office in the United States. There will not, however, be a simple or direct relationship between personality and the exercise of presidential power. Once he assumes office, a new president will be subject to an independent set of influences rooted in the constitutional order. While these influences may have varying impacts on different presidents, for all they will shape the potentialities of executive power in American government. Before this can be more fully elucidated, we must examine in greater detail the nature of executive power under the United States Constitution.

Executive Power and American Constitutionalism

To many contemporary observers, the exercise of presidential power for the past half century or so (perhaps since President Harry Truman sent troops to Korea without formal congressional authorization) has violated one of the central principles of American constitutionalism: the need to channel and restrain executive power through a fabric of law. Presidents seem to do whatever they wish, unrestrained by effective legislative or judicial checks. Indeed, checks and balances seem particularly necessary to limit that power of government that is least subject to internal checks, that is, to the procedural safeguards of discussion, deliberation, and consensus-building that moderate the exercise of legislative and judicial power.

This absence of formal internal checks on the exercise of executive power is no accident. The architects of the presidential office consciously rejected a plural executive or one checked by a council to ensure that the presidency would possess those capacities that, they believed, characterized every well-constructed executive branch: decision, activity, secrecy, and dispatch.[23] These qualities enable the chief executive to act with speed and decisiveness when need arises; whereas legal and constitutional restraints might inhibit the executive's ability to take actions he deems necessary. Consequently, the very qualities that make for an effective executive (and therefore effective government generally) contribute also to the tension between executive power and the law. We are led to the curious conclusion that, in the kind of office it created, the Constitution itself contributes to the difficulty of constitutionally directing and restraining presidential power.

We can begin to make sense of this fact by realizing that the Constitution not only restrains, it also empowers. It assigns broad responsibility to the executive branch of government—command of the armed forces, pardoning power, nominating the principal officers of government, the veto, and recommending measures to Congress—and then makes these the possession of a single individual so that they might be exercised in a direct and forceful way. The framers chose neither a timid grant of power nor internal checks to prevent abuses and usurpation by the executive branch.

This was not because the framers were unmindful of the dangers of an unchecked executive, but because there were alternative means of control that less jeopardized governmental effectiveness. First, as discussed above, they designed the office so that the occupant would have a positive incentive to act responsibly. Second, they created competing structures of power that would have both the inclination and the means to oppose aggrandizement by another branch. The institutions of government would be so carefully constructed and the distribution of powers so artfully contrived that as the members of the several branches acted to promote their own interests they would serve, as it were, as "sentinel[s] over the public rights."[24]

If, for example, presidential power became a threat to popular liberties, this would likely involve an encroachment on the constitutional sphere reserved to Congress or the federal courts. Because the members of these branches have a personal stake in the power and status of their own institution, they could be expected to fight improper presidential designs. This kind of institutionalized conflict would be much more effective in preventing governmental abuse than "parchment barriers," mere constitutional prohibitions of the type that failed to preserve political balance in the state constitutions during the revolutionary period.[25] And equally important, this scheme frees the president to make effective use of the executive power in the first instance, reserving to Congress and the courts the opportunity to act subsequently to combat executive overreaching. So viewed, the constitutional design positively encourages presidential initiative, balanced by the fact that on many matters Congress or the Supreme Court will have final say.

Thus, in neither the structure of the office, the grant of powers, nor the provision for controls is the United States Constitution unfriendly to the exercise of executive power. On the contrary, it is striking how far the framers went to make the fundamental law hospitable to an energetic executive. In this their actions conform to their broader purpose to fashion a constitution fully adequate to national needs. In *The Federalist* Hamilton argued that the new government "ought to be clothed with all the powers requisite to complete execution of its trust" and that "it is both unwise and dangerous to deny the federal government an unconfined authority in respect to all those objects which are intrusted to its management." The danger of establishing a government incapable of achieving its proper ends is that, in any struggle between "parchment provisions" and "public necessity" necessity, will invariably win out. When certain actions are demanded by the force of events, political leaders will take them whether or not constitutionally authorized to do so. History proves that

> nations pay little regard to rules and maxims calculated in their very nature to run counter to the necessities of society. Wise politicians

will be cautious about fettering the government with restrictions that cannot be observed, because they know that every breach of the fundamental laws, though dictated by necessity, impairs that sacred reverence which ought to be maintained in the breast of rulers towards the constitution of a country, and forms a precedent for other breaches where the same plea of necessity does not exist at all, or is less urgent and palpable.

A constitutional government that cannot meet the dangers posed by extraordinary circumstances will soon lose, through the precedent of disobedience, much of its restraining force in more ordinary times. A properly framed constitution, then, must embrace two distinct and seemingly conflicting characteristics. On the one hand, it must ensure that "a power equal to every possible contingency . . . exist[s] somewhere in the government." On the other hand, it must genuinely channel, moderate, and restrain governmental power in normal circumstances.[26]

Armed conflict poses the most severe such challenge. The problem is whether the president, charged with "directing and employing the common strength," will have the means and flexibility to meet the common danger without subverting the original constitutional balance.[27] In 1866, a year after the Civil War ended, the Supreme Court for the first time addressed the problem of whether and how constitutional restraints should be preserved during periods of military emergency. The issue presented to the Court in *Ex parte Milligan* was whether a civilian citizen of Indiana could be lawfully executed for treasonous activities by order of a military tribunal acting under authority of the president. In issuing a writ of habeas corpus for Milligan's release from custody, the Court held that "it is the birthright of every American citizen when charged with crime, to be tried and punished according to law." Consequently, military authority could not lawfully supersede civilian authority "where the courts are open and their process unobstructed," as was the case in Indiana when Milligan was arrested and tried. To allow otherwise would place in jeopardy "the rights of the whole people" by violating one of the fundamental principles of American constitutionalism:

> The Constitution of the United States is a law for rulers and people, equally in war and in peace, and covers with the shield of its protection

all classes of men, at all times, and under all circumstances. No doctrine, involving more pernicious consequences, was ever intended by the wit of man than that any of its provisions can be suspended during any of the great exigencies of government. Such a doctrine leads directly to anarchy or despotism, but the theory of necessity on which it is based is false; for the government, within the Constitution, has all the powers granted to it, which are necessary to preserve its existence; as has been happily proved by the result of the great effort to throw off its just authority.[28]

In holding that the Constitution extends its protection to "all classes of men, at all times, and under all circumstances," the Court appeared to deny martial law any trace of legitimacy. Yet, later in the same opinion the Court maintained that "there are occasions when martial rule can be properly applied":

> If, in foreign invasion or civil war, the courts are actually closed, and it is impossible to administer criminal justice according to law, then, on the theatre of active military operations, where war really prevails, there is a necessity to furnish a substitute for the civil authority, thus overthrown, to preserve the safety of the army and society; and as no power is left but the military, it is allowed to govern by martial rule until the laws can have their free course. As necessity creates the rule, so it limits its duration; for, if this government is continued after the courts are reinstated, it is a gross usurpation of power. Martial rule can never exist where the courts are open, and in the proper and unobstructed exercise of their jurisdiction.[29]

The Constitution itself, of course, authorizes the suspension of the privilege of the writ of habeas corpus "when in Cases of Rebellion or Invasion the public Safety may require it." The Court is not fully clear on the distinction between the suspension of the writ of habeas corpus and "martial rule," but the controlling principle seems to be the following: the suspension of the writ of habeas corpus authorizes the limited action of arresting and holding dangerous individuals during periods of rebellion or invasion, even when the civil authority remains unobstructed; martial rule, on the other hand, includes a much wider range of activities—virtually whatever is necessary "to preserve the safety of the army and society"—but may only be instituted when the necessity is "actual and present; the invasion real, such as effectually closes the courts and deposes the civil administration."[30]

Although the Constitution makes explicit provision regarding the writ of habeas corpus, it says nothing about martial law or martial rule. If the Court's doctrine that none of the provisions of the Constitution "can be suspended during any of the great exigencies of government" is to be maintained, then we must conclude that the institution of martial law in the limited circumstances described by the Court has implicit constitutional sanction. Otherwise, how could it be said that the government under the Constitution "has all the powers . . . necessary to preserve its existence?" Necessity, then, the Court suggests, can make constitutional actions that would not be legitimate in normal circumstances.[31]

This is essentially the justification Lincoln presented for the extraordinary actions he took throughout the Civil War: "I felt that measures, otherwise unconstitutional, might become lawful, by becoming indispensable to the preservation of the Constitution, through the preservation of the nation."[32] Lincoln's point was not that "the constitution is different in time of insurrection or invasion from what it is in time of peace and public security" but rather that "the constitution is different, in its application in cases of Rebellion or Invasion, involving the Public Safety, from what it is in times of profound peace and public Security."[33] The clearest sign of this difference in application is the habeas corpus clause, but Lincoln also recurred to the commander-in-chief clause, the take care clause, and the presidential oath to support the argument that the Constitution itself authorizes the president to take certain actions to meet military necessities that would not be lawful in the absence of a grave danger to the nation.[34]

In justifying as constitutional extraordinary actions necessary to the preservation of the nation, both Lincoln and the Court in *Milligan* present a view of American constitutionalism broadly consistent with Alexander Hamilton's description of the new order as fully adequate to meet the demands of necessity. Hamilton, Lincoln, and the Court were all fearful of the precedent that would be set if leaders found it necessary to go outside the Constitution to protect the nation. Others, however, have argued that on balance the constitutional order is less threatened when the extraordinary actions demanded by extraordinary circumstances are not given the color of law. Perhaps the most comprehensive contemporary statement of this view is to be found in Arthur Schlesinger Jr.'s influential *The Imperial Presidency*.[35]

Schlesinger recognized that there are times when the president must undertake actions to protect the nation's security that are not authorized during normal circumstances: "[T]he question of necessity cannot be burked. Crises threatening the life of the nation have been happily rare. But, if such a crisis comes, a President must act." Such action, Schlesinger urged, should be clearly identified and recognized for what it is: an extra-constitutional resort to raw political power, necessary but not lawful. To try to defend emergency actions on constitutional grounds is to threaten to stretch the Constitution all out of shape, weakening its ability to restrain executive power in more normal times.

Schlesinger's view, then, shifts the issue from one of constitutional interpretation—does the document authorize the specific actions that appear to be necessary to preserve the nation—simply to a determination whether a true national emergency exists. If there is "a clear, present and broadly perceived danger to the life of the nation," then the Constitution may be temporarily set aside and the requisite actions undertaken. The legitimacy of presidential action appears to depend primarily on the seriousness of the danger. On this criterion, Schlesinger argued, both Lincoln during the Civil War and Franklin Roosevelt before and during World War II were justified in undertaking strictly illegal actions; but other presidents who faced less serious threats—he named Jefferson, Truman, Nixon, and Reagan—were not.[36]

Schlesinger based his argument on the theory of executive prerogative developed by the philosopher John Locke in Chapter 14 of his *Second Treatise*, a work, he noted, with which the founding fathers were well acquainted. To put it simply, Locke maintained that because the law cannot provide for every possible contingency—"all accidents and necessities"—that a political community may face, the executive must possess a "power to act according to discretion, for the public good, without the prescription of the Law, and sometimes even against it." When "a strict and rigid observation of the laws may do harm," law must give way to discretion.[37] Although this "idea of prerogative was *not* part of the presidential power as defined in the Constitution," according to Schlesinger, the framers understood, as did later American leaders, that presidents might need to step outside of the Constitution to preserve the nation. To conclude otherwise would mean that "it would be better to lose the nation than to break the law."[38]

Fully cognizant, however, of the dangers of unfettered executive discretion, Schlesinger cautioned that "prerogative is not unqualified. It is not a mandate to the President to do as he pleases." In his original 1973 manuscript, Schlesinger listed six criteria that must be met to justify the exercise of prerogative. A year later in the epilogue to the paperback edition, he expanded these to eight; and then in 1989 in a new lengthy epilogue he presented a revised list of eight criteria:

1. There must be a clear, present and broadly perceived danger to the life of the nation and to the ideals for which the nation stands.
2. The President must define and explain to Congress and the people the nature and urgency of the threat.
3. The understanding of the emergency, the judgment that the life of the nation is truly at stake, must be broadly shared by Congress and the people.
4. Time must be of the essence; existing statutory authorizations must be inadequate; and waiting for normal legislative action must constitute an unacceptable risk.
5. The danger must be one that can be met in no other way than by presidential initiative beyond the laws and the Constitution.
6. Secrecy must be strictly confined to the tactical requirements of the emergency. Every question of basic policy must be opened to national debate.
7. The President must report what he has done to Congress, which, along with the Supreme Court and ultimately the people, will serve as the judge of his action.
8. None of the presidential actions can be directed against the political process and rights.[39]

Thus, the justification for presidential exercise of emergency prerogative depends not simply on the nature of the threat to the nation's well-being, as first appeared, but also on how broadly and accurately that threat is recognized by the body politic. If the danger is not "clear" and if the "understanding of the emergency" is not "broadly shared by Congress and the people," then the president may not undertake strictly illegal actions believed by him to be essential to the nation's very survival. In his 1974 list of criteria, Schlesinger wrote that the danger must also be "uncontestable." He does not say why he dropped this adjective in 1989, but the natural inference is that he came to believe that this was too restrictive a condition. Also, in the earlier list, Congress would "serve as the judge of [the president's] action"; but by 1989, "Congress ... along with the Supreme Court and ultimately the people, will serve as the judge of his action." Again, Schlesinger does not note or explain the change, but the more recent version seems to allow for a public judgment that could possibly side with the president against Congress (or the Court).

The problem with these conditions is that they contradict the essential logic of the justification for prerogative in the first place. Certain actions, though strictly illegal, may occasionally be necessary to preserve the nation; the preservation of the nation is a greater good than perfect fidelity to the letter of the law. In principle what justifies prerogative is simply the factual situation, the nature of the danger, not how clearly that danger is perceived by legislators or the people. Certainly, in a given case the president might have a more accurate perception of the common danger than Congress or the citizenry. Indeed, many would say that this was the case in the United States just before its entry into World War II. Schlesinger summarizes President Franklin Roosevelt's emergency actions in 1941: "Roosevelt, on his own, without congressional authorization, dispatched troops to Iceland, instituted a convoy system, issued a 'shoot on sight' order to the navy, and launched an undeclared war in the North Atlantic." And why not simply seek authorization from Congress? Because, as Schlesinger notes, Roosevelt doubted that Congress would act, especially in light of its near defeat of the draft in August. Are we to conclude that a president in such a situation should forgo actions he judges essential to American survival?[40]

Schlesinger also contradicts the logic of prerogative when he stipulates that "none of the presidential actions can be directed against ... rights," a condition that did not appear in the 1974 list. Surely, one can imagine many needful acts in the midst of a grave crisis that might (temporarily) infringe or deny rights, including property rights, rights to travel and speak freely, and normal due process protections. Are all these to be excluded from the range of permissible emergency measures?

The necessity that justifies prerogative cannot support "stringent" conditions controlling its exercise.[41] This is because, as Locke makes clear, the exercise of prerogative depends finally on the discretion or judgment of the executive: "the good of the Society requires, that several things should be left to the discretion of him, that has the Executive Power." We do not fully understand the issue of prerogative until we recognize the radical nature of the original concession. According to Locke, law qua law is intrinsically incapable of fully realizing the public good; consequently, personal discretion—which, of course, the law was designed expressly to replace ("a government of laws and not of men")—must be given leeway to operate.

If this discretion by its nature operates outside the sphere of law, how can it be restrained? Or must we simply trust the good intentions of the executive? Locke suggests that the only way to control prerogative, once the principle of the thing is granted, is through a public judgment after the fact, perhaps after a series of measures that create an "inconvenience . . . so great, that the majority feel it, and are weary of it, and find a necessity to have it amended."[42] The executive's accountability to the public for his actions (and the public's ultimate right to revolution) is the only proper check on prerogative. This check, however, is not introduced procedurally in the midst of the action (as Schlesinger's conditions would have it) but operates only when enough time has passed that the consequences of the action can be accurately assessed.

One could say that the Constitution effectually institutionalizes a version of this principle by its openness to and even encouragement of presidential initiative balanced by the ability of Congress and the Court to act decisively after the fact to endorse or oppose presidential actions. Opposition can take the form of judicial or legislative mandate, the denial of funds, and finally impeachment and removal from office. The *Milligan* case is a pertinent example. With the cessation of hostilities and therefore any possible justification for martial law, the court quite vigorously reasserted the primacy of civil law (and of the federal judicial system) in matters regarding personal rights.

The decisive fact is that under the Constitution the functioning of the coordinate institutions of American government is not suspended nor is their authority dissolved (as would be the case under a fully consistent theory of prerogative as extraconstitutional) when the president undertakes extraordinary actions. Retaining their constitutional status,

Congress and the courts have a voice in determining the scope and duration of the president's special powers. Whether the president will abide by the actions of these institutions will depend in part on the degree to which the public regards their activity as legitimate. Because the Constitution is the source of authority for the actions of Congress and the courts, as well as for those of the president, this public sense of legitimacy will be more effectively supported by a view, like Lincoln's, that relies on the Constitution to meet emergency needs, than by a view which would have presidents go outside the Constitution; for when presidents adopt and articulate an extraconstitutional view of prerogative, they foster the notion that the Constitution must be "set aside" during emergencies, thereby undermining the claim of Congress and the courts to moderate presidential power.

All of this is not to say that the Constitution solves the problem of accommodating executive discretion to the rule of law. By its nature the problem is incapable of a full resolution. Although the exercise of emergency prerogative is a rare occurrence, we have tried to show that it most clearly reveals the more general tension between discretion and law. A fabric of law is necessary to control the abuses of power so common to political life; but that same law, if rigidly adhered to, can prevent the actions vital to the welfare of the community. The task that confronts us is to find the best practical answer to this insoluble problem. We suggest that a constitutional arrangement that allows for a substantial degree of executive initiative and discretion within a framework of political checks is more effective and less dangerous than a set of arrangements that so constrains and restricts the executive power as to render it incapable of carrying out its proper tasks or that makes it necessary to set aside the Constitution to do what the good of the community requires. Thus the principles that underlie the particular provisions of the original Constitution may serve as standards for evaluating contemporary practice.

Conclusion

Presidential scholarship quite understandably reacts to assessments of how presidential power at different times contributes to the commonweal. These assessments vary as scholars reflect on particular presidents, their political and policy successes and failures, formative political events, and the needs of the nation. At times scholars tend to conclude that the nation would be better served by a stronger and more effective chief executive; at other times the dominant message is that the presidency must be reined in by Congress and the courts. Effectiveness and safety are the poles between which scholarly reflections and public attitudes will continue to oscillate. We have tried to show that these poles were, and continue to be, an intrinsic part of the American constitutional order.

It is often said that the Constitution virtually guaranteed an unending conflict or struggle between the political branches of American government. But this was not simply because the Constitution assigned the political powers to two distinct institutions; for with some small changes in the executive provisions the Constitution could have resulted in a presidency decidedly subordinate to Congress. The abolition of the veto, a reduction in term of office to one year, and the institution of presidential selection by Congress would surely have been sufficient to deny the occupant of the executive office the will and the means to thwart congressional predominance over American government. And as the specific language of the document written in 1787 has given rise to conflict between the political branches, so has it influenced the nature and scope of that conflict. The Constitution's qualified veto, for example, ensures that with rare exceptions Congress must make some accommodation to strongly held policy views of the president. Conversely, other constitutional provisions determine that presidents must generally give serious consideration to senatorial views on treaties and appointments.

Although the Constitution does not lack ambiguity, it is clear enough on many specific points to define the arena and fashion the weapons of congressional-presidential conflict. And when the boundaries of power are not clear, legally questionable actions by the president or Congress quickly precipitate a constitutional debate, bringing the focus again to the meaning of the fundamental law. Consequently, much of the "political" conflict between president and Congress occurs within a horizon of law.

This conflict generally sets something like the upper limit to the exercise of executive power in American government. Representatives and senators will not long tolerate what appears to them to be a usurpation of their prerogatives by the president, even when they agree with him on basic policy direction. It is this dynamic that gives the language of the Constitution, its specific distribution of powers between Congress and president, a real weight in influencing the reach of presidential power. And if congressional assertiveness usually puts a ceiling on presidential power, it is presidential assertiveness that determines the floor. Both illustrate the Constitution's effectiveness in attaching the interests of the officeholder to the rights and duties of the office. At his least assertive the constitutional chief executive is firmly committed to preserving the independence and integrity of the executive branch, takes his responsibilities seriously as commander in chief and as director of foreign relations, and does not shrink from fashioning and recommending legislative proposals or from vetoing what he judges to be unwise measures passed by Congress.

Although this constitutional floor and ceiling are not unbreachable barriers, they do constitute the range within which presidential power will generally operate. It is remarkable that throughout American history even the "weak" presidents have nearly always measured up to the minimal constitutional standards, while the "strong" presidents have been so well checked that for only a few very brief periods has American government been tantamount to one-branch government. This means, then, that the Constitution eliminates a wide variety of types of executives known to us from the historical record and from contemporary practice in other nations. As long as the Constitution remains effective, the president will not be reduced to the status of a city manager or a mere figurehead, nor will he achieve the power of a despot or tyrant.

We do not mean to deny the importance of political skill, popularity, or historical circumstance in contributing to the successes or failures of particular presidents at particular times. Each of these will help to explain the functioning of the executive office. But without radical transformation of the system, these factors will not drastically alter the broad probabilities of presidential power. Nor do we mean to suggest that such transformations are impossible, that under no circumstances could an especially skilled and popular president, anxious to promote his own power or some uncompromising view of the public good, undermine the constitutional safeguards and subvert the separation of powers and checks and balances system. The most effectual checks on such a design will come initially from the willingness of representatives, senators, and federal judges to fight to uphold the constitutional balance; but the ultimate check will come from the attachment of the people to constitutional principle. These will be fostered by a presidential scholarship that focuses attention on the constitutional order, that is sensitive to the difference between the Constitution and a strict legal code, and that recognizes the sometimes uneasy blending of effectiveness and safety characteristic of our fundamental law.

CHAPTER TWO

The Powers and Duties of the President

Recovering the Logic and Meaning of Article II

JOSEPH M. BESSETTE *and* GARY J. SCHMITT

IN HIS AUTHORITATIVE TEXT on the constitutional and legal foundations for executive power in the United States, Edward Corwin describes Article II on the presidency as "the most loosely drawn chapter of the Constitution."[1] Similarly, in his well-known intellectual history of the presidency, Forest McDonald calls the article "imprecise, even muddled."[2] And in his famous concurring opinion in the Korean War case *Youngstown Sheet and Tube Co. v. Sawyer*, U.S. Supreme Court Justice Robert Jackson describes the effort to understand the president's constitutional powers as relying on "materials" (apparently including the text of the Constitution) "almost as enigmatic as the dreams Joseph was called upon to interpret for Pharaoh."[3]

These characterizations reflect, at least in part, a frustration that many have experienced when trying to find in the Constitution answers to questions about the reach of executive power, especially during crises. May a president, for example, order troops into combat overseas without prior congressional approval? Once war is upon us, may the president suspend the writ of habeas corpus on his own authority, seize private industries vital to the war effort, or establish military tribunals to try "unlawful combatants"? May a president abrogate a treaty with a foreign nation without Congress's (or at least the Senate's) approval? May the president legitimately withhold information requested by Congress or the courts to protect national security secrets or to preserve the confidentiality of communications with aides?

When such questions arise, we naturally turn first to Article II. Does the vagueness of its language render such an exercise pointless? Are the president's constitutional powers, then, whatever the temporary occupant wishes or what current public opinion will accept? We think not. We believe that Article II is more tightly drawn, more precise, and less enigmatic than is often thought and is thus a more reliable guide to the reach and limits of the president's constitutional authority than many recognize. In particular, we argue here that Article II is structured, or organized, around the distinction between powers and duties; that, broadly speaking, the former are the means, or instruments, for achieving the latter; and that consequently it is duty that lies at the heart of the constitutional presidency.

Modern political science has much to say about presidential powers but rather little to say about presidential duty. One might usefully ask, for example, what a book, or series of books, on presidential duty would look like. What topics would be covered? How would presidential performance be assessed? How would such a treatment differ from those that focus on power? We dwell a lot on assessing presidential success at wielding power; but how often do we ask how successful presidents are at fulfilling their constitutional duties? If we had to choose between a president who was very good at getting his way and one who was very good at meeting his constitutional obligations, wouldn't we prefer the latter?[4] Something important is missing in our treatment and understanding of the constitutional presidency, something that a careful analysis of Article II can help us uncover and recover.

An Office of Powers and Duties

Article II begins with the well-known "vesting clause": "The executive Power shall be vested in a President of the United States of America." At least since Alexander Hamilton made the argument in 1793, many have noted that this differs from the opening of Article I: "All legislative Powers herein granted shall be vested in a Congress of the United States."[5] To many, this is strong textual support for the view that Congress possesses only enumerated powers—those "herein granted"—while the president possesses a general executive power. Indeed, in the famous "removal power" debate in the House of Representatives in 1789, just weeks after the new Congress first convened, James Madison and others argued successfully that the vesting clause implicitly gave the president the power to fire heads of executive departments, because this was by its very nature an executive power.[6]

In the second sentence of Article II, the Constitution stipulates that the president "shall hold his Office during the Term of four Years, and, together with the Vice-President, chosen for the same Term, be elected, as follows." Six more times in Section 1 the Constitution refers to the "Office" of the president. It specifies, for example, that if a president is removed from office, dies during his term, resigns, or is unable "to discharge the *Powers* and *Duties* of the said Office, the same shall devolve on the Vice President" (emphasis added). And two paragraphs later the Constitution requires that before the president "enter on the Execution of his Office," he take an oath, in part, to "faithfully execute the Office of President of the United States." We know from the previous provision on vice-presidential succession that to faithfully execute the office of president is to faithfully discharge its powers and duties.

Although American constitutional history is replete with references to the "powers and duties" of the president, there has been a marked tendency to refer to the authorities vested in Article II principally as "powers." If, for example, we speak of the "constitutional powers of the president," this would be understood to include whatever authority the Constitution vests in the office. This tendency to collapse "powers and duties" into "powers" simply is at odds with the fact that both historically and etymologically an office is more directly associated with duty than power. Indeed, the Latin word, *officium,* from which the English word "office" derives, meant duty. As Edward Corwin noted,

> etymologically, an "office" is an *officium,* a duty; and an "officer" was simply one whom the King had charged with a duty. In the course of time certain frequently recurrent and naturally coherent duties came to be assigned more or less permanently, and so emerged the concept of "office" as an *institution* distinct from the person holding it and capable of persisting beyond his incumbency.[7]

If at its core an office is best understood as a duty or set of duties, then the powers assigned to an office are essentially instrumental: means to accomplish the assigned duties. Thus, within an office powers and duties are related to each other like the convex and concave sides of a curve. Duties require, or perhaps imply, powers; powers exist not for their own sake but to serve duties.

It is our contention that this powers-duties distinction, though overlooked by modern commentators, is an extremely powerful conceptual tool for analyzing and understanding the authorities vested in the president by the Constitution, as the following discussion will try to demonstrate.[8] (Despite the slight awkwardness, we will use the term *authority* to refer generically to either a constitutional "power" or "duty," preserving as best we can the distinction between a "power" and a "duty" throughout.)

The Work of the Constitutional Convention

The Constitutional Convention met in Philadelphia in 1787 between Friday, May 25, and Monday, September 17. Fifty-five men from twelve states (Rhode Island did not send delegates) attended at least some part of the deliberations. Forty-two delegates were present at the end, thirty-nine of whom signed the document.

We sometimes forget just how much executive experience the delegates brought to the task of building a more effective national government for the new nation. Nearly all (fifty of the fifty-five) had served in one or more executive positions at the national, state, or local level. Fully two-thirds (thirty-seven of the fifty-five) had held a position of considerable executive responsibility, especially for public safety: nine as a state governor; nine as a member of a governor's council (in their state or colonial government); ten on a state's committee of safety during the early revolutionary period; and fourteen as an officer in the Continental Army.[9] Keenly aware of how both the Articles of Confederation, with no independent executive branch, and the state governments, with mainly weak governors, failed to provide for effective government, these men would have been especially alert to the need to provide a sturdy structure and ample authorities to the nation's new chief executive.

Article II was their response to this need. The nature of the specific executive authorities and the form in which they were vested were the result principally of two key committees of the Constitutional Convention: the Committee of Detail and the Committee of Style. The former, which met from July 27 to August 6 (during a recess of the convention) took the various and sundry measures passed to that point and formed them into a draft constitution. The latter, which did its work from September 8 to 12, provided the final form and style to the document. Both committees were quite small: just five members each. On the Committee of Detail served Oliver Ellsworth of Connecticut, Nathaniel Gorham of Massachusetts, Edmund Randolph of Virginia, John Rutledge of South Carolina (chair), and James Wilson of Pennsylvania. On the Committee of Style were Alexander Hamilton of New York, William Johnson of Connecticut (chair), Rufus King of Massachusetts, James Madison of Virginia, and Gouverneur Morris of Pennsylvania.

In its first two months of deliberations, the convention devoted little time or effort to the question of what authorities to vest in the new chief executive. When it created the Committee on Detail in late July and charged it with producing a draft constitution, it had agreed on only three: "to carry into execution the national laws"; "to appoint to offices in cases not otherwise provided for"; and the authority to veto legislative acts, subject to override by a two-thirds vote of both houses of the legislature.[10] The delegates also submitted to the committee two other sets of propositions, which they had not formally approved, with additional language on executive power: a draft constitution introduced by Charles Pinckney of South Carolina and what was known as the "New Jersey Plan," formally proposed by William Paterson and around which many small state delegates had rallied.[11]

Paterson's proposal vested four authorities in the new "federal Executive": (1) a "general authority to execute the federal acts"; (2) "to appoint all federal officers not otherwise provided for"; (3) "to direct all military operations; provided that none of the persons composing the federal Executive shall on any occasion take command of any troops, so as personally to conduct any enterprise as General, or in other capacity"; and (4) the authority to "call forth [the] power of the Confederated States . . . to enforce and compel an obedience to [federal laws and treaties]."[12] The New Jersey Plan did not include a veto power.

Pinckney's proposal, by contrast, went well beyond the three executive authorities approved by the convention or the four in the New Jersey Plan. Although Pinckney's original plan does not survive, historians have reconstructed it from documents found among James Wilson's papers related to the work of the Committee of Detail. It set forth a lengthy list of authorities to be vested in the new president:

In the Presidt. the executive Authority of the U.S. shall be vested.

It shall be his Duty to inform the Legislature at every session of the condition of the United States, so far as may respect his Department—to recommend Matters to their Consideration such as shall appear to him to concern their good government, welfare and prosperity—to correspond with the Executives of the several States—to attend to the Execution of the Laws of the U S by the several States—to transact Affairs with the Officers of Government, civil and military—to expedite all such Measures as may be resolved on by the Legislature—to acquire from time to time, as perfect a knowledge of the situation of the Union, as he possibly can, and to be charged with all the business of the home department. He will be empowered, whenever he conceives it necessary to inspect the Department of foreign Affairs—War—Treasury—and when instituted of the Admiralty—to reside where the Legislature shall sit—to commission all Officers, and keep the Great Seal of the United States.

He shall, by Virtue of his Office, be Commander in chief of the Land Forces of the U.S. and Admiral of their Navy.

He shall have Power to convene the Legislature on extraordinary occasions—to prorogue them, when they cannot agree as to the time of their adjournment, provided such Prorogation shall not exceed——Days in the space of any——He may suspend Officers, civil and military.

He shall have a Right to advise with the Heads of the different Departments as his Council.

Council of Revision, consisting of the Presidt. S.[ecretary] for for. Affairs, S.[ecretary] of War, Heads of the Departments of Treasury and Admiralty or any two of them togr wt the Presidt.[13]

Here for the first time at the convention we see both a detailed list of executive authorities and a distinction between the powers and duties assigned to the president. After vesting "the executive Authority" in the president, Pinckney's proposal listed eight specific "Dut[ies]." Then in the same paragraph it "empowered" the president to carry out four distinct functions. It followed this with a short paragraph making the president, "by Virtue of his Office," the "Commander in chief" of the nation's military forces. The next paragraph gave the president the "Power" to convene and prorogue the legislature and to suspend officers of the government. The penultimate paragraph gave him the "Right" to consult with his department heads. The final paragraph created a "Council of Revision" (which would have the power to veto acts of the national legislature).[14]

On August 6, the Committee of Detail made its report to the convention, distributing a printed copy of its draft constitution to every member. In twenty-three articles, it laid out a detailed plan of government including a bicameral legislature, an executive power vested in "a single person," and a judicial power headed by a Supreme Court. Article X established and empowered the new executive office. Section 1 opened with the words, "The Executive Power of the United States shall be vested in a single person. His stile shall be 'The President of the United States of America;' and his title shall be, 'His Excellency.'" It then reaffirmed the delegates' prior decisions to have the national legislature elect the president for a single seven-year term.

Then, Article X, Section 2, the draft constitution, like Pinckney's plan, vested in the new president numerous specific authorities:

> He shall, from time to time, give information to the Legislature, of the state of the Union: he may recommend to their consideration such measures as he shall judge necessary, and expedient: he may convene them on extraordinary occasions. In case of disagreement between the two Houses, with regard to the time of adjournment, he may adjourn them to such time as he thinks proper: he shall take care that the laws of the United States be duly and faithfully executed: he shall commission all the officers of the United States; and shall appoint officers in all cases not otherwise provided for by this Constitution. He shall receive Ambassadors, and may correspond with the supreme Executives of the several States. He shall have power to grant reprieves and pardons; but his pardon shall not be pleadable in bar of an impeachment. He shall be commander in chief of the Army and Navy of the United States, and of the Militia of the Several States.[15]

The veto power approved by the convention survived in Article VI.

Having preserved the convention's decisions to vest the executive with the appointment and veto powers, the committee dramatically expanded (or added to) the authority "to carry into execution the national laws" by including such potentially significant authorities as recommending measures to Congress, convening the legislature on extraordinary occasions, receiving ambassadors, granting reprieves and pardons, and serving as commander in chief of the army and navy and of the state militia. While we do not know whether the Committee of Detail believed that this was a comprehensive list, it began its provisions on the presidency with language that could reasonably be read as itself a grant of authority: "The Executive Power of the United States shall be vested in a single person." However one interprets the vesting clause of the committee's proposal, it is clear that the essential authorities of the office would rest not on congressional will, but on a constitutional grant.

Although the list of executive authorities in the draft constitution does not, like Pinckney's, formally distinguish "duties" from "powers" or "rights," it captures some sense of this distinction by its varied use of "shall" and "may" in introducing all but two of the specific authorities. Some of the authorities read like discretionary powers: he "may" recommend measures, convene Congress on extraordinary occasions, adjourn the House and Senate if they cannot agree when to adjourn, and correspond with state governors. And others read like mandatory duties: he "shall" give information to the legislature, take care that the laws are faithfully executed, commission and appoint officers, and receive ambassadors. Moreover, the authority to grant reprieves and pardons is specifically identified as a "power," suggesting a discretionary authority, not a mandated duty: that is to say, the president *may* grant a reprieve or pardon, but need not. The one exception to this pattern is the commander-in-chief authority: "he shall be commander in chief." Whatever duties might inhere in such an office (more on this below), it is obviously a position of real power, vesting significant discretion, over the operations of the military.

Some of the concluding language of Article X is also relevant to the powers-duties distinction. The president must swear (or affirm) to "faithfully execute the office of the President . . . before he shall enter on the duties of his department." Why not write, "before he shall exercise the powers of the presidency"? Oaths, it appears, are more naturally connected to duties than to powers. One takes an oath to fulfill one's duties, employing powers as appropriate. Indeed, one might think of the oath of office as imposing an overarching duty that supervenes or informs the more specific "duties of his department."

Immediately following is the language making the president removable from office if impeached by the House of Representatives and convicted by the Supreme Court of "treason, bribery, or corruption." Any of these offenses would, of course, be a violation of the president's duty to "faithfully execute" his office. Then, if the president is removed from office, dies, resigns, or is unable "to discharge the powers and duties of his office, the President of the Senate shall exercise those powers and duties."

In a broad sense we might say that the executive article of the Committee of Detail's constitution begins with power—"The Executive Power of the United States shall be vested in a single person"—and ends with his overarching duty to "faithfully execute" his office and with the consequences that befall him if he fails to do so. In between the broad power and the encompassing duty come a variety of specific powers and duties, all of which devolve upon the President of the Senate in the case of a vacancy in the office or an inability to carry them out.

During the month between the report of the Committee of Detail and the appointment of the Committee of Style, the delegates made several, mostly minor, changes in the executive authority. Most importantly, they withdrew from the Senate the sole authority "to make treaties" and to appoint ambassadors, other public ministers, and judges of the Supreme Court and made these shared powers with the president, with two-thirds of the Senate required to ratify treaties and a majority to confirm presidential nominations to high office.

Two relatively minor changes, both pushed by Gouverneur Morris, bear on our understanding of the powers-duty distinction. On August 24 Morris moved that the word "may" in the clause, "he may recommend to [the legislature] . . . such measures as he shall judge necessary, and expedient," be replaced with "shall." This was done "in order to make it the *duty* of the President to recommend, & thence prevent umbrage or cavil at his doing it."[16] Here is an explicit recognition of the difference between a discretionary power and a positive duty.

The other change of note is the one case where the convention deleted a power from the draft constitution. On August 25 Morris moved "to strike out the section—'and may correspond with the supreme Executives of the several States' as unnecessary and implying that he could not correspond with others."[17] There was no debate and the motion passed, nine states to one. Apparently, the vast majority of delegates agreed that the president would be fully authorized to correspond with the chief executives of the states (as well as with others) without a specific grant of power to this effect.

One could hardly find clearer evidence of the notion of implied executive powers. As the possessor of the "Executive Power of the United States," the president possessed at least some powers not specifically enumerated.

Strikingly, throughout this phase of the deliberations no one rose to oppose in general the apparent enlargement of executive authority introduced in the draft constitution, despite the contrast between the impressive list of authorities in the committee's draft and the three general provisions formally approved by the convention in its first two months. Indeed, the debate on the specifics of the executive powers, though occurring on parts of three separate days (August 24, 25, and 27), appears to have filled no more than one day's worth of discussion. There were a few efforts to trim specific powers, but these were easily defeated. By a vote of nine states to one the delegates turned down a proposal to allow Congress by statute to determine what appointments the president could make on his own authority; and by a vote of eight states to one they defeated a motion to replace the general authority to grant pardons and reprieves with a more limited power to grant reprieves until the next session of the Senate and to require senatorial consent for pardons.

Similarly, when the convention held its final debate on the treaty power —which now resided in the president and Senate—no one proposed returning the power to the exclusive control of the Senate. The change had proven remarkably uncontroversial. Madison did, however, move to deny the president authority over treaties of peace, lest a president continue a war longer than he should. But a large majority of his colleagues disagreed, and the motion failed eight states to three. Although Madison did succeed temporarily in authorizing the Senate to ratify peace treaties by a simple majority, the delegates later reversed this decision, placing peace treaties on the same footing as other treaties.

Three other actions completed the list of the president's authorities. The convention authorized the president to (1) "require the opinion in writing of the principal officer in each of the executive departments, upon any subject relating to the duties of their respective offices"; (2) convene either house of Congress separately (so that the Senate, for example, could consider treaties in a timely fashion); and (3) make temporary appointments to fill vacancies that occur during a recess of the Senate.

On September 8 the Convention appointed its final committee, the five-member Committee of Style, "to revise the stile of and arrange the articles which had been agreed to by the House."[18] Unlike previous committees, this one was not balanced by region or between the large and small states. The Deep South was not represented, and four committee members came from the most populous states. Presumably, what mattered at this final stage of constitution writing was not a balance of political forces but skill at legal craftsmanship.

The committee, through its chairman William Johnson, made its report to the delegates on September 12.[19] The twenty-three articles of the Committee of Detail's draft constitution were now reduced to seven, introduced by a revised preamble. The first and longest of the articles was on Congress; the next in order and length was on the presidency; and the third was on the judiciary. Articles IV–VII covered a variety of miscellaneous topics. Other than a few minor modifications, the authorities of the president previously agreed to by the convention were adopted by the committee with at most stylistic changes.

Nonetheless, in fashioning a single executive article, the committee fundamentally restructured the vesting of executive authority. As noted above, the draft constitution of the Committee of Detail had divided Article X on the executive into two sections, with the list of detailed authorities comprising most of Section 2. Then during its subsequent deliberations the convention modified some of these powers and added others. The Committee of Style now reorganized the executive authorities in its new Article II into four sections. The first, and longest, section again began with the vesting clause, rewritten to read, "The executive power shall be vested in a president of the United States of America." It also included provisions on term of office, mode of appointment for the president and vice president, qualifications for office, succession by the vice president, compensation, and oath of office. The second and third sections listed the specific authorities vested in the executive office. Section 2 included the commander-in-chief power and the powers over opinions in writing, reprieves and pardons, treaties, and appointments. Section 3 included the authority to inform Congress and recommend measures, the limited powers over convening and adjourning Congress, and the provisions governing receiving ambassadors, taking care the laws are faithfully executed, and commissioning officers. Finally, Section 4 stipulated that the president, vice president, and all other civil officers would be removed upon impeachment and conviction of "treason, bribery, or other high crimes and misdemeanors."

Comparison of Article II with the Constitution of New York of 1777

Given the care with which the Committee of Style arranged the numerous and various provisions passed by the convention—historian Clinton Rossiter, for example, called the committee's product "a masterpiece of draftsmanship"[20]—it seems reasonable to presume that when the committee divided the president's specific authorities into two distinct sections it did so because of some difference in kind between the items listed in each. (Contrast this with the single lengthy list of Congress's powers in Article I, Section 8.) Although there is nothing in the convention record itself that addresses this issue, we do have significant circumstantial evidence that this distinction is indeed one between *powers* and *duties*. Most telling is a comparison of the contents and structure of Article II of the Committee of Style's report with the various state constitutions. This reveals a striking similarity between the form used in the Constitution of New York of 1777 to vest authority in that state's governor and the form employed by the Committee of Style to empower the U.S. president. Table 2.1 presents a side-by-side comparison of the two.

Of the twelve state constitutions written between independence and the Constitutional Convention (Connecticut and Rhode Island kept their charter governments and South Carolina had two constitutions during this period), only New York's began its grant of executive authority with a vesting clause in one section (Article XVII) followed by two major sections detailing specific authorities (Articles XVIII and XIX). Other similarities between the New York constitution and the Committee of Style report include the following: beginning the second section with the commander-in-chief power, including the pardoning power in the second section, beginning the third section with the responsibilities for providing information and recommending measures to the legislature, and locating the "take care" clause near the end of the third section.

There are, of course, differences between the documents, mainly because the specific authorities vested in the two executives were not identical. The president, for example, was not specifically granted the authorities, found

TABLE 2.1 Vesting of executive authority in the Constitution of New York (1977) and the Committee of Style report

New York constitution (1777)	Committee of Style report
XVII. the supreme executive power and authority of this State shall be vested in a governor	Article II, Section 1. The executive power shall be vested in a president of the United States of America
XVIII. the governor shall . . . by virtue of his office, be general and commander-in-chief of all the militia, and admiral of the navy of this State;	Section 2. The president shall be commander in chief of the army and navy of the United States, and of the militia of the several states when called into the actual service of the United States:
that he shall have power[:]	he may require the opinion, in writing of the principal officer in each of the executive departments, upon any subject relating to the duties of their respective offices, and
to convene the assembly and senate on extraordinary occasions;	
to prorogue them from time to time, provided such prorogations shall not exceed sixty days in the space of any one year; and,	he shall have power to grant reprieves and pardons for offences against the United States, except in cases of impeachment.
at his discretion, to grant reprieves and pardons to persons convicted of crimes, other than treason or murder, in which he may suspend the execution of the sentence, until it shall be reported to the legislature at their subsequent meeting; and they shall either pardon or direct the execution of the criminal, or grant a further reprieve.	He shall have power, by and with the advice and consent of the senate, to make treaties, provided two-thirds of the senators present concur; and
	he shall nominate, and by and with the advice and consent of the senate, shall appoint ambassadors, other public ministers and consuls, judges of the supreme court, and all other officers of the United States, whose appointments are not otherwise provided for.
	The president shall have power to fill up all vacancies that may happen during the recess of the senate, by granting commissions which shall expire at the end of their next session.
XIX That it shall be the duty of the governor[:]	Section 3. He shall from time to time give to the Congress information of the state of the union, and recommend to their consideration such measures as he shall judge necessary and expedient:
to inform the legislature, at every session, of the condition of the State, so far as may respect his department;	

TABLE 2.1 *Continued*

New York constitution (1777)	Committee of Style report
to recommend such matters to their consideration as shall appear to him to concern its good government, welfare, and prosperity;	he may, on extraordinary occasions, convene both houses, or either of them, and in the case of disagreement between them, with respect to the time of adjournment, he may adjourn them to such time as he shall think proper:
to correspond with the Continental Congress, and other States;	
to transact all necessary business with the officers of government, civil and military; to take care that the laws are faithfully executed to the best of his ability; and to expedite all such measures as may be resolved upon by the legislature.	he shall receive ambassadors and other public ministers:
	he shall take care that the laws be faithfully executed, and
	shall commission all the officers of the United States.

in the New York constitution, to prorogue temporarily the legislature, to correspond with the Continental Congress and the states, to transact business with the officers of the government, and to expedite the measures passed by the legislature. Conversely, he was vested with some authorities not granted the New York governor: specifically, to require the opinion in writing of department heads, to make treaties (with the Senate's advice and consent), to settle disputes between the two branches of the legislature regarding adjournment, and to receive ambassadors. (The New York governor's authority to make appointments, shared with the council of appointment, and to commission all the state's officers were vested in Articles XXIII and XXIV, respectively.)

The Committee of Style, however, had no control over the powers themselves, just the style and arrangement of what the delegates had already approved. And here they seemed to follow closely the New York constitution. In every case but one where the national executive had an authority comparable to what could be found in the three principal executive articles of the New York constitution, the committee located such authority in the parallel place in Article II. The one exception is the authority to convene the legislature on extraordinary occasions, which the New York constitution located in the second of the three executive articles and the Committee of Style in the third. The only other structural deviation between the Committee of Detail's report and the New York constitution was the committee's decision to include the executive's appointment power and his responsibility to commission officers with the other express authorities, which the New York constitution had not done.

If this textual similarity is not enough to demonstrate that the New York constitution was the model for the structure of Article II of the U.S. Constitution, we have strong supporting evidence. Virtually all we know about the work of the Committee of Style is that Gouverneur Morris was the principal architect of its final report. Abraham Baldwin, a delegate from Georgia, made this claim in December of 1787. Morris, himself, in a letter to Timothy Pickering written in 1814, maintained that the Constitution "was written by the fingers, which write this letter." Also in an 1831 letter James Madison reported that "the *finish* given to the style and arrangement of the Constitution fairly belongs to the pen of Mr Morris; the task having, probably, been handed over to him by the chairman of the Committee, himself a highly respectable member, and with the ready concurrence of the others."[21] Morris's preeminent role in preparing the Committee of Style's report is particularly relevant to the comparison with the New York constitution because although Morris served in 1787 as a delegate from Pennsylvania, in 1776–77 he was a member of the New York legislature that prepared that state's constitution. In fact, Morris was a leading figure, second only to John Jay, in formulating the original draft of the New York constitution and guiding it through the legislature.[22]

It can hardly be doubted that, when he put his hand to the executive authorities submitted to the Committee of Style, Morris knew full well that his rearrangement followed the structure of his native state's constitution. And lest we forget, the Committee of Style also included one member, Alexander Hamilton, who represented New York and was presumably familiar with the details of its constitution. Scholars have long noted that the institutional provisions of the New York constitution that made for an unusually strong state governorship—a relatively lengthy three-year term, indefinite re-eligibility, and election by the people rather than by the legislature—were in some broad sense a model for the U.S. presidency.[23] We should not be surprised that that modeling extended to the specific executive authorities and their arrangement in the respective constitutions.

The importance of recognizing the parallel between the New York and U.S. constitutions is that the New York constitution explicitly groups the authorities of the chief executive into *powers* and *duties*. Article XVIII begins by naming the governor "commander-in-chief" and then stipulates that "he shall have power" to convene the legislature on extraordinary occasions, prorogue them temporarily, and grant reprieves and pardons. Article XIX begins "That it shall be the duty of the governor" and follows this with six specific provisions. It seems reasonable to conclude, then, that the provisions of Section 2 of Article II were understood by the Committee of Style as powers and the provisions of Section 3 as duties. It is these "powers and duties" that would now "devolve on the vice-president" in the case of the removal of the president from office, his death, resignation, or "inability to discharge" the responsibilities of office.

In its four days of deliberations on the Committee of Style's draft, the convention made two changes to the president's authorities, but both of these changes were in Article I on the role of Congress. Previously the convention had given Congress the power to appoint the nation's treasurer. Now it removed this power from Congress, thus leaving it to the president, by a vote of eight states to three. The other change, which somewhat reduced presidential power, was a reduction in the ratio of votes needed to overturn a presidential veto from three-fourths to two-thirds.

How, then, does this powers-duties distinction help us in understanding the nature of the specific authorities vested by Article II in the American president?

Interpreting Specific Presidential Authorities

In interpreting a particular presidential authority, one begins, of course, with the precise words used by the Constitution. We have argued that even at this level the powers-duties distinction is evident, with the use of "he may" or "he shall have power" to designate discretionary powers and "he shall" to designate duties. Yet if we are right that there is a principled distinction between the authorities of Section 2 and those of Section 3, then location within Article II may provide additional guidance. Note, for example, that the "he may," "he shall have power," and "he shall" language vesting executive authorities in Article II corresponds closely, but not perfectly, with the division of specific authorities into Sections 2 (powers) and 3 (duties).

In Section 2, for example, three of the six grants begin with the statement that the president "shall have Power." Another begins, "he may require the Opinion in writing," implying a general discretionary authority to require opinions in writing—the equivalent of saying, "he shall have power to require opinions in writing." A fifth provision, his military authority, is vested in the form of an office; yet by its own terms it is an office of command—that is, of power. (As noted above, the office of commander in chief may also imply certain duties.) The only grant in this "powers" section that seems to employ "duties" language is the appointment provision: "he shall nominate, and by and with the Advice and Consent of the Senate, shall appoint Ambassadors, other public Ministers and Consuls, Judges of the supreme Court, and all other Officers of the United States, when Appointments are not herein otherwise provided for, and which shall be established by law."

Correspondingly, in Section 3 five of the seven grants use the mandatory term "shall" and only two use the more discretionary "may." The uses of "may" refer to the related functions of convening and adjourning Congress: "he may, on extraordinary Occasions, convene both Houses, or either of them," and when the branches cannot agree on the time of adjournment, "he may adjourn them to such Time as he shall think proper." What, then, to make of these few exceptions to the overall scheme?

The inconsistency between the precise language vesting authority over making appointments, convening Congress, and adjourning Congress and the location of these authorities in Sections 2 and 3 may reflect, perhaps, their mixed nature. Consider first appointments. Does the president have a duty, a mandatory responsibility, to appoint the high officers of the government—"he shall nominate, and . . . shall appoint"—or is this a general discretionary power—as suggested by its location in Section 2? Certainly, it seems to be both. The president, for example, is not free not to nominate judges of the Supreme Court. If he were, he (with his successors) could let the institution expire by waiting until the last justice died or resigned. Moreover, were a president to do this, we would rightly say that he had not fulfilled his constitutional duty. The mandatory "shall" language of the appointment clause drives this home. But the appointment authority gives the president some real discretionary power to shape American national government and especially his own administration. The president retains, of course, broad discretion as to whom to nominate for high office, and at least his appointees within the executive branch act to some degree as extensions of his own power and authority. His subordinates give him the means or ability to carry out his constitutional and legal duties. Without them, he would lack the "power" to fulfill his obligations.

An example from Andrew Jackson's administration illustrates just how much real power over public policy the appointment authority, combined with the implicit removal power, can give a president. After successfully vetoing an 1832 statute rechartering the Bank of the United States, Jackson sought to hasten the death of the bank, whose charter had four more years to run, by having the federal deposits withdrawn and distributed to state banks. The problem was that legal authority over the federal deposits had been vested not in the president, but in the secretary of the treasury. To effectuate his policy Jackson found it necessary to remove from office two consecutive secretaries of the treasury, both of whom had refused to do his bidding. It took his third appointee, Roger B. Taney, then attorney general and later to become chief justice of the Supreme Court, to consummate Jackson's desires. Here the "duty" to nominate department heads became the basis for enhancing "power" over public policy.

As for the limited authority to control the convening and adjourning of Congress, we may also ask whether these authorities are best understood as discretionary powers, as implied by the use of "may" in introducing them, or as duties, as suggested by their location in Section 3. These also appear to have a mixed character. If, for example, the authority to convene Congress "on extraordinary occasions" vests a pure discretionary power, then the president would be under no obligation to convene Congress at all during a national emergency, even if Congress were not scheduled to meet for many months. (The early Congresses typically met only three to six months per year.)

Consider in this respect the most "extraordinary Occasion" ever to face the American nation: the attempted secession of southern states and the outbreak of armed hostilities at the beginning of President

Abraham Lincoln's first term. When Lincoln assumed the presidency on March 4, 1861, seven southern states had already voted to secede from the Union. Five weeks later, on April 12, Confederate forces fired upon Fort Sumter in Charleston harbor and the Civil War began. At this critical moment, however, Congress was not in session, having adjourned on March 3, and was not scheduled to reconvene until December 2, 1861.[24] Under a strict reading of the president's convening authority, Lincoln was not required to convene Congress at all; for to say that "he may, on extraordinary Occasions, convene [Congress]" is to imply necessarily that he also "may not" convene them. Lincoln, it would follow, could have governed with a free hand for nearly eight months after war had begun.

The structure of Article II, however, shows us that this is too loose a reading of the President's authority to convene Congress; for its location in Section 3, with the other specific duties, points to the obligatory nature of this authority. The Constitution implies that the president has a positive duty to convene Congress when circumstances seem to warrant. And, indeed, Lincoln did call Congress into special session for July 4, 1861, or five months before the scheduled date. But note that Lincoln issued this call back in mid-April (in his April 15 proclamation that called out a militia force of 75,000 "To cause the laws to be duly executed"), allowing more than two and half months for the members to make their way to Washington. At a time when telegraphs and railroads were common, Congress surely could have been convened sooner. Implicitly obliged to convene Congress to deal with the national crisis, Lincoln used both the independence of his office and the discretion built into the convening authority to give himself a bit more leeway—and thus a bit more power to control the national government's response to the crisis—than would have been the case if Congress had been convened at the earliest possible moment. That said, Lincoln did call Congress back into session, fulfilling his obligation to give Congress the opportunity to fulfill its constitutional role to enact legislation regularizing the government's handling of this unprecedented crisis.

As for the president's apparently discretionary authority to adjourn Congress when the two houses cannot agree—"he may adjourn them to such Time as he shall think proper"—it must be noted that there may well be occasions when it is proper for the House and Senate to adjourn at different times, when, for example, the Senate wishes to remain in session to consider appointments or treaties. The presumption, however, of locating this clause in Section 3 is that at bottom this is really an obligatory duty: if the House and Senate simply cannot agree when to adjourn, the president must act to settle the matter.

Powers and Duties in Action: The Whiskey Rebellion

The early history of the presidency affords us an excellent example of the relevance of the powers-duty distinction to the exercise of executive authority: President George Washington's actions during the Whiskey Rebellion.[25] In 1792 resistance in western Pennsylvania to the recently passed excise tax on distilled liquor prompted Washington to consider extraordinary measures to enforce the law. "It is my duty," he wrote his secretary of the treasury, Alexander Hamilton in September, "To see the Law executed: to permit them to be trampled upon with impunity would be repugnant to it."[26] One week later the president, citing "The particular duty of the Executive 'to take care that the laws be faithfully executed,'" issued a formal proclamation exhorting the resisters to obey the law.[27] Although resistance subsided for a while, it flared anew in the summer of 1794.

Washington remained resolute in his determination to enforce the law. He required of his cabinet members written opinions as to what to do, and then, following Hamilton's advice, prepared to call out a militia force of 12,000 men.[28] In accordance with the law of May 2, 1792—"An Act to provide for calling forth the Militia to execute the laws of the Union, suppress insurrections and repel invasions"[29]—the administration transmitted evidence of the resistance to Associate Supreme Court Justice James Wilson for certification that the laws could not be enforced by the ordinary judicial process and Washington issued a new proclamation stating the intentions of the government to enforce the law and calling for an end to the resistance. Before resorting to military measures, however, Washington made one last effort to defuse the insurrection peaceably. He sent a commission of three to the area of resistance to offer concessions to the resisters, including a general pardon for those who had not yet been indicted for violating federal law, in exchange for assurances of future compliance with the excise law.[30]

With the failure of these measures to restore order, the military operation commenced, a fact announced by Washington on September 25, 1794, in his third proclamation on the subject. The president acted, said the proclamation, "in obedience to that high and irresistible duty, consigned to me by the Constitution, 'to take care that the laws be faithfully executed.'"[31] Washington joined the military force at Carlisle, Pennsylvania, and accompanied it part way to its destination. He supervised the training and organization of the forces, determined the order of command, and labored to instill a due sense of responsibility in the officers and soldiers.[32]

Clearly, Washington believed that the "take Care" clause of Article II, Section 3, imposed on him a duty—"that high and irresistible duty"—to enforce the law. To that end he employed all the powers granted to him in the first paragraph of Section 2: the powers to require opinions in writing, to grant pardons, and to command the military. Constitutionally granted powers, or means, were made to serve a constitutionally imposed duty, or end. The Constitution itself both imposed the duty and provided the means for fulfilling it.

We should note here just how broadly Washington interpreted the duty imposed by the "take Care" clause. At its narrowest, the clause—"he shall take Care that the Laws be faithfully executed"—could be understood as requiring little more than administrative oversight: taking care that those who actually execute the laws do so honestly, consistently, and in conformity with both the letter and spirit of the law. Yet Washington's reading of the clause went far beyond this to embrace citizen obedience. That Washington so understood the clause and that he publicly announced this understanding on more than one occasion is itself powerful evidence that this broad interpretation was widely accepted at the time. And indeed, this view is quite consistent with the precise meaning of the verb "execute," which from the Latin *ex* and *sequi* means, "to follow out." Citizens themselves have a duty to follow out the law. When they obey the laws—by, for example, paying their taxes—they are contributing to the execution of the laws. It was, in fact, an essential element of early American republican thought that the principal way in which the laws are executed in a republic is through voluntary citizen obedience. As the Anti-Federalist Richard Henry Lee wrote, "In free governments the people, or their representatives, make the laws; their execution is principally the effect of voluntary consent and aid."[33] In a word, the people execute the laws by freely obeying them.

Thus, when the Constitution authorizes Congress to pass laws "To provide for calling forth the Militia to execute the Laws of the Union," this has, of course, nothing to do with using military force against recalcitrant or corrupt executive officials and everything to do with enforcing popular obedience to the laws. Similarly, in language even closer to the president's duty to "take Care that the Laws be faithfully executed," Congress in 1807 passed a law authorizing the president to use the nation's military "for the purpose of . . . causing the laws to be duly executed" whenever there was an "obstruction to the laws, either of the United States, or of any individual State or Territory." It would be odd indeed if the congressional language "causing the laws to be duly executed" referred broadly to ensuring citizen obedience, but the constitutional language "take Care that the Laws be faithfully executed" applied only to administrative oversight.[34]

This interpretation of Washington's actions during the Whiskey Rebellion in light of the powers-duties distinction of Article II also sheds important light on the commander-in-chief clause. In *Federalist* No. 69 Hamilton argued that the commander-in-chief authority "would amount to nothing more than the supreme command and direction of the military and naval forces, as first General and Admiral of the confederacy." By "nothing more" Hamilton meant that a U.S. president, unlike a British king, could not on his own authority declare war or raise armies and navies, since these authorities were specifically assigned to the Congress by the Constitution. Modern scholars often cite this as evidence that Hamilton understood the commander-in-chief power narrowly. Yet there is nothing in Hamilton's formulation to deny that a president may properly use his power of military command to serve duties constitutionally assigned to him, such as taking care that the laws are faithfully executed or, from his oath, preserving, protecting, and defending the Constitution.

The opening clause of Section 2 of Article II places the military might of the nation in the hands of the single person who occupies the executive office. This is power in its most obvious, awe-inspiring, and potentially dangerous form. In itself the commander-in-chief clause does not define the ends to which military command may be put, although it may well imply responsibilities for the proper management of the military forces. In a word, military command is a means, or power, placed in the president's hands to serve the ends, or duties, associated with his office. These duties are found elsewhere in Article II, and are limited, of course, by Congress's constitutional powers to raise and support military forces and to declare war.

Powers and Duties Writ Large

The centrality of powers and duties to the framers' understanding of the executive office is evident in more than the distinction between Sections 2 and 3 of Article II. Indeed, both Section 1, standing alone, and Article II as a whole begin with considerations of power and end with concern for duty. Section 1, for example, begins with the vesting of the "executive Power," and it ends with the two great duties imposed by the oath of office: to "faithfully execute the Office of the President of the United States" and "to the best of my Ability, preserve, protect and defend the Constitution of the United States." As is well known, the Constitution imposes this second overarching duty on no one but the president. All other federal and state legislators and executive and judicial officers are required to take an oath only "to support this Constitution." The president's unique duty to "preserve" the Constitution might well authorize actions that a less emphatic duty merely to "support" it would not.

Why give this special responsibility to the president? Because he, and only he, possesses the nation's "executive Power." "The power of directing and employing the common strength," Hamilton wrote in *Federalist* No. 74, "forms an usual and essential part in the definition of the executive authority." Once the great executive power has been placed in a single hand, the oath is necessary both to ensure that that power will be safely exercised—that it will not be used to subvert the Constitution—and to stimulate the occupant of the office to use his energies "to the best of [his] Ability" to preserve the constitutional order.

Finally, where Article II as a whole begins by vesting executive power, it ends by defining the price a president may pay for violating his duties: removal from office upon impeachment by the House of Representatives and conviction by the Senate. The specific offenses that can lead to this result are "Treason, Bribery, or other high crimes and Misdemeanors."

When the Committee of Detail drafted its constitution in early August, it revised the standard for impeachable offenses from "malpractice or neglect of duty," previously passed by the delegates, to "treason, bribery, or corruption."[35] Some weeks later the Committee on Unfinished Business dropped "corruption," leaving only "treason" and "bribery."[36] This is how matters stood as late as September 8, when the issue came before the delegates. Here George Mason objected that as the clause then stood "many great and dangerous offenses" were not covered. Mason noted specifically that the "treason and bribery" standard would not have reached the case of Warren Hastings, the former British governor of India who was then undergoing lengthy and highly contentious impeachment proceedings in the British House of Commons. "Attempts to subvert the Constitution," Mason argued, ought to be impeachable but might not amount to "treason or bribery." To broaden the standard to cover such cases, Mason proposed adding "maladministration" as an impeachable offense. In the face of an objection from Madison that this would be "equivalent to a tenure during pleasure of the Senate," Mason withdrew "maladministration" and substituted "other high crimes and misdemeanors against the State." This was then changed to "against the United States," which phrase was dropped entirely a few days later by the Committee of Style.[37]

Although we have very limited evidence as to how the framers understood "high crimes and misdemeanors,"[38] at least this much can be said: All agreed that a president who committed either of the two political crimes, treason and bribery, ought to be subject to removal from office. Yet there appeared to be other dangerous acts, potentially subversive of the Constitution itself, that were not actually treason or bribery but were more serious than general maladministration. Such subversive acts would obviously be contrary to the president's high duties to faithfully execute his office and to preserve, protect, and defend the Constitution. The duties in the president's oath of office, imposed on him alone among all those in positions of public trust, constitute the ultimate standard against which to judge his stewardship.

Conclusion

As we noted at the beginning, many who are otherwise impressed with the framers' legal craftsmanship tend to withhold their praise from Article

II of the U.S. Constitution. They believe that there is no particular rhyme or reason to its content and structure, that its particular authorities were vague and were assembled more or less randomly. But, on its face, does this make sense? Does it comport with what we know about those who crafted the Constitution?

The framers of the country's second constitution knew perfectly well that in establishing a largely independent, unitary chief executive with a potentially unlimited tenure in office, they were breaking new ground. As men of broad experience in matters of law and government, it seems unlikely that they would have settled for a haphazard construction of the president's essential authorities. That we have forgotten how to read Article II properly probably owes more to the fact that, for the framers, the distinction between powers and duties and the logic connecting them were so obvious that no extended explication or commentary was required. As we have seen in the case of Washington and the Whiskey Rebellion, this understanding of the president's authorities was indeed part of the governing grammar.

Reading Article II as we have remains highly relevant today. Consider, for example, the president's pardon power. On first glance at the Constitution, it appears to be a plenary power; for the Constitution does not limit whom the president may pardon or for what federal crimes (except that he may not pardon in cases of impeachments). But what if a president were found to have granted a pardon to cover up his own role in breaking the law? What if a president opposed to "criminalizing" some behaviors punishable under federal law pardoned everyone convicted under the applicable criminal statute? Wouldn't such a president have violated both his specific duty to "to take Care that the Laws be faithfully executed" and his larger obligation to "faithfully execute the Office of President"? Having violated those duties, wouldn't this president legitimately face impeachment and possible removal from office? It is the logic of Article II that powers serve duties, and that a serious violation of duty may justify impeachment.

The Constitution, as we have pointed out, gives the president a unique oath, and therefore a unique responsibility. Once the new government was functioning in 1789, plans were drawn up to give the president a home to live in — the only constitutional officer so privileged. Both the president's oath and his home point to the exceptional nature of the executive office. It is the one branch of government that operates, as we say, 24/7. It should be no surprise then that the framers took some care in crafting not only the institutional features of the new "energetic" executive but also the office's specific authorities. Read as intended, Article II's interplay of powers and duties should remind us not only of the president's potentially expansive authorities, but also of the large and specific responsibilities that inform and limit how he should exercise them.

CHAPTER THREE

President Washington's Proclamation of Neutrality

GARY J. SCHMITT

CONSTITUTIONAL INTERPRETATION, as a rule, tends to divide scholars, judges, and commentators between two camps: those looking to
find some "original intent" on which to hang their hats and those want-
ing to "see into" the Constitution some principle that time, knowledge,
and circumstances should now bring to the fore regardless of whether the
founding generation would recognize it as belonging to the constitutional
order they intended. But a striking exception to this split occurs when it
comes to interpreting the powers of the presidency in the area of national
security. Here, more than in any other area of constitutional disputation,
one finds both defenders and critics of presidential decisions racing to
find quotes, arguments, and precedents from the founding period to bol-
ster their views on what the president should or should not do when it
comes to foreign affairs and national security. This is even more salient
when one thinks about the fundamentally altered position of the country in world affairs from 1787 to today. If there were ever a situation ripe
for reading the Constitution as a "living" document, one would think this
would be it. Yet, there is something about such a fundamental civic issue
as war and peace that we are continually drawn back to the founding
period for guidance. Indeed, few today would argue that we should jetti-
son the framers' allocation of the war and foreign affairs powers between
the Congress and presidency.

Complicating these efforts, however, is the fact that the actual powers
of the presidency were not widely discussed in the Constitutional Convention and the follow-on state ratification conventions. In Philadelphia,
the overwhelming portion of the debate about the executive focused on
working out the office's structure—a plural or singular executive, the president's tenure, and his mode of selection. Far less time was spent discussing

the meaning of the particular powers that came to be vested with the president. Even *The Federalist* is, from a constitutional lawyer's point of view, short on explication of the president's authorities and, arguably, not always clear in the few instances where those powers are discussed.

Naturally enough, this less-than-definitive record in the convention and ratification period leads one to look at the early precedents on the use of executive power. What decisions the first presidents made, what authorities they wielded, and how the other branches of government and the political opposition reacted to the use of executive power are seen as telling examples of what the Constitution's framers had in mind when they created the executive office. Hence, it is no surprise that those interested in divining the framers' intentions would look at Washington's handling of the first major foreign policy crisis under the new constitution — war in Europe and the issuance of the Neutrality Proclamation in 1793.

Yet, the examination of the debate surrounding Washington's proclamation has often generated more confusion than clarity, as scholars and commentators see not one, but two key framers — Hamilton and Madison — squaring off over the proper understanding of the president's constitutional powers. As this chapter attempts to show, however, there is more to the precedent than just the debate between Pacificus and Helvidius. Indeed, there is even more to that particular debate when examined more closely. This episode, taken as a whole, provides us a unique look into this earliest of important exercises of presidential power. Equally important, a thorough examination of this precedent also gives us a unique perspective on the possibilities and paradoxes of the exercise of executive power itself, touching directly on that core issue raised by Publius in *Federalist* No. 70, that "there is an idea which is not without its advocates, that a vigorous executive is inconsistent with the genius of republican government."

The Crisis Unfolds

Whatever the United States' long-term advantage in being separated from Europe by the Atlantic Ocean, the immediate problem the nation faced in the wake of independence was encirclement by the colonial possessions of two imperial powers: Spain and Great Britain. Through its North American possessions in the west and in the south, Spain controlled navigation rights on the Mississippi and, as such, had a significant say over the commercial life of Americans living west of the Appalachians. Spain also held Florida and was asserting claims over large areas of what eventually would become parts of Alabama, Mississippi, Tennessee, and Kentucky. Concerned about possible U.S. plans to expand to the west and south, Madrid was not above stoking secessionist fires among disgruntled American frontiersmen. To the north, Great Britain retained control over Canada. From there, the British provided assistance to Vermonters conspiring to rejoin the empire and, with trade and aid, supported the Indians of the Northwest Territory in their effort to impede American settlers from moving into the region. In the east, London had closed its West Indian ports to U.S. trade. And, in retaliation for the Americans' failure to carry out fully the terms of the peace treaty ending the Revolutionary War, Britain still manned strategically placed forts on U.S. soil in the Northwest Territory.

Accordingly, before the United States could enjoy its splendid isolation from Europe and the world's great powers, it first had to address its encirclement in North America. But it had to do so, if possible, without getting involved in a war that it could not afford at this stage in its development. For American statesmen of the time, the central difficulty was that Great Britain, the country that posed the greatest threat to the United States, was also the nation's largest trading partner. And it was on the back of that trade—and the federal revenues it generated—that the new government's plans for the country's fiscal stability and commercial prosperity rested.

Further complicating America's security were the turmoil and wars brought about by the French Revolution. Initially, most Americans were favorably disposed toward events in France, believing that the establishment of a second liberal republic in the world might lesson the United States' own international isolation. In the years following 1789, however, American public opinion began to divide as the revolution took on a more radical cast and the French regime grew increasingly unstable. The division was essentially between those who retained some hope for what the revolution might eventuate in and those who dismissed it for what it had become.

The split in American opinion largely mirrored, and became a partisan touchstone for, the division between the Federalists, who supported

Secretary of Treasury Alexander Hamilton's London-centric fiscal and commercial policies, and the emerging party of Democratic-Republicans, led by Secretary of State Thomas Jefferson and Congressman James Madison, who saw closer ties to France as a means to break the Anglophilia they thought animated the Washington administration's policies. For Republicans, it was particularly significant that America's only treaty-based alliance was with France. Two treaties had been signed in 1778 with the *ancien régime*: a Treaty of Amity and Commerce and a Treaty of Alliance.[1] Under the terms of the latter, the United States had committed itself to defending France's West Indian possessions in a time of war.

"Strict Neutrality"

Through this maze of strategic interests, treaty obligations, and domestic politics, it was not evident that the United States could stay clear of war. Matters were coming to a head in 1792. While France had suffered a spring and summer of disastrous military campaigns in its war with Austria and Prussia, the autumn brought a sudden reversal of fortune with success on the battlefield and the conquest of the Southern Netherlands. Flush with this success, the French government announced in November its willingness to support revolutionary efforts outside of France and promised assistance to any people trying to "recover their liberty" by toppling their monarch. Two months later, France beheaded its own king, Louis XVI. Then, on February 1, 1793, Paris formally declared war against its remaining monarchic neighbors: Spain, Great Britain, and Britain's ally, the Netherlands.

Word of these events made their way slowly across the Atlantic. By early April, Secretary of State Jefferson was convinced that the reports of a general war in Europe were true and so wrote the president at Mount Vernon. Washington responded with notes to Jefferson and Hamilton, saying he was canceling his plan to stay in Virginia for the month and would make his way back to Philadelphia immediately. In his response, the president made it clear that he was especially worried that American ship owners and seamen would find the opportunity provided by the war to make large sums of money by privateering for either France or Great Britain too attractive to resist. He insisted that the cabinet give prompt attention to determining what measures were needed "to prevent" U.S. citizens "from embroiling us with either of those powers." His goal, he wrote, was to establish a policy of "strict neutrality" between London and Paris.[2]

As promised, Washington hurried back to Philadelphia, arriving on Wednesday, April 17. The Second Congress had adjourned a month before and the Third Congress was not scheduled to meet until December. The day after his return, Washington circulated to his cabinet a list of thirteen questions, answers to which, he indicated, would form "a general plan of conduct for the executive" in addressing the crisis at hand. On Friday, Washington and his cabinet met. It was "agreed by all" that a proclamation should be issued by the president "forbidding" U.S. citizens from undertaking any activities that might undermine U.S. neutrality between the two powers. Prepared by Attorney General Edmund Randolph, the proclamation declared that it was the United States' intention to "pursue a conduct friendly and impartial towards the belligerent powers." Washington signed and issued the proclamation the following Monday, April 22.[3]

Interpreting the Proclamation

Despite the unanimity within Washington's cabinet over the desirability of issuing the proclamation, questions immediately arose about the proclamation's precise character and, in turn, the president's authority to issue it.

Many Republicans initially interpreted the proclamation as a binding declaration of U.S. policy that, they also believed, exceeded the president's constitutional powers. Madison complained to Jefferson that the proclamation's "unqualified terms" established America's position as one of "unconditional neutrality," a position that seemed to ignore the country's existing treaty obligations with France. By "express articles," the United States had guaranteed, Madison argued, French possessions in the West Indies. Yet, with his proclamation the president had unilaterally determined that the United States was not bound to guarantee French possessions and would not go to war to protect them. Madison did not think this was a matter the president could legitimately determine on his own. The "right" to choose between "war and peace," he wrote Jefferson, was "vested in the Legislature" by the Constitution.[4]

Essays appearing in the Republican-leaning *National Gazette* in May and the early part of June 1793 made similar points. The president had assumed kingly powers, it was argued. Not only had Washington annulled existing treaty obligations on his own, he was also threatening, without the benefit of a duly-enacted law, criminal proceedings against U.S. citizens exercising their "sacred rights" as free individuals to assist the French.[5]

It was in response to these public attacks that Secretary of Treasury Alexander Hamilton set out to defend both the president's authority to issue the proclamation and the wisdom of doing so. Writing under the pseudonym "Pacificus," Hamilton penned seven essays that appeared in Philadelphia in the *Gazette of the United States* from the end of June through late July. Pacificus argued that the president had in fact issued a formal and binding "Proclamation of Neutrality," that he was within his constitutional powers to do so, and that, for solid reasons of state, the United States was not bound by its treaty with France to defend its island possessions from attacks by Great Britain.[6] The heart of the constitutional defense is found in the first and longest essay: Article II of the Constitution vests "the executive power" in the president, and this authority includes not only the power to execute the laws but also (following the analysis of the executive power found in the writings of Locke, Montesquieu, and Blackstone) the "federative power" to manage a country's foreign affairs.[7] And, although the Constitution admitted exceptions to the executive power by giving Congress the right to declare war and the Senate a say in making treaties, these were merely exceptions to the wider compass of executive power and were not to be viewed as anything but. Accordingly, Pacificus argued, it was Washington's constitutional prerogative, as the executive, to interpret and determine the country's obligations under its existing treaties.[8] In the six essays that followed, Pacificus set about cataloguing the arguments that justified Washington's determination that, despite the terms of the treaty with France, the United States was not bound to become "an *associate* or *auxiliary* in the War."[9]

Initially, then, both the defenders and critics of the proclamation interpreted it in a similar fashion: the proclamation was a formal declaration of U.S. policy that not only proscribed Americans from provocative activities but also announced to the world that the U.S. government believed that it was under no obligation to defend France's West Indian possessions.

The proclamation's critics, however, faced a particular political problem. Despite the existence of considerable sympathy for France within the American citizenry, most Americans seemed to favor keeping the country out of war.[10] As a result, Republican essayists often decried the fact that the administration was turning its back on France at a critical time but, then, typically, went on to suggest that American assistance need not include U.S. military involvement in the war.[11] In short, although the proclamation's critics disliked its reach and the assertion of executive authority it seemed to rest on, like the population as a whole they were largely in agreement with the proclamation's overarching goal.

Led by Jefferson, Republicans eventually attempted to square this circle by arguing that the proclamation was not in fact a formal "Proclamation of Neutrality." To his friends, Jefferson pointed out that the proclamation did not actually use the term "neutrality" and did not explicitly repudiate the treaty or the U.S. guarantee. Moreover, the United States had no military force capable of fulfilling the guarantee in any case. There was little chance, then, that France would force the issue by asking for American military help in protecting its possessions in the West Indies.[12] Jefferson's position was that there was no reason for the Republicans to concede that the proclamation had formally determined an answer to a question that had not, and likely would not, be raised.[13]

Having found a way to save, at least nominally, the alliance with France, Republicans could turn their efforts to contesting the nature of the precedent that Washington seemed to be setting with the proclamation's issuance. It was obvious that the president's decision to issue the proclamation—and do so without Congress's involvement—was an important precedent. The task at hand for Jefferson and the Republicans was to limit it by narrowing the grounds on which the president's action could be constitutionally justified. By mid-summer 1793, the issue was no longer the president's policy, but rather Hamilton's claims about what the president's actions meant constitutionally. It was with some urgency, then, that Jefferson wrote to Madison complaining, after the first three essays of Pacificus had been published, that "nobody answers him." If left unchallenged, "his doctrine will . . . be taken for confessed."[14]

With some reluctance it appears, Madison took up his pen in response.

Writing under the pseudonym "Helvidius," Madison authored five essays.[15] The first was published in late August and the last in mid-September. Ignoring everything but Pacificus' claims regarding the nature of the president's "executive power," Helvidius argued that the president's essential function—his "natural province" as the official vested with "the executive power"—is "to execute laws."[16] From this it follows that Congress's power to declare war cannot be read as an exception to a general grant of executive authority when, according to Madison, that power is properly understood as limited in scope. In fact, the power to authorize war, along with the power to make treaties, is more akin to the legislative function of enacting laws than executing them. Hence, if Washington's decision to issue the proclamation is to be justified constitutionally, it cannot rest on the exaggerated claims about the meaning of "the executive power." Helvidius argues instead that it must rest on the implicit obligation of the president, as the nation's chief executive, to maintain the country's existing legal condition—in this case, a state of peace—until Congress has met and voted to declare war or not.[17]

Under the Constitution, as Helvidius reads it, power over war and peace lies with Congress and it is the president's duty, given the limited reach of "the executive power," not to infringe on the exercise of Congress's prerogative.[18] Properly understood, Washington's decision to issue the proclamation was an example of executive deference, not presidential prerogative. The proclamation was not establishing new policy; rather, it was keeping the nation at peace until Congress determined otherwise.[19] Hence, the precedent being set by the proclamation's issuance was, under Helvidius's reading, considerably different from what Pacificus had claimed.

As for the president himself, Washington never explicitly clarified what his own views were about the proclamation's reach or the constitutional grounds for issuing it.[20] On the one hand, in his correspondence Washington was more likely than not to refer to the proclamation as the "Proclamation of Neutrality," terms suggesting a broad reading of what he had done.[21] On the other hand, when it came time to inform Congress in his "state of the Union" address in December 1793 of what he had done, he described the proclamation as "a declaration of the existing legal state of things" and noted that it was within Congress's power "to correct, improve, or enforce" the rules subsequently issued by him in carrying out the proclamation.[22]

From the latter, Madison biographer Irving Brant has concluded that

> Washington's address to Congress . . . left no doubt of the effect of
> Madison's reply to "Pacificus." Jefferson, who wrote the passage on
> foreign affairs, was able to describe the neutrality proclamation
> merely as a declaration of the legal state of things, designed to pre-
> vent Americans from engaging in hostile acts. This was the same as
> saying that Hamilton ("Pacificus") had no warrant for calling it a
> denial of future obligations under the treaty of France.[23]

The House of Representatives' reply, which Madison helped craft, attempted to seal this interpretation by declaring that "the maintenance of peace was justly regarded as one of the most important duties of the Magistrate charged with the faithful execution of the laws" and, thus, the proclamation's defense of "the existing legal state of things" was an appropriate measure taken by the president.[24]

Brant's reading of this exchange, however, is not definitive. For one thing, the Senate's response to the president's message was different from that of the House. The Senate described the proclamation as having declared "the disposition of the nation for peace . . . to the world," suggesting a somewhat broader understanding of what the president had done.[25] Moreover, Washington's use of the phrase "existing legal state of affairs" and his stated deference to Congress's right to pass new legislation changing what he had done were not at odds with the views of any of his Federalist defenders, including Pacificus. No Federalist defender of the president denied Congress' potential role in regulating these matters.

Even though Pacificus believed it "advisable" to provide a "broad and comprehensive" constitutional justification for the proclamation's issuance, even he argued at the end of the first essay that it was not "absolutely necessary to do so." It is "entirely erroneous" that the proclamation's critics have "represented [it] as enacting some new law." Seen within the context of existing U.S. treaties (including a peace treaty with Great Britain) and the law of nations, Pacificus argues that the proclamation "only proclaims a fact with regard to the existing state of the nation, informs the citizens of what the laws previously established require of them in that state, & warns them that these laws will be put in execution against the infractors of them." Accordingly, Washington's duty under the Constitution to execute the laws was, Pacificus claims, sufficient to justify what he had done. In short, Washington's description of the proclamation as "a declaration of the existing legal state of things" was one both Republicans and Federalists could agree on.[26]

This last point is significant. The initial reaction to Washington's proclamation was partisan and heated, with much of the heat directed at Washington personally. By late fall 1793, however, the partisanship had given way to general support for the policy of neutrality, if not the precise grounds to justify it. The president had been inundated by resolutions from around the country—from areas controlled by Federalists and Republicans alike—that praised both him and his policies. With this new unanimity in hand, and still concerned about the level of partisanship within and outside his administration, Washington might have concluded that the most politically prudent course was to justify the proclamation and the rules to carry it out in terms likely to generate the least debate. This was not the time to renew a fight. The Federalists were expected to lose control of the House in the next session of Congress, and Washington might well have thought it best not to put the new Congress in a mind to challenge him and his policies.[27] If this was Washington's stratagem, it was successful: both houses of Congress formally praised the president for the actions he had taken and, with minor exception, enacted into law the policies he had already put in place.

The Proclamation's Administration

Washington was never forced to make a final choice between the arguments of Pacificus and Helvidius, and he didn't. As divergent as the two sets of essays were on the fundamental question of the nature of "the executive power" vested by Article II, both provided the president with sufficient constitutional authority to issue the proclamation. And because Paris was unlikely to call on the United States to fulfill its pledge to protect France's American possessions, there seemed to be no issue on the horizon that might force Washington to abandon his silence and assert the proclamation's ultimate meaning. But the proclamation's significance as a precedent for the exercise of presidential power did not begin and end with its issuance. Between April 1793, when Washington signed the proclamation, and the following December, when the Third Congress convened for the first time, the administration took a number of steps to ensure that the policy outlined in the proclamation was implemented. In carrying out the proclamation, the Washington administration exercised authorities that, in certain respects, revealed as much about the nature of the new executive office and its institutional capacity as the decision to issue the proclamation in the first place.

To start, shortly after Edmond Charles Genet, the new French ambassador, had arrived in America, news reached the capital that French warships and newly commissioned privateers had seized a number of British merchant ships as prizes. When the vessels were brought into American ports, it was learned that most of the captures had taken place close to U.S. shores. George Hammond, Great Britain's representative in the United States, immediately asked the administration to take the ships from French control and return them to their owners. Since the British ships had not been captured on the high seas as allowed by the laws of war, he argued that the seizures were illegal. The problem the administration faced, however, in responding to Hammond's demarche was that the United States had never set its maritime boundaries. What constituted "U.S. waters" had not been formally established. Pushed by the necessity of giving the British ambassador an answer, the administration, after a bit of deliberation, fixed the country's home waters at one sea league (three maritime miles) from shore. That determination then became the binding rule used to determine future disputes over captures and claims of illegal seizures.[28]

In an effort to maintain the country's neutrality, the Washington administration was also determined to prohibit U.S. citizens from enlisting in the service of any of the belligerents.[29] Without the benefit of any guiding federal statute, and in the face of complaints that he was exercising "despotic" powers in doing so, the president outlawed Americans from joining in the fray: there would be no U.S. citizens serving on board French privateers, no U.S. citizens joining British-sponsored expeditions against French West Indian possessions, and no U.S. citizens involving themselves in French schemes to launch a military campaign from Kentucky aimed at the Spanish-held city of New Orleans.[30]

But of all the decisions taken by the administration to implement the proclamation, perhaps the most significant was its determination to prohibit France and its ambassador from outfitting privateers in American ports. Under the 1778 Treaty of Amity and Commerce with France, the United States had agreed to deny France's enemies that privilege. The treaty was silent, however, on the question of whether Paris could use American ports as a base from which to commission its privateers. Read one way, the silence could be interpreted as implying a French right to use U.S. ports for that purpose. Moreover, there was a matter of America's debt to France for allowing American naval captain John Paul Jones to use its ports to raid British shipping during the early years of the Revolutionary War and before France had formally sided with the United States. Nevertheless, the president and his cabinet were unanimous in the view that the treaty's prohibition against France's enemies did not, in turn, imply a positive right for France. Although the French government had some expectation that the American government might allow —or at least turn a blind eye to—the outfitting of French privateers from its ports, the administration consistently operated under the assumption that the policy of neutrality required denying Paris that privilege.[31]

Like the decision to fix the country's maritime boundaries, the administration's ruling on French use of American ports arose in response to cases that followed pretty quickly in the wake of the proclamation's issuance. By mid-summer 1793, Washington and his cabinet were convinced a more systematic and prescriptive approach to this and related questions was necessary. During the second half of July, the cabinet crafted a relatively comprehensive code ("Rules Governing Belligerents") that was intended to regulate the arming, repair, and equipping of vessels of the belligerent states in U.S. ports. Described as being "deductions from the laws of neutrality," the rules established, in effect, a kind of "administrative law of neutrality."[32]

Implementing the proclamation was a complex and, at times, difficult task. But the most potentially explosive problem facing the administration came in the person of Genet, France's ambassador to the United States. Buoyed by the enthusiastic public reception he received upon his arrival in the United States, and misconstruing Jefferson's initial willingness to confide in him the comings and goings of cabinet politics, Genet was unwilling to accept the administration's decisions when he thought they conflicted with either French interests or what he believed French rights were under existing treaties. By summer, Genet was not only taking steps to challenge the substance of many of Washington's decisions, but he was also questioning the authority of the president to make them. Again, acting unilaterally, the administration responded to Genet's actions, in one case, by revoking the privileges of the French consul in Boston and, finally, by requesting that the French government recall Genet himself.[33]

These efforts to implement the proclamation and to request Genet's recall could have been constitutionally justified by the arguments of either Pacificus or Helvidius. For Pacificus, this authority naturally followed from "the executive power," understood broadly. For Helvidius, however, the president's power fell into his hands by a kind of constitutional "back door." In carrying out what Helvidius describes as an essentially ministerial role in maintaining the legal status quo, Washington was apparently authorized to wield authorities that were themselves not simply ministerial, nor minimal.[34] Between the goal of maintaining "the existing legal state of things" and the actual establishment of a regime of neutrality, there existed considerable room for the exercise of executive discretion. And while this discretion was not without limits, it was considerable: so much so that the president appeared at times to be less engaged in executing the laws than in creating them. As the cabinet's administration of the proclamation revealed, even Madison's narrow account of executive power had the potential, under certain circumstances, to expand into an authority that was anything but narrow.[35]

Moreover, the possible consequences resulting from the proclamation's administration were not of an order normally associated with the exercise of ministerial-like functions. Although a system of "strict neutrality" was adopted by the Washington administration, international practice at the time appears to have not required this degree of impartiality. A state might have retained its neutral status, and the privileges associated with that status, even while it provided material assistance of various kinds to the powers at war. This was especially true in those instances in which the neutral power had, by virtue of a treaty, obligations of some sort to the belligerents. Accordingly, because the United States observed "strict neutrality" between France and Great Britain in every particular, Paris might have accused the Americans of adopting a policy more favorable to the British than was absolutely necessary.[36] Thus, if it had been in Paris's interest to do so, France could have used the request for Genet's recall to end friendly relations between the France and the United States.

Although unlikely, it was even possible that Genet's recall would have led to hostilities.[37] As British Ambassador Hammond speculated in a note back to his own government, should the French government "determine to support its minister—this order of things must issue in war between France and this country."[38]

For a number of reasons, events did not unfold as Hammond conjectured they might. Nevertheless, we should not lose sight of the fact that Washington's efforts to keep the United States from becoming involved in Europe's war required him to make decisions that might have entangled the country in a major foreign policy crisis and, perhaps, even armed conflict. In such circumstances, a president who understood his role as chief executive to be fairly circumscribed and believed his principal duty was to keep the country at peace until the Congress had met would presumably have thought it his constitutional duty to call Congress into session early to get from it a firm set of directives on what U.S. policy should be. But, as noted above, the Second Congress had closed its doors in March 1793—before word of the war in Europe had reached the United States—and the Third Congress was not due to meet until December. Washington and his cabinet twice considered calling the new Congress into session early, but they decided not to.[39] For seven event-filled months, the Washington administration established and managed a system of neutrality on its own. The fact that Washington did not call Congress into session and no public outcry arose as a result strongly suggests that the Madisonian model of active presidential deference to Congress was not the prevailing understanding of the time.

Actually, the sharpest criticism of the administration's decision not to involve Congress more directly in these matters came from the French ambassador and not members of the House or the Senate. Frustrated by Washington's minimalist reading of the United States' obligations to France, Genet told Secretary of State Jefferson that these were decisions that "ought not to have been made by the Executive without consulting Congress, and that on the return of the President [to Philadelphia from a visit to Mount Vernon] he would certainly press him to convene the Congress."[40] According to Jefferson, his own reply was blunt: on questions related to the interpretation of treaties, "the constitution had made the president the last appeal." The U.S. government, he told Genet, had "divided the functions of government among three different authorities . . .

each of which were supreme in all questions belonging to their department and independent of the others." On those "questions" that had arisen between France and the United States, it was up to "the Executive department" to decide. Even "if Congress were sitting," such issues "could not be carried to them, nor would they take notice of them." When it came to these matters, Jefferson informed Genet, the president was "the highest authority."[41]

Seeking Support

Despite having both a constitutional justification for taking the initiative and the institutional capacity to do so, the administration was uneasy as it began to implement the proclamation. Political tensions were high. Pro-French sentiment among the public was considerable and "the republican interest" would, it was thought, be in control of the incoming Congress. Although the basic goal of staying free of the conflict was shared by most everyone, there was still plenty of room for debate about how to do so.

Moreover, Washington and his cabinet did not have the luxury of easing into the proclamation's enforcement. Disputes immediately arose over the proclamation's meaning and how to apply it in particular cases and circumstances. Handling each case as it arose was a considerable administrative and political burden. The cabinet quickly came to the conclusion that a comprehensive set of rules needed to be promulgated to put an end to some of the uncertainties that were producing this steady stream of mini-crises.

Crafting the "Rules Governing Belligerents" involved the administration in interpreting and applying existing treaties, international law, and the common law. Given the nature of the task, Washington and his cabinet decided in mid-July to submit a list of twenty-nine questions to the Supreme Court (to those "learned in the laws") for their opinion on various legal issues related to neutrality's enforcement. In the letter accompanying the submission, Secretary of State Jefferson explicitly took note of the fact that the administration was asking the Court to involve itself in a matter outside its normal "cognisance." There was no case to be decided in this instance. But, he suggested, the administration was also a bit at sea since the issues facing the president were "little analogous to the ordinary functions of the Executive." By providing their expert legal opinions on these matters, the Court would help protect the administration "against errors dangerous to the peace" of the United States. In addition, as Jefferson seemed to admit, the Court's role as a nonpartisan body could be useful politically, should it decide to provide its advice. By connecting the reputation of the justices to the administration's decisions, the administration was hoping to "ensure the respect of all parties" to the rules and, implicitly, the policy they rested on.[42]

In July, when the cabinet submitted its questions to the Court, there appears to have been little, if any, discussion about the possible precedent being set by the executive seeking an opinion about foreign affairs from the judicial branch. The matter had come up previously, however. In May, Hamilton had argued in a memorandum submitted to the president that involving the Court in a dispute over the restitution of illegally seized British ships was to involve the justices in an issue they were not "competent" to decide. As the treasury secretary reasoned at the time, this was fundamentally an issue "between the Governments" and, as such, should be "settled by reasons of state, not rules of law." Asking the Court for advice would inevitably invite questions about the president's own constitutional authority to decide these matters. Once the precedent had been set of involving the Court, the president might be hard-pressed not to defer to its judgment in future controversies.

Perhaps Hamilton didn't raise any objections in July over the cabinet's submission since he had already made the case against seeking such advice and because he was confident that the Court would not respond positively to the administration's request in any case.[43] Moreover, none of the twenty-nine questions concerned the president's own authority to issue or enforce the rules under discussion.[44] And, in fact, the administration did not wait for the Court's guidance. The cabinet completed the "Rules for Belligerents" even before it received word that the Court rebuffed its request.[45]

Hamilton may (or may not) have had serious reservations about seeking assistance from the Court—and thus support from *within* the constitutional order—for the administration's policies. Surprisingly, he was apparently not shy about seeking support from *outside* it by rallying public opinion to the president's side. To understand Hamilton's actions, one should begin by remembering that the war in Europe presented the new

American government with its first major challenge. Many thought that the stability, prosperity, and even the existence of the country were at stake. The country could not afford mistaken or erratic policies. But most observers, including Washington and his cabinet, were unsure how the public would react in that spring and early summer to the administration's decisions. Hamilton and other Federalists were keenly aware of the favorable reception Genet had received from the public on his arrival in the United States and were quite worried about the harsh, and, from their perspective, Jacobin-like attacks on Washington and his policies.[46] They had never faced this kind of crisis before. The bitter partisanship was new, and they were uncertain whether the public's tacit support for the administration's policy of strict neutrality would last.[47]

To the Federalists' good fortune, the increasingly impolitic behavior of France's ambassador provided them with the opportunity to rally support for the president and his policies. Genet had not only publicly questioned the administration's policies, but, as his frustration with the president's decisions boiled over, made the mistake of threatening to go over Washington's head with an appeal to Congress and, if necessary, directly to the American people.[48] As soon as Hamilton and other Federalists found out about Genet's threat, they believed they had a way of moving opinion in the administration's favor. They assumed that once the French ambassador's slights of Washington and the constitutional order were made public, Americans' pride in their president and new constitution would turn them against Genet and increase their sympathy for Washington's efforts to maintain the country's neutrality.[49]

This was not an opportunity Hamilton could let pass by and, in Jefferson's words, the treasury secretary "pressed" Washington to use this information and make "an appeal to the people . . . with an eagerness I never saw before." Although the president was apparently attracted to the idea initially, he eventually agreed with Jefferson that Genet's behavior should first be taken up with the French through the normal diplomatic process. This did not stop the treasury secretary, however. Writing under the pseudonym "No Jacobin," Hamilton catalogued Genet's misconduct in a series of essays. He was joined in this effort by other Federalists, notably John Jay and Rufus King of New York. The cumulative impact was as they hoped: popular indignation toward the French ambassador and increased support for the president.[50]

But promoting general support for the president was not enough. If it was to have an impact politically, especially on the members of the incoming Congress, a means had to be found to give that support an effective voice. To this end, the Federalists resurrected from the country's revolutionary period the practice of calling mass meetings at which resolutions on public disputes would be debated and then voted up or down by the gathered crowd of citizens. Although the first of these town meetings was held in Boston before the No Jacobin essays appeared, the revelation of Genet's threats generated dozens of similar meetings and the passage of resolutions of support for the president in cities throughout the Northeast and mid-Atlantic areas. The meetings and resolutions were reported on locally and those stories, in turn, were reprinted by newspapers in neighboring cities and states. It soon appeared as though the whole nation was rallying around the president and his policies.[51]

And it was not just an impression. Jefferson himself admitted that there had been a real and substantial change in public opinion:

In N[ew] York, while Genet was there, the vote of a full meeting of all classes was 9 out of 10 against him, i.e., for the Proclamation . . . All the towns Northwardly are about to express their adherence to the proclamation and chiefly with a view to manifest their disapprobation of G[enet]'s conduct. Philadelphia, so enthusiastic for him, before his proceedings were known, is going over from him entirely.

The Federalists were even able to organize a public meeting in support of the president in Richmond, Virginia, normally a stronghold of Republican views.[52]

Stung by this avalanche of resolutions, Madison and James Monroe drafted their own model resolution, designed to reflect what they thought to be "the true and general sense of the people." Hoping to generate meetings at which resolutions would be passed along the lines proposed by them, the two distributed copies of their draft to allies in various Republican strongholds.[53] A more resigned Jefferson, however, had warned them that Genet's behavior made it imperative that Republicans "abandon" him "entirely." And since the American public's "desire for neutrality" was now "universal," there was little room left for the Republican-styled resolutions to differentiate themselves from those that had already been passed. As Stanley Elkins and Eric McKitrick conclude: "Except for matters of shading and emphasis—on the Proclamation and on friendship for the French people—there was now little in substance to choose between Republican resolutions and Federalist resolutions, and Washington benignly welcomed them all."[54]

With Hamilton's encouragement and possible direction, the Federalists won the "war of the resolutions." By exploiting Genet's behavior in this revolutionary-era fashion, they were able to help shape and solidify public opinion in favor of the president and his policies. Although it is obviously impossible to measure with any precision the effects of this campaign, the short-term political result seems to have been a quiescent legislature. In spite of the fact that the new Congress that convened in December 1793 was decidedly more Republican than its predecessor, it fully supported Washington's decisions.[55]

The long-term consequence, however, was to make way for a presidency tied to populist politics. With the exception principally of James Wilson, the Federalists had argued that insulating the chief executive to some degree from the tides of popular sentiment by creating a stable and independent office of some independence was one of the new constitution's principal advantages. Putting distance between the chief executive and the demands of popular politics allowed presidents to act, if necessary, against existing opinion for the greater and more permanent good of the country. But, by playing the public card as they had, Federalists were, in James Monroe's words, "seiz[ing] a new ground whereon to advance their fortunes."[56]

Not all Federalists were sure they had done the right thing. As Rufus King, Federalist senator from New York and organizer of New York City's own rally, reminded Hamilton, "We have with great trouble established a Constitution, which vests competent powers in the hands of the Executive." By relying on such "irregular measures" as mass rallies to generate support for the president, the administration's friends were legitimating a political stratagem that over time could "destroy the salutary influence of regular government." In particular, King worried that a reliance on these kinds of efforts had the effect of "render[ing] the magistracy a mere pageant," implying as they did that the public should have some immediate say in judging the executive's decisions. Despite his own role in orchestrating the public campaign on behalf of the president, King wondered whether what he had done was "altogether wrong."[57]

Setting a Precedent

The war between France and Great Britain was the first major crisis faced by the country under the new constitution. It was a test that the Washington administration helped the nation pass with flying colors. Lacking any congressional guidance, uncertain about public support, and facing unprecedented partisan opposition, the administration was still able to provide the kind of leadership that the Constitution's architects hoped would result from the creation of an independent and unitary executive office.

However, most presidential scholars, when they turn to Washington's issuance of the proclamation, focus chiefly on the debate over the president's powers between Pacificus and Helvidius. Given who was involved in the debate and the importance of the arguments themselves, this is certainly understandable. But the debate itself—as one might have predicted—did little to settle questions about the president's specific authorities. In part, this was because Washington never thought it necessary to provide an extended constitutional justification for his actions and, in part, because both Madison and Hamilton believed that Washington's actions could be justified under their respective but divergent accounts of "the executive power." At most, the controversy surrounding Washington's decision to issue the proclamation generated not one but two "authoritative" interpretations of presidential power, setting a "precedent" of sorts for subsequent debates down to this day.[58]

Yet, as important as the debate between Pacificus and Helvidius was in outlining two distinct constitutional paradigms for the exercise of presidential power, focusing simply on that debate can lead us to miss the actual decisions taken by Washington and the reactions to them by the body politic. As Charles Thach Jr., among others, has reminded us, a total absence of a distinct executive branch under the Articles of Confederation had left the United States with a federal government severely handicapped in the administration of the country's day-to-day affairs as well as in the management of crisis situations. A unitary and independent executive was needed not only to check legislative excesses in policymaking (a lesson learned particularly in the new states with their weak governors) but also to imbue the government with a facility for effective and decisive action. Creating such a capacity through the new presidential office was a critical priority of the framers.[59] From this perspective, Washington's behavior was not only well within the intent of the creators of his office but perhaps even predictable given the office's independence and unitary structure. Moreover, the fact that Washington did not call Congress back into session early to deal with this crisis suggests that although he voiced his willingness to abide by Congress's subsequent decisions on neutrality, he did not accept Helvidius's most fundamental assertion that the chief executive should do nothing that would impinge on the legislative branch's say over matters of war and peace. Here, at least, Washington's actions speak louder than his few words.

Finally, the arguments put forward by Madison as Helvidius and Hamilton as Pacificus, when examined in the context of the politics and policies of the time, highlight the latent paradoxical character of executive power in a republican government. Madison depicts an executive whose formal authority appears quite limited but who, in certain narrow circumstances and in supposed deference to Congress, can nevertheless wield extensive prerogatives in service of the limited goal of maintaining the status quo. In contrast, Hamilton, when his words and actions are taken together, offers up a president who is formally powerful but seems weak politically.

Under Hamilton's understanding of "the executive power," the president retains broad formal authorities to initiate new policies and to do so without Congress's sanction. Yet it was precisely Hamilton, the author of this position, who appears most concerned with bolstering the exercise of these discretionary authorities with extraconstitutional, popular support. The treasury secretary might have told himself that this was a one-time effort, which did not involve the president directly and was justified by the extraordinary dangers and politics of the day. But, the fact remains, Hamilton and his Federalist allies helped open the door to a form of presidential politics that has never been quite shut again. Although the attempt to use public opinion in this fashion was bound to happen sooner or later given the underlying republican character of the regime, the surprise is that this precedent was set so quickly and, interestingly, set first by the Federalists and not Jefferson and Madison's Republicans.

The controversy over Washington's Proclamation of Neutrality in just the fourth year under the new Constitution reminds us of the tendency, capacity, and perhaps necessity for the president to act first and decisively to protect vital national interests. As we have seen, this does not always require an expansive view of executive power under the Constitution. In 1793, even Madison's more modest interpretation of Article II powers was firm enough ground to support a range of presidential initiatives and a large degree of executive discretion. That such initiatives during crises constrain Congress is unavoidable. The legislative branch finds itself confronting two basic options: supporting the president's acts in the interests of continuity of policy and national unity or challenging the president at a time when it seems most necessary for the nation to speak and act with one voice. Congress, of course, retains its constitutional ability to resist, and perhaps even thwart, the president, and the Constitution gives it the tools to do so. But it is naive to think, as the Federalists learned in 1793, that a separation of powers clash will be resolved simply independent of the character and direction of public opinion, an opinion likely to be energized by the stakes at hand.

CHAPTER FOUR

Theodore Roosevelt and William Howard Taft

The Constitutional Foundations of the Modern Presidency

LANCE ROBINSON

The most important factor in getting the right spirit in my Administration, next to the insistence upon courage, honesty, and a genuine democracy of desire to serve the plain people, was my insistence upon the theory that the executive power was limited only by specific restrictions and prohibitions appearing in the Constitution or imposed by the Congress under its Constitutional powers. My view was that every executive officer, and above all every executive officer in high position, was a steward of the people bound actively and affirmatively to do all he could for the people, and not to content himself with the negative merit of keeping his talents undamaged in a napkin. I declined to adopt the view that what was imperatively necessary for the Nation could not be done by the President unless he could find some specific authorization to do it. My belief was that it was not only his right but his duty to do anything that the needs of the Nation demanded unless such action was forbidden by the Constitution or by the laws.

THEODORE ROOSEVELT

The true view of the Executive function is, as I conceive it, that the President can exercise no power which cannot be fairly and reasonably traced to some specific grant of power or justly implied and included within such grant as proper and necessary to its exercise. Such specific grant must be either in the Federal Constitution or in an act of Congress passed in pursuance thereof.

There is no undefined residuum of power which he can exercise because it seems to him to be in the public interest, and there is nothing in the Neagle case and its definitions of a law of the United States, or in other precedents, warranting such an inference.

WILLIAM HOWARD TAFT

TOGETHER WITH WOODROW WILSON, Theodore Roosevelt and William Howard Taft form the troika of twentieth-century presidents who wrote seriously about the office of the presidency.[1] Between 1908 and 1916, these presidents offered three distinct views of the character of executive power. Wilson wrote on the presidency both theoretically and prior to actually holding the office, and his expressed affinity for ministerial party government easily differentiates him from Roosevelt and Taft, who rhetorically hew closer to traditional American constitutional arguments about executive power. Also, Roosevelt and Taft, unlike Wilson, wrote after serving as president and drew on their practical experience in office.

That Roosevelt and Taft wrote as deeply as they did would surprise many who are familiar with their thoughts on executive power only from the passages cited above.[2] Also, many modern scholars, apparently following Roosevelt's dictum that history to be useful must be readable, pass over Roosevelt's and Taft's works because of a perceived turgidity or torridness in their prose.[3] Regardless of the aesthetics of their writing, however, the mere fact that these twentieth-century presidents wrote extensively and thoughtfully on the office they held during a period of progressive political foment is reason enough for some deeper investigation. Roosevelt and Taft also wrote about the constitutional character of the office without offering an explicit alternative to the existing Constitution, and they convey their thoughts on the expansive power of the presidency, which each exercised beyond its traditional reach. They thus contributed to the origins of what has become known as the modern presidency, offering two grand alternative views of the bounds of executive power within the American constitutional order.

The brief passages captured above appear over and over in anthologies and texts about the American presidency.[4] Typically, scholars interpret Roosevelt as invigorating the exercise of executive power in a way necessary to cope with the social and political challenges that faced an industrializing America. In contrast, they present Taft as a throwback to a more pinched and restrictive understanding of executive power. Taft's more formally constitutional view is commonly thought insufficient to meet the challenges of twentieth-century America, challenges so very different from those that the country faced when the Constitution was written. This is the conventional, progressive explanation of the Roosevelt-Taft debate on executive power, one found in most accounts of the development of the American presidency.

As we will see, however, this interpretation misses the extent to which Roosevelt and Taft agreed on the need for an expansive executive power. Taft, it turns out, favored a powerful presidency, though one whose powers were informed and limited by law. The primary difference between Roosevelt's and Taft's views is not that between loose construction and strict construction of the Constitution but rather between an explicitly extralegal and an explicitly legal foundation for the exercise of executive power. Properly understood, the Roosevelt-Taft debate—and particularly a reconsideration of Taft's views—illuminates the potential for executive power to be exercised for the good of the republic on explicitly constitutional grounds, regardless of the challenges posed by changing conditions in society, technology, economy, industry, commerce, or any other of a myriad of factors.

The Meaning of Stewardship

Although Roosevelt periodically invoked the authority of the Constitution in a general way to justify an expansive view of presidential power, he did not appeal, perhaps surprisingly, to specific constitutional grants of authority. He did not cite the vesting clause, the oath of office, or other specific provisions of Article II in his claims for extraordinary presidential authority. Such were the grist of previous justifications for the exercise of extraordinary power made by presidents such as Lincoln and Jackson, as well as by statesmen of the founding generation such as Hamilton and Madison. They are also present in Taft's work. Even the essay Roosevelt wrote in 1902 entitled "The Presidency" omits an elaboration of constitutional powers and duties in favor of a discussion on the immense power of the American president.[5] Instead of drawing on the words of the Constitution, in this essay Roosevelt elaborates the concept of the president as "a steward of the people."

The word "steward" is derived from a combination of the Anglo-Saxon word for house or hall and the word for warden and dates from the eleventh century.[6] The steward is an official of the king or of a household who carries out the instructions of his employer, administering the tasks for which he is responsible. In each sense, the steward is in the service of a king, head of household, or senior officer whose instructions or wishes he is expected to carry out. The steward is to execute the will of his master; that is, he is to follow out the instructions of his master and carry into effect his purposes. In no sense is the steward justified in exercising a will contrary to that of his employer; though the word does admit of the capacity for some flexibility in determining the best means by which to achieve the given ends. The steward, in other words, is responsible and accountable to his employer for fulfilling his defined duties. It is a very direct and limited responsibility. The nature of this responsibility or accountability, and the meaning that Roosevelt invests in it when he speaks of stewardship, diverges from the historical understanding of executive magistracy, especially as expressed in the United States Constitution.

From a Hamiltonian perspective, the problem with the notion of the president as steward of the people is that it seems to make the president the agent for fulfilling the immediate desires of the voters. Yet central to the framers' design was a distinction between public reason and public passions: "it is the reason, alone, of the public, that ought to control and regulate the government. The passions ought to be controlled and regulated by the government."[7] The Constitution, and its principles and institutions in practice, provides a filter by which the reason of the people may be discerned and applied without the constant direct involvement of the people. Thus can the people both govern (their reason) and be governed (their passions). In this respect the president was to be a steward of the constitutional people, guided by the people through their chosen instrument, the Constitution, and not the steward of direct popular will as suggested by Roosevelt.

Roosevelt declared in his *Autobiography* that he ultimately considered the "executive as subject only to the people."[8] This formulation puts him at odds with the principles of the Constitution, which, through the president's oath of office, places the president subject to the Constitution itself. The president swears an oath to "execute the Office of President of the United States," not the will of the people directly. He further swears to "preserve, protect and defend the Constitution of the United States." Again, there is neither a duty to make himself directly subject to the will of the people nor does Article II in any other place contain this stipulation. What is remarkable about Article II is the absence of any direct popular connection to the people. The president is elected indirectly through the chosen electors and he deals with Congress, the judiciary, and the departments directly in the performance of his duties but not with the people in a collective sense. Roosevelt's steward here directly challenges Hamilton's executive, who is to be governed by "the deliberate sense of the community" rather than by "every sudden breeze of passion."[9] Insofar as the president is to accomplish the ends of government identified and established by the people in their sovereign capacity in the preamble to the Constitution, he is to do so in accordance with the Constitution; for the people "do ordain and establish this Constitution" to achieve those ends. The presidency is therefore one of the means established in the Constitution to provide the energy necessary to achieve those ends.

The people, by constitutional intention, are not directly involved in the daily operation of the government. Thus, Roosevelt, by his construction of a direct connection with the people disrupted what Harvey Mansfield Jr. has called "a certain constitutional space between the people and their government allowing the government a certain, limited independence so that it can develop a certain character and responsibility of its own."[10] The people have identified the ends that their government is established to secure and have instituted that government through a Constitution that establishes the institutional means by which that government will pursue those ends. In doing this, "the sovereign people has been replaced by the constitutional people," as Mansfield argues.[11] This does not eliminate the sovereign capacity of the people but instead defines their role within the Constitution. That is, the people choose under the Constitution who will exercise the duties of government and occasionally may reappear in a semi-sovereign capacity in making constitutional amendments.

Roosevelt collapsed this space by drawing the sovereign people into policy disputes that would normally be handled within the institutional structure of the government itself by the political interaction between the branches in the normal course of business.[12] This not only distorted the institutional structure by upsetting the responsibility the institutions have of governing in the name of the people, but it also corrupted the people in their sovereign capacity by drawing them into a direct role in the daily operation of government. Thus Roosevelt's stewardship theory worked to circumvent precautions included in the Constitution by reinterpreting the roles of the executive and of the people under the Constitution.

This reinterpretation of roles led Roosevelt into the problem of popular leadership, a problem for which he had no adequate solution. In governing in accordance with his stewardship theory, Roosevelt was ostensibly following the dictates of a people freshly reincorporated into the daily operations of government. Yet there is not a comprehensive popular will by which a president can be directed because of the normal division in the population along lines of party or interest. This requires the president either to lead in the formation of public opinion and thus fashion the will that he is supposedly following or to choose among existing partisan interests and act in response to only a portion of the public, making that interest his own and that of the government as well. This requirement to keep pace with current opinion places an enormous burden on the president. It also places stresses on the Constitution by reintroducing the classic notion of the partisan regime into a system that was designed in part to ameliorate the destructive tendencies found in violent regime changes of the past. The founders attempted to do this by incorporating all citizens into the "regime" and reducing their differences to differences of interest rather than justice.[13] That is, there would be competition among interests over how to achieve the ends of government but fundamental agreement over the ends themselves.

In stepping outside the institutional structure and limitations of the Constitution, Roosevelt also subtly altered the ends of the government as well, emphasizing the securing of the public welfare as a government responsibility rather than pursuing liberty and its blessings.[14] According to Roosevelt, it was the responsibility of the steward to "do all he could for the people" and "to do anything that the needs of the Nation demanded." Thus, as president he "acted for the public welfare . . .

for the common well-being of all our people, whenever and in whatever manner was necessary."[15] The introduction of the notion of popular leadership, then, carries along with it an enhanced responsibility to direct and to secure the public welfare and to resolve the various conflicts regarding material benefits and social justice.

The tendency of Roosevelt's theory, as expressed in his speeches and writings and as practiced by him as president, is to weaken formal deliberation between constitutionally separated institutions and its moderating effects upon American government. Deliberation is transferred to the public at large and thus removed from public institutions in which knowledge, experience, persuasion, and argument may refine the debate on issues of national importance. And once in the realm of unreflective public opinion, ideology, and self-interest, it is altogether too subject to the vicissitudes of low political oratory, if not coarse demagoguery.[16]

The check Roosevelt relied on to protect the people of the United States from such demagoguery was not an institutional one but rather a faith in the race characteristics of Anglo-Saxons and their inherited capacity for self-government. According to Roosevelt, "during the past three centuries the spread of the English-speaking peoples over the world's waste spaces has been not only the most striking feature in the world's history, but also the event of all others most far-reaching in its effects and its importance." [17] The American colonies were among the most important examples of that spread. America was unique in that

> under any governmental system which was known to Europe, the
> problem offered by the westward thrust, across a continent, of so
> masterful and liberty-loving a race as ours would have been insoluble.
> The great civilized and colonizing races of antiquity, the Greeks and
> the Romans, had been utterly unable to devise a scheme under which
> when their race spread it might be possible to preserve both national
> unity and local and individual freedom.[18]

The first chapter of Roosevelt's *The Winning of the West* and the first three chapters of his *Thomas Hart Benton* in particular are descriptions of the capacity of these people to spread beyond their borders, conquer and occupy territory, and institute self-government almost unconsciously. Roosevelt describes this capacity beautifully in one assessment of the accomplishments of the early American pioneers:

The first duty of the backwoodsmen who thus conquered the west was to institute civil government. Their efforts to overcome and beat back the Indians went hand in hand with their efforts to introduce law and order in the primitive communities they founded; and exactly as they relied purely on themselves in withstanding outside foes, so they likewise built up their social life and their first systems of government with reference simply to their special needs, and without any outside help or direction. The whole character of the westward movement, the methods of warfare, of settlement, and government, were determined by the extreme and defiant individualism of the backwoodsmen, their inborn independence and self-reliance, and their intensely democratic spirit.[19]

In relying on what he perceived to be the innate capacity of Anglo-Saxons for self-government, Roosevelt seemed to reject the founders' reliance on constitutional and legal structures to regulate, moderate, and filter majority influence in the regime. And in promoting a presidency that represented the particular and discrete interest of what he called the common man, Roosevelt also seemed to reject a larger and more comprehensive public interest. Thus, Roosevelt advanced a more democratic regime but did so potentially at the expense of constitutional and legal protections that guard against the tyranny of the majority.

Taft's Chief Magistrate

In his reflections on his and his predecessor's administrations and political thought, William Howard Taft explored the sharp contrast in thought, temperament, and action that existed between the two men. That contrast is the not-so-subtle and ever-present undercurrent to his book on the presidency. Its emphasis on the legal draws constant attention to the extralegal methods advocated by Roosevelt. That Taft developed a "legal" defense of the exercise of extraordinary presidential power nearly as broad as Roosevelt's is one of the major surprises in his book, and one not made clear by the common reference to the short passage that denies the existence of a residuum of power. Taft's work was also more systematic than Roosevelt's and, unlike Roosevelt's, addressed in some detail the specific constitutional powers and duties of the president.

Taft's book on the presidency follows the form of a series of lectures on executive power delivered at Columbia University and elsewhere and was published in its most common form as *Our Chief Magistrate and His Powers* in 1916. The lectures were delivered while Taft was professor of constitutional law at Yale University, where he taught from 1913 to 1921, and drew heavily on his recent experience as president (1909–13). In a refreshing manner, Taft's book refers routinely to the formal powers and duties of the president, which takes the modern reader back to an era in academic discourse before the proliferation of studies of presidential attributes, personality or leadership styles, media strategies, organizational constructs, or the permanent campaign. Taft's is a clear and persuasive recitation of the primary constitutional powers and duties of the chief magistrate and of how the Constitution provides for the legal development of executive obligations not specified. In six chapters he treats six major and six minor powers.[20] This analysis is preceded by a discussion of the principle of distribution of governmental powers and is followed by, and summed up in, a theoretical and practical discussion of the limits of presidential power. His constitutional and legal exegesis is thus bounded at each end by more theoretical discussions. The central discussion of the specific powers and duties is eminently practical in its approach.

Taft expounds his theoretical principles early and forcefully in his book. The distribution of power is of central importance to him theoretically. The lack of abundant court case law "makes the definition of Executive power somewhat more difficult . . . than that of Congress."[21] "There is," though, "in the scope of the jurisdiction of both the Executive and Congress a wide field of action," and "in this field, the construction of the power of each branch and its limitations must be left to itself and the political determination of the people who are the ultimate sovereign asserting themselves at the polls."[22] This wide field of action, though, does not include the area where "individual rights" may be "affected in such a way that they can be asserted and vindicated in a court."[23] The boundaries of the remaining political activities of the branches were further constrained according to Taft, by the court's decision in *Marbury v. Madison*, which "made the judicial branch of the government the branch which could effectively determine the limits of power of the other two branches."[24] While the immediate question in Marbury was one of individual right, Taft argues that Chief Justice Marshall took the opportunity to snub Jefferson and Madison and offer a "broad, liberal Federalistic construction of the Constitution."[25] The actions of the executive and the legislature, according to Taft, are conditioned by interest in a way that conduces to inefficiency in the administration of government.[26] The presidency is conditioned to an interest in reelection by the continual eligibility allowed under the Constitution, while Congress is conditioned by division into electoral districts that amplifies local interests and increases pressure on the government, particularly on budget matters. The locus of deliberation shifts to the courts for Taft, where the major issues of right and justice are resolved, whereas in Roosevelt's thought institutional deliberation was weakened in favor of stimulated and focused public sentiment. The discussion of the legal character of executive power that follows from this theoretical foundation is the great strength of the book. Law is central to the exercise of legitimate executive power for Taft, while it is peripheral, and at times an impediment, for Roosevelt.

It is in the chapters on the executive powers that Taft shines, particularly on the central subject of "The Duty of the President to Take Care That the Laws Are Executed." This is the "widest and broadest duty which the President has,"[27] and, interestingly, this power is discussed in the same chapter as the commander-in-chief powers and duties. In this chapter we see combined the dual character of the executive: the rather more benign civil magistrate and the violent prosecutor of the nation's wars, the enforcer of the national interest and wielder of the nation's power. It is here that Taft introduces the Supreme Court's 1890 decision *In re Neagle*, in which the executive power is explained to include duties inferable from laws duly enacted.[28] In this case, the inference is that a federal marshal serving in the Department of Justice has a lawful authority to protect a judge despite the fact that there is no law authorizing that specific executive function. He cites the Supreme Court as having "declared that any obligation inferable from the Constitution, or any duty of the President or the Attorney-General to be derived from the general code of his duties under the laws of the United States is a law within the meaning of the phrase."[29] Taft, as Louis Fisher understands, had in effect added "to the Constitution a 'necessary and proper' clause for Presidential powers."[30]

Under the same reasoning used to defend the government's case in *Neagle*, Taft also defends the commander-in-chief power of the president in language reminiscent of Pacificus' assertion that "the Executive, in the exercise of its constitutional powers, may establish an antecedent state of things which ought to weigh in the legislative decisions."[31] Taft cites as an appropriate action under law the compelling of an Austrian vessel by the commander of an American vessel to surrender a Hungarian who had merely stated an intent to become a U.S. citizen.[32] He also defends Roosevelt's administrative governance of the Panama Canal Zone by the War Department in the absence of congressional authorization and his own landing of Marines in Central American countries absent a declaration of war. In this case Taft makes a distinction between the army and the marines, because the use of marines exhibited an intent to police rather than engage in war, which use of the army would have signified.[33] In fact, Taft uses language that could have been penned by Pacificus himself: "only Congress has the power to declare war, but with the army and the navy, the President can take action such as to involve the country in war and to leave Congress no option but to declare it or recognize its existence."[34] Here Taft seems to go even beyond Pacificus in the extent to which he will allow the executive to commit the country to war absent congressional involvement or approval. In his own way, Taft asserts and defends the exercise of extraordinary executive power comparable in extent to Jackson and Lincoln, and nearly comparable to Theodore Roosevelt himself.

In addition to the take care clause and the commander-in-chief power, Taft includes the veto, appointment power, foreign relations, and the pardon as major powers. In each case, he follows a similar pattern of principled explanation of the legal and constitutional meaning of the power or duty, followed by explanatory examples of the principle in question, and the breadth of scope to which they may be exercised, often drawing from his own experience as president. This same form is used in regard to what he refers to as the minor executive powers of consulting department heads; informing Congress of the state of the union; recommending wise, expedient, and necessary legislation; issuing commissions; convening Congress in special session; and adjourning Congress. Throughout, he follows his practice of tracing the legal thread that connects the practice in question to the formal constitutional grant or legal statute that authorizes it.

In this legal explication, Taft follows the pattern of Alexander Hamilton when Hamilton defended Washington's neutrality proclamation in the Pacificus letters. Hamilton laid down four principles of constitutional interpretation in his argument to justify Washington's exercise of executive power. According to Hamilton, to be proper, a president's practice must be within his constitutional authority and duty, it must be in regard to a power clearly the responsibility of the national government, it must be in conformity with other constitutional provisions and the principles of free government, and it must be subject to the exceptions and qualifications to the vesting of executive power in the president.[35] Taft is careful in his explanations, consistent with Hamilton's example, to delineate each practice with regard to the other constitutional branches, the states, and other provisions of the Constitution. Taft clearly shows the constitutional authority and duty, as well as the national character of executive actions in the examples he selects to elaborate upon.

It is in regard to Hamilton's third and fourth points that Taft and Hamilton diverge. Taft chooses to omit the vesting clause from his reasoning and restricts himself to the Constitution and laws rather than including the principles of free government as does Hamilton. While the attachment to law is one of the great strengths of the book, it is perhaps its greatest weakness as well. As much as Taft is able, through an extremely expansive understanding of the law, to justify most active exercises of the executive power, his argument seems incomplete. As expansive as is his understanding of the limits of the law, he does not provide a satisfactory answer for those situations in which the Constitution and laws, or even customary practice, do not provide the grounds of even a tenuous legal defense.

Hamilton offers the principles of free government and the open-ended interpretation of the vesting clause as opportunities to deal with such contingencies. How is the president to act absent law? What legal grounds would Taft find to answer the challenge Lincoln faced in 1861 of undertaking "measures, whether strictly legal or not . . . ventured upon, under what appeared to be a popular demand, and a public necessity?"[36] To Taft's credit, he recognizes the importance and potency of public opinion, but mainly as an instrument to break a logjam among the branches on political questions rather than something to be refined by constitutional deliberation or wielded in defense of executive action. In this he follows Roosevelt's model by emphasizing the tools of pressure group politics rather than those of constitutional politics. Despite having had Lincoln's example as precedent, Taft simply did not confront the extreme, or crisis, situation in his arguments, that situation when law may have to be augmented by discretion in order to preserve free government. Taft's emphasis on law, while following Hamilton's grounding in the constitution, omits Hamilton's openings for action in those cases where law is not definitive.

Taft viewed Article II of the Constitution as containing the positive grants of executive powers and duties as well as the foundation for powers and duties not specified. He closely associated the oath of office with both his duty to veto unwise or unconstitutional measures and his obligation to "take Care that the Laws be faithfully executed," which he called his "widest power and the broadest duty."[37] In his writings, Taft only hints that there may be broader powers associated with the office itself that the oath would bind the president to exercise. He rhetorically associates the power of statutory construction and rule-making with the faithful execution of the laws rather than with the executive power itself. Thus, he does not, as Hamilton did, look to the vesting clause for anything more than descriptive power, until, that is, his ruling in *Myers v. United States* in 1926, while serving as chief justice of the Supreme Court. In this case, though, Taft does not go beyond the argument that "the vesting of the executive power in the President was essentially a grant of the power to execute the laws," even though he also recognizes that there is a significant difference between the more limited vesting of the legislative power in Article I—"All legislative Powers herein granted shall be vested in a Congress"—and the more general vesting of executive power in Article II—"The executive Power shall be vested in a President."[38]

Hamilton's more forceful reliance on the vesting power as a source of executive powers not specified or specifically limited in his fourth principle offered a means to cope with the exigent circumstance that is superior to Taft's crafting of broad legal principles. Hamilton understood the vesting clause to carry meaning for undefined, or discretionary, powers in itself. Hamilton viewed the list of powers and duties as only partial and incomplete or as defining the exceptions and qualifications that the Constitution makes to natural executive power. Therefore, according to Hamilton, the Constitution provides legally for the discretion to meet those exigent circumstances unforeseen by any of the formal or customary methods of creating legal obligations used by Taft. Furthermore, as in the example of Lincoln, the Constitution does so while maintaining a scrupulous regard for constitutional propriety within the constitutional and legal structure that Taft so values. The flexibility of the president to act under law while remaining just and the value of law to society in promoting stability and orderly change are what Taft offers to counter what must have appeared to him as rampant populism in Roosevelt's approach to the exercise of executive power. Taft approved of Roosevelt's judgment as president, but an individual's judgment is not always as reliable over time as sound legal foundations, a principle the worth of which would be vindicated in Taft's later political relations with Roosevelt.

Stewardship, Magistracy, and the Modern Presidency

According to Theodore Roosevelt, as we have seen, the Constitution withholds certain powers from the president rather than granting powers to the executive. This we see in his assertion that "the executive power was limited only by specific restrictions and prohibitions appearing in the Constitution or imposed by the Congress under its Constitutional powers."[39] This is further amplified by Roosevelt's proud claim that "during the seven and a half years of my administration we greatly and usefully extended the sphere of Governmental action," and yet with perfect equanimity he claims that he "did not usurp power, but . . . did greatly broaden the use of executive power."[40] What becomes apparent in the course of his argument is an attempt to read the American Constitution in the light of British constitutional development. At times this extends so far as to seem to read the royal power of the British monarchy into the American executive power. He claimed to be able on his own, as president, to expand the scope of executive power, whether the nation is in crisis or not, to accomplish any objective that is not at the time covered by a law.[41] Roosevelt even argued, in the case of presidential commissions he convened for a number of purposes, the right to act against statutory law should he so desire.[42]

We learn from Roosevelt's early writings that in his opinion the Constitution was not a document representing a higher principle of any kind other than fostering a beneficial and powerful union among the several states. In accomplishing this union, the Constitution itself was just a "bundle of compromises."[43] The structure and stated ends of the Constitution did not lend anything to this union beyond the convenience of being acceptable enough to all parties to permit the union of the separate states to be preserved. In Roosevelt's opinion, the Constitution did not represent a significant change or development in either republican government or constitutional government but rather carried on a centuries-old tradition in a manner that was suited to the specific time and conditions of the American people and their physical environment.[44]

Stewardship, on reflection then, held a meaning for Roosevelt that was not fully conveyed by the terms and examples he invoked in the exposition of his theory. The term *stewardship* itself conveys a rhetorical message that would not be alarming to a republican people, a message that was also amplified through Roosevelt's choice of supporting terms and analogies. But this rhetorical message is equivocal at best when the message conveyed by these elements of the theory is contrasted with Roosevelt's speeches and writings as a whole. What emerges is a more expansive and unlimited understanding of executive power than is conveyed by those rhetorical elements, and which, in many ways, is more consistent with historical treatments of executive power outside the American constitutional and modern republican tradition. Roosevelt's concept of the executive in many ways evokes the British king, the Machiavellian prince, or the Roman dictators.

The tendency of the stewardship presidency to draw the American people into an active participation in policy debates, to undermine the auxiliary precautions that create the constitutional space between the people and the government, to undermine deliberation by concentrating power in an executive who appeals over the head of Congress to the people directly, and to expand the powers of the national government and the presidency beyond the bounds of the enumeration, even broadly read, contained in the Constitution, all work to weaken the constitutional framework that was intended by the founders to provide an indispensable support to republican government. The founders' Constitution was designed to spare America the fate suffered by republican governments throughout history. Thus, Roosevelt's writings refer to an earlier understanding of republican government that was rejected as too unstable by the founding fathers. In his constitutional theory, Roosevelt places a greater emphasis on civic virtue, enlightened statesmanship, and the progressive unfolding of evolutionary history, and thus nudges American political practice away from the original constitutional principles.

William Howard Taft, as we have seen, preferred a more overtly legal and constitutional approach to the description and definition of presidential power and duty. The judge in Taft comes out in his view of the presidency, as does the extrovert in Roosevelt's more personal approach to the exercise of presidential power in his stewardship theory. Taft, however, gave very little ground to Roosevelt in the exercise of presidential power, despite his legalistic view. We have seen that Taft's understanding of the application of law is quite broad indeed. By incorporating customary usage and actions necessary and proper to the exercise of either constitutional or statutory powers and duties in the way that he did, Taft's view of the legitimate extent of the normal exercise of presidential power expanded on the traditional view considerably. By restraining even this expanded view of executive power to the limits of the law, Taft made the energetic executive of the progressive era more palatable to a republican citizenry.

Despite Taft's generous view of the president's legal powers, Roosevelt attacked it with some vehemence in his *Autobiography*. In a passage nearly as famous as the statement of the stewardship theory itself, Roosevelt argued that

> there have long been two schools of political thought, upheld with equal sincerity. The division has not normally been along political, but temperamental, lines. The course I followed, of regarding the executive as subject only to the people, and, under the Constitution, bound to serve the people affirmatively in cases where the Constitution does not explicitly forbid him to render the service, was substantially the course followed by both Andrew Jackson and Abraham Lincoln. Other honorable and well-meaning Presidents, such as James Buchanan, took the opposite and, as it seems to me, narrowly legalistic view that the President is the servant of Congress rather than of the people, and can do nothing, no matter how necessary it be to act, unless the Constitution explicitly commands the action. Most able lawyers who are past middle age take this view, and so do large numbers of well-meaning, respectable citizens. My successor in office took this, the Buchanan, view of the President's powers and duties.[45]

He then goes on to take Taft to task for what Roosevelt perceived to be a tepid defense of a cabinet officer.

> Perhaps the sharp differences between what may be called the Lincoln-Jackson and the Buchanan-Taft schools, in their views of the power and duties of the President, may be best illustrated by comparing the attitude of my successor toward his Secretary of the Interior, Mr. Ballinger, when the latter was accused of gross misconduct in office, with my attitude towards my chiefs of department and other subordinate officers. . . . The Jackson-Lincoln view is that a President who is fit to do good work should be able to form his own judgment as to his own subordinates. . . . My successor took the opposite, or Buchanan, view when he permitted and requested Congress to pass judgment on the charges made against Mr. Ballinger as an executive officer.[46]

Here Roosevelt attacks Taft for being insufficiently conservationist and for conceding to a congressional inquiry of a cabinet official, even though Ballinger, the official in question, had requested such an investigation to clear his name.[47] Roosevelt, in addition to castigating Taft as effectively a do-nothing president, here also gilds his own lily by likening his own actions as president, and his understanding of presidential power, to that of Jackson and Lincoln. In doing so, he inappropriately cloaks himself and his stewardship theory with the mantle of constitutional propriety.

With deftness and humor Taft responds that "the identification of Mr. Roosevelt with Mr. Lincoln might otherwise have escaped notice, because there are many differences between the two, presumably superficial, which would give the impartial student of history a different impression."[48] Taft continues to point out "that Mr. Lincoln with the stress of the greatest civil war in modern times" did things that were quite fairly questioned as to their constitutionality. Still, even in such circumstances, "Mr. Lincoln always pointed out the source of the authority which in his opinion justified his acts, and there was always a strong ground for maintaining the view he took." Taft then more forcefully states that "Mr. Lincoln never claimed that whatever authority in government was not expressly denied to him he could exercise."[49] Taft forcefully recounts Lincoln's commitment to the law and his appeals to constitutional authority but also omits here, as in the comparison with Hamilton, Lincoln's appeal to the principles of free government that guided his legal interpretations in defense of his expansive exercise of executive power.

Taft in this argument not only proceeds to lay a claim to the mantle of Lincoln himself, in opposition to Roosevelt's characterization, but also then goes on to compare Roosevelt's theory with President Jefferson. Jefferson, according to Taft, started as "a strict constructionist of the Constitution in theory," but "when he had power things looked differently to him," and he was able to justify more expansive actions "on the theory that he was doing good and working for the public welfare."[50] Taft deftly turns Roosevelt's argument on its head and comes out the better for it. Taft is able through this example to clearly demonstrate the weakness of Roosevelt's argument by its position outside the Constitution and law. All this name slinging, in the meantime, obscured the fact that Taft was as active an executive as Roosevelt and more successful in some areas, such as regulation of the trusts.

It remains for us, then, to return to Taft's famous paragraph that forms the impression most have of Taft as president, or at least Taft as presidential commentator. As we recall, Taft's oft-quoted passage is as follows:

> The true view of the Executive function is, as I conceive it, that the President can exercise no power which cannot be fairly and reasonably traced to some specific grant of power or justly implied and included within such grant as proper and necessary to its exercise. Such specific grant must be either in the Federal Constitution or in an act of Congress passed in pursuance thereof. There is no undefined residuum of power which he can exercise because it seems to him to be in the public interest, and there is nothing in the Neagle case and its definitions of a law of the United States, or in other precedents, warranting such an inference.[51]

The words in this passage that leap out are "no undefined residuum of power." This is commonly seen as the main point of contention between Roosevelt and Taft, and indeed it does capture a fundamental difference between the two. Paolo Coletta, a Taft biographer, has observed that "where Taft disagreed most notably with Roosevelt . . . was not in objective, but in method and interpretation," and this primarily "in their conception of the office of president."[52] He also notes that "Taft was convinced of the righteousness of Roosevelt's reforms"[53] and had expressed himself in support of those and other progressive reforms.[54] *Our Chief Magistrate and His Powers* in no way indicates any opposition by Taft to progressive reforms and principles. Indeed, his own "conception of the office of president," as we have seen in the context of the book as a whole, requires no undefined residuum of power but instead has all the power necessary and proper through legal construction of both the Constitution and statute law. There was, then, a significant difference in means between Taft and Roosevelt, if not necessarily a difference in ends. Taft viewed the law, whether constitutional or statutory, as providing opportunity to an executive, whereas Roosevelt viewed the law as a constraint to be circumvented by appealing to the people directly.

A second, critical difference between Taft and Roosevelt has to do with the interest represented, or the source of presidential authority. It is not just that Roosevelt declared the president's right to act beyond permissions to be found in the constitutional text or statute, but that Roosevelt justified his actions on the basis of a perceived need among a portion of the population, which he referred to as the common man. Here, again, Taft parted ways with Roosevelt on a point of means that did not indicate or necessitate a disagreement over ends. In Taft's view, representing what is legal, or finding authority in the Constitution and the laws, is a much firmer foundation on which to build the desired progressive reforms. In this preference, he is not that far off from Hamilton's ambitious arguments in favor of presidential power writing as Pacificus in the 1790s. Taft and Hamilton appealed to the common good, in the Constitution and the laws, to justify controversial exercises of executive power. Taft more than Roosevelt allowed for cooperation between the institutions of American politics to achieve desired, even progressive, policy ends. Roosevelt, in turn, offered to lead a more combative, visionary end run around the institutions of government to achieve the public interest as he defined it.

Both Roosevelt and Taft have laid claim to the mantle of Lincoln by appealing to him to justify the expansive exercise of executive power. Yet, the challenges they faced fall far short of those that confronted Lincoln. In the way they made routine the exercise of powers typically reserved for periods of crisis or threats to national survival, both Roosevelt and Taft were essentially modern in the way they viewed the powers and duties of the presidency. That Taft chose to articulate his views in a more traditional legal rhetoric differentiates him significantly from Roosevelt, who erased the traditional boundaries of executive power by declaring that the president could do all that was not specifically prohibited. Roosevelt offered a pinched, Jeffersonian view of constitutional power (one might almost go so far as to call it Buchanan-like) and therefore appealed to the personal and popular power of the executive rather than the formal and legal. Roosevelt was willing to exercise power, wanted to exercise power, and so needed some conception of an undefined residuum of executive power. The stewardship theory gave him all the power he needed to act to ameliorate the condition of the common man. Taft, frightened by the prospect of a populist president drawing upon an inexhaustible source of power, emphatically rejected the undefined residuum of power but nonetheless found within the Constitution and laws sufficient authority to support his own version of the modern energetic executive.

CHAPTER FIVE

Constitutional Controversy and Presidential Election

Bush v. Gore

DAVID K. NICHOLS

THE 2000 PRESIDENTIAL ELECTION is destined to remain one of the most controversial in American history. It became clear on election night that Florida's electoral votes would decide the outcome of the race. Before the polls had even closed in the Florida panhandle, the television networks announced that Al Gore was the projected winner in the state. However, as more votes were counted, Gore's lead evaporated and George W. Bush was declared the victor. Gore called Bush and conceded defeat; but as additional votes were tallied, Bush's lead began to shrink and Gore withdrew his concession. Thus began the thirty-six-day struggle to arrive at a definitive vote count in Florida that ended only when the U.S. Supreme Court reached its decision in *Bush v. Gore* on December 12 and Gore conceded the election on December 13.[1]

It is hardly controversial to suggest that the case of *Bush v. Gore* was inextricably entangled with issues of electoral politics. Many commentators have decided that the case, or at least its outcome, can be explained fully in those terms. Alan Dershowitz, for example, concluded that "the justices were so determined to ensure a Republican victory that they engineered a short-term resolution locking in that victory at the risks of considerable long-term costs to the Bush presidency and the credibility of the Supreme Court."[2] It was his belief that the justices acted out of partisan motives rather than any concern with the constitutional validity of their decision or actions.[3]

Dershowitz might be right, but motivations are difficult to determine with any certainty. As Alexander Hamilton said in *The Federalist*, all we can do is to examine the arguments. I will suggest, however, that the arguments rest not merely on the Republican or Democratic prejudices of the justices, but at a deeper level reflect different understandings of the democratic and republican philosophical assumptions underlying the Constitution. These assumptions are neither fully articulated in the opinions nor are the justices consistent in the application of those principles within their discussion of this case or in relation to some of their previous opinions. But unlike Dershowitz, I would contend that this inconsistency is a bipartisan phenomenon.[4] Neither the majority nor the dissenting justices have advanced a coherent account of their constitutional principles.

Nonetheless, if it can be demonstrated that the argument is about more than just politics, that the justices' opinions reflect some deeper constitutional dispute, then we may see that the divisions in the case are both more profound and less disturbing than many have claimed. I contend that *Bush v. Gore* is about more than who wins an election. It is about fundamental questions regarding the character of constitutional democracy. The case does indeed reveal some confusion and even some hypocrisy regarding the use of constitutional principles, but it also reveals the complexity of those principles. If this contention is correct, then the arguments in the case may move us beyond partisanship to a more complex and more coherent view of the place of the presidency and the Court in the democratic republic established by our Constitution. It may also help us to better understand that a more political approach to constitutional interpretation may elevate rather than diminish the status of both the Constitution and contemporary politics.

Partisan Division

One does not have to look far to find evidence of partisanship in the Supreme Court decision that halted the recount of the Florida vote and resulted in the election of George W. Bush. Frequently quoted is the conclusion of Justice John Paul Stevens's dissent: "Although we may never know with complete certainty the identity of the winner of this year's Presidential election, the identity of the loser is perfectly clear. It is the Nation's confidence in the judge as an impartial guardian of the rule of law."[5] Justices Stephen Breyer and David Souter explicitly argued that the Court should have never taken the case, and Justice Ruth Bader Ginsburg's opinion closed with the words "I dissent," rather than the more typical phrase,

"I respectfully dissent." One might conclude that there was very little mutual respect among members of the Court after this 5–4 decision.

Only five members of the U.S. Supreme Court wanted to review the Florida Supreme Court's decision, and only five justices supported the initial stay of the recounts issued on December 9 and the decision to end the recounts announced on December 12. But lost in this picture of acrimony and partisan division are some broad areas of agreement. On the central legal question, whether the recount as it was being conducted violated constitutional standards, there was in fact a 7–2 majority.[6] One Democratic appointee, Justice Breyer, and one liberal Republican appointee, Justice Souter, joined Justices Anthony Kennedy, Sandra Day O'Connor, William Rehnquist, Antonin Scalia, and Clarence Thomas in arguing that the recount mechanisms established by the Florida Supreme Court violated the equal protection clause of the Fourteenth Amendment. The disparate standards used in the recounts failed to guarantee that each vote would receive equal scrutiny. Justices Breyer and Souter broke with the other five on the appropriate remedy, not on the question of the unconstitutional character of the recount. As the per curiam opinion noted, "Seven justices of the Court agree that there are constitutional problems with the recount ordered by the Florida Supreme Court that demand a remedy."[7]

Why has this 7–2 majority received such little attention in the commentary on the case? First, it does not fit the popular narrative of deep division and partisanship. The 5–4 vote is the better story. Second, however, is the fact that although Justices Breyer and Souter agreed with the majority on this crucial point, most of their opinions were devoted to an attack on the reasoning of the majority and particularly on the majority's remedy.[8] Four justices were very unhappy with the outcome of the case.

Nonetheless, the seven-vote majority deserves more attention, because it undercuts the argument that the case turned on mere partisanship. Justice Souter admitted that the recount lacked uniform standards for determining voter intent and concluded: "I can conceive of no legitimate state interest served by these differing treatments of the expressions of voters' fundamental rights. The differences appear wholly arbitrary."[9] Justice Breyer was more tentative in his support of the equal protection claim stating, "I agree that, in these very special circumstances, basic principles of fairness may well have counseled the adoption of a uniform standard to address the problem."[10] He immediately went on to say, however, that "in light of the majority's disposition, I need not decide whether, or the extent to which, as a remedial matter, the Constitution would place limits upon the content of the uniform standard."[11] The Court's decision to halt the recount allowed Breyer to sidestep the question of the appropriate standard for a recount under the equal protection clause, but the important point is that he recognized that there was a constitutional "problem" with the existing recount.

It is hard to imagine partisan motivations that would have led Justices Souter and Breyer to reach this conclusion. They clearly believed that the majority was wrong about the appropriate remedy and that it was wrong in much of its legal analysis. Souter and Breyer had no reason to toss the majority a bone in this contentious fight. One would have to assume that they thought the majority made a legitimate point regarding equal protection, and however grudging or narrow that agreement, it was not based on partisanship.

There was even more agreement in the earlier case of *Bush v. Palm Beach County Canvassing Board*.[12] In that case Bush had challenged the constitutional validity of the decision of the Florida Supreme Court to require manual recounts in some counties and to extend the deadline for completing those recounts. In a per curiam opinion and without dissent the Court argued:

> As a general rule, this Court defers to a state court's interpretation of a state statute. But in the case of a law enacted by a state legislature applicable not only to elections to state offices, but also to the selection of electors, the legislature is not acting solely under the authority given it by the people of the State, but by virtue of a direct grant of authority made under Art. 1, §1, cl. 2, of the United States Constitution.[13]

The United States Supreme Court has authority to determine whether actions taken by the state courts were consistent with the Constitution of the United States on this matter. The opinion goes on to raise two possible problems with the Florida Supreme Court's decision. First, it was not clear that the Florida Supreme Court had recognized the deference owed to the state legislature under Article II, Section 1, Clause 2, of the U.S. Constitution. The U.S. Constitution placed authority for the selection of electors in the hands of the state legislatures, not in the state governments as a whole. Thus, in addition to the normal deference due to the legislative branch, the state legislatures were owed additional deference in the matter of the selection of electors because their authority came from the U.S. Constitution and not the state constitutions. Second, the Court was unclear as to the consideration that the Florida Supreme Court accorded to 3 U.S.C., Section 5, the federal statute that establishes procedures for the conduct of elections.

> Since §5 contains a principle of federal law that would assure finality of the State's determination if made pursuant to a state law in effect before the election, a legislative wish to take advantage of the "safe harbor" would counsel against any construction of the Election Code that Congress might deem to be a change in the law.[14]

Thus, there was both a constitutional and a federal statutory basis for the U.S. Supreme Court's interest in this case.

The Court concluded "that there is considerable uncertainty as to the precise grounds for the decision." The Florida Court had not established that it was acting within the bounds of its discretionary authority, and its decision was vacated. Bush had a possible justiciable claim under Article II and under 3 U.S.C., Section 5, but the decision was far from a complete victory for Bush. The Court deferred review of these federal questions and remanded the case to the Florida Court for explanation. Bush would not necessarily prevail on the merits; nor was the possibility of further recounts ruled out.

The point here, however, is not to examine the persuasiveness of the legal arguments offered in the per curiam opinion but to point out that the Court's opinion produced no dissents. No one disagreed that both Article II and 3 U.S.C., Section 5, provided a basis for Supreme Court oversight of the actions of the Florida courts in this matter. Moreover, no one disagreed with the arguments that the Florida courts owed greater deference than usual to the Florida legislature or that the "safe harbor" provisions of 3 U.S.C. placed serious constraints on any action to be taken by the Florida Supreme Court.

Dershowitz, however, provides two scenarios that would explain this unanimous opinion on a deeply divided Court. First, following the speculation of Linda Greenhouse in the *New York Times*, Dershowitz suggests that Justices Breyer, Ginsburg, Souter, and Stevens "by joining the per curiam opinion and remanding the case back to Florida" thought they would avoid any major damage, because, as Greenhouse argues, "The election would be over before the case could come back to haunt the Supreme Court again."[15] The four dissenters calculated that they could obtain the results they wanted by going along with the argument of the five-member majority. Dershowitz's second, and by no means contradictory explanation, is that the four justices "were duped, or at least outmaneuvered, by the majority five."[16] The majority lured their four opponents into a seemingly harmless decision that "set a trap for the Florida Supreme Court from which it could not escape."[17]

The dissenting opinions by these four justices in *Bush v. Gore* lend some support to this thesis. To varying degrees, each of these dissents dismisses the concerns with the safe harbor provisions of 3 U.S.C., Section 5, or the possible constraints placed on the Florida Supreme Court by Article II. They would all appear to be at odds with the reasoning of the per curiam opinion they joined in *Bush v. Palm Beach County Canvassing Board*. But if Dershowitz is correct, and the four joined the per curiam opinion only because they thought it would give them the result they wanted, then it is they, and not the majority, who are guilty of unprincipled inconsistency in the two cases.

There is, however, another possible explanation for the differences in the two cases. The Court was seeking a principled consensus in both cases. In the first, *Bush v. Palm Beach County Canvassing Board*, the Court was successful in establishing such a consensus. Even though four justices may have been reluctant to take the case, they were willing to sign on to the opinion because they accepted the proposition that decisions of the Florida Supreme Court must be consistent with Article II of the U.S. Constitution and with federal election statutes. Indeed, it is difficult to imagine how anyone could disagree with that proposition.

The question was how to determine whether the Florida Court had violated either of those standards in its decision. It is reasonable to assume that there were significant differences of opinion among the justices on this question and that the per curiam opinion represented a compromise among those differing opinions. In what was undoubtedly a nod to Justices Breyer, Ginsburg, Souter and Stevens, the opinion did not claim that the Florida Supreme Court was in violation of either the Constitution or federal statutes. Moreover, it gave the Florida Court the opportunity to explain the grounds of its decision and their consistency with the

Constitution and federal statutes. Justices Kennedy, O'Connor, Rehnquist, Scalia, and Thomas in effect admitted that there was some ambiguity in the application of the agreed-on constitutional and legal standards in this case. So, there might be a violation or there might not be.

The decision to vacate the Florida Court's decision and remand for further action consistent with this opinion represented a concession by both sides. All of the justices were willing to concede that there might be more ambiguity in the case than they had initially assumed. Justices Breyer, Ginsburg, Souter, and Stevens granted that the Florida Court had not provided an adequate defense of the grounds of its decision, while Justices Kennedy, O'Connor, Scalia, Rehnquist, and Thomas admitted that the Florida Court, given the opportunity to do so, might well be able to provide a persuasive constitutional defense.

Rather than emphasize the partisan divisions in this case, which are hardly surprising given the politically charged atmosphere, I would suggest that what is truly remarkable is the fact that the justices were able to reach agreement about certain constitutional principles that should guide their decisions and that they were able to reach a compromise on the question of the application of those principles in such a short time in the face of such intense political pressure. It is hard to identify any other institution that took seriously the range of differing opinions in the dispute or that made a more reasoned or deliberate attempt to find common ground where possible and to create it through compromise where none had existed before.

This was true not just in *Bush v. Palm Beach County Canvassing Board* but also in *Bush v. Gore*. Kennedy and O'Connor have been criticized by both liberals and conservatives for their use of an equal protection argument in this case, and we will examine the merits of those criticisms below, but the point here is that Kennedy and O'Connor were hardly the most partisan judges on the Court. In fact, they were often praised for their moderation, for their willingness to step across the Court's ideological divide, and for their role in balancing the competing claims of left and right on the Court. It is possible that Kennedy and O'Connor eschewed their usual moderation in this case and decided to use any argument that they could to gain victory for Bush, but it seems more likely that Justices Kennedy and O'Connor were looking for common ground. As John Yoo points out: "One can even view the emergence of the per curiam opinion

—clearly the work of Justices Kennedy and O'Connor—as evidence of an ultimately failed effort to rebuild the coalition that had produced the unprecedented *Casey* plurality. As in *Casey,* the Court sought to end a national debate that it feared was tearing the country apart."[18] Kennedy and O'Connor were fulfilling their long-established reputations as coalition builders on the Court.

Seven justices in *Bush v. Gore* could agree that any recount must avoid arbitrary decisions and follow established rules if it was to pass constitutional muster, and, moreover, they were willing to agree that the Florida recounts did not meet such standards. Justices Breyer and Souter were not willing, however, to accept the argument of Justices Rehnquist, Scalia, and Thomas that the Florida Court was acting outside its authority under either Article II or federal statue. They could accept the equal protection argument, because it left the Florida Court room to fashion an acceptable remedy. Justices Rehnquist, Scalia, and Thomas would have preferred to rest their argument on Article II grounds or perhaps a due process claim, but they were willing to go along with the use of the equal protection argument in the per curiam opinion because it allowed them to address their constitutional concerns about the conduct of the recount.

There were divisions, even bitter ones over this case, but what is too often missed is the extent to which even in the face of such divisions the Court sought common ground, looked for compromise, and tried very hard to narrow the scope of that division. They were not as successful in doing so in *Bush v. Gore* as they were in *Bush v. Palm Beach County.* Two justices wanted nothing to do with the per curiam opinion of the Court in *Bush v. Gore.* Two more found the remedy proposed by the Court to be much worse than the problem it was intended to solve. But any decision would have had partisan implications and led to partisan interpretations. In such a situation it takes a little more effort to see the legitimate concerns expressed on both sides of the case.

The Principled Basis of the Partisan Divisions

A few commentators have argued that the opinions in the case rested less on rank partisanship than on a fundamental debate over political principles. These arguments arise on both sides of the political spectrum. On the right, Harvey Mansfield claims:

The two parties were very much themselves throughout. The Republicans stand for the rule of law, and the Democrats for the rule of the people. And the Democrats, because they stand for the rule of people, believe that rule should be paramount, and that technicalities are subordinate to that will. Whereas the Republicans believe in doing things properly or legally. It really was a contest of principle between two parties.[19]

Mansfield may think the republican perspective is the more "proper" of the two, but the thrust of his argument is to suggest that both sides were acting on principle.

On the left, Richard Pildes has developed a remarkably similar thesis:

Whether democracy requires order, stability, and channeled, constrained forms of engagement, or whether it requires and even celebrates relatively wide-open competition that may appear tumultuous, partisan, or worse, has long been a struggle in democratic thought and practice. . . . Of course, the answer is that democracy requires a mix of both order (law, structure, and constraint) and openness (politics, fluidity, and receptivity to novel forms). But people, including judges and political actors, regularly seem to group themselves into characteristic and recurring patterns of response to new challenges that arise. These patterned responses suggest that it is something beyond law, or facts, or narrow partisan politics in particular cases, that determine outcomes.[20]

Pildes goes on to argue that the Court's intervention in *Bush v. Gore* was based on the "fear that democratic institutions would be unable to secure their own stability, and the perceived need for constitutionally imposed order."[21] Without doubt, Pildes believes that this fear was exaggerated but like Mansfield he agrees that the opinions in *Bush v. Gore* were not an aberration but the product of two distinct principled approaches to democratic politics.

Much of the disagreement in the case can be understood in these terms. On the one hand, Democrats and democrats argue that the essential function of an election is to determine the intentions of the voters. Republicans and republicans, on the other hand, emphasize the importance of formal legal procedures to avoid corruption or arbitrariness. Republicans would admit that elections entail democratic values; rules that place extraordinary limits on the franchise or that make it extremely difficult to exercise the right to vote would not be acceptable. Conversely, Democrats would admit that there must be some rules and regulation for participation in elections and tabulating the results.[22] But as Mansfield suggests, it is not surprising to see that Republicans would emphasize formal procedures and Democrats would emphasize voter intention.

These differing perspectives are obvious at almost every stage of the disputed election. The fact that Gore won the national popular vote but was to be denied the victory because of the Electoral College was an affront to many Democrats' concept of democracy.[23] Ultimately, however, the Democrats understood that this was a fight that would have to wait for another day. They had to fight the battle under the existing rules of the game. An Electoral College victory was possible if democracy could triumph in the state of Florida.

The problem was that democracy had run into a number of obstacles in the Florida vote. First was the issue of the now-infamous butterfly ballots used in Palm Beach County. Some voters reported that they had mistakenly cast votes for Pat Buchanan, the Reform Party candidate, or David MacReynolds, the Socialist Party candidate, instead of for Al Gore, and others had voted for Gore and either Buchanan or MacReynolds thinking that they were voting for Gore and Lieberman. Although there was some room for confusion among Bush voters, the design of the ballot clearly presented a much greater problem for the Democrats than for the Republicans.

But even Dershowitz admits that Gore was not likely to prevail on this issue.[24] First, the flawed ballot had been designed by a Democrat and had been approved by the Democrats.[25] There was no intention to aid Bush, and the Democrats had had an opportunity to object before the election. Second, the only possible remedy for this problem would be to revote, and given past cases it was highly unlikely that the Court would pursue such a remedy.

"Count all the votes" became the most promising and most persuasive rallying cry for the Gore campaign. Gore claimed that the Votamatic punch-card voting machines used in some heavily Democratic counties consistently undercounted legitimate votes. Gore believed that a more accurate count would give him a victory, and from a rhetorical standpoint it was a difficult argument to resist. Who would not want to count all the votes?

Florida Secretary of State Katherine Harris took up the challenge, claiming that the time for counting was over. There would never be a flawless count. At some point officials had to act on the best available information. She claimed that by statute she had a right to declare that that time had come and certify the election results favoring Bush. Her argument was not without appeal, especially to Bush supporters, but it played into the hands of the rhetoric of the Gore campaign. By stopping the recount, one woman was usurping the power of the voters to choose the next president. The courts must step in to defend democracy, and they did.

The Florida Supreme Court, basing its argument on the primacy of the principle of voter intent, ordered manual recounts. The deadlines established by the legislature and the discretionary authority granted to the secretary of state to certify election results were trumped by the state's interest in guaranteeing a full and accurate accounting of the intention of the voters. The Florida Court agreed with the Gore campaign that democratic principles were fundamental.

The Bush campaign countered with its republican arguments, foremost of which was the claim that democratic intentions can only be determined legitimately according to pre-established rules and procedures. As in the case of the butterfly ballots, the time to complain about the accuracy of the punch-card voting machines was prior to the election, not after the fact. Once the Democratic-controlled election boards had decided on ballots and voting machines, the legal requirements for a fair election had been determined and could not be changed in the hope of producing a different outcome.

The Gore campaign objected to this conclusion for two reasons. First, they argued that machines had malfunctioned and failed to record legitimate votes. A recount was not changing the rules but correcting a mechanical malfunction. Second, they contended that even though in some cases it was the voter and not the machine that had malfunctioned, for example when a voter failed to dislodge the chad associated with a particular candidate, such minor technical mistakes by the voter should not prevent the recording of a vote where there was in fact a clear expression of intent.

But according to republican principles, voters should be responsible for following instructions, and voting machines, whatever the error rate, were superior to hand counts because machines were not subject to political bias. Predetermined procedures and mechanical tabulation were the best way to avoid arbitrariness. It was this concern regarding the arbitrariness of the recount process that led seven members of the U.S. Supreme Court to call into question the recounts.

Five members of the Court, however, took the additional step of calling for a halt to any further recounts, but this too can be explained on republican grounds. In addition to the belief in the rule of law, the modern republicanism of the American founders also was characterized by a concern for effective and decisive government. Earlier republics and democracies had foundered because they were unable to act decisively. Modern popular governments must be able to overcome this defect if they are to succeed. We often forget that the immediate reason for the Constitutional Convention was the widespread belief that the government under the Articles of Confederation was incapable of governing.

A narrow, legalistic interpretation of the Constitution neglects that fact that the purpose of constitutional rules and procedures is not merely to restrain government action but also to empower the government to make decisions. These two sides of republicanism are illustrated in the practice of providing fixed terms of office. Fixed terms, as opposed to life tenure, can be seen as a protection of the people against the arbitrary exercise of power by a permanent governing class. Seen in this light, fixed terms allow for a popular or even democratic check on the exercise of government power. But seen in comparison to a parliamentary system that allows for a vote of no confidence and early elections, fixed terms are a means of insulating government officials from short-term popular control. Once elected, government officials can exercise power with discretion for a fixed term. If they do not plan to seek reelection, their discretion is limited only by the legal constraints on their office and on their personal behavior. If they wish to seek reelection, it is up to them to determine the extent to which they wish to take that desire into account when exercising their authority. Fixed terms, thus, allow officials some room to act, without having to be immediately accountable to the people.

The 2000 election forced an even closer look at this distinction between democratic politics and republican government. Although the Democrats would certainly claim that the Republicans' use of the rhetoric of republican government was in the service of Republican politics, the Republican argument did in fact have its roots in its modern republican principles. The call for an end to the recounts was consistent with a belief that elections must give way to governing. Democratic elections must end so that the business of governing can begin. This desire for decision, added to the belief that democratic elections are only legitimate to the extent that they follow republican procedures, provided the principled core for the arguments of the Bush campaign and for the Supreme Court's five-member majority.

The Appearance of Hypocrisy: Equal Protection

Although it is important to recognize the principled basis of the partisan arguments in this case, it would be a mistake to ignore both the perceived and real inconsistencies in those arguments. The anomalous positions of the justices in regard to both equal protection and federalism might well give rise to cries of hypocrisy. Indeed, both conservatives and liberals saw flaws in the Court's equal protection argument. The conservatives claimed that the Article II and 3 U.S.C., Section 5, arguments made by Justices Rehnquist, Scalia, and Thomas were more than adequate and that use of the equal protection argument implied an acceptance of a liberal interpretation of the equal protection clause that would come back to haunt conservatives in later cases.[26] The liberals claimed that it was disingenuous for conservatives to have discovered the equal protection clause in this case when they had traditionally tried to restrict its application, and that it was particularly egregious to do so here because the effect was to disenfranchise the very voters it was intended to protect, the minority voters of Palm Beach, Broward, and Dade counties.[27]

Even Richard Epstein, a defender of the majority decision, complained that "the Florida scheme is devoid of any suspect classification needed to trigger the equal protection analysis."[28] Cass Sunstein further noted that "nothing in the Court's previous decisions suggested that constitutional questions would be raised by this kind of inequality."[29] In spite of his criticisms, however, Sunstein concluded that there was some merit to the equal protection claim.[30] And, Bruce Ackerman, who called the majority decision an act of "sheer willfulness," defended the equal protection claim arguing:

I do not suggest that the majority's equal protection rationale is silly. It isn't. The Constitution obviously applies to vote-counting, and the Court has an obligation to intervene if a recount is systematically skewed in favor of one side. The majority's application of this basic principle in this case was controversial, but this is often true. And if the Court had simply ordered the Florida recount to proceed under its newly minted standards, I would not be protesting in the name of the rule of law.[31]

According to Ackerman, the problem with the decision was the remedy provided and not the diagnosis of an equal protection problem. Not everyone accepts the equal protection argument of the Court, but it is hardly without its defenders.

The more common complaint is that the judges were being disingenuous. As Mark Tushnet argued, "Although there are legal principles that might justify the equal protection holding . . . it is exceedingly difficult to conclude that the five justices in the majority were committed to legal principles that required the result they reached."[32] Sunstein elaborated that the equal protection claim was subject to three criticisms: "[that it] lacked support in precedent or history, that it raised many unanswered issues with respect to scope, and that it might well have authorized problems as serious as those it prevented."[33] If the majority was really serious about equal protection, they would have (1) established a much stronger record in support of it in the past, (2) not limited the ruling in *Bush v. Gore* to the facts of this particular case, and (3) shown more concern for the abuses of equal protection in the different voting systems throughout the state of Florida and the nation.

Pamela Karlan, on the other hand, lamented that "unfortunately for equal protection law, *Bush v. Gore* is not an aberration. Rather, it is yet another manifestation of the newest model of equal protection, a model laid out in the Court's decisions regarding race-conscious redistricting and Congress's power to enforce the Fourteenth Amendment."[34] Karlan identified the Court's theory as "structural equal protection." "In this newest model of equal protection, the Court deploys the equal protection clause not to protect the rights of an individual or a discrete group of individuals, particularly a group unable to protect itself through the operation of the normal political process but rather to regulate the institutional arrangements within which politics is conducted."[35] According to Karlan, the Court developed this conception of equal protection in a line of cases including *Shaw v. Reno, Miller v. Johnson, Bush v. Vera, Hunt v. Cromartie, Kimel v. Board of Regents*, and *Board of Trustees v. Garrett*.[36]

Karlan was highly critical of this model. Building on the work of Pildes, she claimed that "the 'image of democracy' that has informed the contemporary Supreme Court's intervention into the political arena . . . is fear of too much democracy, of too robust and tumultuous a political system."[37] Mark Tushnet agreed, claiming that "the contemporary Court sees itself as the guardian against the disorders to which democracy is prone."[38] But if Karlan and Tushnet are correct, the majority is innocent on the charge of hypocrisy. The equal protection theory of *Bush v. Gore* is not novel and is likely to be used in future cases, much to the dismay of Karlan and Tushnet. Indeed its roots go very deep in American history. The authors of *The Federalist* would have no trouble recognizing a theory of popular government that took into account the dangers of instability in democratic governments or the need to protect individual rights against majority tyranny. The forms of the Constitution are necessary to make political power safe and effective.

Those fears may become exaggerated or they may be neglected, either of which may cause great peril to the nation. Constitutional government requires a delicate balancing act, but if it is to work neither side should be too eager to push the other off the scale. The debate over equal protection in *Bush v. Gore* is at its core a debate over two competing principles of popular constitutional government. Each of those principles has a long history in the American political tradition.

The Appearance of Hypocrisy: Federalism

Even if a case can be made for consistency in the use of the equal protection clause, surely both the majority and the dissenters must blush when faced with their arguments regarding federalism. The Republicans called for the U.S. Supreme Court to overrule a state court on a matter of state election law, and the Democrats defended the supremacy of the state in deciding its own election procedures. Those positions might have been consistent with party principles in 1900 but were hardly so in 2000.

Listening to David Boies, Gore's lawyer, defend the primacy of state courts in deciding matters of state law in *Bush v. Gore* and Theodore Olson, Bush's legal counsel, argue for the principle of national supremacy, one might be justifiably confused and even a little suspicious of their motives. But lawyers are supposed to use any available argument to defend their clients. The more troubling inconsistency is the one between the judges' opinions in this case and their earlier opinions.

A comparison of the opinions of the justices in *Bush v. Gore* with those in the 1995 case of *U.S. Term Limits v. Thornton*[39] is particularly instructive. *Thornton* was also a case about election law. In 1992 Arkansas voters adopted an amendment to the state constitution preventing the names of candidates who had served three or more terms in the U.S. House of Representatives or two or more terms in the United States Senate from appearing on the ballot for those respective offices. The intended effect of these ballot restrictions was to introduce term limits for Arkansas' congressional delegation. The division of the U.S. Supreme Court in this case was remarkably similar to that in *Bush v. Gore*. On one side were Justices O'Connor, Rehnquist, Scalia, and Thomas. On the other were Justices Breyer, Ginsburg, Kennedy, Souter, and Stevens. Only Justice Kennedy would have appeared to switch sides in the two cases; but on closer examination we will see that it is Kennedy who remained consistent and the other eight justices who swapped arguments.

Justice Thomas's dissenting opinion in *Thornton*, which Justices O'Connor, Rehnquist, and Scalia joined, argued that the state of Arkansas had the right to determine ballot access rules for congressional elections. According to Thomas, "the people of each state have retained their independent political identity."[40] The U.S. Supreme Court "cannot override the decision of the people of Arkansas unless something in the Federal Constitution deprives them of the powers to enact such measures."[41] To do so would violate the Tenth Amendment. The majority, however, argued that by establishing qualifications for members of Congress, the U.S. Constitution preempted the states from adding additional qualifications. Thomas, however, contended that if the Constitution did not forbid the exercise of such authority by the state, it allowed it. The states could not ignore the standards set by the Constitution, but they were free to enact additional qualifications. On any subject on which the Constitution is silent, the power remains with the states and the people.

In addition to the Tenth Amendment arguments, Thomas made two additional claims. He maintained that although the framers intended to create "a direct link between members of the House of Representatives and the people, the link was between the Representatives from each state and the people of that state"[42] The Constitution did not create a national system of representation. Representatives were to be identified with their particular states. Moreover, Thomas claims that the times, places and manner clause of Article I, Section 4, is not a delegation to the states of a power over elections but a duty placed on them to insure that Congress continues to exist. The power of the states over the selection of their representatives is not a delegated power but a reserved power.

The obvious question is whether Thomas's opinion in *Thornton* is consistent with the concurring opinion he signed onto in *Bush v. Gore*. Thomas might argue that in one case we are dealing with congressional elections and in the other with a presidential election. Whereas Congress represents the people of the states, the president represents the nation as a whole. The presidency is a more national office and therefore its selection should be guided by national rather than state standards. The problem with this argument, however, is that the Constitution grants more discretion to the states in the selection of the president than in the selection of members of Congress. The state legislatures are free to adopt any methods they wish in the selection of electors. If, as in the case of Florida, state law provides for the participation of the courts in determining election results, Thomas's view of federalism should have led him to defer to the state courts to determine matters of state law.

It is possible, however, that Thomas was correct in *Bush v. Gore* but wrong in *Thornton*. Ironically, the best case for that conclusion may be found in Steven's majority opinion in *Thornton*. Quoting Justice Story, Stevens explained: "the states can exercise no powers whatsoever, which exclusively spring out of the existence of the national government, which the constitution does not delegate to them . . . No state can say that it has reserved, what it never possessed."[43] The selections of members of Congress and of the president are national functions. Without the Constitution these offices would not exist.

Justice Thomas's argument might be persuasive if we were still operating under the Articles of Confederation, but once the Constitution created national sovereignty, the argument falls apart. The states may possess the sovereign powers of states under the Constitution, but those powers are limited to the internal affairs of the state. National sovereignty is created through the Constitution and any participation by the states in that sphere of sovereignty must be derived from the Constitution. The states' role in the selection of members of Congress or of presidential electors is limited to those powers or duties delegated to the states by the U.S. Constitution. There is no reservoir of reserved powers from which the states may draw in regard to the election of federal officials. National supremacy should be the rule for both congressional and presidential elections.

If Thomas is therefore wrong in *Thornton* and right in *Bush v. Gore*, then by implication the reverse is true for Stevens. Stevens should have applied his standard of national supremacy for national elections in *Bush v. Gore* as well as in *Thornton*. But Stevens attempted to avoid this conclusion with the following argument:

> The Constitution assigns to the States the primary responsibility for determining the manner of selecting the electors. See Art. II, §1, cl. 2. When questions arise about the meaning of state laws, including election laws, it is our settled practice to accept the opinions of the highest courts of the States as providing the final answers. On rare occasions, however, either federal statutes or the Federal Constitution may require federal judicial intervention in state elections. This is not such an occasion.[44]

The logic seems straightforward. The Constitution gives the states the power to control the selection process, which means that the selection process will be conducted under state law. State courts are ordinarily the final authority for the interpretation of state law. Federal intervention is therefore the exception and not the rule in state elections. The problem with this logic, however, is that it moves from the premise that the Constitution gives the states the power to conduct an election to the conclusion that presidential elections are simply "state elections."

Even Justice Thomas might blush at this extraordinarily state-centric interpretation of the Constitution. Justice Stevens was, in effect, arguing that presidential elections are no different from a state representative race and that the authority of state courts and state laws are as binding in one case as the other. Stevens might claim that he believed the Constitution's delegation of power to the states was much greater in the case of presidential elections than it was in congressional elections, but even granting this point it is difficult to reconcile his claim that this is simply a "state election" with his argument in *Thornton* that the authority over the selection of national officials ultimately belongs to the nation and not the states.

Only Justice Kennedy remained consistent in his position in both *Thornton* and *Bush v. Gore*. In his concurring opinion in *Thornton*, Kennedy explains his view of the federal system:

> In one sense it is true that "the people of each State retained their separate political identities," for the Constitution takes care both to preserve the States and to make use of their identities and structures at various points in organizing the federal union. It does not at all follow from this that the sole political identity of an American is with the State of his or her residence. It denies the dual character of the Federal Government which is its very foundation to assert that the people of the United States do not have a political identity as well, one independent of, though consistent with, their identity as citizens of the State of their residence.[45]

Justice Thomas is correct in affirming the sovereignty of the state when dealing with state matters. We are citizens of the state in which we reside. But for Justice Thomas's opinion to prevail, one would have to deny the equally important principle that we are citizens of the United States. There is a sphere of national sovereignty the states are obliged to respect. Federalism is based on dual sovereignty, not state sovereignty.

In both *Thornton* and *Bush*, Kennedy supported the intervention of the Court to protect the integrity of a national election process. It is difficult to explain his actions in terms of partisan motives. Most Court watchers would agree that Justice Kennedy drifted to the left during his tenure, but it is in the earlier case, *Thornton*, that he breaks with his conservative colleagues on the Court, and in the later case of *Bush v. Gore* that he sides with the conservatives over the liberals. Perhaps this pragmatic moderate justice has a greater claim to principled consistency than his more ideological colleagues on the left and right.

Justice Kennedy's eight colleagues are certainly open to the charge of hypocrisy in their federalism arguments, but even here we should remember that hypocrisy is not merely a sign of division or partisanship but also a kind of tribute to one's opponent. The dissenters' appeal to the principles of federalism is much like the majority's appeal to the equal protection clause. It is an attempt to make the case for one's position by appealing to the fundamental principles of one's opponent. This is not a bad way to try to reach consensus, neither is it simply unprincipled.

The principles on each side remain clear: democratic participation and voter intent versus republican rules and finality. The question is about the appropriate constitutional means for defending these principles. Ordinarily the dissenters might see federalism as an obstacle to democratic decision-making, just as the majority might conclude that equal protection is often used as a justification for arbitrary action on the part of the Court. But in this case, we might say the two sides return to their roots. They remember that Democrats once defended the states as the true home of democracy and that Republicans wrote the equal protection clause to protect one group from the arbitrary use of power by another. In attempting to undercut the position of their opponents, Democrats and Republicans were forced to recover a more complex understanding of their own positions.

Missed Opportunities

A better understanding and more consistent application of republican and democratic principles might have led to an even more satisfactory consensus. On one level, it is not surprising to see Justices Breyer, Ginsburg, Souter, and Stevens defending the Florida Court's attempt to defend democratic participation, or Justices Kennedy, O'Connor, Rehnquist, Scalia, and Thomas argue that that same Court had engaged in standardless judicial activism. These are positions we have come to associate with modern Democrats and Republicans. The difficulty is that neither position was applied consistently in this case. The dissenters were willing to allow an activist Florida judiciary to intervene in the election, but they were appalled by the intervention of the U.S. Supreme Court in this matter. The majority rejected the activism of the Florida Court but was unwilling to allow either the Florida courts or the U.S. Congress the opportunity to settle the dispute before jumping into the fray.[46]

Let us look first at the majority's inconsistent republicanism. The majority failed to take advantage of two possible republican solutions to the problems presented by the state recounts. First, the Court could have simply remanded the case to the Florida courts, allowing them to attempt to conduct a proper recount in the time allotted. By refusing this option, the majority left itself open to Justice Ginsburg's charge that the "Court's conclusion that a constitutionally adequate recount is impractical is a prophecy the Court's own judgment will not allow to be tested."[47] Courts are supposed to decide the case after all the facts are in, not before.

But given the fact that this decision was being handed down on December 12, the deadline for certifying the vote under the "safe harbor" provision, the distinction between before and after made little difference, or at least that was the contention of the majority. Justice Breyer, however, was not persuaded that the Supreme Court was bound to enforce the safe harbor provision. He argued:

> The Chief Justice contends that our opinion in *Bush v. Palm Beach County Canvassing Bd.* (*Bush I*) in which we stated that "a legislative wish to take advantage of [§5] would counsel against" a construction of Florida law that Congress might deem to be a change in law, now means that this Court "must ensure that post-election state court actions do not frustrate the legislative desire to attain the 'safe harbor' provided by §5." However, §5 is part of the rules that govern Congress' recognition of slates of electors. Nowhere in *Bush I* did we establish that this Court had the authority to enforce §5. Nor did we suggest that the permissive "counsel against" could be transformed into the mandatory "must ensure." And nowhere did we intimate, as the concurrence does here, that a state court decision that threatens the safe harbor provision of §5 does so in violation of Article II.[48]

The safe harbor provision is an option, not a requirement, and even if it were a requirement it would be up to the state courts rather than the federal courts to enforce it. Thus, Justice Breyer concludes that at the very least the state of Florida would not have to certify a slate of electors until the date when the electors were scheduled to meet, December 18.

Justice Ginsburg, in her dissenting opinion, reminded us that in addition to the December 18 "deadline," there was also a December 27 deadline. Under federal law, if Congress has not received a state's electoral votes by the fourth Wednesday in December, it is authorized to request the state secretary of state to send a certified return immediately. Implied in this statutory provision is the assumption that Congress may not only receive but also solicit electoral votes until the end of December. Even more significant, Justice Ginsburg claimed, is "Congress' detailed provisions for determining, on 'the sixth day of January,' the validity of electoral votes."[49] Congress is free to accept votes until that date. Justice Ginsburg might have added that in addition to federal statute, the U.S. Constitution itself makes clear that Congress has the ultimate authority to determine the validity of electoral votes. A more republican Supreme Court majority might have deferred to this explicit constitutional mechanism rather than fashion its own remedy.[50]

The dissenters, however, could have been more consistent in their support of democratic values. They should have been willing to apply the same standards of judicial restraint to both the U.S. Supreme Court and the Florida Supreme Court. If action by the U.S. Supreme Court threatened to disrupt the democratic process, so to did the actions of Florida Supreme Court. But the dissenters largely ignored the claims of those who feared that the court-ordered recounts might themselves violate democratic principles. For example, Justice Ginsburg maintained that "no one has doubted the good faith and diligence with which Florida election officials, attorneys for all sides of this controversy, and the courts of law have performed their duties."[51] But in fact many people did express such doubts.

A major premise of Bush's complaint was that the recounts were manufacturing rather than counting votes. The vague standard of "voter intent" being applied in obviously disparate ways in different jurisdictions and even in different ways within the same jurisdiction could hardly be described as a democratic process. Giving the counters such leeway in determining the meaning of a ballot in effect substituted the will of the counters for the will of the people.

Justices Breyer and Souter at least acknowledged this problem by joining in the seven-vote majority that questioned the legitimacy of the recounts under the equal protection clause, but Justices Ginsburg and Stevens rejected any concern with the legitimacy of the recounts. They argued that although they might have preferred more objective standards, it was within the legitimate discretion of the Florida Supreme Court to conduct the recount in this way. The Florida Supreme Court was under no obligation to adopt standards that would provide some assurance that the vote counters were not substituting their own discretion for that of the voters. The discretion of the Court and of the counters would thus appear to be more important than the determination of voter intent. The dissenters were willing to leave a large degree of discretion with the Florida courts, hardly the most democratic branch of the Florida government.

The dissent also ignores the legitimate discretion of the Florida secretary of state to certify the election results. If the federal courts owe great deference to the Florida courts in this case, why should the Florida courts not owe equally great deference to the decision of the secretary of state? She was the elected official responsible for certifying the election. If she had determined that the vote count was as accurate as we were likely to obtain, then the Florida Supreme Court should be reluctant to second guess her decision. She might have been mistaken, but it was her call. In the absence of fraud or a rigged election, the Florida Supreme Court had no need to become involved in an essentially political and administrative process.

From the perspective of Justices Kennedy, O'Connor, Rehnquist, Scalia, and Thomas, the U.S. Supreme Court intervened to defend democracy against an attack by the Florida Supreme Court. But from the perspective of Justices Breyer, Ginsburg, Souter, and Stevens, the U.S. Supreme Court undermined the institutional prerogatives and legal mechanisms established at both the national and state levels, in both statutory and constitutional law. Each side could have learned something about their principles from the arguments of their opponents.

Who was right? In a sense it probably did not matter. The nonpartisan recount conducted by the National Opinion Research Center at the University of Chicago concluded that if the U.S. Supreme Court had allowed the recount to continue Bush would still have carried the state of Florida.[52] The proposed recounts would have supported the legitimacy of Bush's victory and undercut Gore's complaints of an unjust process. Thus one may find a kind of poetic justice in the outcome of the case.

But was the decision just from a constitutional perspective? I would argue that it was, but I would also suggest that the opinions of Justices Breyer and Souter might also have led to a constitutional result. In the end the case turned on a judgment of the constitutional discretion of various state and federal judges and elected officials. And although there are constitutional and legal standards that help us to define the scope of discretion, in the end some cases will remain a judgment call. There was no hard and fast legal or constitutional standard that could determine if the majority should have allowed more time for the process to play out or if the dissenters should have been more sensitive to the complaints of a flawed recount. A formal legal analysis cannot lead us to a final judgment.

In the absence of such clear-cut standards, we find room for discretion. But how is discretion defined or circumscribed by either democratic of republican principles? Both Democrats and Republicans have had difficulty developing and maintaining a consistent position on the role of discretion in our constitutional framework. Public doubts about the constitutional validity of the arguments presented in *Bush v. Gore* make sense in a political environment in which neither party can provide a coherent account of the proper extent and limits of judicial or executive discretion under the Constitution.

Democracy, Discretion, and Republican Government

As partisans it is natural to approve of discretion when we are in control and to oppose it when power is the hands of our opponents. Partisan attitudes toward executive and judicial power typically reflect the partisan composition of those institutions.[53] For much of our history parties have defended discretion for one branch while opposing it in the other. For example, New Deal Democrats embraced broad discretionary authority for the executive but wanted a restrained judiciary; whereas by the 1970s Democrats had become suspicious of executive power but defenders of judicial activism. The simple explanation for this phenomenon is that the life tenure of the Court tends to institutionalize the political perspective of earlier presidencies. The Court is a conservative institution, although at times what it conserves might be considered to be liberal political principles. The president's desire to act is often constrained by the Court's desire to preserve or promote the principles of the previous presidents who nominated them.

There are, however, exceptions to this pattern. If one party tends to prevail in presidential elections over a long period of time, defenders of executive discretion may come to appreciate the virtues of judicial discretion and opponents of executive discretion may come to distrust judicial discretion. Even prior to *Bush v. Gore*, we have seen growing evidence of such a trend. There is a substantial literature in which liberal commentators attack the Supreme Court's increasing conservative activism.[54] The consensus that developed in the mid-twentieth century behind the belief that judicial activism would provide the best protection for liberal democratic values has started to crumble. The recent liberal critics of the Court are now arguing that courts are inherently undemocratic institutions. There is no justification for judicial policy-making in a democratic government, and the courts should stop meddling in the political process. Just as New Deal defenders of a powerful executive, such as Arthur Schlesinger Jr. turned against executive discretion when faced with a strong Republican executive, liberal legal commentators have come to appreciate the problems for democratic theory posed by judicial activism.

On the other hand, Republicans have been increasingly willing to use the courts to impose republican constraints on legislative actions. In commerce cases such as *United States v. Lopez* and *Printz v. United States*, conservative justices have placed limits on congressional authority under the commerce clause.[55] And in a series of takings clause cases going back almost two decades, the conservatives on the Court have attempted to place constitutional restraints on regulation of private property by the states.[56] In this way conservative judges have come to appreciate the important role that courts may play in supporting republican restraints on democratic politics as well as the importance of republican decisiveness for effective government.

The opinions in *Bush v. Gore* represent, if not the culmination of these trends, at least a major step in support of them. The political motivations behind the decision are far more complex than most commentators have suggested. The partisan motives are entangled with a debate over the relative importance of the democratic and republican foundations of our Constitution. The political implications of that debate may be much more far-reaching than the outcome of a single election. We might see an even greater divide between Republicans and Democrats, as they become more consistent adherents to their democratic and republican principles. But such division might also be an occasion for greater reflection on the relationship between the democratic and republican principles underlying our Constitution.

Both the judiciary and the executive were created in recognition of the need for discretion within the bounds of constitutional government. Laws could neither interpret nor could they execute themselves. General rules could not always be applied mechanically to specific cases. But what legitimizes the exercise of such discretion? The democratic answer is that discretion is legitimate to the extent that it promotes popular will or popular participation. Thomas Jefferson used this argument to defend his use of prerogative powers. Theodore Roosevelt developed it more fully in his stewardship theory, and contemporary scholars have come to identify the modern presidency as the popular presidency. The democratic argument for judicial discretion is of more recent origin. But at least by the time of the Warren Court, judges had begun to justify their discretionary authority in terms of what Sunstein calls a theory of "democracy reinforcement."[57] It is this democratic perspective that is reflected in the arguments of the Gore campaign as well as the dissenters in *Bush v. Gore.*

But there is also a republican defense of discretion. Discretion may be necessary to make government both safe and effective. Majorities may ignore individual rights, and democracies may find it difficult to act quickly and decisively. That is why Hamilton turned to the Constitution rather than popular will as a source of executive authority. Hamilton wanted to find room within the Constitution for an institution that would counter these dangerous democratic tendencies. An executive that could act decisively and stand up against the dangers of short-term majorities that may arise in the legislature would make the new government competent and free. Hamilton's vision of executive power serves to correct both the more narrow and legalistic readings of the Constitution by Edward Corwin and his intellectual descendents, as well as the views of Richard Neustadt and his followers, who have paid scant attention to the Constitutional sources of executive power.[58]

John Marshall developed a similar defense of judicial power. The judiciary would defend the Constitution against attacks by the legislature, the executive, or the states. The Court would use its discretion to defend the more considerate, long-term will of the people as expressed in the Constitution against short-term political pressures. Both Hamilton's and Marshall's view are reflected in the arguments of defenders of the contemporary Republican presidents and justices.

As Tushnet, points out, however, "the difficulty with *Bush v. Gore* is that legal conservatism has only been selectively suspicious of democracy . . . When it suits the cause, legal conservatives become populists, decrying the arrogance of a liberal elite in imposing its will on a more sensible public."[59] Of course, one might add, that liberal Democrats have discovered the virtues of judicial restraint only after they lost control of the Supreme Court. *Bush v. Gore* should be an occasion for contemporary Democrats and Republicans to think more seriously about their fundamental principles. Not only might they become more consistent in their arguments, but Republicans might be forced to admit that a powerful Supreme Court and a powerful executive cannot operate without democratic support, and Democrats may come to appreciate that democracy may be either self-destructive or incompetent without republican restraint and republican energy. In this way we may escape not only the perspective of mere partisanship but also encourage presidency scholarship that recognizes that constitutional forms shape political behavior and that constitutional provisions create as well as restrain political power.

CHAPTER SIX

Military Tribunals, Prerogative Power, and the War on Terrorism

RICHARD M. PIOUS

W E WILL PROTECT AMERICA," President George W. Bush pledged on the first anniversary of the 9/11 attacks, "But we will do so within the guidelines of the Constitution, confines of the Constitution ... the American people got to understand that the Constitution is sacred as far as I'm concerned."[1] These were noble sentiments, but earlier Bush had taken a different stance: "The enemy has declared war on us," he said in a speech on November 29, 2001, "And we must not let foreign enemies use the forums of liberty to destroy liberty itself."[2]

The purpose of this chapter is to describe one decision President Bush made in the "war against terror"—the creation of military tribunals—and then to raise several questions: What constitutional and legal doctrines did the president use to justify his decision? How did Congress and the judiciary respond, and how did the response by the other branches affect the exercise of this prerogative? These are questions that political scientists specializing in public law can help to answer.

Presidents defend and their opponents attack the legitimacy of presidential prerogative powers. The debate leads to three alternative outcomes. First, in the "frontlash" effect the policy succeeds, the president's party unites while the opposition is divided and demoralized, Congress is supportive or at least acquiescent, and the federal courts rule for the executive or decline to take jurisdiction. Second, in the "backlash" effect the presidential policy may succeed, but at a high cost, or the result does not meet public expectations; the president's decision is called into question; his party is demoralized while most of the opposition unites against him; Congress is likely to modify his policies or even abandon them, while increasing oversight and possibly passing framework legislation to create a new pattern of policy codetermination; and courts are likely to rule in ways that check and balance executive action. Finally, in extreme cases there is an "overshoot and collapse" effect, which results in investigations of wrongdoing that reach the highest levels of the White House, a shake-up of senior staff, criminal investigations and indictments, and informal or formal censure or impeachment proceedings.

Which of these possibilities best describes the reaction to President Bush's creation of military tribunals? What is the likelihood that military tribunals will be incorporated into "the living presidency?" And what do the actions of Congress and the Supreme Court tell us about the politics of prerogative power?

The Establishment of Military Tribunals in the War on Terror

In the aftermath of the 9/11 attacks by al Qaeda on the World Trade Center and the Pentagon, President Bush requested that White House Counsel Alberto Gonzales organize a working group, headed by Pierre-Richard Prosper, a State Department official and expert on war crimes, to determine what procedures to use as members of al Qaeda were captured. While some task force officials wanted to use regular military courts-martial (established by Congress under the Uniform Code of Military Justice [UCMJ]) and others suggested that special military tribunals be established, Attorney General John Ashcroft and his deputy Michael Chertoff proposed that terrorists be tried in federal courts. President Bush, on the advice of Gonzales and Vice President Dick Cheney, issued a military order establishing tribunals, based on his powers as president and commander in chief and on powers delegated by Congress.[3]

Under the terms of the president's order, noncitizens, including resident aliens, could be subject to military tribunals at the discretion of the president. Those subject to the tribunals would be members of al Qaeda, persons involved in "acts of international terrorism," or persons who had "knowingly harbored" others in the first two categories. The president would determine whom the tribunals would try, with some detainees tried in federal courts and others held without trial.

Tribunal proceedings had elements of due process. Defendants would be presumed innocent, and the burden of proof would remain with the government. They would be given notice of charges before trial; they did not have to testify against themselves; they could call witnesses and see evidence presented by the government; their attorneys could cross-examine witnesses; they could choose their own counsel (if they could afford to do so), but all defendants under subsequent Pentagon guidelines were also assigned military counsel.[4]

By design, some due process protections of civilian courts were lacking.[5] No definition of "international terrorism" was provided in the order or regulations. Group association and membership, rather than commission of concrete acts, could be the basis for detention and trial.[6] A person could be charged and tried solely at the discretion of the president, without any judicial review. Anyone charged could be held indefinitely at any location in the world, a provision that went far beyond congressional intent in the USA Patriot Act, which specified only a limited seven-day detention period, after which a person held must be charged with a crime or immigration violation and which provided for judicial review in habeas corpus proceedings. The judges, prosecutors, and military defense lawyers would be appointed by the president—a power later delegated to the secretary of defense or his designees in the chain of command. Any civilian defense attorney would have to be cleared for "secret" information.[7] Private defense counsel and the accused would not have the right to be present if the commission's presiding officer or the secretary of defense ordered "closed" proceedings to guard "classified or classifiable" information, to protect physical safety of members of the tribunal, or to "safeguard intelligence and law enforcement sources, methods or activities" or other "national security interests." Military defense counsel, however, could not be excluded from any proceedings, and military guidelines started with the presumption that proceedings would be public. Later, Congress provided that illegally and unconstitutionally obtained evidence (such as confessions after maltreatment) would be permissible if it had "probative value to a reasonable person." (This stands in sharp contrast to courts-martial, in which rules of evidence similar to civilian courts apply.) Evidence would not have to be authenticated, nor a "chain of custody of incriminating evidence" demonstrated to guard against tampering.

There would be no jury trials. A two-thirds vote of the judges on the tribunal would be sufficient to convict. To vote guilty, members of the commission would have to be certain "beyond a reasonable doubt," which corresponds to the standard in civilian trials. Guilty verdicts could be appealed to an independent appeals board on which civilians might serve, but the appeals board could only review the evidence and could not apply the Constitution or federal laws to review procedures of the tribunals. The commission would determine penalties, with unanimity required to impose the death penalty. The president could reduce the penalty (though he could not change a not guilty verdict to guilty).[8] Even if a defendant were acquitted, he or she might be kept in custody if thought to be dangerous.[9]

No civilian court could review tribunal decisions. (In courts-martial the verdicts are reviewed by the Court of Criminal Appeals, then by the Court of Appeals for the Armed Forces, and the U.S. Supreme Court may undertake a final review.[10]) The absence of judicial review stands in contrast to Section 412 of the USA Patriot Act, which provides for habeas corpus proceedings so that civilian courts may review any detentions of noncitizens "reasonably believed" to be involved in terrorism. It also stands in contrast to the Constitution, which provides that the privilege of obtaining the writ of habeas corpus may not be suspended, except in cases of invasion and rebellion, although it should be noted that foreign nationals held as prisoners of war (POWs) do not enjoy the same constitutional protections as American citizens. Since the federal courts have already recognized a presidential power under the commander-in-chief clause to establish commissions until such time as peace is finalized, the tribunals established by President Bush could continue until hostilities ended. Thus, to the extent that a "war" on terror might last for a generation—as had the cold war—these tribunals would become a long-standing fixture of the American legal system.[11]

The Relevance of International Law

A major issue in the debate over the president's order is the relevance of international law. Does the government have an obligation to enforce treaty obligations relating to prisoners apprehended in international conflicts? Do these obligations or the norms of customary international law conflict with the president's order? And if so, would the order remain valid?

The Bush administration's policy was to take an "intelligence gathering" approach to those it apprehended and to treat terrorists as unlawful combatants rather than common criminals or formal POWs. It focused on the enormity of the potential damage from terrorism: strikes at nuclear waste facilities, fuel storage tanks, dams and reservoirs; the potential use of weapons of mass destruction; the possibility of cyberwarfare against information systems; the use ground-to-air missiles against civilian jet airliners; and the potential for martyrdom acts in mass transit that can instill terror in the population and completely disrupt normal commercial, social, and cultural life.[12] Terrorism could lead to panic, with Americans stampeding out of cities or away from nuclear reactors, so that the impact of a single horrendous act committed by a handful of terrorists could be leveraged. Even if the probability of such acts is low in a given year, over the long term the probabilities multiply. Threats of reprisal against terrorists are meaningless and deterrent factors limited. Almost always the advantage lies with the attackers rather than the defenders. Gaining intelligence from detainees might reduce those advantages, and many in the administration believed that such intelligence could be gained through aggressive interrogation that would enable the military or covert agents to discover the operatives planning new attacks and then disrupt their operations.

Under international law the United States had the right to try combatants for violations of the laws of war (battlefield atrocities), humanitarian law (genocide), or criminal law (airplane hijacking and murder). This holds true even if operatives are captured outside a zone of combat or are not engaged in combat activities. The Bush administration rejected an approach—standard in American practice prior to 9/11—that treated terrorists as criminals and tried them in civilian criminal courts with due process guarantees (though some accused of terrorist acts or conspiracies since 9/11 have been tried in civilian courts). It did so because al Qaeda had been harbored by the Taliban regime in Afghanistan, therefore creating an issue of self-defense between the United States and another sovereign state.

International law governing the conduct of belligerents (*jus in bello*) divides into two parts: conduct on the battlefield (Hague Conventions) and the treatment of POWs and civilians (Geneva Conventions). There are four Geneva Conventions on the Protection of War Victims (last revised in 1949), with the Third Convention applying to POWs and the

Fourth Convention applying to civilians, both ratified by the United States in July 1955. There are two Additional Protocols of 1977 (which the United States has not ratified). The Geneva Conventions apply in all cases of armed conflict between two or more signatory states. Since both the United States and Afghanistan had ratified the conventions, both states were required to adhere to them in their mutual relations.[13]

The Bush administration early in 2002 labeled the al Qaeda operatives and their Afghan Taliban allies enemy combatants who had committed an act of war against the United States. It also determined that the al Qaeda operatives were unlawful enemy combatants and therefore not entitled to POW status.[14] This designation was based partly on what they did and partly on how they were organized. They had committed acts that violated the laws of war. Some of these, dealing with behavior in combat, are codified in treaties, such as the Hague Convention Respecting the Laws and Customs of War on Land, and others are based on customary practices in warfare. The laws of war prohibit certain tactics and weapons (such as gas attacks), and include prohibitions against attacks on civilians and destruction of civilian buildings. International law makes a distinction between individuals who may lawfully engage in combat and those who may not: members of a non-state organization such as al Qaeda fit in the latter category, because they are not members of the armed forces of a state, do not have a chain of command, do not wear uniforms or have distinctive identifying signs on the battlefield, do not carry arms openly, and do not adhere to the laws and customs of war.

Critics charge that the Bush administration determinations violated the Geneva Conventions. Article 5 of the Third Convention requires that if there is "any doubt" about the status of a detainee, a "competent tribunal" must determine his or her lawful or unlawful status.[15] Even if a detainee were judged an unlawful combatant, he or she must be given the protections guaranteed by Common Article 3, which appears in all four of the 1949 Geneva Conventions.[16] These protections include the rights: to "be treated humanely"; to be protected from "violence to life and person, in particular murder of all kinds, mutilation, cruel treatment and torture"; not to suffer "outrages upon personal dignity, in particular, humiliating and degrading treatment"; care for the "wounded and sick"; and to be sentenced or executed only after a "judgment pronounced by a regularly constituted court affording all the judicial guarantees which are recognized as indispensable by civilized peoples." Also, "an impartial humanitarian body, such as the International Committee of the Red Cross, may offer its services to the Parties to the conflict." "Grave breaches" of the conventions by captors mistreating "protected persons" are war crimes, including "unlawful confinement of a protected person."

A decision that detainees are *unlawful* combatants has important consequences for their conditions of detention. Under the Geneva Convention, *lawful* combatants held as POWs do not have to provide information beyond "name, rank and serial number" or other basic identification and may not be coerced or intimidated. Article 102 of the Third Geneva Convention provides that "a prisoner of war (POW) can be validly sentenced only if the sentence has been pronounced by the same courts according to the same procedure as in the case of members of the armed forces of the Detaining Power, and if, furthermore, the provisions of the present Chapter have been observed."[17] Article 105 includes the same rights of appeal as those granted to detaining forces.[18] POWs must be repatriated after cessation of active hostilities (unless convicted and sentenced by courts). But al Qaeda detainees were not considered lawful combatants, and so the Bush administration denied these protections to them. This decision raised several questions: What international treaty and customary international law applied to the treatment of these detainees? Could they be held indefinitely for interrogation? Were there any limits on how they might be interrogated? And could they be tried by the special tribunals?

As noted above, a fair trial is to be held by "a regularly constituted court, affording all the judicial guarantees which are recognized as indispensable by civilized peoples."[19] But what is a "regularly constituted" court? Does a military tribunal established by the president qualify?

Customary international law sheds some light on the legality of military tribunals.[20] During the Civil War, Attorney General James Speed, in a formal opinion to President Abraham Lincoln, observed that if Congress failed to create military tribunals, the executive could do so "according to the laws and usages of civilized warfare."[21] This would suggest that they would qualify as "regularly constituted." But although military commissions and tribunals were justified in the nineteenth and early twentieth centuries according to the laws and customs of war (they were used, for example, in the Revolutionary War, during the Mexican-American War to discipline American troops, during the Civil War against Confederate spies and others, against conspirators in the Lincoln assassination, during the occupation of the Philippines, during World War II against Nazi saboteurs, and after the war against Japanese and Germans), in modern times they are placed in a suspect category in human rights treaties such as the Inter-American Convention on the Forced Disappearance of Persons, because of their abuse by dictatorial military regimes.[22]

Proponents of a due process approach argue if the United States establishes military tribunals, these courts should comply with Article 14 of the International Covenant on Civil and Political Rights, which recognizes a set of customary and treaty-based due process protections: the right to be tried by a competent, independent, and impartial tribunal established by law; presumption of innocence; right to be informed of charges promptly; the right to have time and resources to prepare a defense and the right to counsel of choice; the right to examine witnesses; the right to have an interpreter; the privilege against self-incrimination; the right of review by a higher tribunal.[23] The United States was not required to provide these protections, but it might have been in its own interest, since member states of the European Union cannot extradite individuals—even those in custody—to the United States when there is a risk that American judicial or military procedures will violate human rights under customary international law.[24]

The president directed the military to treat al Qaeda detainees in a manner consistent with the "principles" of the Geneva Conventions but to do so only "to the extent appropriate and consistent with military necessity."[25] Bush used (as have other presidents) the sovereign power to determine whether or not to comply with international obligations, as well as the power to interpret and reinterpret such obligations. Although the administration held in reserve as a sovereign right of the United States the claim that the president had the prerogative to suspend the nation's adherence to international law, it argued that it was meeting its international obligations.

Bush used his power to reinterpret international law rather than his power to abrogate American adherence to it. He decreed that Common Article 3 did not apply to al Qaeda. He argued that the combatants in Afghanistan did not have lawful combatants' privilege because of their practices in combat. They were "common enemies of humankind" and a stateless band of terrorists not acting with any legitimate authority, according to the precept in international law that defines acts of private warfare as *malum in se* (wrong in itself). The administration observed that Common Article 3, applies to "an Armed conflict not of an international character occurring in the territory of one of the High Contracting Parties."[26] According to the Bush administration reinterpretation of that clause, Article 3 due process guarantees would not apply, because the conflict involved the United States against a terrorist group crossing state boundaries and represented a threat to many nations, therefore making the conflict one of an "international character." The more common interpretation of the language of Article 3 is that it applies to a conflict other than between two nation states, in which case it would apply to acts of terrorism carried out by a non-state organization (al Qaeda) against the United States. The fact that the organization was not a nation-state had been crucial in the administration's determination that al Qaeda operatives were unlawful combatants.

The Bush administration claimed that these facts were self-evident and so there was no need for adjudicatory proceedings under the Third Geneva Convention's Article 5 to determine combatant status and entitlement to POW status. As unlawful combatants, al Qaeda operatives under the laws of war could be interned without criminal charges or access to legal counsel until hostilities ended. Until charges were brought, they would have no right or access to legal counsel, leaving them to be incarcerated and interrogated indefinitely.

The administration further claimed great latitude in conducting the interrogations of unlawful combatants. If they were not to be protected either by the rights granted defendants in civilian court proceedings or by the customary protections accorded prisoners under the UCMJ (and overseen by military courts-martial), the way was open to instituting an interrogation approach to prisoners that would go well beyond Article 17 of Geneva Convention III Relative to the Treatment of Prisoners of War, which prohibits "any form of coercion" in interrogation.[27] The administration argued that Geneva Convention IV Relative to the Protection of Civilian Persons in Time of War protects civilian detainees who qualify as "protected persons" from coercion, but that not all detainees qualify as protected persons, especially those engaging in terrorist acts. And although Article 75 of Additional Protocol I protects all detainees captured in international or internal armed conflict, regardless of their legal status, the United States is not a party to this protocol (having rejected it during the Reagan administration in 1987).

The Department of Defense developed guidelines for the interrogation of these prisoners. Memoranda argued that the prisoners were not entitled to protection under the Geneva Conventions. If there were no violations of the Geneva Conventions, then the prohibitions contained in the UCMJ against commission of war crimes in treating prisoners could not be violated, because the UCMJ requires that the Geneva Conventions be violated to demonstrate such war crimes. A Justice Department memorandum offered a narrow definition of torture that would permit harsh interrogation tactics being devised by the Department of Defense.[28] (A companion memorandum, which remains classified, outlined specific methods that the Central Intelligence Agency could use.) The evidence obtained by mistreating or torturing prisoners could be admitted in proceedings to determine if a detainee can be held indefinitely at Guantánamo Bay detention camp and in panels determining combatant status. (In contrast, statements produced under torture may not be introduced into civilian courts or military courts martial established by Congress.) The Detainee Treatment Act of 2005 (DTA) authorized the panel to consider the probative value of such evidence—the first time Congress had ever legitimated the use of evidence obtained through inhuman treatment.[29]

Sole or Concurrent Constitutional Powers

Does the president have an inherent constitutional prerogative to establish military tribunals without obtaining authorization from Congress? Is there a concurrent authority to administer military justice? And if so, are there any limits to presidential power that might be inferred or implied from the doctrines of separation of powers and checks and balances? Put differently, how can an executive power to create tribunals be inferred, when there is a specific power to provide rules and regulations for the Armed Forces that was granted in the Constitution to Congress, and therefore one might assume that providing such rules is an exclusive legislative power? Even if the authority were concurrent, would congressional intent always trump presidential action? If not, what principle would determine which institution's intent should prevail?

In determining the constitutionality of a presidential action, Justice

Jackson's three-fold test in the Steel Seizure case is helpful. Jackson suggested that when the president acts with the concurrence of Congress, the constitutionality of his action is at the highest presumption. When he acts alone there is a lower presumption, and when he acts against the express or implied will of Congress, then the presumption is at its lowest.[30] The Bush administration argued that the military order should be in the first category since provisions of the UCMJ acknowledge that presidential military commissions may conduct trials during armed conflicts: Article 36 grants the president the authority to establish procedures for both courts-martial and military commissions; Article 27 notes that they will have concurrent jurisdiction; and the establishment of parallel military courts has been recognized in subsequent legislation.[31]

President Bush claimed that there was "joint concord" with Congress on ways to conduct a war on terror, and it is a long-standing presidential position that courts should defer when a presidential action is clearly consistent with congressional intent expressed in statutes, particularly when the commander-in-chief power is at stake. Federal courts have tended to agree in war powers and national security matters. In the war on terror, the Authorization for Use of Military Force (AUMF) that Congress passed as a joint resolution in the aftermath of 9/11 allows the president, stating: "To use all necessary and appropriate force against those nations, organizations, or persons he determines planned, authorized, committed, or aided the terrorist attacks on September 11, 2001, or harbored such organizations or persons, in order to prevent any future acts of international terrorism against the United States by such nations, organizations, or persons."[32] The White House claimed that this authorizes any means the president deems fit to employ in waging a war on terrorists.

The White House had another line of argument: the power to create military courts is not a sole congressional power but rather a concurrent power: even if there were no joint concord, the president had the constitutional prerogative to create the tribunals. The defense of a "common law" of military justice had been made as early as 1912, when Army Judge Advocate General Enoch Crowder argued in a Senate hearing that, irrespective of congressional establishment of courts-martial, presidential war courts would have concurrent jurisdiction.[33] The claim of concurrent powers is based on the doctrine of partial rather than complete separation of powers, a doctrine developed originally by James Madison in *The Federalist* to keep Congress from exercising all legislative powers and therefore prevent all powers of government from being swallowed up in "the impetuous [legislative] vortex."[34] Overlapping authority and concurrent exercise of power means that the executive exercises some legislative and some judicial powers, Just as Congress exercises some executive and judicial powers, and the federal courts exercise some legislative and executive powers. Creating military tribunals involves such overlapping authority.

The Bush administration argued that establishment of military tribunals flows out of both the presidential war powers as commander in chief and the delegation of power granted from Congress through the AUMF. However, it has never argued that these are "Lockean" emergency prerogatives that allow the president to go beyond the powers granted to him by the Constitution and delegated to him by the laws of the land or that allow him to dispense with the obligations of the United States flowing from its adherence to international conventions or treaties.[35] While other presidents have occasionally made these arguments during other crises, they were not part of the administration's defense of military tribunals.

Presidents and their legal counsel argue that the courts should defer to the judgment of the executive because the cases are nonjusticiable: judges lack the institutional competence to make determinations about the proper balance between preserving individual rights and ensuring national security. They argue that courts do not have and should not gain access to classified information that would be needed to make that determination. As in cases involving war and diplomatic powers, the government also argues that courts have no jurisdiction because the issues involve political questions best left to Congress and the president to work out.[36]

The Bush administration turned to a body of case law previously decided by the courts to argue that precedents provide the president with ample latitude to develop any and all procedures involving military tribunals. Although *Ex parte Milligan* had held that U.S. citizens must be tried in federal courts rather than in military tribunals when the civilian courts were open, no such protections adhere to noncitizens or noncivilians. Even so, the Bush administration held some American citizens in indefinite detention and denied that courts had the power to review the detentions, claims that were rejected by the Supreme Court in *Hamdi v. Rumsfeld* and *Rumsfeld v. Padilla*.[37] In *Ex parte Quirin* the Supreme

Court during World War II had held that the president, as commander in chief, had the power to enforce all laws relating to the conduct of war "and to carry into effect . . . all laws defining and punishing offenses against the law of nations, including those that pertain to the conduct of war." The justices also had held that the president had the power "to seize and subject to disciplinary measures those enemies who in their attempt to thwart or impede our military effort have violated the law of war."[38] The Court had ruled that the German saboteurs who had been caught by the FBI after infiltrating into the United States were not criminal defendants but belligerents who had violated the laws of war: "An enemy combatant who without uniform comes secretly through the lines for the purpose of waging war by destruction of life or property, are familiar examples of belligerents who are generally deemed . . . to be offenders against the law of war subject to trial and punishment by military tribunals."[39] Even a saboteur who claimed U.S. citizenship (Haupt) had been deemed to be subject to the tribunal because he was an unlawful combatant in the service of a foreign state, thus distinguishing *Milligan*'s protections of a citizen because Milligan had not been a combatant and had not been subject to the laws of war. Supreme Court precedent has repeatedly upheld the use of military commissions to try individuals who have committed violations of the laws of war, as demonstrated in *In re Yamashita* (327 U.S. 1 (1946)).[40]

Bush's military order establishing the tribunals provided that anyone subject to its proceedings would not be "privileged to seek" any remedy or maintain any proceeding in any court of the United States or any state court, or any court of a foreign nation, or any international tribunal.[41] The term "privileged to seek" was taken from the proclamation issued by President Franklin Roosevelt entitled "Denying Certain Enemies Access to the Courts of the United States," when he established a tribunal to try the eight German saboteurs.[42] In both cases, the word "privileged" refers back to the clause allowing the government under certain conditions to suspend the "privilege of the Writ of Habeas Corpus." It was a way for the president to suspend the writ in practice without promulgating a formal suspension of the writ—and Bush's military order did not mention the writ of habeas corpus—and therefore a way of avoiding the question of whether Lincoln's precedents in suspending the writ during the Civil War remained valid constitutional law. Since Bush did not formally suspend the writ (though he did so in all but name), a petition of habeas corpus remained a potential remedy for those believing conditions of detention or trial procedures violated the Constitution or international law.

When detainees' counsel have petitioned federal courts for writs of habeas corpus challenging the legality of the detentions and the jurisdiction and procedures of the military tribunals, the government has argued that the protections of the Geneva Conventions are not judicially enforceable by federal courts and that courts have no right to entertain habeas corpus petitions. The administration claims that even if detainees are held in violation of treaties ratified by the United States, and even if Congress has provided for jurisdiction involving such claims, the claims are unreviewable.[43] Lawyers representing detainees held at Guantánamo claimed that the bases are equivalent to U.S. territory and that therefore those detained there must have access to the U.S. courts through writs of habeas corpus. The government insisted that Guantánamo was not sovereign territory of the United States, since the land was leased from Cuba and the 1903 treaty reserved sovereignty to Cuba.

The Supreme Court in *Rasul v. Bush* (2004) decided two questions: the status of Guantánamo and whether or not a 1950 case upholding the use of special military tribunals outside the territory of the United States, *Johnson v. Eisentrager*, was controlling precedent. In that case the Supreme Court had held that a group of German officers detained in China after World War II could be tried by a special military commission and that they did not have a right of habeas corpus review by federal courts, because they were noncitizens who had never been held in custody within the territory of the United States. In *Rasul* the Supreme Court distinguished two circumstances from *Eisentrager*: first, the status of German officers as POWs had never been contested, whereas the detainees in Guantánamo claimed not be combatants at all; and second, because Guantánamo was territory under the sole control of the United States—even if the United States were not technically sovereign—those detained at Guantánamo had the right to have their habeas corpus petitions reviewed in federal courts.[44] It based the decision on its reading of the habeas corpus statutes passed by Congress, without reaching the constitutional powers of the president. Based on this ruling, the Pentagon established a review process to determine the status of the detainees. The Supreme Court decision in *Rasul* complemented a series of other cases in which federal courts have found a right of habeas corpus review, even where laws seemed to bar such review.[45]

Not only has the Supreme Court upheld the right to petition for habeas corpus review, it has also insisted on additional due process protections for detainees. "The laws and Constitution are designed to survive, and remain in force, in extraordinary times," Justice Anthony M. Kennedy wrote for the majority in the court's 2008 *Boumediene v. Bush* decision, which mandates habeas proceedings before a federal district court if a detainee challenges his indefinite detention after proceedings before the Pentagon's Combat Status Review Tribunal.[46] "The detainees in these cases are entitled to a prompt habeas corpus hearing. . . . The costs of delay can no longer be borne by those who are held in custody," Kennedy held, concluding that the procedures that had been used to classify detainees as enemy combatants through the Combat Status Review Tribunals were inadequate. The decision provides significant due process protections: detainees held for a significant period of time (i.e., well past the battle-field situation) have a right to contest their detention if they argue that they are not combatants, they have a right to competent counsel, and the counsel can be cleared by civilian courts to see classified evidence.

The decision expands their opportunities to present evidence on behalf of detainees and requires factual findings and a record on the decision to detain. The Combat Status Review Tribunal's detention decision may be reviewed in civilian federal court, and the court can correct errors in the combat status designation. The opinion holds that the judges handling habeas cases "must have adequate authority to make a determination in light of the relevant law and facts and to formulate and issue appropriate orders for relief, including, if necessary, an order directing the prisoner's release."[47]

Based on these cases and others involving the war on terror, it is clear the federal courts are not willing to give up their power to review habeas corpus petitions. After the *Rasul* and *Hamdi* cases, other federal courts entertained suits about the specifics of some tribunal procedures, such as the right of detainees facing war crimes charges to represent themselves rather than accept military lawyers.

Opponents of the presidential prerogative to establish military tribunals argue that the president does not have the constitutional authority he claims. To begin with, the take care clause of Article II of the Constitution refers to the law of the land, and that law includes treaties and other international agreements. Most of the protections in the Geneva Conventions are not confided to the president by virtue of the commander-in-chief clause but rather involve congressional powers. These include, in Article I, Section 8, paragraphs 10, 11 and 14, that "Rules for the Government and Regulation of the Land and Naval Forces" are to be established by Congress, and that Congress shall define and punish "Offences against the Law of Nations," make "Rules concerning Captures on Land and Water," and deal with piracy, brigandage, and other actions of lawless non-state actors through issuance of letters of marque and reprisal. Thus the president and Congress share responsibility for enforcement of the laws of war. Under the define and punish clause, Congress can incorporate international law, the laws and customs of war, and treaty obligations into its domestic law. It can and has passed statutes establishing criminal liability for violations of treaty or customary international law.

The Anti-Torture Act enforces customary international humanitarian law.[48] Even though some international obligations also involve the war powers of the president, the fact that the Senate consented to the Geneva Conventions empowers Congress, using the necessary and proper clause, to regulate matters that in the absence of the treaty might be considered exclusively under executive authority.

It is understood by courts and Congress that executive orders stand below statutory law, and therefore courts cannot enforce them if they conflict with such law. It is also understood that executive agreements with other nations are below treaties, are not the supreme law of the land, and therefore their provisions are not enforced if they conflict with treaties or statute law, which are supreme law. It follows that presidential military orders would also be subordinate to treaties and laws and would not be enforceable by the courts if they contained provisions inconsistent with treaties and laws. This is not the same as saying that a president cannot claim a concurrent authority to make policy through executive orders or executive agreements—simply that there are limits to their enforceability by courts when their provisions conflict with statute law.

Congress has directed the president to establish courts-martial and military tribunals that follow "to the extent practicable" the procedures and rules of evidence followed by district courts.[49] One interpretation of this phrase would leave the matter of "extent practicable" to the final judgment of the president or to view it as a "political question" not suitable for judicial determination. But another interpretation could be that federal courts may consider whether the president has complied when examining whom he requires be tried by tribunals, on what grounds, and under what procedures.

The Supreme Court Decides

On the substance of the legal challenges rather than on procedural issues, the lower federal courts gave the administration great leeway for several years, culminating in a Circuit Court of Appeals for the District of Columbia decision in the summer of 2005 holding in *Hamdan v. Rumsfeld* that, although an initial combat status review would be required for each detainee, the president himself could be the initial "competent tribunal" to determine a detainee's status and that a subsequent status review could occur during the tribunal's proceedings.[50] The Appeals Court ruled for the government's position that on issues of international law and treaty obligations the president's power as commander in chief in a time of war would be determinative, particularly since Congress, in passing the Authorization to Use Military Force, had created a situation of joint concord.

In the summer of 2006 in *Hamdan v. Rumsfeld*, the Supreme Court decisively rejected these positions in a 5–3 decision.[51] (Chief Justice John Roberts recused himself because he had been a part of the Appeals Court decision.) The Court did, however, uphold certain principles that the Bush administration and its supporters could view as a victory. All justices rejected the contention that establishing military commissions without specific statutory authorization was unconstitutional. They followed Attorney General Francis Lieber's 1863 opinion that the president derived these powers as commander in chief. None required trials in civilian courts for detainees, and none insisted on closure of Guantánamo or other military detention facilities. Continuing a line of cases based on the Supreme Court's 2004 decision in *Hamdi v. Rumsfeld*, Justice John Paul Stevens (himself a veteran of World War II) noted that "*Hamdan* does not challenge, and we do not today address, the Government's power to detain him for the duration of active hostilities." The Court's decision did not deal with the power of the government to detain but rather with conditions of detainees and with the right of the government to pass sentence by using military commissions.

Writing for the majority, Justice Stevens rejected the Bush administration's procedures for the commissions. He held that Congress by statute had required that military commissions comply with the laws of war, which was the condition by which Congress, in Article 21 of the UCMJ, recognized the president's authority to establish tribunals. Unless Congress otherwise provides, the president's conduct is subject to limitation by statutes and treaties and must comply with the international laws of armed conflict. Neither the AUMF nor the DTA provided authorization to go beyond the UCMJ or laws of armed conflict. The Court pointed to UCMJ Article 36, Paragraph b, providing that rules and regulations for such commissions be uniform so far as practicable with rules for courts martial.

The Court likewise indicated that the military tribunals established by President Bush violated the UCMJ and the Geneva Conventions in several ways: the possibility of excluding the detainee from the proceedings, the denial of the detainee's or private counsel's right to see certain evidence, and the admissibility of evidence obtained under duress. These procedures could only be permitted through explicit statutory authorization by Congress that would allow the president to go beyond the UCMJ or would exempt the tribunals from the laws of armed conflict. Alternatively, the president could follow a statutory provision and justify departures from the laws of armed conflict and courts-martial (which he had not done)—justifications that then could be reviewed in subsequent court proceedings. The Court based all of its reasoning on its construction of laws passed by Congress, and therefore did not reach the question of the president's constitutional powers as commander in chief. Justice Breyer's concurring opinion invited Congress to clarify its intent about procedures for future trials of detainees.[52]

The Court held that Common Article 3 of the Geneva Conventions applied to alleged al Qaeda terrorists. They could only be tried and punished by a "regularly constituted court," which meant an "ordinary military court" that is "established and organized in accordance with the laws and procedures already in force in a country."[53] A military commission can be "regularly constituted" only if some practical need explains deviations from court-martial practice. The Court found that no such need had yet been demonstrated by the administration. Four justices agreed with Stevens that the phrase "all the guarantees . . . recognized as indispensable by civilized peoples" in Common Article 3 must be understood to incorporate at least some trial protections recognized by customary international law. Stevens held that the procedures adopted to try *Hamdan* failed to afford the requisite guarantees.

President Bush, putting the best face on the decision, claimed that the high court had tacitly approved the use of tribunals, announced that he would ask Congress to determine whether military tribunals would be the right approach, and supported congressional authorization.[54] Attorney General Alberto Gonzales took issue with the reasoning of the Court, especially in its discussion of Common Article 3 protections for detainees. The Pentagon pointed out that it could continue to hold detainees without charges and continue to run Guantánamo. It did seem likely that it would accelerate its policy of transferring detainees back to their home countries: by late 2006 no trials had ensued, only ten prisoners had been charged, perhaps another two dozen might have been charged. The Pentagon planned to release nearly one-third of the prisoners at Guantánamo because they posed no threat to U.S. security, and Pentagon officials indicated that most of the remaining would eventually be sent to their home countries or released because they no longer had any intelligence value.

Congress held hearings after *Hamdan* on new statutory authorization. Justice Department lawyers, including Steven G. Bradbury, the Justice Department's Office of Legal Counsel acting head, insisted that *Hamdan* had limited reach and called on Congress to authorize what the president had established. They prepared (without initial input from military lawyers) a thirty-two-page draft bill with a preliminary statement that military courts-martial procedures were "not practicable in trying enemy combatants."[55] The bill was modeled after the military tribunal system: indefinite detention of all enemy combatants until the end of hostilities, no statute of limitations for trial, definition of offenses to be made by the Secretary of Defense rather than by Congress, use of hearsay evidence, withholding of classified evidence from the accused, exclusion of some defendants from part or all of their trials, admission of evidence gained through mistreatment of detainees, and power to detain defendants even if found not guilty.

The administration also proposed to retroactively immunize military and CIA officials who may have ordered or been involved in mistreatment of prisoners. Defense Secretary Donald Rumsfeld said that the provision would clear up ambiguities so that military personnel would not be "charged with wrongdoing when in fact they were not engaged in wrongdoing."[56] The draft of the bill stated that the Geneva Conventions "are not a source of judicially enforceable individual rights." It would make enforcement of the War Crimes Act passed by Congress in 1996 subject to the Bush administration's interpretation of the Geneva Conventions — interpretations that would be limited to "shock the conscience" acts of torture, rather than the more widely used interpretation that war crimes under Common Article 3 of the Geneva Conventions also include humiliating and degrading treatment. Under the draft only ten categories of illegal acts, such as torture, murder, rape, and hostage-taking would be punishable, but U.S. interrogators who had threatened detainees with physical, mental, or sexual violence or had put them in degrading conditions of confinement, would be immunized.

Opponents, including six present and retired judge advocates general of the military services, such as Major General Scott C. Black, judge advocate general of the Army, and Brigadier General David M. Brahms, retired judge advocate general of the Marine Corps, called on Congress to establish procedures that would more closely adhere to courts-martial, though providing for exceptions in some narrow respects to deal with alleged terrorists. None of the military lawyers endorsed the administration's position that Congress should authorize the presidential commissions with their existing procedures, and they opposed many of the provisions of the draft bill, especially those involving handling of evidence, exclusion of defendants from trials, and definition of offenses without a statutory base. They were also highly skeptical of the draft legislation provisions regarding mistreatment of prisoners. With House Republican leaders backing the administration's position, and a bipartisan group of Senators urging closer adherence to court-martial rules, the stage was set for an eventual compromise, which was reached in the fall of 2006. As a result of the Supreme Court ruling, congressional authorization was now to be substituted for presidential prerogative power. The provisions of the law came close to what the administration favored because of the president's influence in Congress, not because of his interpretation of his constitutional powers.

The law stripped federal courts of their jurisdiction over habeas corpus petitions from detainees. It authorized the president "to establish military commissions" dealing with violations of the laws of war. Information extracted from detainees violating the ban on "cruel, inhuman or degrading treatment" would be permitted into evidence obtained prior to December 30, 2005, when the Detainee Treatment Act of 2005 went into effect. But it barred the president from issuing an executive order authorizing any interrogation technique that involved war crimes, including torture; mutilation, maiming, or serious bodily injury, or cruel and inhuman treatment. It did permit the president to "interpret the meaning and application" of Geneva Convention standards.

The Supreme Court ruling and the congressional activity that followed quickly became part of the election-year debate. Republican House Majority Leader John Boehner went on talk shows to denounce Democrats for advocating "special privileges for terrorists." After Democratic House Minority Leader Nancy Pelosi hailed the Court ruling, conservative commentator Rush Limbaugh referred to her as "deranged." On the specifics of the decision, Democrats seemed to have the advantage, as one national opinion poll had 71 percent of the public supporting the idea that detainees should be given POW status or charged with a crime, and not held indefinitely without charges.[57]

Although critics of the administration hailed *Hamdan* as a landmark, this assessment seemed premature. To begin with, had Chief Justice Roberts been able to participate, the decision would have been 5–4. Had a Republican president made one more conservative appointment to the high court, it would likely have created a majority that either would have overturned *Hamdan* or have whittled down its reach. The composition of the federal district and appeals courts also made it likely in the short term that the opinion would be construed narrowly (especially since Congress subsequently provided authority to the president in new legislation), though it is likely that new appellate court appointees by a Democratic president after 2009 will construe the decision more broadly.

The prospect that the system of military justice will provide significant elements of due process of law to prisoners in the war on terror will continue to rest on military defense lawyers, who, at the risk of ending their careers in uniform, have mounted strong challenges to the proceedings. They have challenged proceedings because the government can monitor lawyer-client communications and because their own offices are shared with counsel representing the government, enabling their conversations to be overheard. Some have refused to participate in the trials rather than expose themselves to the charge that they participated in proceedings that were below minimum procedural standards—a criminal offense in itself.[58] Even two senior military prosecutors complained of changes in procedures designed to deprive defendants of evidence that might exculpate them, as well as of "handpicking" of the members of the military commission to ensure a conviction. One prosecutor refused to write a legal motion, claiming that the proceedings would not be "full and fair."[59] Several have requested reassignment.

Illusory Checks and Balances

Congress has subordinated itself to the executive, passing presidential requests for greater statutory authority in the war on terror and delaying and limiting investigations of interrogation excesses so that the responsibility generally tended to stop with lower-level miscreants. Interrogation abuse has been treated as an aberration from policy rather than as the administration policy itself.

Congress did pass Senator John McCain's "anti-torture" amendment. McCain, along with Senator Lindsey Graham (a reserve officer in the Air Force JAG), sponsored an amendment to a $440 billion Department of Defense Appropriation Act of 2006 (the Detainee Treatment Act, or DTA), requiring that detainees in the custody of the military could be subjected only to interrogation techniques of the *Army Field Manual*, and that "no individual in the custody or under the physical control of the United States Government, regardless of nationality or physical location, shall be subject to cruel, inhuman, or degrading treatment or punishment."[60]

After the House passed the measure, Bush agreed not to exercise his veto, but there was no reason for him to do so. First, the Pentagon was already in the process of revising the *Army Field Manual* to increase authority for extreme interrogations. Second, the amendment did not define cruel, inhuman, and degrading treatment. Third, McCain had already compromised on a key point: CIA officers and other civilians accused of abusive interrogation techniques could raise as a defense their belief that they were obeying a legal order.

A provision of the DTA sponsored by Senators Lindsey Graham and Jon Kyl provided that "to the extent practicable" courts would assess whether testimony was obtained as a "result of coercion." If so, the courts were to consider the "probative value" of the evidence in military tribunals in determining whether to admit the testimony. In effect Congress had decided through the McCain amendment to ban torture, but then through the Graham-Kyl amendment that it would allow evidence obtained from torture. This was the first time Congress had legitimated using the fruit of torture in the courts, tribunals, or preliminary proceedings.[61] The DTA also stripped the federal courts of the right to review detentions through habeas corpus petitions from detainees.[62] And by implication, in passing the measure Congress was recognizing the constitutionality of the military tribunals themselves.

Bush issued a signing statement dealing with the McCain amendment. "The executive branch shall construe [the law] in a manner consistent with the constitutional authority of the President . . . as Commander in Chief," Bush wrote, adding that this approach "will assist in achieving the shared objective of the Congress and the President . . . of protecting the American people from further terrorist attacks." And so the president immediately reopened the loophole that the McCain amendment was to have closed.

As the bill moved through the Senate, Senators Levin and Graham reached an agreement whereby cases already before the courts would not be subject to a provision removing habeas corpus jurisdiction. President Bush's signing statement interpreted the amendment to apply to "existing" as well as "future" action, including writs of habeas corpus.[63] Subsequently the Solicitor General informed the Supreme Court that it no longer had jurisdiction over 186 detainee cases pending in federal courts and asked the Court to drop jurisdiction over the *Hamdan* case as well. The Court rejected this position when it accepted the case.

Military Tribunals and Presidential Power

Bush's reliance on presidential faits accomplis was masked at every turn by claims that he was acting in "joint concord" with the legislature and that he was authorized to act by the initial anti-terrorist authorization, as well as by other statutes. This approach was a variant of the "soft prerogative" governing style, which can be defined as: the White House relies on an expansive interpretation of presidential prerogative for authority to act while claiming that the action involves joint concord since it is based on a combination of constitutional authority and statutory law.[64]

But when presidents rely on prerogative power—even "soft" prerogative power—it may not always result in a "frontlash" effect in which their policies are vindicated and their powers are upheld and become a part of the "the living Constitution." (This hoped-for incorporation of novel interpretations of international obligations would be rather ironic for an administration that railed against judicial activism.) As noted above, sometimes a president's tactics result in a judicial or legislative "backlash" in which checks and balances overturn presidential authority to act, thereby diminishing presidential powers.[65] And under some circumstances presidential tactics may lead to an "overshoot and collapse" scenario that puts the president or his top aides in legal as well as political jeopardy. This may occur in the war on terror if the measures taken to thwart terrorist activity seem way out of proportion to the probability and magnitude of the threat, particularly if the war leads to excesses by national security operatives. In such a case, the very legitimacy of the presidency may be put to the test—as happened in Watergate and in the Iran-Contra affair.

At every turn the administration has opted for the "Hamiltonian" approach, relying on prerogative power fused with the most expansive interpretation of statute law. In establishing military tribunals, the Bush administration becomes legislator, prosecutor, judge, and jury. "The accumulation of all powers legislative, executive and judiciary, in the same hands, whether of one, a few or many, and whether hereditary, self-appointed or elective," James Madison wrote in *The Federalist*, "may justly be pronounced the very definition of tyranny."[66] Presidential reliance on prerogative violates the doctrine of checks and balances, which in operational terms requires "that two branches of government concur for almost every major form of government action."[67]

This was not the only option open to President Bush. It is a maxim in international law that a state is obligated to adhere closely to the norms of international law, even when it has not formally ratified a particular convention—as the United States has not ratified the Geneva Convention Additional Protocols of 1977. Bush could have used the practice of "close adherence" in developing the procedures for the tribunals, which would have garnered the United States legitimacy and support, while not compromising their legitimate judicial function. And, had such close adherence been adopted, the use of pressure tactics at Guantánamo and elsewhere would probably have been minimized or eliminated. There seems little reason to believe that the United States would have lost significant intelligence, and there is every reason to believe that America's standing in the world would have benefited. Similarly, according to the UCMJ, military tribunals must conform as closely as practicable to courts-martial. Meeting the "close as practicable" standard would have inoculated the administration from the close scrutiny it subsequently received from federal courts. As a result of the *Hamdan* decision, the administration is now obligated to do what it should have thought of doing on its own volition.

The military tribunals constituted by the Bush administration in the war on terrorism are an integral part of an overall approach to intelligence gathering that relies on mistreatment of detainees. This is clear from initial memos written by administration officials in the immediate aftermath of 9/11 and from in the extraordinary lengths the administration has gone to ensure that the fruits of such mistreatment may be used in tribunal proceedings It is also clear from its successful efforts to get Congress in the Military Commissions Act of 2006 to immunize those who mistreated prisoners through 2005, as well as to prevent counsel representing detainees from discussing such techniques unless they have undergone classification review. This not only compromises America's position in the international community, but it also leaves officials who have authorized such treatment of prisoners, or who have participated in judicial proceedings that violate international law, vulnerable both to international sanctions and to punishment under domestic law. The Supreme Court has decided that under the Alien Tort Claim Act there can be a lawsuit for violations of customary international laws.[68] It is possible that prolonged or indefinite detention, and the maltreatment of prisoners during that detention, might be a cause of action against administration officials in the future.

The 9/11 Commission recommended that the United States and its allies "develop a common coalition approach toward the detention and humane treatment of captured terrorists."[69] It urged the U.S. government to "draw upon Article 3 of the Geneva Conventions on the law of armed conflict," which was "specifically designed for those cases in which the usual laws of war did not apply." Congress had the powers under the Constitution to legislate on these issues but did not act to put the tribunals on a statutory basis until after the Supreme Court ruled in *Hamdan*. No real checks and balances are likely to occur when Congress is controlled by the president's party; when public opinion is focused on other issues; when the legal issues are complex, unsettled, and debatable; and when the impact of tribunals is minimized by the fact that few have been constituted. At such times, a High Court decision can act as a catalyst, but it is unlikely to have transformative impact if congressional majorities remain protective of presidential prerogative and act to legitimize rather than curtail it. When Congress is controlled by the opposition party, however, the prospect for serious checks emerges. In the aftermath of the Democratic victory in the midterm elections of 2006, congressional committees prepared to review their newly passed legislation, with the intent of striking out the court-stripping provisions Congress had just passed and barring the use of evidence obtained through mistreatment of the detainees. Other proposals would give to the U.S. Court of Appeals for the armed forces the power to review decisions of the military commissions.

Many federal judges, prosecutors, and others in the criminal justice system have joined their colleagues in the Judge Advocate General's Corps in questioning the value as well as the legality of these tribunals. After the successful prosecution in the summer of 2005 of Ahmed Ressam, charged with planning to bomb Los Angeles Airport during the millennium celebrations, U.S. District Judge John C. Coughenour observed: "We did not need to use a secret military tribunal, detain the defendant indefinitely as an enemy combatant or deny the defendant the right to counsel." And he added, "The message to the world from today's sentencing is that our courts have not abandoned our commitment to the ideals that set our nation apart." To a packed and suddenly somber and hushed courtroom, the judge noted that some believe that the terrorist threat "renders our Constitution obsolete," but he warned his audience, "If that view is allowed to prevail, the terrorists will have won."[70]

CHAPTER SEVEN

Executive Orders

KENNETH R. MAYER

M ORE THAN TWENTY-FIVE YEARS ago, when Joseph Bessette and Jeffrey Tulis urged us to recognize the importance of constitutional structure and formal powers to the president, they were swimming upstream. Political scientists had largely abandoned the public law approach to the presidency over the previous two decades, and most scholars saw presidential power as a function of strategy, not authority. Presidents got what they wanted—whether legislation, policy, coordination, appointments, or anything else—because of their bargaining skill and political acumen, not because they were the president. "Presidential on the title page means nothing but the President," wrote Richard Neustadt. "Power means his influence."[1] In one of the most frequently quoted passages in all of political science, Neustadt concluded that "presidential power is the power to persuade."[2]

This observation was both empirical and prescriptive. Neustadt warned presidents not to rely on command to get what they want, because that is a sign of weakness. A command is "a forced response to the exhaustion of other remedies, suggestive less of mastery than of failure—the failure of attempts to gain an end by softer means."[3] The risks of issuing orders are magnified by the fact that they don't work. To Neustadt, commands are "self-executing" only in a narrow set of circumstances that rarely converge. Harry S Truman explained the differences Dwight D. Eisenhower would find on moving from the army to the Oval Office. "He'll sit here, and he'll say 'Do this! Do that!' *And nothing will happen.* Poor Ike—it won't be a bit like the Army."[4]

This focus on persuasion and the limits of command framed a generation of presidential scholarship, emphasizing the limits of presidential authority and the difficulties of decisive action in a system of separated powers. Political scientists studied presidential popularity, legislative success rates, public appeals, reputation, bargaining strategies, press relations, mass opinion, advisory networks, coordination processes, and many other aspects of presidential persuasion. Far less time was devoted to the study of presidential authority, which was presumed to be less interesting, in part because the grants of constitutional power are the same now as they were in 1789.

That view may be changing. Presidential scholars have taken another look at the formal authority that presidents possess, and have noticed — or rediscovered — that presidents can actually accomplish a great deal relying on their formal powers. There are indeed times when a president says "Do this! Do that!" and something happens, even when the president's strategic situation suggests that it should not. Both theory and practice have demonstrated the importance of unilateral power or of the general class of actions that presidents can take on their own authority, based either on constitutional or on statutory grants of power. After years of attracting no notice in the political science literature, the study of executive orders and unilateral powers has surged in the past decade.[5]

Constitutional and statutory vestments turn out to matter a great deal and give the president some decisive advantages in disputes over policy or control. Presidents have always leaned heavily on their executive powers, and even the most vigorous proponents of limited presidential authority see things differently from the perspective of the Oval Office.[6]

Executive orders fit into this framework because they are an embodiment of the formal exercise of presidential authority. An "executive order" may refer to a specific document published in the *Federal Register* in that form or it may refer more generally to any unilateral presidential decision or policy. From the president's perspective, the initial promise of the executive order is that it reaches as far as the executive power itself.[7] From the social scientist's perspective, the executive order gives us a window through which we can view the nature of executive power.[8]

Here, I set out what we know (or think we know) about executive orders, and situate the state of empirical knowledge within the key theoretical frameworks.

Using Executive Orders to Implement Major Policy Change

Until recently, the consensus view was that executive orders were useful only for routine administrative tasks and minor policy changes. A president might be able to give federal employees a half-day off on December 24, correct errors in the schedule of federal salaries, or require federal employees to use seat belts.[9] But major policy innovations, the thinking was, required at a minimum legislative action.

In *With the Stroke of a Pen*, I argued that this view stemmed from Neustadt's conception of the presidency as one of weak formal powers and the subsequent influence of his strategic paradigm of presidential power, which assumed that command equaled failure. If this were true, it made little sense to even examine commands as a source of presidential influence. Consequently, our conceptions of executive power were tied to the belief that Congress was the appropriate agent for major change. Keith Whittington and Dan Carpenter state the problem in more general terms, suggesting that much of the literature on American political institutions is driven by a "congressional-dominance narrative," in which Congress is the primary branch of government.[10]

Research into executive orders and other unilateral instruments has demonstrated that this view of executive power is incorrect. Presidents have used executive orders to create and modify crucial programs, institutions, and policies: defining the information classification process, organizing the intelligence community, establishing cost-benefit requirements for federal regulations, creating new units within the White House Office, authorizing the internment of Japanese Americans during World War II, seizing private property, desegregating the military and requiring government contractors to abide by affirmative action programs, and expanding the scope of central clearance within the Executive Office of the President.[11]

Relying on their commander-in-chief authority, presidents have routinely ordered U.S. military forces into combat without any congressional authorization.[12] While there is no official count of the number of instances, the number is undoubtedly large. A 2006 Congressional Research Service study identified sixteen instances of congressional authorizations for the use of military force since 1789: five formal war declarations and eleven statutory authorizations. But the uses of military force number in the hundreds: one count is 383 instances between 1945 and 2000; another is 119 instances since 1973.[13]

Looking at the broader category of unilateral presidential action, it is incontestable that presidents have always relied on their ability to make important—often landmark—policy. Even a quick sweep identifies some of the most important events in American history.

LOUISIANA PURCHASE

In 1803, Thomas Jefferson negotiated the purchase of the Louisiana Territory. In agreeing to purchase over 830,000 square miles of land from France, he doubled the size of the United States.[14] It was, according to historian Joseph Ellis, "one of the most consequential executive actions in all of American history."[15] The Constitution said nothing about how the United States should go about acquiring foreign territory or even whether such a step was permitted. Jefferson expressed serious doubts about his authority to enter into the agreement but kept his reservations to himself. Publicly, he relied on the opinion of his secretary of the treasury, Albert Gallatin, that the nation had an inherent right to add territory and that the power was indirectly vested in the presidency through the treaty-making power. Jefferson did present the finished treaty to the Senate for ratification, and Congress subsequently passed legislation giving him the authority to construct a government for the new territory. Even so, a recent review of the purchase argues that it was, in fact, an unconstitutional use of the treaty power.[16]

LINCOLN IN THE SPRING OF 1861

In 1861, Abraham Lincoln suspended the right of habeas corpus, ordered a blockade against southern ports, expanded the size of the army and the navy, and spent funds without any congressional appropriation.[17] Lincoln's suspension of habeas rights gave military personnel the authority to arrest and detain people without the normal protections of the civil courts. Under Lincoln's orders, individuals could be arrested and held without being charged with a crime. The suspensions were imposed in a series of presidential orders issued between April and July 1861.

Not only did Lincoln engage in some of the most significant uses of unilateral powers of any president, ushering in what some scholars have called a constitutional dictatorship, he did so without even a shred of what contemporary political scientists would regard as political capital: the federal government had only a minimal administrative capacity, there was no electronic mass media to give him access to the public, Congress (or what was left of it after the South seceded) was very nearly in open rebellion, and he came to office having won with only 39.9 percent of the popular vote.

CREATION OF THE EXECUTIVE OFFICE
OF THE PRESIDENT

The expansion of the federal government's size during the 1930s made it clear that the president could no longer manage the executive branch with the resources that were at hand; the government was simply doing too much. The lack of formal administrative support meant that nobody could help the president keep track of everything the executive branch was doing. After failing to get all the administrative authority he wished from Congress and in the midst of an increasingly dire situation in Europe, President Franklin Roosevelt created the Executive Office of the President (EOP) via Executive Order 8248. The order established six units within the office, including an unnamed branch that would perform whatever responsibilities the president might assign. FDR activated this open-ended self-delegation of authority in May 1940, when he set up the Office of Emergency Management, a presidential office that coordinated much of the war effort in the early stages of World War II. One prominent presidency scholar, Clinton Rossiter, claimed that FDR's creation of the EOP probably "saved the Presidency from paralysis and the Constitution of radical amendment."[18]

TRUMAN AND THE KOREAN WAR

When North Korea launched a surprise attack against South Korea in June 1950, Harry S Truman decided on his own to commit the U.S. military to the fight. He never sought formal congressional approval of the deployment and notified congressional leaders only after he had issued his orders. Truman claimed that his legal authority to issue this order came from the United Nations charter. Truman had his way, even though most legal scholars consider the commitment patently unconstitutional.[19]

In 1952, after a strike by steelworkers threatened to disrupt the supply of steel and other materials to defense contractors, Truman ordered the secretary of commerce to take possession of eighty-six steel mills (over 80 percent of the entire industry).[20] The president justified his action by claiming an emergency presidential prerogative to ensure the continuation of supplies necessary to fight the war in Korea. Truman argued that his decision was not subject to judicial review. The steel companies immediately sued to block the order and prevailed in one of the most significant Supreme Court cases addressing the reach of presidential power (*Youngstown Sheet and Tube v. Sawyer*).

These examples are outliers, to be sure, as they can hardly be said to describe the common aspects of presidential leadership. However, they are cases where a president took decisive action on his own, acting without congressional cooperation or even in the face of congressional opposition (the fact that both Jefferson and Lincoln had their decisions retroactively ratified does not minimize the significance of the initial steps). And of these five historic decisions, the president was turned back only once.

President George W. Bush continued this pattern, using his executive authority to implement significant policy changes. Since 9/11 he granted the Air Force authority to shoot down hijacked commercial airliners, created the Office of Homeland Security as a unit within the Executive Office of the President, authorized the indefinite detention of suspected terrorists and unlawful combatants and created a system of military tribunals to try them, asserted the constitutional authority to conduct warrantless surveillance inside the United States, claimed the power to authorize coercive techniques in interrogation, and said that he will ignore statutes that try to limit the president's constitutional authority.[21] Though Bush has been partially rebuffed on the interrogation and tribunal system, the basic structure of his initial decisions remain intact.

I have estimated that, since 1949, about 15 percent of executive orders have involved significant policy changes. Howell arrived at the same number, even though he used a different method to evaluate an order's significance.[22]

Taking Advantage of Gaps and Ambiguities in Constitutional and Statutory Language

A valid presidential order must be based on the president's constitutional authority or on a power conferred or delegated by statute. This, as far as it goes, is obvious, as our tradition of limited constitutional government requires some kind of formal authorization as a justification for state action.

But this statement obscures the tremendous ambiguities of the executive power. The difficulty is that no comprehensive and consistent legal framework of presidential power exists, nor is it likely that one ever will. The very concept of executive power—with the power to implement the will of the legislature but with an independence designed to check legislative excess—embodies a contradiction that cannot easily be reconciled.

For all of the detail of *The Federalist*, the authors never quite get around to saying what, precisely, the executive power is. Alexander Hamilton spends considerable time justifying the allocation of specific powers that the president will exercise, particularly in comparison with the powers of the British monarchy, arguing in favor of a single executive, and defending the selection process. All students of the presidency can recite Hamilton's equation of "energy in the executive" with "decision, activity, secrecy, and dispatch."[23] But in the end, we know a great deal about what president does but very little about what an executive is.

This is no accident. As Harvey Mansfield put it: "The beauty of executive power . . . is to be both subordinate and not subordinate, both weak and strong. It can reach where law cannot, and thus supply the defect of law, yet remain subordinate to law. The ambivalence of the modern executive permits its strength to be useful to republics, without endangering them."[24]

Article II does not solve these problems; indeed, its ambiguity, and the uncertainty about why the framers chose the specific language that made its way in, probably adds to them.[25] The text of Article II contains too many internal contradictions and gaps to permit a definitive resolution of every dispute that can arise. It is easy to pose hypothetical questions that simply cannot be answered solely by looking at specific constitutional or statutory language but instead require a broader interpretive framework: Can the president refuse to execute an unconstitutional law? Can Congress shut down the presidency? Does the president have inherent or extraconstitutional powers? Can the president begin military action without a congressional declaration of war? Sometimes the answer to these questions is yes, sometimes no, with much depending on the specifics. Sometime the answer is that nobody is quite sure, and disputes are often resolved on the basis of which branch—Congress, the presidency, or the Supreme Court—is more willing to commit political resources to the fight or on what the public is willing to put up with.

Justice Robert H. Jackson recognized this even as he set out his own framework for analyzing the constitutionality of presidential action:

> A judge, like an executive adviser, may be surprised at the poverty of really useful and unambiguous authority applicable to concrete problems of executive power as they actually present themselves. Just what our forefathers did envision, or would have envisioned had they foreseen modern conditions, must be divined from materials almost as enigmatic as the dreams Joseph was called upon to interpret for Pharaoh. A century and a half of partisan debate and scholarly speculation yields no net result but only supplies more or less apt quotations from respected sources on each side of any question.[26]

In their casebook on presidential power, Peter Shane and Harold Bruff note that "the vagueness of Article II presents special problems for the interpreter. These problems are only magnified by the tendency of great crises of our national history to pose questions of executive power."[27]

The Constitution strives for equilibrium through checks and balances. Each branch has a limited ability to check the actions of the other two, and these overlapping and recursive chains of authority make it hard for any single branch to usurp the powers of the others.

But the president has an advantage, in that he has the ability to move first and then to leave it up to either Congress or the Court to reject what he has done. By changing the default policy, the president forces Congress or the Court to take positive action to undo the change (this process is, in fact, the basic tenet of the unilateral powers model of presidential behavior).[28] Even when Congress has the constitutional power to overturn a presidential action—which it will often have, especially in cases where the president is acting on the basis of statutory authority—this advantage is usually tempered by practical difficulties. Congress is a majoritarian institution, famously unable to act quickly, and even when it reverses what a president has done, it will have to muster a two-thirds majority if the president vetoes the initial legislative response. Similarly, even though the federal courts have the final say on the constitutionality of a presidential act, judges must wait for an actual case to be brought to them, and the process can take years. These structural obstacles do not preclude effective response, and in the event of a direct confrontation the president will not always win (as occurred in *Youngstown* or in the congressional response to Nixon). They do, however, make effective response more difficult.[29]

These two characteristics of the presidency—a set of formal powers with ambiguous boundaries and the ability to act first in many cases—often mean that the president initiates policy change through unilateral action. In their theoretical treatment of unilateral presidential powers, Terry Moe and William Howell explain the consequences of this ambiguity combined with structure:

> Because presidents are executives, and because of the discretion, opportunities, and resources executives have available to them in politics, presidents are particularly well suited to be first-movers and to reap the agenda powers that go along with it. If they want to shift the status quo by taking unilateral action on their own authority, whether or not that authority is clearly established in law, they can simply do it—quickly, forcefully, and (if they like) with no advance notice. The other branches are then presented with a fait accompli, and it is up to them to respond. If they are unable to respond effectively, or decide not to, the president wins by default. And even if they do respond, which could take years, he may still get much of what he wants anyway.[30]

Apart from the war in Iraq, the most controversial aspects of George W. Bush's assertions of constitutional power involved decisions made in the war on terror. Chief among those were the unilateral imposition of a military tribunal system to try suspected terrorists, the assertion of a power to deny enemy combatants due process rights or access to civilian courts, and the decision to allow the National Security Agency to conduct certain types of electronic surveillance without first obtaining a warrant from the Foreign Intelligence Surveillance Court (FISC). While critics of these actions typically object to the policies themselves, the most interesting problems actually arise from the fact that these actions constitute direct challenges to the constitutional power of the other two branches: in the first, by arguing that the judiciary lacks jurisdiction to review the status of unlawful combatants and, in the second, by asserting a constitutional power that appears to trumps a clear statutory prohibition. In each of these cases, Congress or the Court resisted these claims and partially overturned Bush's initial move. But the president only "lost" —in the sense that the initial position was invalidated—on the assertion that the Courts had no power to review the status of enemy combatants. In the other two cases, Congress would up giving the president legislative foundations for the original unilateral actions, in the process moving the final policy very close to the president's position.

Both of these assertions of unilateral power are anchored to core executive functions: the president's constitutional authority as commander in chief and the president's historical control over foreign intelligence gathering. At the same time, each also exists at the boundary of another branch's power, which is why the precise degree of authority is unclear.

Below, I present evidence on the overall success in Congress and the Court in overturning unilateral actions. The general pattern of presidents exploiting ambiguities in both constitutional and statutory language has been well established. Presidents seek out opportunities to assert control over institutional processes, independent of era. Moe analyzes in detail Ronald Reagan's executive order requiring agencies to justify major regulations with cost-benefit analysis, subject to Office of Management and Budget (OMB) approval.[31] The post-1981 history of OMB review is remarkably similar to Taft's efforts to insist on central clearance of executive budget requests in 1910–1911, when (in the face of a statute that explicitly forbade it) he demanded that cabinet secretaries submit their budget requests to him.[32]

The dispute over National Security Agency's warrantless surveillance illustrates this dynamic in canonical form. In response to the intelligence abuses of the 1970s, which included domestic spying and infiltration of political groups, covert destabilization of foreign governments and attempts to assassinate foreign political figures, Congress enacted a series of reforms designed to control the intelligence agencies. A key part of these reforms was the Foreign Intelligence Surveillance Act of 1978 (FISA), a law designed to clarify and limit the president's authority to collect intelligence information domestically.[33]

As a general rule, the executive branch may not use intelligence agencies to conduct surveillance on people inside the United States; that task is left to law enforcement, although the wall separating the two functions is lower now than it was prior to 9/11. At the same time, intelligence agencies have a much freer hand in collecting information abroad and can spy on foreign governments, plant bugs and monitor conversations, operate in secrecy, recruit double agents, or even carry out covert action, without worrying about warrants or probable cause or constitutional limits.[34]

But there is an ambiguity at the boundary of foreign intelligence and domestic surveillance: the case of a foreign agent operating inside the United States. Is this considered a domestic situation because of the agent's location, with the government's ability to conduct surveillance constrained by warrant requirements and other constitutional limitations? Or do the international rules apply because the agent is working for a foreign government, in which case the government can proceed as if the agent were operating abroad? FISA resolved this haziness by establishing a special court that had the authority to issue warrants for electronic surveillance of people suspected of being agents of a foreign power. Unlike regular criminal courts, FISC operates in secret and allows surveillance under a lower standard than that used for ordinary criminal warrants.[35]

After 9/11, President Bush issued a secret order allowing the National Security Agency to conduct electronic surveillance without going through the FISC, when a conversation or transmission involves a person inside the United States and someone outside the United States who is suspected of involvement in terrorist groups. When the program—called the Terrorist Surveillance Program (TSP)—was revealed in 2005, critics charged that it was a flagrant violation of FISA and a usurpation of Congress's constitutional authority to put limits on the executive branch.[36] The White House responded that the president's constitutional authority to conduct foreign intelligence could not be curtailed by any statute and that Congress had implicitly allowed the program when it passed the Authorization to Use Military Force in September 2001.[37] The president and key advisors continued to press the constitutional argument, insisting that FISA could not constrain powers granted under Article II.[38]

The legal issues are complex. Eric Posner and Adrian Vermeule point to authorities and precedent on each side of the debate, concluding that the constitutional arguments could reasonably go either way. They do, however, criticize the immediate denunciations of the program as over-heated.[39] Even inside the Bush administration, there were conflicts over the legality of the program.[40]

Ultimately the dispute distills into a contest between a presidential claim of constitutional power laid against a congressional effort to limit that power. Presidents sometimes win these fights, and sometimes lose them.[41] For my purposes, the important aspect of the program is that despite congressional opposition, even from Republicans, Congress took no formal action to stop it and ultimately changed the underlying statute to permit what the TSP was already doing. Even though the president, in the end, eventually backed away from his initial assertion of plenary constitutional power, he succeeded in framing the congressional response in a way that shifted policy in the direction he favored.[42]

Initially, the legislative reaction consisted of general statements of opposition, some bills introduced, and a handful of oversight hearings.[43] In April 2006, Senator Arlen Specter (R-PA), chair of the Senate Judiciary committee, threatened to introduce legislation to cut off NSA funding but only as a signal that the White House needed to be more forthcoming with information about the program.[44] In September 2006, the House, still controlled by the Republican party, passed legislation that enhanced the president's authority to engage in warrantless surveillance under FISA.[45]

After the 2006 midterm elections gave the Democrats control of both chambers, the administration offered a few minor concessions. In January 2007, Attorney General Gonzales announced that the administration had asked for and received authorization from the FISC to conduct TSP-like surveillance under its auspices. The move meant that Bush was no longer relying solely on his constitutional authority and was taken as a significant concession to the realities of Democratic congressional control. Still, it "also help[ed] Bush undercut congressional oversight of the program and possibly judicial review by regular federal courts."[46] Two weeks later, Gonzales agreed to provide Congress with documents related to the new FISC order.[47]

Throughout the spring and summer of 2007, though, the White House kept pressure on Congress, arguing that FISA had failed to keep up with technological changes.[48] In August 2007, Congress enacted legislation that permitted warrantless electronic surveillance as long as the target was outside the United States, with a six-month sunset provision designed to give legislators enough time to work out permanent FISA reforms.[49] The six-month period passed with no permanent legislation, and the new authority lapsed in February 2008.[50] In the weeks that followed, Republican leaders charged the Democrats with making the country vulnerable to future terrorist attacks.[51]

The key sticking point in congressional deliberation over a permanent change to FISA was whether telecommunications companies should be immunized from civil litigation arising out of their cooperation with the federal government in early stages of the program. To conduct surveillance, the NSA had to have access to the actual message traffic and therefore had to work with the companies to install equipment at key transmission and routing points. By the summer of 2008, there were dozens of civil lawsuits alleging that companies had violated customers' constitutional rights (because the companies were acting as an agent of government) and statutes protecting the privacy of electronic communications.[52]

The nature of this dispute shows how President Bush had changed the terms of the debate. It was no longer about the merits of NSA surveillance, which had become accepted as a necessary part of the global war on terror and homeland security. Even if retroactive immunity did not pass, the NSA program itself would continue (though, presumably, with the telecom industry becoming a less-than-enthusiastic partner).[53]

In the end, though, President Bush got what he wanted, which was a permanent revision to FISA that codified in statute most of what the NSA had been doing all along. The legislation, finally enacted in July 2008, also granted the retroactive immunity that the White House insisted on.[54] Despite the opposition of many Democrats, and even though Bush's popularity was at record lows, the political risks of opposing the legislation had simply grown too large:

> The pressure that the Bush administration exerted skewed the Democratic leadership's calculus of the costs and benefits toward scheduling the [FISA] legislation. If Congress left for its recess without

passing a FISA fix, the administration would have spent August berating Democrats for endangering the country and, were a terrorist attack to occur, the Democrats would have been blamed. Once the Senate passed the bill Bush wanted and recessed, protecting the party's reputation dictated allowing the bill to pass the House. Doing so angered the Democratic base—and many editorial boards—but, on balance, the alternative was perceived to be more costly.[55]

On the NSA surveillance program, the president unilaterally changed policy in a way that challenged congressional authority. Seven years later, rather than taking action to overturn the program, Congress instead authorized it. Bush began the program in secret, with his own legal advisors disagreeing on the president's underlying legal authority. But the sequence of events confirms the basic logic of the unilateral action model, which suggests that presidents can change the focus of policy debates simply by making the first move and leaving it up to the other branches to "undo" the president's act. This is precisely what happened here. Congress—in the end under control of the opposition party—was not only unable to reverse the president's initial program, but it even wound up granting the executive branch the very authority that was in dispute.

How Difficult Is It to Undo Unilateral Policy?

One mark against executive action is that it is ephemeral. What one president does can be undone, either by the other branches or (more likely) by the next president. At times, the policy reversals become routine. In April 1992, President George H.W. Bush issued an executive order requiring federal contractors to post a notice informing workers of their right to not join a union and to ask for a refund of a portion of their dues.[56] Unions despised this order, seeing it as a deliberate attempt to limit their political effectiveness and a ploy to help Bush mobilize his base.[57] But one of Bill Clinton's first official acts as president was an executive order of his own revoking the Bush order.[58] In February 2001, President George W. Bush reversed Clinton's order with another executive order, reinstituting his father's policy on union notices by federal contractors. It seems likely that President Obama will reverse this reversal of a policy reversal with a subsequent order of his own. The same pattern occurred in federal funding for overseas groups that perform abortions as part of their family planning activities. The elder Bush banned the practice; he was reversed by Clinton; and the younger Bush reversed Clinton, restoring the original policy. Obama will likely reverse Bush, reverting to the Clinton position.[59]

But not all unilateral actions are subject to this kind of policy Ping-Pong. Presidents have the chance to commit their successors, either by imposing new policies that are not easily reversed or by raising the costs of reversion to unacceptable levels. Presidents may hustle through final regulations, issue pardons, commit to or withdraw from treaties, negotiate executive agreements, deploy U.S. troops, or create national monuments, all in ways not easily undone. Even as a lame duck, when, presumably, his strategic resources were at their lowest, Clinton managed to impose new policies that the incoming Bush administration opposed but had to accede to. President Bush did the same thing to President-elect Obama.[60] Hyperactive lame-duck unilateralism is, in fact, a general pattern of presidential behavior, because presidents can impose policies that stick. As William Howell and Kenneth Mayer put it: "Precisely when powers of persuasion abandon them, when presidential command over the legislative process reaches its low point, presidents regularly strike out on their own, set vitally important public policies, and leave it up to Congress and an incoming administration to try and recover an old status quo."[61]

If unilateral policies are hard for presidents to undo, they pose even more difficulties for Congress or the Court. Earlier I set out the logic of this argument when I claimed that the structures and processes of congressional and court decisions give presidents a clear advantage in policy struggles.

Indeed, even though Congress or the Court *may* step in to overturn what the president has done, they don't choose to do so very often. I have found only two cases since 1970 in which Congress explicitly overturned an executive order by enacting a statute. Howell and Moe found only three cases between 1973 and 1998, and only thirty-seven attempts, during a period when presidents issued over a thousand executive orders.[62] Howell identified eighty-three federal court challenges to executive orders between 1943 and 1997, with the president losing only fourteen (during a period when presidents issued over four thousand orders).[63]

Although Bush suffered some partial defeats in the Supreme Court—losing the argument that the courts have no jurisdiction over the detention of enemy combatants in Guantánamo and the claim that the government can detain an American citizen indefinitely without due process—the sweep of judicial opinion was as deferential as that shown any other president.[64]

Bush, moreover, raised the stakes by asserting the right to ignore statutory constraints on presidential power. In a number of his signing statements—a controversial practice in which a president seeks to add to the legislative history of a law by announcing his own interpretation when he signs it—Bush claimed the right to reinterpret, or even ignore, certain statutory language that purportedly intrudes on the president's constitutional powers. The 2006 Defense Department Appropriations Act included a section prohibiting the use of "cruel, inhuman, or degrading treatment or punishment" against anyone detained by the U.S. government.[65] This language, opposed by the White House, was explicitly inserted into the bill as a response to the administration's hairsplitting about what, exactly, constituted "torture."[66] Facing overwhelming congressional support for the language, the president agreed to it.

On signing the bill, however, the president qualified his support with language suggesting that he was not constrained by the anti-torture provisions:

> The executive branch shall construe Title X in Division A of the Act, relating to detainees, in a manner consistent with the constitutional authority of the President to supervise the unitary executive branch and as Commander in Chief and consistent with the constitutional limitations on the judicial power, which will assist in achieving the shared objective of the Congress and the President, evidenced in Title X, of protecting the American people from further terrorist attacks.[67]

Many observers have noted Bush's use of signing statements as a tool of executive interpretation.[68] The American Bar Association criticized the practice in 2006, arguing that Bush's extensive use of signing statements was "contrary to the rule of law and our constitutional system of separation of powers."[69] Bradley and Posner, however, conclude that signing statements pose no threat to separation of powers, and, further, that signing statements can even enhance accountability by creating a public record of how the president intends to interpret a statute.[70]

There has been no definitive judicial ruling on how much influence these signing statements should have on subsequent interpretations. Members of Congress, to be sure, see them as an affront to legislative supremacy.[71] But if signing statements have any effect at all, they would give presidents even more of an advantage over the other branches. Not only does Congress face the enormous hurdle of mustering multiple majorities (or supermajorities, if the president threatens a veto), but the president then gets the last word, and in doing so might be able to contest even an explicit statutory constraint. Whatever the eventual fate of the signing statement, it is yet another indicator that presidential unilateral action can be hard to undo.

Unilateral Action and the President's Strategic Resources

Apart from the different positions on the importance of formal authority, the unilateral powers literature departs from Neustadt on the role that strategic resources play in presidential decision-making. In the strategic model, if we wish to asses a president's ability to get things done, we need to know how popular he is, how he is regarded by legislators and members of the Washington political community, and how the president's interests match up with those of other stakeholders.

In the unilateral powers model, rather, we look to the extent of the president's constitutional and statutory powers, the nexus between what the president wants and what those powers suggest the president can have, precedent, and the likelihood that other actors may try to overturn a particular act. A president's strategic position can enter in to this assessment, but it is not the first thing we need to know.

Under the logic of unilateral action, a president might even make the first move based on his political weakness, not his strength. The conventional wisdom holds that presidents who are stymied by congressional opposition, or who are unpopular or otherwise weak, will look toward unilateral action to achieve what cannot be obtained through legislative channels. A president may well favor a legislatively enacted policy because of the legitimacy, institutional endurance, and budgetary authority that congressional action can confer. But unilateral action provides an alternative.

Here, empirical work has reached conflicting conclusions about the relationship between executive orders, presidential popularity, and congressional majorities. Models of unilateral action generally predict that as presidents become weaker politically, they are more likely to fall back on their unilateral powers to accomplish policy change. Nevertheless, scholars have been attacking this question for less than a decade and there are important areas of disagreement or ambiguity.

Most models of executive order issuance conclude that presidents are more likely to issue executive orders or other unilateral actions when they are less popular, as a way of compensating for their weakness.[72] George Krause and Jeffrey Cohen find no relationship, though they do conclude that presidents issue more orders when the economy is struggling (either because of high inflation, high unemployment, or both).[73] These findings, ironically, are actually consistent with Neustadt's strategic model of presidential leadership, as they suggest that presidents resort to command when other avenues of policy choice are closed off.

A quick look at George W. Bush's history of executive orders and popularity casts some doubt on the strength of this relationship (see Figure 7.1). If anything, the frequency of his order issuance appears directly related to his popularity, a reverse of what the existing literature predicts.[74]

Of course, formal executive orders by themselves do not capture the full range of Bush's unilateral decision-making. He did issue some important orders after September 11, 2001, establishing the Office of Homeland Security, mobilizing the Ready Reserve, blocking terrorist financing, and invoking some emergency authorities. But he also set policy for handling unlawful combatants in a military order, and (we now know) authorized warrantless surveillance by the NSA. This is consistent with the established pattern of relying heavily on unilateral authority during wars and other crises.

More interesting are the contrasting results on the relationship between congressional strength and unilateral action. It is generally accepted that unified government makes it easier to obtain congressional majorities, even if divided government does not preclude significant legislation.[75] As a consequence, the conventional wisdom on executive orders

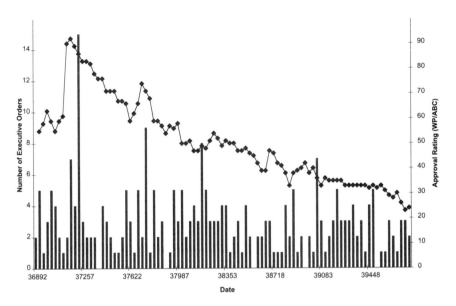

FIGURE 7.1. Executive Orders and Popularity, January 2001 to November 2008

—based largely on anecdotal impression—is that presidents are more likely to use them in the face of congressional opposition.[76] This certainly makes sense in the context of the strategic model, as the presumption is both that presidents need congressional action for major change and that they must rely on their popularity and reputation to persuade legislators. It is also consistent with Clinton's public face after the 1994 midterm elections. The president's critics accused him of overusing his unilateral authority to countermand Republican majorities; it did not help that Clinton advisor Paul Begala publicly mused "Stroke of the Pen . . . Law of the Land. Kind of Cool."[77]

Empirical work, however, has come to decidedly mixed results (and Begala's view notwithstanding, Clinton issued fewer executive orders after the Republicans took over). Some scholars have found no relationship between order issuance and congressional majorities.[78] Others have found that, contrary to the conventional wisdom, executive orders are more frequent when the president enjoys party majorities in Congress or that unified government reduces the number of domestic policy orders but not foreign policy orders.[79] Deering and Maltzmann find that presidents do respond to congressional opposition by issuing more orders but only when they are confident that Congress will not overturn them.[80] This view is consistent with Clinton's experience with his promise to overturn the military's ban on gay and lesbian members of the military: although he had the authority to alter the military rule unilaterally, he opted not to, in the face of overwhelming congressional opposition (even within his own party).[81]

Howell, putting this in theoretical perspective, concludes that congressional majorities can either increase or decrease the frequency of unilateral action, depending on the nature of congressional preferences and the potential for court action. With respect to Congress, Howell writes:

> Congress' (or any legislature's) ability to overturn the president is not constant over time. When members' preferences are widely dispersed, it is relatively difficult for legislative coalitions to form, and presidents can seize upon new opportunities to exercise their unilateral powers. By contrast, when members' preferences line up tightly around one another, it is relatively easy to enact legislation, and the president's freedom to act unilaterally declines. With each election Congress is made weaker or stronger depending on the composition of members within it, and the strength of the parties that organize them.[82]

Subsequent research validates this constitutional relationship: William Howell and Jon Pevehouse find strong evidence that presidential decisions on the use of military force are strongly constrained by a president's assessment of congressional opinion.[83]

So, presidents might rely more (or less) on unilateral action, depending on whether they face congressional support (or opposition), the type of policy (foreign or domestic, military or civilian), and the nature and distribution of congressional preferences. In other words, we do not yet fully understand the dynamics of how presidents take Congress into account when they resort to unilateral action.

Executive Orders and American Constitutionalism

The recent surge of work on unilateral presidential action serves as a direct challenge to the long-dominant model of presidential politics. Presidents can make significant policy on their own, and even if we have not completely worked through the interinstitutional dynamics of presidential action, we have better theoretical and empirical accounts of what presidents do. Just as Neustadt saw *Presidential Power* as describing the reality of presidential activity, the unilateral power model captures a great deal of what actually occurs. Presidents think about their constitutional powers and are impelled to seek out ways of putting their stamp on policy within the limits of their authority. The structural features of American national government give the president important advantages in the fight for policy control. It is safe to say that the focus on unilateral powers has proven to be one of the more important theoretical and empirical developments in the presidency literature.

The empirical claims set out here offer a framework for future research. There are some factual claims that capture what we know about the use of unilateral action to initiate policy change. But other questions remain open; in particular, we have yet to understand how divided government, or congressional opposition more generally, affects decisions to rely on unilateral powers. Theory predicts that unilateral action should become more frequent as congressional opposition to the president increases. This is not, however, what we observe. The problem might be the theory itself. More likely, we need better ways of understanding congressional opposition, and how presidents take it into account when making choices.

In any case, continued rigorous specification and testing of the theory underlying these empirical claims—what I have called the unilateral powers model—will give us further insight into the nature of presidential authority as it is exercised.

There is a second benefit to the study of unilateral powers. A focus on presidential authority and formal powers reconnects the study of presidential action to normative considerations of constitutional propriety. If our concern is presidential bargaining or public opinion or media relations or legislative strategy, it is difficult to make normative arguments as to whether the president is acting legally, or wisely. What matters, rather, is only whether the president wins. Indeed, presidential scholars are often criticized for promoting a view of the presidency where constitutional anchors are less relevant than the effectiveness of presidential action. In one of the stronger criticisms of Neustadt's influence on presidency scholarship, David Gray Adler argued that "Neustadt evinced virtually no interest in constitutional powers and limitations. On the contrary, Neustadt's *Presidential Power* was a virtual political manual written in the tradition of Machiavelli's *The Prince*, in which he explained how a president might acquire, maintain, and exercise power. Above all, it was devoted to the effort to maximize power."[84]

In a similar vein, Louis Fisher, who has spent his career writing about constitutional and legal parameters of presidential power, asks

> how can we teach the presidency divorced from the idea of constitutional limits? What happens when public law is downgraded and we focus on how well the president can dominate policy making even if the results violate or do damage to the constitution? On such occasions, it is not enough to report the results of roll call analysis in Congress. While presidential policy making, politics, and elections are worthy of study, they ought not to be pursued at the expense of constitutional considerations. The presidency is a creature of the Constitution, which was and remains the source of its powers and defines its limitations.[85]

Certainly, the Bush administration has embraced an expansive view of executive power, even to the point of making claims of unlimited presidential discretion that parallel the arguments Truman made to justify his seizure of the nation's steel mills in 1952. Key legal advisors subscribe to the legal theory of a "unitary executive," which posits that within a broad sphere of constitutional executive authority, the president's power is plenary and not subject to statutory limits.[86] In one sense this argument is a truism, because in those areas wholly committed to presidential discretion—the motivations behind a veto, for example—his authority *is* plenary. This only begs the question, though, of what kinds of authority actually fall into that category.

Taking the NSA warrantless surveillance program as the example, if we are interested solely in Neustadtian power stakes, what matters is the program's effect on the president's overall strategic balance sheet. How does the policy affect the rest of the president's program, relations with Congress, or public opinion? Did the president misread the congressional response or the media reaction? Did it have any impact on the midterm election results? Was the program effective?

These are all interesting questions, but they miss the most important one: is it legal? Even if we cannot reach a definitive answer, we can at least analyze the program within the framework of executive authority and identify where it fits into the historic debates over presidential power. The unilateral power model explains, so far at least, the sequence of events: the president makes the first move, establishing a new policy based on an assertion of constitutional or statutory authority (in this case, the president has the additional advantage that the program was not public, although there is a dispute over how much Congress knew about it). Congress and the Court are relegated to a reactive mode, although a definitive Supreme Court ruling against the president would likely settle the matter.

As I noted above, the key to the conflict is the president's assertion of an inherent constitutional authority running into an explicit congressional effort to regulate that authority. Whether or not the president is considered to have "won," the advantage of analyzing the program constitutionally is that it provides a context and informs us that the NSA program is only the latest example in a 220-year history of presidential-congressional disputes over their respective authorities.

Explicitly connecting the study of unilateral powers to constitutional approaches to presidential authority neither implies nor requires that we will have clear answers to every question that can come up; precisely the opposite is true. But accepting the ambiguities of executive power is not the same as insisting that there are no limits at all, or that the president can do whatever he can get away with. Mansfield argued that executive power is contradictory, in that it takes a strong executive to protect against populist usurpation of political freedom.[87] Hamilton himself had trouble reconciling the contradiction, arguing that the president had narrowly prescribed powers, while at the same time insisting that "energy in the executive is a leading character in the definition of good government."[88] This tension exists as well in our views of presidential greatness. Lincoln and Franklin D. Roosevelt are at or near the top of any presidential ranking, even though it is generally agreed that both committed significant constitutional violations.

By tying empirical research to explicit concerns about formal powers, we are in a better position to evaluate the normative aspects of presidential action. This research can cut both ways—in the face of the Bush administration assertions of unitary powers, some might conclude that he has dramatically overstepped the boundaries of legitimate action and others that his actions are no different than what any other president has done in similar circumstances. The unilateral action model suggests that President Obama will find many Bush administration precedents useful as he pursues his own agenda and that he will not retreat as much on executive power as his supporters hoped.[89] But unlike the purely strategic framework, which focuses mainly on the how the president gets what he wants and how he can maximize his power, the unilateral powers model offers a common starting point, which is the nature of the president's formal powers.

CHAPTER EIGHT

Budget Power, Constitutional Conflicts, and the National Interest

JASMINE FARRIER

NEITHER THE CONSTITUTION'S TEXT nor *The Federalist* explicitly reveals what an ideal budget process would look like, let alone what good fiscal policy entails. But there are key constitutional details as well as a larger spirit that can supply the ingredients of stable and responsible budgetary policy-making: a filtering of constituent desires through representation in Congress, a fragmented lawmaking process that promotes deliberation and compromise, and executive leadership with institutional resources for broad action. In budgeting, as in other policy areas, the ultimate goal is to balance somehow the nation's wants, needs, and capacities. The Constitution's framers were pessimistic that the public and their leaders could forge such outcomes naturally, so they established separation of powers to promote different perspectives on the "national interest" and protect the country from narrow and insufficiently considered policy.

Separation of powers and checks and balances only work, however, if elected officials develop an attachment to the rights and duties of their institution and work to foster its distinctive contribution to American government. Over the course of American history, this institutional ambition has changed dramatically in Congress. For the past century or so on many policy fronts, Congress has alternated between delegating and expanding its legislative and oversight powers to fit the institutional, political, and cultural moment. Meanwhile, the president's branch has expanded its scope and policy tools as a result of a lively and relatively steady institutional ambition. One result of these inconsistent developments is the creation of fiscal policy that is a messy hybrid of conflict, cooperation, and abdication by the institutions of power.[1]

In recent decades Congress has shown signs of ambivalence about the value of its legislative powers. Although the Democratic-controlled Congress of the 1970s acted vigorously to assert its institutional prerogatives on the budget, in the 1980s and 1990s Congress repeatedly limited its own powers by approving a variety of procedural fetters to help balance spending and revenue. These included deficit and spending caps, restrictive rules governing floor debate and amendments, the "line-item veto," and the near-passage of a proposed balanced-budget constitutional amendment. Other than the item veto, presidents were wary of these reforms because of concerns that they would curtail some executive prerogatives. Congress, however, was more than willing to delegate authority to satisfy critics, even in times of divided government, and almost always rejected the policy alternatives that protected member, committee, and majority powers the most.[2]

Yet this period also witnessed occasional bursts of congressional ambition and assertiveness that were interspersed with these moments of low institutional confidence. The mixed partisan Congress in the 1980s demonstrated conflicting institutional signals by treating presidential budget proposals as "dead on arrival" and then going on to blame itself for fiscal imbalances in two rounds of Gramm-Rudman-Hollings (G-R-H) deficit caps in 1985 and 1987. Although the Budget Enforcement Act (BEA) of 1990 was an unusually useful set of fiscal restraints compared with the overly ambitious and arbitrary G-R-H rules, and even more so after its renewal in 1993 and 1997, the premise of the BEA was also that Congress could not budget responsibly with normal member, committee, and majority prerogatives. During the 104th Congress, House speaker Newt Gingrich used his legislative weapons to shut down the government to protest President Bill Clinton's fiscal proposals. Paradoxically, at the same time he pushed to *lose* institutional power in the item veto and budget amendment. Despite such institutional ambivalence in Congress about its proper fiscal powers, divided government during these decades still ensured a healthy dose of interbranch conflict. The budget surplus at the end of the 1990s probably would not have occurred absent such fights on the nation's proper fiscal course under George H.W. Bush and Bill Clinton and a roaring economy.[3]

By contrast, after 2001, the economic and political landscape changed dramatically. For a variety of reasons, surpluses turned to deficits and economic health turned to unease and later downright sickness. Unified government, in all its meaning, emerged stronger during the middle of Bush's presidency than any time since the 1960s, but the effect of the resulting policies on the national interest, like then, is a topic of hot debate. The costliest fiscal items shaped by the executive branch were often controversial during and after passage (tax cuts, Iraq war, Medicare expansion, hurricane recovery, and the 2008 economic "bailout") in part because of incomplete information about long-term cost and management. But these items passed as a result of close coordination between the White House and leaders of Congress under both parties' rule.[4] It is true that a more vibrant interbranch debate on these issues and the budget in general took root at the start of the 110th Congress when the Democratic majority leaders took office. However, while the new leadership organized its members well enough to obstruct the president's favored bills and even overturned vetoes of domestic spending bills, the Democrats still failed in their main goal to translate unrelenting criticism of the war and President Bush's economic priorities into new policy.

Regarding the budget specifically, in a typical inward gaze, despite years of bipartisan criticism of the Bush administration's management of hundreds of billions of dollars spent at home and abroad, the members of both parties took considerable time "reforming" Congress's prerogatives to appropriate money in earmarks in 2007 and 2008 and even seriously debated giving President Bush an item veto in 2006. While potent as a symbol of government waste, all programs denigrated as "pork" taken altogether were less than 2 percent of the budget and thus paled in comparison with Bush's signature policies.[5]

Then, in a dramatic contrast to such perennial attention to budgetary crumbs, the more significant economic and budgetary coda of the Bush years was executive-led legislation designed to shore up the nation's finance industry beginning in October 2008. In response to the sudden perception of a far-reaching economic crisis, the Democratic Congress worked closely with the administration to delegate enormous power to the secretary of the treasury, Henry Paulson Jr. to spend up to $700 billion to buy "troubled" or "toxic" assets. Charles Rangel (D-NY), Chairman of the House Ways and Means Committee described the moment: "So, in a sense, we have a political gun at our heads that we can't afford to say that we know better."[6] Within weeks of passage, Congress demanded more transparency as the means and ends of the program strayed from the original legislation. Senator James Inhofe (R-OK), who voted against the plan, referred to Mr. Paulson in November 2008 by saying "it is clear that it was a mistake to sign a blank check to one man for such a tremendous amount of money."[7]

Rather than simply reiterate such details further to explain these and other confusions and minutiae surrounding the annual budget process, this chapter instead emphasizes how patterns in such moments are important windows on the health of the contemporary separation of powers system. Although President Bush has been compared to President Richard M. Nixon in a variety of ways meant to be unflattering to both, it is the difference between the Congresses that these presidents faced that demands further scrutiny. As other contributions to this volume imply, President Bush may have behaved like a Hamiltonian executive in certain ways, but Congress in recent years has hardly been a Madisonian one, even before September 11, 2001. On more distant inspection, occasional bursts of institutional ambition in the House and Senate over the past three decades are often the middle part of a persistent cycle of delegation of power, regret, and more delegation on a particular policy issue. This pattern transcends short-term partisan and policy fluctuations, although they can be exacerbated by them. If such institutional ambivalence holds, it is unlikely that Congress can sustain a rebirth of institutional will.

The post-9/11 Congress (under both parties' rule) is therefore not a wholly new creature so much as an exaggeration of already-present forces that have prevented or discouraged members and leaders from maintaining a consistently high national profile. The reasons for these changes over the course of the twentieth century are numerous: executive-centered media coverage of national issues and elections, members' channeling their legislative energies into district-level policy and reelection, committee fragmentation, the culture of legislative individualism, the limited life span and lack of interest in institutional maintenance from congressional party leaders, and increasing emphasis on after-the-fact oversight. These barriers to effective coequality are compounded by the many differences between the House and Senate that were designed to prevent a unified mind-set even under conditions of more unified government.[8]

All of this helps to explain why Congress has largely avoided sustained institutional ambition on major issues of the day from base closings and trade policy to war powers and budgeting. Of course, on other issue fronts in recent years, such as immigration, energy policy, and Social Security reform, the Congress has held onto policy power through preserving the status quo and resisting presidential leadership. And the Congress even led the executive branch into agreements on economic and housing policies in 2008. Between moments of institutional ambition and abdication lies ambivalence. Congress's members and leaders sometimes believe that their powers, interests, and expertise can help resolve national problems and at other times, they blame themselves and say the very nature of their institution undermines the national interest.

As these and other examples of congressional ambivalence continue in a new political landscape, so will other underappreciated constitutional ironies surrounding the national budget. First, despite a variety of internal political and structural problems aired freely for all to see, Congress has retained significant potential to contribute to the nation's fiscal health through its fragmented, but potentially deliberative, budget mechanisms and the expertise of its long-serving members and staff on budget-related committees as well as its own nonpartisan Congressional Budget Office. Despite the common presidential presumption that he alone can speak and act broadly for the national interest while finger-pointing at Congress for serving narrow or local "special interests," one is hard-pressed to find a modern president who was never accused of favoring certain regional, economic, or ideological interests at the expense of others.

Second, this imperfect state of constitutional affairs, in combination with the unending fiscal pressures of old and new spending commitments, has led to another strain on the original intentions of separation of powers: representation and deliberation through hands-on legislative processes. Since the return of large budget deficits at the dawn of the twenty-first century, adding to an already staggering national debt inherited from the previous decades, there have been widespread calls in the budget policy community (left, right, and center) for the renewal of artificial, but perhaps more reliable, fiscal "leadership" in the form of automatic budgeting rules that would restrict what the Congress and the president can do with annual fiscal policy and how they do it.

The crucial constitutional issues of the day are therefore not only the uneven trajectories of institutional ambition in the branches but rather a consistent assumption today by many budget actors that elected officials are inadequate to the fiscal tasks at hand. The logic goes that it is not the Congress that is overwhelmed but so the entire system of separation of powers. The perennial issue of budget reform throughout the twentieth century and beyond is often a shorthand way for political actors and watchers to express a need to stanch seemingly bottomless demands for government programs and services from all partisan corners. The main dilemma is a painful acknowledgement of the limits of democratic representation: if voters and elites are uninterested in fiscal responsibility, can automatic mechanisms save us from ourselves?

At the same time, in the midst of this complex fiscal tangle is consistent self-confidence in the executive branch that its view of the budget landscape is correct due to its unitary and hierarchical structure (regardless if that is true) and almost pathological insecurity in the Congress that its view of the budget landscape is flawed due to its divided and decentralized structure (regardless if that is true). There is indeed a crucial relationship between recent budget politics and the renewed growth of the presidency; but this is as much the result of congressional deference as of presidential assertiveness.[9]

In the next section I describe how these trends raise questions about the framers' understanding of the sources and effectiveness of institutional ambition and budgetary checks and balances. I then compare budgetary politics under Presidents Nixon and George W. Bush. These cases show that allegedly "imperial" executive behavior is only as real as its congressional support. Even today, the purposes and tools of separation of powers remain there for the taking, as we see in periodic moments of especially intense partisan and interbranch rivalry. Yet the question remains in the concluding section of this chapter whether these most basic constitutional presumptions are fully relevant to twenty-first-century fiscal challenges. Even if we can recapture the keen sense of congressional ambition of the Nixon years, the fiscal fact remains that most of the budget is technically not even controllable by normal legislative processes, even in the absence of automatic antideficit mechanisms. It is therefore doubtful that we could ever go back in the policy arena to theory of interbranch relations pitting ambition against ambition in the style of *Federalist* No. 51. However, there are still key ingredients of constitutional thinking relevant to the contemporary budget world.

Virtues of Constitutional Budgeting: Filtration, Leadership, and Conflict

Budget creation is not given much direct attention in *The Federalist*, but this crucial task touches many of the papers' themes surrounding the virtues of institutional specialization and the representative and deliberative components of the legislative process. Simply put, the legislative and executive branches are designed to see the national interest very differently. Because they have such different political perspectives on policy problems, conflict between the president and Congress should produce more reasonable laws than either institution could easily produce alone. If both branches pursue their visions vigorously, the ensuing conflicts should produce deliberation and compromise. However, the founders do not treat all the branches with equal suspicion. There is also a great sense of ambivalence on the proper role of Congress, which is undoubtedly related to the contemporary problems of sustained institutional will.

The legislative branch, especially the House of Representatives, was rather feared and disparaged by the framers for being closest to the people and thus infused with more passion than reason, but it was still given formidable budgeting powers. *Federalist* No. 55, the same paper that says "had every Athenian citizen been a Socrates, every Athenian assembly would still have been a mob," explains in part why such a seemingly disdained institution is still given so much responsibility in the Constitution.

> As there is a degree of depravity in mankind which requires a certain degree of circumspection and distrust, so there are other qualities in human nature which justify a certain portion of esteem and confidence. Republican government presupposes the existence of these qualities in a higher degree than any other form.[10]

Article I, Sections 7 and 8, of the Constitution include several provisions related to national economic life, including appropriations, taxation, debt, commerce, and monetary regulation. Therefore, it is not surprising that variations on the phrase "power of the purse" are used by James Madison and Alexander Hamilton in *The Federalist* in describing legislative power. In *Federalist* No. 58, which also discusses the powers of the House of Representatives, Madison says "this power over the purse may, in fact, be regarded as the most complete and effectual weapon with which any constitution can arm the immediate representatives of the people, for obtaining a redress of every grievance, and for carrying into effect every just and salutary measure."[11] And in the famous paragraph in *Federalist* No. 78 in which Hamilton describes the federal judiciary as the "least dangerous branch" for the powers it does not possess, he says "the legislature not only commands the purse but prescribes the rules by which the duties and rights of every citizen are to be regulated."[12]

Yet, in light of the fears of majority factions and the passions of the people spelled out in *Federalist* No. 10 and elsewhere, there are several remedies for the possibility that the House of Representatives can be dangerous to the whole polity. One of the key remedies is the difference in the broader view of senators described in *Federalist* Nos. 62 and 63, which emphasizes the need for stability in the upper chamber to counter the "mutability" of personnel and policy in the lower one.

There are equally important executive powers in the Constitution designed not only to balance both chambers of Congress but also to provide a different viewpoint on the national interest. These executive resources can be used to shape and lead the budget process and fiscal policy generally. First, the president has direct and indirect legislative power through the veto and state of the union address, in which he would "recommend to [Congress's] consideration such measures as he shall judge necessary and expedient." Second, the president has numerous administrative powers and duties (in the Bessette-Schmitt sense of the words as set out in chapter 2 of this volume) that would ultimately include nominating executive branch officials to enforce economic regulations, giving life to new economic offices created by Congress to meet national economic needs, as well as shaping specific fiscal outcomes by way of the executive power and the take care clauses in Article II.

In the sections of *The Federalist* that describe executive power, Alexander Hamilton discusses several themes related to the president's unique role in government that depends on an electoral base and institutional perch organically unlike Congress. These institutional virtues can be connected to budgeting. In *Federalist* No. 70, "energy in the executive" is connected to good government. In No. 71, Hamilton ties the executive branch to the "public good" and the kind of representative distance necessary to achieve the interest of the people, even if they do not see it.

> When occasions present themselves in which the interests of the people are at variance with their inclinations, it is the duty of the persons whom they have appointed to be the guardians of those interests to withstand the temporary delusion in order to give them time and opportunity for more cool and sedate reflection.[13]

However, *The Federalist* is unclear on whether this proper role of the president is to be found in executing the law as understood by Congress or via a more independent position hinted at above. What is striking about these papers is their relatively sanguine attitude about the national purposes and use of executive power, which is a strong contrast to its overall pessimism regarding the ability of the legislature to see the best interest of the whole. In the opening paragraph of *Federalist* No. 72, for example, the president does not appear tied to Congress's view of the administrative universe.

> The administration of government, in its largest sense, comprehends all the operations of the body politics, whether legislative, executive, or judiciary; but in its most usual and perhaps in its most precise signification, it is limited to executive details, and falls peculiarly within the province of the executive department. The actual conduct of foreign negotiations, the preparatory plans of finance, the application and disbursement of the public moneys in conformity to the general appropriations of the legislature, the arrangement of the army, the direction of the operations of war—these, and other matters of a like nature, constitute what seems to be most properly understood by the administration of government.[14]

In an overview of these particular papers in *The Federalist*, Herbert J. Storing concludes that all these parts of the executive duty fit together quite nicely. In this way, although it can be easily misunderstood, the constitutional virtues of the executive arise within separation of powers arrangements, not above them.

> [Hamilton] shows that administration is the beginning and end of government. . . . He shows that the president's responsibility for

administrative details implies a responsibility for the administration in the greatest and most comprehensive sense. He shows that the president's duty to check the legislature and even the people, when they are wrong, carries a duty, not merely to resist but to lead, to provide the direction that finally only he can provide.[15]

In Storing's view, such presidential leadership would engage, not supplant, the other branches through a unique perspective on the national interest that should shape, if not inherently elevate, national discourse rather than exist outside of it. And if a presidential faction behaves in the same way as a legislative one, multiple layers of representation, deliberation, and power distribution among the branches will remain potent weapons for slowing down majority will and the potential for the tyranny of repressive, and simply bad, ideas. *Federalist* No. 42 says "the mild voice of reason, pleading the cause of an enlarged and permanent interest, is but too often drowned, before public bodies as well as individuals, by the clamors of an impatient avidity for immediate and immoderate gain."[16]

Deliberation then becomes the key mechanism to balance representative forces.[17] Although the framers appeared to fear legislative more than executive power, there is no reason for the president to be spared from this deliberative separation of powers mix. As *Federalist* Nos. 47, 48, and 51 emphasize, constitutional values depend upon a vibrant and overlapping system of powers and prerogatives that harnesses individual and institutional ambition through an arsenal of constitutional weapons rather than relying on firm structural borders of institutional responsibilities.

Congress, however, was given an extra handicap regarding its ability to articulate and act on institutional will. The two-chambered Congress, each elected by different constituencies and for different terms of office in (originally) different manners of selection, was an explicitly planned obstacle to national consensus, and still is, as these structures were meant to encourage local, state, and national perspectives on legislation. For these structural reasons, deep institutional ambition in Congress is more difficult to sustain within and between the chambers than in the other branches.[18]

So while it is not too surprising that presidents are more eager and able to expand their own powers than Congress generally, these actions can alter separation of powers but need not destroy it. Sometimes Congress can overcome its institutional barriers to unified action and rise up against the president, as seen most vividly in the early 1970s. As the next section shows, in the Hamilton-Storing sense President Nixon was working for himself and his branch through the rhetoric of working for the entire polity. In a Madisonian sense, the Democrats in Congress were likewise working for more than themselves—they had a national policy vision that was also designed to maintain a better separation of powers equilibrium. Economists will differ on the fiscal outcomes of the separation of powers clashes of the early 1970s. This chapter instead focuses on the historical constitutional value of the interbranch conflict. As we will see, however, the tenure of President George W. Bush was characterized not by interbranch conflict but by Congress's timidity to see itself as coequal on a variety of policy fronts.

Constitutional Virtues in Action: President Nixon versus Congressional Ambition

President Nixon and the Democratic-dominated Congress engaged in years of political and constitutional clashes over the budget that ultimately led to the 1974 Congressional Budget and Impoundment Control Act. This near-ideal separation of powers moment brought together politically charged policy differences between the parties and branches with broader debate over which branch had the resources and perspective to see the national economic picture clearest and why. Although the complicated issues of controllable spending versus automatic entitlement spending and other forms of "backdoor" appropriations arose at this time, the basic mechanisms of separation of powers worked as they were utilized by the interested actors to further a broader policy and institutional agenda. Individual ambition was indeed harnessed to institutional ambition via a contemporary twist: divided government. Madison's larger hopes were realized, as seemingly pedestrian political conflicts were elevated to full-blown constitutional confrontations that would, somewhat ironically, help maintain polity stability and power balance (see *Federalist* No. 49).

President Nixon triggered one important component of the budget conflict by repeatedly impounding congressionally authorized funds and justifying this action as a necessary tool for spending and deficit reduction. Nixon argued that Congress was incapable of reining in its spending for both ideological and institutional reasons. Among other budget process criticisms, Nixon disagreed with the prevailing incremental budgeting strategy of continuing programs previously approved and arguing only about new increases, not the budgetary bases. Acting on this argument, he attempted to reduce or eliminate the bases of several programs, touching agriculture, health, education, housing, and economic development. But his main point was not only that these small programs needed paring but also that Congress could not get a handle on the big picture:[19]

> The Congress suffers from institutional faults when it comes to federal spending. . . . Congress not only does not consider the total financial picture when it votes on a particular spending bill, it does not even contain a mechanism to do so if it wished. . . . The Congress, thus, has no sure way of knowing whether or when its many separate decisions are contributions to higher prices, or possibly to higher taxes.[20]

During the ensuing reform movement, Congress did not rebut this point and actually closely echoed Nixon's criticism in its attempt to recover budgeting primacy. It appeared that the president's more national perspective on the budget dysfunctions of Congress had a profound effect on Nixon's congressional opposition, even from the institutionally protective House Rules Committee:

> The excessive fragmentation of the budget process in Congress makes it difficult for Congress to effectively assess program priorities or to establish overall budget policy. At the very least, priority-setting means that competing claims on the budget are decided in some comprehensive manner rather than in isolation from one another. This is not now the case. . . . The total is the sum of many individual actions, most of which are taken without any real cognizance of their impact on the economy.[21]

But members of Congress did not take this argument to the next level that Congress was permanently incapable of taking a national perspective. If that were true, the executive would have an inherently powerful role to reshape congressional preferences. This Hamiltonian viewpoint was articulated by Arthur Burns, then chairman of the Federal Reserve's Board of Governors, during 1973 hearings on budget process reform. Burns said, "procedures that produce deficits that the Congress itself does not desire invite corrective actions by the Executive."[22] Representative Claude Pepper (D-FL) disagreed in a later exchange as he argued that despite Congress's big-picture budget problems, presidential impoundments are violations of the oath of office and the Constitution by a failure to execute the law: "The President is not the protector of the country against the Congress. The Constitution did not give him that prerogative."[23]

The ad-hoc Joint Study Committee on Budget Control in charge of the reform bills laid out Congress's challenges in the language of institutional ambition that has become rare: "It is essential that Congress develop ways of making its own decisions on budget priorities so that realistic control over the purse can be regained by the Congress, as intended by the Constitution."[24] Rep. George H. Mahon (D-TX) concurred: "Congress demonstrates its power of the purse when it delivers it to some modified degree to the Executive. It can give or it can take away, demonstrating that it does have control."[25]

Along these lines, the dominant argument of the bipartisan 1974 Congressional Budget and Impoundment Control Act's legislative history was that Congress had ceded far too much budgetary power to the executive branch over the course of the century. At the same time, the reform was prompted by Congress's admission that the various institutional problems that Nixon seized on to justify his impoundments were real. Yet the House Rules Committee rejected reform alternatives that included the types of fetters that had been used in the past, like restrictive spending ceilings and related floor rules, which ultimately would be resurrected in the 1980s and 1990s. Institutional ambition in the early 1970s was not ambivalent, as it became later. As the House Rules Committee said, "Budget reform must not become an instrument for preventing Congress from expressing its will on spending policy."[26]

The final tally shows how solidly members tied their personal ambition to an institutional one—only six votes were cast against the reform—but the moment was fleeting. The 1974 Budget Act is a rare moment of Congress's viewing its own power as crucial to budget control. The 1974 reform is thus a stark contrast to subsequent episodes of congressional budget process changes in the 1980s and 1990s, which emphasized temporary reductions of congressional power through external delegation and automatic spending-reduction procedures through the G-R-H bills of 1985 and 1987, the 1990 Budget Enforcement Act, and the Line-Item Veto Act of 1996.

For its scope and longevity, though, the 1974 Congressional Budget and Impoundment Control Act was the most important bundle of budget process changes since the 1921 Budget and Accounting Act that created the annual presidential budget proposal. The newly created Congressional Budget Office, the House and Senate Budget Committees, and the annual budget resolution and reconciliation processes were all created to enhance congressional control and coordination of annual budget and appropriations decisions. And unlike a short-lived experiment with congressional budgeting in the late 1940s, the 1974 act's processes are still the core of the annual budget process. Today, if Congress wants to take back the budget from the current president, or a future one, it has much of the institutional capacity it needs, if not the will, to do so. As the process add-ons have come and gone, the core Budget Act still stands.

However, even the 1974 reform's impoundment controls still accepted Nixon's premise that there is a strong need for presidential scrutiny of appropriations outlays and the act continued to allow presidents to use their administrative judgments to refuse to spend money approved in appropriations bills, known as impoundment or rescission. The 1974 processes gave Congress an explicit and easy mechanism to stop these withholdings if Congress disagreed with the president's actions. After 1974, if Congress wanted to stop a rescission it did not have to do anything because each rescission under the 1974 act required a bill of congressional approval within forty-five days or the funds in question would be released. Although Congress had utilized these 1974 provisions regularly to allow or stop presidential withholdings totaling billions of dollars over the decades, the short-lived Line-Item Veto Act of 1996 altered this legislative process to make it much more difficult for Congress to override presidential preferences.[27] Regardless of the name, it is clear that any permanent process that allows any one president to not spend funds authorized previously by Congress rests on the assumption that all presidents have a special vantage point on good policy that can elude other more narrowly focused actors and citizens.

Ironically, around the same time, other budgetary developments directed by Nixon were at odds with this assumption by being explicitly designed to decrease policy objectivity in the executive branch. President Nixon's budgetary legacy also included a new tool for more narrow and partisan policy-making that survives to this day as a perennial source of alleged budgetary mischief: the Office of Management and Budget (OMB). The Reorganization Act of 1939, which created the Executive Office of the President (EOP) and moved the Bureau of the Budget (BOB) from the Treasury Department to the EOP, expired just prior to President Nixon's first term. Nixon submitted a plan to Congress to abolish essentially the politically isolated BOB and replace it with a new budget office, which would be more responsive to presidential policy objectives regarding agency management and budgeting. The reorganization plan was contentious, especially in the House, not least because the top officials of the proposed OMB were not going to be subject to Senate confirmation. But the old BOB was quite unpopular, even in Congress, and Nixon's Reorganization Plan No. 2 passed and OMB replaced BOB in 1970.

Under its first three directors, George Schulz, Caspar Weinberger, and Roy Ash, OMB was heavily criticized for its partisan bent, extensive reach into the executive branch, and role in Nixon's impoundments. In response, Congress did more than just complain. In 1973, Congress passed a bill requiring that the director and deputy director be confirmed by the Senate (for both present and future officeholders) rather than appointed directly by the president. Nixon vetoed the bill arguing that it violated his constitutional removal power since Congress was in effect creating a new position title by abolishing and recreating the offices to circumvent the president's appointment prerogative. The Senate overrode the veto, but the House did not, and compromise legislation was passed to confirm future directors only.[28]

This transformative moment in presidential budgeting is subtle and momentous at the same time. The old Bureau of the Budget had long enjoyed a grudging political respect encapsulated in its reputation as the "abominable no man." Now that the budget office became politicized, both branches and parties became more highly engaged in competition over economic interpretation and fiscal needs. In 1975, Hugh Heclo's important article from *Public Interest*, "OMB and Neutral Competence," described the tensions evident in this transformation from BOB to OMB, which showed the need for, and result of, a more politically sensitive executive approach to budgeting that is still relevant today.

> There were good policy reasons for increasing political control over the agency and agency identification with the president. Increasingly interventionist policies—with civil servants dealing in questions of birth control, consumerism, medical care, environment, energy, transportation, civil rights, and so on—provide a legitimate justification for a much greater political interest in civil service decisions. . . . In the eyes of the White House, administration policy faced not only an opposition Congress but also an opposition executive, a collection of agencies and departments with a vested interest in the ways of the past. . . .
>
> However well-intentioned some of these efforts have been, the fact remains that the easiest way for an organization to become politicized and lose neutral competence is to become visibly identified with a given political bargain or piece of public advocacy. . . . As OMB's visibility has grown, it is understandable if others fail to make the distinction between OMB's governmental authority as an institution of the presidency and its political power as the president's personal staff. . . . Even more threatening than problems with outsiders is the fact that members of the Executive Office of the President themselves may become less able to distinguish service to the president from service to the presidency.[29]

While this and other institutional developments of this period are complex, they still echo with a recognizable constitutional spirit. First, despite the obviously political bent of President Nixon's actions that affected budget processes and outcomes, Congress took the institutional aspects of Nixon's national interest rhetoric seriously by trying to improve internal budget mechanisms while also accepting the president's special role in the budget process. Second, at the same time, Congress attempted to combat the president on specific policy differences by rising to the occasion as an institution committed to self-improvement and fiscal discipline to preserve its coequal place. If the new OMB was going to be a partisan weapon for the president, Congress would fight back with new confirmation requirements and its own source of objective budget information in the Congressional Budget Office.[30]

In the 1980s and 1990s, however, an external and internal backlash against Congress began when huge deficits brought the wrath down on its budget powers at every level (member, committee, and partisan). Congress did not consistently rebut Presidents Ronald Reagan, George H.W. Bush, and Bill Clinton's accusations of particularism and waste. Members alternated between giving away and coveting their budget powers for two decades.[31] At the turn of the new century, iterations of this ambivalence characterized the Republican and Democratic Congresses, with semi-bipartisan abdication to President Bush in 2001–4 giving way to semi-bipartisan obstruction from 2005–8. In this extraordinary time, the budget process became unhinged.

Constitutional Virtues on Hiatus: President George W. Bush versus Congressional Ambivalence

From beginning to end, the George W. Bush presidency reached a high-water mark for presidential power and a low one for Congress as the result of extreme ambition in the former and extreme, if inconsistent, deference in the latter under mostly unified government and the shadow of 9/11. Many of the goals and tools of separation of powers went by the wayside on both domestic and foreign policy as members and leaders of both parties accommodated much of the president's agenda relatively quickly, even though there was often disagreement in the membership and controversy in the public sphere about policy specifics. In the final Bush years, however, more traditional obstructionism and agenda battles were temporarily resurrected by members of both parties as President Bush's poll numbers dropped after his reelection in 2004 and the 2006 election delivered a new majority to the House and Senate, largely on dissatisfaction with Bush's executive branch management of the wars, the hurricanes of 2005, and the economy. However, a fresh round of congressional deference and delegation re-emerged in the final months of the administration surrounding a series of executive-led actions to shore up the finance industry as evidence of a recession mounted. These and prior executive and congressional actions led to a record deficit for fiscal year 2009 for the years since WWII—in both nominal terms and as a percentage of the economy—nearly one trillion dollars.[32] Congress held its nose and went along.

By any measure, though, Bush's first term was marked by a smooth legislative process and time after time, these policies had extraordinary impact on the immediate and long-term budget commitments of the United States. In spring 2001, Congress, then under split-chamber party control, passed Bush's favored tax cuts with sunset provisions. At the same time, the federal government continued to grow its spending commitments in a manner that did not match revenues each year, producing repeated budget deficits. Most notably, in Bush's first term, Congress authorized a war against Iraq and (with more resistance from Republicans in Congress) a large-scale expansion of Medicare for prescription drug benefits, with the costs of both actions seriously underestimated at the time by the Bush administration. Even as the president and Republican members of Congress lobbied in 2006 to make the 2001 tax cuts permanent, the administration estimated the cost of new Medicare policy alone would exceed one trillion dollars within its first decade. The Iraq war exceeded 600 billion dollars in direct military costs by 2008, despite the original 50- to 60-billion dollar estimate. The Congressional Budget Office pegs the overall cost of the war, including veterans' benefits, nation building, and other indirect costs, to be one to two trillion dollars, but some economists say it could be even more.[33]

This dramatic turn in fiscal policy was made possible in part by both branches allowing the expiration of restrictive rules and procedures of the Budget Enforcement Act (BEA) that were extended through the entire decade and widely viewed as crucial to controlling spending and new entitlements in the Clinton years. These rules were set to expire in 2002 after their last extension in 1997. The director of the Congressional Budget Office, Dan L. Crippen, testified in Congress in June 2001, in favor of keeping the law on the books, especially its provisions for annual limits on discretionary spending and the scoring of "pay-as-you-go" rules for new mandatory spending and tax reduction policies. His testimony provided a prescient warning that the surplus might not last, stating: "Budgeting is a process for setting priorities and allocating resources. Large surpluses do not make those tasks unnecessary. Moreover, baseline projections of surpluses depend largely on continued economic growth and assumptions of fiscal constraint, which may or may not come to pass."[34]

September 11, 2001, was less than three months later. Between the new tax cuts and the "war on terror," the budget process and fiscal policies of the United States became as unpredictable as the new world order. For example, almost all the money for the Afghanistan and Iraq wars during the Bush years was approved through annual emergency spending provisions not subject to regular budget rules, even during years after the war was authorized in October 2002. In June 2006, the Senate approved an amendment to force the president to submit future requests via his normal budget proposal in February. The administration argued that is impossible because war costs are unpredictable. The amendment's sponsor, John McCain (R-AZ) seemed to cast blame widely for the situation: "We are blowing the budget process. We are carving gigantic holes in the system. Since 2001, the administration has sought to fund the war operations almost entirely through emergency appropriations measures. . . . During the 11-year Vietnam War, there were four supplemental appropriations bills."[35]

And yet, also in 2006, despite these and other more serious cries of fiscal mismanagement in Iraq and the U.S. response to Hurricanes Katrina and Rita in 2005, the Republican House and Senate seriously considered giving President Bush a new version of the item veto. The return of the item veto as a legislative possibility began in the state of the union address in 2006 where Bush said, "I am pleased that the members of Congress are working on earmark reform, because the federal budget has too many special interest projects. And we can tackle this problem together, if you pass the line-item veto."[36] However, what the president was really asking for was not a "true" item veto, which most governors have to delete an item and sign the rest of the bill into law but rather enhanced rescission power to prevent spending of certain items after a spending bill is passed and signed by both branches. As a new bill to give the president these new powers moved to the House floor in March 2006, the acting director of the Congressional Budget Office argued that even if the president had the expedited rescission power being proposed, it would have a negligible affect on the deficit today for a variety of reasons. Despite an epidemic of earmarks during the Republican years in the congressional majority, these items of "pork" are not the main problem of the U.S. budget:

[Although this bill] includes the authority to propose rescissions of new mandatory spending, it would not apply to existing mandatory programs. Those programs now constitute a majority of the federal budget, and are likely to pose significant fiscal challenges in coming years. . . . Additional budgetary tools can assist in bringing about budgetary restraint, and improved accountability is desirable . . . Such tools, however, cannot establish fiscal discipline unless there is political consensus to do so. Competing priorities can make such consensus difficult to reach. . . . The Congress will have to weigh the potential for possibly modest budgetary benefits against possible drawbacks, which include a shift of power to the executive branch and effects on the legislative process.[37]

In these debates on the item veto in the House, proponents and opponents showed various shades of ambivalence about their institution. Proponents of the new item veto measure said outright that Congress needed new external controls. The House Rules Committee's report on the enrolled bill said it "marks the continuation of a monumental and long-standing effort to change the way Congress does business and restore public confidence in its ability to manage the Nation's finances." But the same section of the report begins with trepidation: "It is the sense of Congress no President or any executive branch official should condition the inclusion or exclusion or threaten to condition the inclusion or exclusion of any proposed cancellation in any special message under this section upon any vote cast or to be cast by any Member of either House of Congress."[38]

However, opponents remained convinced that the item veto could be used to threaten members' projects. In addition, Democrats chided Republicans for not reining in the allegedly irresponsible earmarks that grew dramatically under their watch over a decade of Republican rule. For example, Rep. Betty McCollum (D-MN) said:

The line-item veto proposed today will expand Presidential power and challenge the separation of powers critical to the function of our government. It is an extreme dilution of the authority of the legislative branch if the President can hold a member's priorities hostage in order to garner votes for other initiatives. . . . Republicans today are decrying the practice of earmarking projects. However, since 1996, under the Republican watch, the number of earmarks has grown. . . .

As the Majority party, Republicans have had the power for the last 12 years to reduce earmarks and to add oversight to this process.[39]

But Rep. McCollum was not as institutionally protective as she implied as she supported an alternative budget process reform bill from John Spratt (D-SC) that contained an even broader variety of spending fetters for Congress, in addition to enhanced rescission. Representative Spratt explained why more restraints are better: "Merely granting the President expedited rescission authority alone . . . will do little to require that Congress set budget priorities, put the budget on the path back to balance, and stick to its budget promises."[40]

Although the House passed the Republican rescission measure in June 2006, it stalled in the Senate, where there was also inconsistent behavior among members. For example, some supporters of the expedited version of the item veto a decade before, including Sen. Robert Byrd (D-WV), changed their minds to deny this type of power to Bush. This bill was also opposed by several Republican Senators who gave a stronger version of the power to Democrat Bill Clinton in 1996. And some key Democrats remained in favor of it, such as John Kerry (MA) and Evan Bayh (IN), both of whom had repeatedly publicly criticized the president's use of the fiscal powers he already had.[41]

This particular item veto idea died and the Democrats won the midterm elections later that year. But, in a typical moment of institutional chutzpah three months after the 2006 election, President Bush again called on Congress to grant him greater authority over budgeting outcomes in an item veto.[42] While the item veto idea was dropped in the 110th Congress under the new Democratic majority, President Bush continued to hammer at congressional earmarks, which had grown from around four thousand in 1994 to over fourteen thousand in 2006, and the Democrats responded with reforms as soon as they took office in January 2007. While earmarks are a still a minority of total discretionary spending, and only around 2.4 percent of the total budget, they loom large in perennial media accounts of government waste and constituent-driven boondoggles.[43]

At the same time that Congress exhibited mixed behavior regarding whether or not its spending powers are necessary for representation or detrimental to the budget, the president balked at using his considerable existing powers to slow federal spending. Even without a new item veto or earmark reform in Congress, President Bush could have all along utilized two other unique and historically potent tools to undermine congressional spending preferences: his regular veto and existing rescission authority. Although the administration asserted vast institutional prerogatives on many fronts, President Bush hardly touched his powers to peel back Congress's large and small budget items. Such hesitance led some conservative critics to wonder if the president's broad rhetoric of protecting the nation from runaway spending was sincere or if he only wished to use his powers in a more narrow and partisan way against the opposition. In 2007, for example, President Bush's sudden interest in criticizing earmarks after the Democrats won the majority prompted a Cato Institute analyst to say this behavior shows "he dislikes Democrats more than he likes big government."[44]

An examination of Bush's initially sparse use of his regular veto power against Congress's budget bills also shows his vulnerability to these charges. President Bush used just one veto against the Republican Congress on a stem cell research bill, but several against the Democrats in 2007 and 2008 (a few of which were overridden) and threatened to veto scores of bills both years, prompting a comprehensive "Veto Watch" on the Web site of speaker Nancy Pelosi. Explaining this new trend in 2007, White House spokesman Tony Fratto said, "We have to be a check on bad policies coming out of Congress." Yet Fratto did not dispute House Speaker Nancy Pelosi's assertion that the proposed spending differences between the White House and the Democrats for Fiscal Year 2008 (the object of this particular veto threat) were less than 1 percent.[45]

The other executive branch budgeting tool that President Bush almost completely ignored was his original rescission authority left over from the 1974 Congressional Budget and Impoundment Control Act. When the Line-Item Veto Act of 1996 was struck down by the Supreme Court in 1998, the 1974 rescission process became the default presidential mechanism for eliminating spending after the branches passed appropriations bills. In 2005, Rep. Jim Cooper (D-TN) of the House Budget Committee published an op-ed in the *New York Times* wondering why President Bush had failed to request any rescissions from Congress. President Bill Clinton, by contrast, had won 111 of 163 rescission requests, many during the six years when he faced an opposition Congress. While the savings were a drop in the budgetary bucket in the 1990s—several billion dollars—Cooper asked, "Why has Mr. Bush kept this knife in a dusty drawer, especially given his stance on the need to curb spending and his close ties with the Republican leadership?"[46] A few months later, Bush submitted his only rescission: $2.3 billion of Hurricane Katrina recovery funds. Bush's rescission record stands in stark contrast to his predecessors' greater interest in refusing to spend congressionally authorized funds for a variety of managerial and political reasons.[47]

Overall, though, President Bush exhibited a deep similarity to his predecessors as his actions and rhetoric did not second-guess his institution's virtues in fashioning sound budget policy. For example, President Bush's message to introduce his Fiscal Year 2007 budget proposal did not include the self-flagellation seen so often from Congress: "As this Budget shows, we have set clear priorities that meet the most pressing needs of the American people while addressing the long-term challenges that lie ahead. The 2007 Budget will ensure that future generations of Americans have the opportunity to live in a Nation that is more prosperous and more secure. With this Budget we are protecting the highest ideals and building a brighter future for all."[48]

Two years later, in June 2008, while Bush's popularity sank further and the accuracy of these statements remained unclear, President Bush's final emergency supplemental war funding bill passed Congress. Members on both sides justified their support for the 258-billion-dollar bill, which ultimately included war funding, veterans' benefits, unemployment extensions, flood relief for the Midwest, and Medicaid support. To the end, Democrats expressed frustration with their institution's and party's inability or unwillingness to use the budget process to force the president's hand on the war. For example, Mark Udall (D-CO) said on the floor "I'm disappointed that the bill gives the President most of what he wants in Iraq spending without any significant policy constraints. Congress has tried and failed to include such constraints in previous spending bills, and here we have failed again."[49]

There was anguish on the Republican side too. Paul Ryan (R-WI), the ranking member of the House Budget Committee showed his own ambivalence as he cast his "aye" vote on this omnibus bill that would fund the troops and help unemployed workers and flood victims in his district, but he did by holding his nose and cast blame internally:

Mandatory spending doesn't belong on an appropriations bill because mandatory spending is forever. . . . In fact, we cannot afford the entitlements we have, much less an expansion in them. We are going to spend over $30 trillion in the next ten years; surely we could have found $63 billion in offsets. But we didn't even try . . . PAYGO does not exist. It is waived every time we have to make a choice. We are sent here to make decisions—to make choices—to govern. Like the floods, this bill takes the path of least resistance; it passes the buck—and the debt to future generations. We shouldn't budget or legislate this way.[50]

But President Bush did not show any lack of confidence in this bill. At the signing ceremony he explained his support for each part of the bill and gave a sanguine conclusion: "This bill shows the American people that even in an election year, Republicans and Democrats can come together to stand behind our troops and their families."[51]

Indeed, the Bush administration and the Democratic Congress did come together again and again to spend money in 2008 to provide monetary help to housing consumers and lenders, taxpayers, and wobbly financial institutions. Yet these rushed agreements in the fall of 2008 belied deep differences between the parties and branches on the nature of the economic situation. For years, members of both parties had a wide variety of housing, banking, and mortgage issues on the agenda. By contrast, neither President Bush nor Bush appointee Federal Reserve Chairman Ben Bernanke argued at first that his branch had a unique structural place and superior national approach to resolving mortgage or credit pressures. In fact, in the summer of 2007, Bush and Bernanke seemed quite restrained in their thoughts and ideas on ramifications of the situation while members of the Congress were relatively proactive.[52]

In this pre-"crisis" period, President Bush acknowledged the pain of foreclosure to the families experiencing it but maintained that overall the downturn in the housing markets was not going to undermine the economy. While Bush did say that housing was a "top priority" and that he would push Congress to enact his proposed reforms to the Federal Housing Administration and other housing and mortgage-related agencies, his rhetoric was decidedly restrained and he made no argument that the executive branch was best suited to solve the problem:

The recent disturbances in the sub-prime mortgage industry are modest. . . . But if you're a family—if your family is one of those having trouble making the monthly payments, this problem doesn't seem modest at all. . . . We've got a role, the government has got a role to play—but it is limited. A federal bailout of lenders would only encourage a recurrence of the problem. It's not the government's job to bail out speculators, or those who made the decision to buy a home they knew they could never afford.[53]

Five months later, in January 2008, Senator Charles E. Schumer (D-NY) gave an indirect response to Bush's relatively sanguine attitude in his opening statement at a hearing before the Joint Economic Committee, which he chaired. His presentation was bluntly titled "What Should the Federal Government Do to Avoid a Recession?"

In some ways, the bad news could have been averted. Last year, with the subprime mortgage crisis staring us in the face, this Bush administration was unwilling to act to stem that crisis and refused to consider the possibility that a recession was on the horizon. As many economists predicted (this committee included), the subprime mortgage meltdown spilled over into the broader housing market, damaged credit markets, and brought us to the precipice of a recession. Because of presidential inaction . . . the economy is now on the edge of recession.[54]

Indeed, eight months after Schumer's statement, these very mortgage and economic pressures came to a head. Treasury Secretary Paulson's initial proposal to engage the federal government in unloading bad private assets gave vast discretion to himself and his then-unknown successor with scant attention to oversight by Congress. At the first public hearing three days after Congress received the three-page proposal, Chairman Christopher Dodd (D-CT) took issue with several points:

Barely 72 hours ago, Secretary Paulson presented a proposal that he believes is urgently needed to protect our economy. This proposal is stunning and unprecedented in its scope and lack of detail. It would allow [Paulson] to intervene in the economy by purchasing at least $700 billion of toxic assets. It would allow him to hold onto those assets for years, and to pay millions of dollars to hand-picked firms to manage those assets. It would do nothing to help even a single family save a home. It would do nothing to stop even a single CEO from dumping billions of dollars of toxic assets on the backs of taxpayers. . . . And it would allow him to act with utter and absolute impunity—without review by any agency or court of law. . . . I can only conclude that it is not just our economy that is at risk, Mr. Secretary, but our Constitution, as well. Nevertheless, in our efforts to restore financial security to American families and stability to our markets, this Committee has a responsibility to examine this proposal carefully and in a timely manner.[55]

Secretary Paulson's opening statement, by contrast, did not acknowledge doubts about the program nor his or the president's possible culpability in the situation:

Over these past days, it has become clear that there is bipartisan consensus for an urgent legislative solution. We need to build upon this spirit to enact this bill quickly and cleanly, and avoid slowing it down with other provisions that are unrelated or don't have broad support. This troubled asset purchase program on its own is the single most effective thing we can do to help homeowners, the American people and stimulate our economy . . . our next task must be to address the problems in our financial system through a reform program that fixes our outdated financial regulatory structure, and provides strong measures to address other flaws and excesses. . . . Many of you also have strong views, based on your expertise. . . . Right now, all of us are focused on the immediate need to stabilize our financial system, and I believe we share the conviction that this is in the best interest of all Americans.[56]

The House voted down the administration's initial proposal, but just days later Congress passed the Troubled Asset Relief Program (TARP), with a few hundreds of pages of added details and additional sweeteners for members. In contrast, however, to his original proposal to purchase mortgage-based assets from institutions, Paulson directed the Treasury Department to provide capital directly to troubled banks. Within weeks, Congress gave him and Chairman Bernanke a bipartisan scolding in oversight hearings. The House Committee on Financial Services's ranking Republican, Spencer Bachus (R-AL), said while I applaud Secretary Paulson for recognizing that capital injections would best serve the taxpayers' interest, I have serious concerns about the improvised and ad hoc nature of Treasury's implementation of the Capital Purchase Program and other elements of the TARP. We all understand that when conditions on the ground change, policymakers must be agile enough to adjust to those changed circumstances. But changing too quickly, without adequately explaining why you've changed or what you're going to do next, risks sending mixed signals to a marketplace that is in dire need of certainty and a sense of direction.[57]

In early December, a nonpartisan Government Accountability Office report also offered a mixed assessment on the executive branch's operations.[58]

As was the case in each of President Bush's signature policies over eight years, this episode in interbranch relations demonstrated institutional ambivalence as Congress veered from delegation to criticism. As President Barack Obama took the reins of the administration and ownership of these economic difficulties, his implicit task was to revitalize as well the reputation of the executive branch. It remains to be seen if the Democratic version of unified government will result in a similar reinvigoration of the strengths of the House and Senate.

Conclusion

If this budget overview of the past few decades shows anything definitively, it is that neither branch nor party has an inherent monopoly on the means or ends of fiscal responsibility. In this way, the federal budget process is a microcosm of the virtues and pathologies of democracy in general and of separation of powers in particular. The budget is the key document that connects constituent desires and representative power and it is shaped and reshaped by many actors of different perspectives but shared authority. If a responsible budget, like all other important policies, is something different than one institution's or party's narrow perspective, or less generous than the sum of all desires, who or what should be charged with sifting through these particular demands to attain an outcome that is closer to the interest of the whole, if such a goal is possible?

Rather than name a person or institution charged with the unilateral responsibility to protect the fiscal national interest, the Constitution gives us a complex, multi-institutional legislative process in which each unique part is supposed to protect and advance its own version of best policy. And yet, under a variety of partisan institutional arrangements, Congress regularly questions its own ability to act for the broadest interests of the nation while the executive branch does not. On the one hand, it is true that Congress's representative and legislative processes create perennial fiscal pressures that are difficult to coordinate in a fragmented system that has long separated revenue and appropriations processes. On the other hand, while the executive branch has long had a more streamlined and hierarchical budget process, its policy wants are no less subject to accusations of being partisan, narrow, and without accompanying funds to pay for them.

The authors of *The Federalist* show how and why each part of the government brings different viewpoints and structural resources. While presidential power waxed and waned over the Constitution's first century on all policy fronts, executive advocates during the Progressive and New Deal eras built vast new fiscal resources for the administration of expanded federal spending and policy reach. While it is up to each president to decide how and when to use these powers, his place in the budget universe is secured not only through these modern structures but also because of the steady application of executive institutional ambition. By contrast, although Congress is still the legislative center of the budget process, as an institution it has long struggled to maintain its place in separation of powers arrangements on many fronts. Such differing institutional trajectories between the branches over time have often brought greater attention and weight to presidential claims of acting for the national interest, while simultaneously making similar claims coming out of Congress inconsistent at best.

However, even the most recent ideal moment of constitutional and political budget clashes seen in the early 1970s did not tackle head-on the central budget challenge of modern fiscal policy: the fact that most of the annual budget actions shape only a minority of the true budget picture. While both branches often discuss the pressures of entitlement funding and mandatory spending, there is little public recognition of how much this issue constrains future leadership opportunities in both branches and parties. The technically "controllable" parts of the annual budget (called discretionary spending) are a minority of the whole, usually in the neighborhood of 35 to 40 percent and sometimes less. The rest of the budget goes to mandatory spending (entitlements), fulfillment of past authorizations, as well as net interest payments, among other things.[59] As discretionary spending includes almost all military spending as well as nonentitlement social programs, this bloc is almost as politically difficult to alter as the mandatory one. The leadership dilemma is more than simply trying to raise taxes on the wealthiest interests or whittling down tiny discretionary programs, it is confronting these long-term fiscal realities in the context of unrelenting and expensive policy desires.

In light of these challenges, executive branch power in the budget process can certainly streamline the policy-making process and help overcome intra- and interbranch paralysis. However, permanent presidential dominance over budgeting, through both aggressive executive centralization and congressional delegation, has yet to be proven to create objectively better fiscal policy. Such power imbalances can also threaten other constitutional values, even if Congress consents. First, excessive concentrations of executive power, especially from delegation by Congress, can significantly reduce deliberation and public debate.[60] Second, dramatic, sustained power shifts cloud responsibility and accountability, thus weakening popular control.[61] Third, extraordinary power growth in one part of the government can negatively affect the institutional virtues of the other branches and the separation of powers system.[62]

Fiscal and institutional developments surrounding the extraordinary growth of the government have certainly altered key constitutional processes and assumptions. While this is not the place to review the debate on the pros and cons of the contemporary administrative state, there is no doubt that the recent occupants of both branches—and the followers of both major parties—have staked their agendas on the premise of expansive government action (regardless of present or past rhetoric to the contrary). And it may be the case that in contemporary budget politics, divided government, and process fetters have become substitutes for institutional ambition and policy leadership. But it may not matter whether the Constitution's framers would approve of these developments.

The more relevant question is whether we still understand and value the aspirations of the separation of powers system Madison and Hamilton described. If members and leaders in Congress want to show the president that they can and should reshape his priorities and not just criticize them, then Congress needs to be more consistently attentive to maintaining its constitutional place. If the president wants to show Congress that he sees the policy landscape more broadly than the people themselves and their representatives, then he will need to transcend the narrow bounds of the political forces that put him in office. Under these conditions, rather than having a one-sided argument, the national interest is more truly open to debate.

CHAPTER NINE

Executive Privilege

DAVID A. CROCKETT

IN THE LONG WAKE OF 9/11, it is becoming fashionable to resurrect the term *imperial presidency*. Coined by historian Arthur Schlesinger Jr. in response to the abuses of the Nixon White House, the phrase refers to the supposed rise of a presidency of nearly absolute powers—running roughshod over Congress, exercising unilateral power in a variety of areas, and operating unrestrained in a system of emasculated checks and balances.[1] While one would be hard-pressed to find those who would describe Presidents Ford or Carter as imperial, various aspects of the Reagan, Bush I, and Clinton presidencies kept the phrase from completely fading into history. There is nothing, however, like a sustained national security threat to focus attention on presidential power. The actions of President George W. Bush's administration in response to the terrorist attacks of September 11, 2001, again raised the specter of a president ruling by decree in defiance of constitutional norms and procedures.[2]

One of the key components of this "imperial" model is the employment of secrecy by the president, usually through the claim of executive privilege. Defined simply, executive privilege is the power of a president to withhold information, whether from Congress, the courts, or the public. It is usually defended by the need to protect national security or the confidentiality of candid advice from presidential advisors.[3] To some, the very idea that a president can keep secrets is dangerous to a republic founded on open deliberation by the people's representatives.[4] Secrecy is associated with spying and palace intrigue and cabal, not open and honest government. If the Nixon presidency was marked by excessive abuse of power, and secrecy was an integral part of that abuse, then any future manifestation of secretive tendencies ought to give rise to similar fears.

Although presidents prior to George W. Bush made executive privilege claims, Bush elevated the issue of secrecy in the White House to new prominence. In November 2001, Bush used an executive order to expand the ability of current and former presidents to claim executive privilege over their papers, establishing a presumption of secrecy when it comes to access to presidential documents. In December 2001, Bush made his first formal claim of executive privilege when he refused access to pertinent documents by a congressional committee investigating closed criminal investigations. Most well known from the early Bush days was the administration's refusal to release information about the composition and activities of Vice President Richard Cheney's energy policy task force to two Democratic members of Congress and the General Accounting Office (GAO).[5]

Controversies over secrecy did not slow down as Bush entered his second term. The creation of two vacancies on the Supreme Court in 2005 led to battles over old White House documents. First, the Bush administration got into a tussle with Congress over the work of Judge John Roberts when he served in the Reagan and first Bush administrations. The White House agreed to release documents from Roberts's days working on the attorney general's staff and White House counsel's office but refused to release documents from his tenure as Deputy Solicitor General.[6] Then, when White House counsel Harriet Miers was tapped to replace Sandra Day O'Connor, the White House flatly refused to release documents related to her work in the White House, an argument that ultimately supplied the pretext for her withdrawal.[7] The indictment of Lewis "Scooter" Libby, Vice President Cheney's chief of staff, for actions related to the leak of a CIA officer's identity raised the possibility of another confrontation over secrecy if the vice president were called to testify.[8] By early 2006, various members of Congress were requesting documents related to the administration's response to the devastating Hurricane Katrina and demanding more information relating to the administration's program of wiretapping international phone calls and e-mail messages without a warrant.[9] The Democratic takeover of Congress in 2007 further raised the profile of executive privilege controversies. The conflict came to a head that summer when Congress issued two sets of subpoenas, one for documents explaining the legal justification of the administration's warrantless wiretapping program and the other to several White House officials in an attempt to investigate the firing of nine federal prosecutors in 2006. This latter case led to three successive claims of executive privilege between June 28 and August 1.[10] Finally, the 2005 CIA leak case led to another claim of executive privilege in July 2008 when President Bush, on the advice of Attorney General Michael Mukasey, sought to prevent Congress from seeing FBI reports of interviews with the vice president and other officials about the leak.[11]

Although the intensity of the Bush administration's fight for secrecy may have been higher than normal, and the partisan divisions much starker due to the polarizing nature of this president, the essential issue is hardly new. Nor does it stretch back only to the Nixon presidency. The question of secrecy in the executive branch goes all the way back to George Washington's quarrels with Congress and even to the arguments outlining the parameters of power established by the Constitution. Although the passions evoked by current controversies make it difficult to exercise practical wisdom, such an attempt is essential if we are to come to a principled and balanced understanding of this important issue. For the presence of unified government does not immunize President Barack Obama from wrestling with questions of secrecy.

In this chapter, I attempt to achieve this understanding with a four-part argument. First, the chapter begins with a summary of the argument against executive privilege, highlighting the core claims of what I call the *argument of congressional supremacy*. The second part of the chapter addresses these core claims and explains why they constitute a deficient understanding of the constitutional system. The third part examines in greater detail the different functions of the executive branch and explores what those different functions suggest about the relative strength of different executive privilege claims. The final part of the chapter highlights the limits to executive privilege in a separation of powers system. The result is a description of a constitutional system that may not appear very neat but that over time allows each branch to possess qualities essential to its functioning, while still providing for a fairly open system.

The Argument of Congressional Supremacy

Perhaps the strongest argument against the idea that presidents can make use of secrecy contrary to the will of Congress is found in Raoul Berger's classic text *Executive Privilege: A Constitutional Myth*. Written at the height of the Watergate scandal, Berger argues that executive privilege has no constitutional warrant—that it is, as the title suggests, a myth. Berger believes that the framers of the Constitution created a system of government in which the executive branch is decidedly subordinate to Congress. He cites James Madison approvingly when the latter argues in *Federalist* No. 51 that "in a republican form of government, the legislature necessarily predominates." Congress, in Berger's eyes, is "the senior partner," and the American democratic system is "bottomed on the legislative process." To Berger, Connecticut's Roger Sherman spoke the truth when he said at the Constitutional Convention that he "considered the Executive magistracy as nothing more than an institution for carrying the will of the Legislature into effect."[12] In such a model, there is no room for an executive branch defying Congress.

Although Berger's argument has been repudiated by other scholars,[13] that fact has not stopped partisans of congressional supremacy from advancing his case. Two recent attempts merit consideration as useful examples of the argument of congressional supremacy. Louis Fisher's book *The Politics of Executive Privilege* presents an exhaustive account of interbranch relations between Congress and the presidency, focused on the question of congressional access to executive branch information. Fisher acknowledges that there is no explicit language in the Constitution giving the president the right to withhold information from Congress, neither is there any language explicitly giving Congress the right to demand documents from the executive branch. Fisher argues that both powers are implied and that the result is often a clash between Congress's need to oversee the executive branch and the executive branch's need to guard the effectiveness of its own functions.[14]

Having made that bow to separation of powers, however, it is clear that Fisher sides in favor of congressional supremacy. For example, he argues that without access by Congress to national security information, "the political system necessarily moves away from the republican model fashioned by the framers toward an executive-centered regime they feared." The nature of this republican model is best illustrated by the fact that Fisher, echoing Berger, also cites approvingly Sherman's argument that the president is "nothing more than an institution for carrying the will of the Legislature into effect." Because representative government constitutes the foundation of the American constitutional system, congressional deliberation requires information. A consistent theme in the book is the fact that Congress "needs information to perform its constitutional duties" and that Congress has "no reason to defer to presidential claims." Fisher believes that there has been "a steady flow of political power" to the presidency since World War II, and the cost has been "to the checks and balances and separation of powers that the framers knew were essential to protect individual rights and liberties."[15] To summarize, the American constitutional order is a republican one centered on Congress; the presidency is principally an instrument of Congress and should work to satisfy its needs; and, when it resists, basic principles and functions of government become endangered.

David Gray Adler is another partisan of congressional supremacy, making his argument most recently in a written debate with Mark Rozell on executive privilege. Adler envisions a Constitutional Convention marked by a "deep-seated fear of executive power" on the part of the framers. At the heart of republican government lies the notion that the "wisdom of the many was superior to the judgment of one." Thus, the very purpose of checks and balances is to serve as a constraint on "executive unilateralism." This vision includes the arena of foreign affairs. In order to perform its functions, Congress requires "access to information possessed by the executive." The doctrine of separation of powers is designed not to create power but to "preserve the Constitution's enumeration of powers against acts of usurpation"—in this case, executive usurpation.

Adler repeats the argument made by Berger and Fisher that the "primary purpose animating the invention of the presidency was to create an executive to enforce the laws and policies of Congress"—quoting again Sherman's "nothing more" comment in an endnote.[16] Both Fisher and Adler criticize the Supreme Court's decision in *United States v. Nixon* for creating a constitutional doctrine of executive privilege and especially for implying that a privilege claim ought to prevail if the issue involves the "need to protect military, diplomatic, or sensitive national security secrets."[17] To summarize again, the constitutional system is marked by a fear of executive tyranny that manifests itself in an executive branch that is subordinate to and in service to Congress; this dynamic includes the arena of national security and foreign policy; and, checks and balances and separation of powers exist to preserve this dynamic.

The congressional supremacy argument can be broken down, then, into a series of connected propositions:

1. The American system of government is a republican one and is best defined as legislative-centered.
2. The presidency is subordinate to Congress and is best described as an institution designed to carry out Congress's will.
3. The president should defer to Congress in all arenas of action, including national security and foreign policy; indeed, there is no arena of action in which the presidency is the privileged actor.
4. The principal political values protected by this system are democracy (defined as responsiveness to the popular will) and the protection of individual rights and liberties.
5. The primary motivation behind these propositions is fear of executive tyranny; thus, the principal function of checks and balances and separation of powers is to constrain executive usurpation.
6. Thus, secrecy in the executive branch is unwise, and a president's attempt to withhold information from Congress violates the structure and intent of the constitutional order.

These propositions rest on twin deficient understandings, first of the framers' fear of tyranny, manifested in constitutional checks and balances, and second of the framers' understanding of competing and complementary functions of government, manifested in the separation of powers system. We must now examine these deficient arguments, constructing in the process a more complete understanding of the constitutional order.

The Argument of Constitutional Order

The first fundamental problem with the argument of congressional supremacy lies with the authors' understanding of the framers' fear of tyranny. Berger, Fisher, and Adler are fiercely committed to republican government. They believe that republican government is best safeguarded by a strong legislature that represents the popular will and protects the rights and liberties of its citizens. Berger says as much when he cites Madison on the predominance of the legislative branch. The locus of potential tyranny rests in the executive branch, which these authors associate with the British crown. The American Revolution was fought to end such tyranny, and in constructing their own executive branch the framers chose to subordinate it to Congress.

The problem with this account is that it is historically and philosophically inaccurate. It is historically inaccurate because it transposes the invention of the presidency from 1787 to the time of the American Revolution. It is true that a principal lesson learned in the run-up to war was that the executive, represented by the crown and its governors, was not to be trusted with power. Thus, in most state governments during and after the Revolution, legislatures were made much stronger than the executive. The result was a collage of abuse that discredited the notion of legislative supremacy. Similarly, the national government under the Articles of Confederation had no true executive branch as we understand it today. Congress created committees to handle various executive branch functions, but no single entity gave direction to executive agencies, and the "president" was simply the presiding officer of Congress. The result was a government incapable of responding adequately to crises and unable to provide for steady administration of the laws. It was this historical context that led to the calling of a Constitutional Convention in 1787 and to the invention of the American presidency. While fear of tyranny was one theme in Philadelphia, the overriding desire to form a more effective government was a far stronger one.[18] The presidency as an institution cannot be understood apart from the fact that it was constructed at a convention primarily concerned with the failure of the system under the Articles of Confederation—the system established in the shadow of executive tyranny—to provide for effective governance, in part because of the lack of a properly constructed executive branch.

The account is also philosophically inaccurate, as an examination of the same Federalist papers cited by these authors demonstrates. Berger, for example, cites Madison's comment in *Federalist* No. 51 that "in a republican form of government, the legislature necessarily predominates." What Berger ignores is Madison's argument immediately following describing how that "inconveniency" is remedied in the constitutional system. Madison makes his case in exceptionally strong terms over the course of several papers stretching from *Federalist* Nos. 47 through 51. It becomes very clear in those papers that the framers did, indeed, share a distrust of power, which they considered to be "of an encroaching nature."

They also recognized that different "departments" would be the principal "source of danger" in different types of political systems. For example, in hereditary monarchies it would be the executive that would tend toward tyranny. In a representative republic, however, it is the legislature that tends to absorb all power "into its impetuous vortex," and this danger is so great that Madison argues that it is against this popular branch that "the people ought to indulge all their jealousy and exhaust all their precautions."[19] This language is hardly consistent with Adler's "deep-seated fear of executive power." It is, however, consistent with the larger theme of *The Federalist*, which can be interpreted as a deep reflection on the strengths and weaknesses of republican government and as a prescription for addressing the latter.

In fact, the framers did not believe that tyranny was a danger restricted to the executive branch. Madison states in *Federalist* No. 47 that "the accumulation of all powers, legislative, executive, and judiciary, in the same hands, whether of one, a few, or many, and whether hereditary, self-appointed, or elective, may justly be pronounced the very definition of tyranny."[20] Tyranny, then, is not simply the old Aristotelian model of rule by one in his selfish interest, which is what motivated the colonists to revolt.[21] Madison redefines tyranny to include any combination of rulers (Aristotle's one, few, or many) who control all the functions of government. Even the elected representatives of the people in the legislature can become tyrannical, as Madison notes, citing Jefferson's remark that despotism by a body of 173 (the size of the Virginia state legislature) is still despotism.[22] The fear of tyranny includes legislative usurpation and legislative unilateralism.[23] The core argument of this sequence of papers by Madison explains how the checks and balances system, coupled with the personal motives—typically ambition—that accompany all those who seek political power, work together to prevent any single branch from becoming tyrannical.

It is worth emphasizing the extent to which Madison thought it necessary to constrain the legislature. In the very paragraph Berger cites to make the case for legislative supremacy, Madison essentially argues that the stronger checks should be placed on this naturally strongest branch. One of the reasons for a bicameral legislature with two chambers structured quite differently from each other is to "guard against dangerous encroachments" by this branch of government, most likely against the executive. Counterintuitively by modern standards, Madison describes the executive in this case as marked by "weakness."[24] While Madison defends popular election of the House for ensuring that its members would "have an immediate dependence on, and an intimate sympathy with, the people," he also argues that lengthy terms in the Senate would make that body "an anchor against popular fluctuations" by blending stability with liberty.[25] Hamilton's later discussion of term length in the presidency mirrors Madison by arguing that the people "sometimes err," and when they do "it is the duty of the persons whom they have appointed to be the guardians of those interests to withstand the temporary delusion in order to give them time and opportunity for more cool and sedate reflection."[26] It would seem that the constitutional order requires something more than simply responding to the popular will. The argument of congressional supremacy misunderstands the framers' fear of tyranny as something focused specifically on the executive, when in fact it is concerned with any branch that usurps the functions of another branch.

The second fundamental problem with the argument of congressional supremacy lies with the authors' understanding of the separation of powers system. This confusion is seen in their tendency to conflate checks and balances with separation of powers, as though the two doctrines perform the same function in the constitutional system. Fisher complains that the flow of power to the presidency since World War II has come at the cost of "the checks and balances and separation of powers that the framers knew were essential to protect individual rights and liberties." Adler argues that the purpose of checks and balances is to serve as a constraint on "executive unilateralism" and that the purpose of separation of powers is to "preserve the Constitution's enumeration of powers against acts of usurpation"—essentially the same function. While it is true that a principal function of checks and balances is to protect the republic against tyranny—from all branches, not just the executive, as demonstrated above —the doctrine of separation of powers has the additional function of providing for more effective governance.[27]

One of the reasons why scholars tend to conflate these two doctrines may be the influence of Richard Neustadt's observation that the Constitution "created a government of separated institutions *sharing* powers." He goes on in an endnote to equate "power" with influence and "powers" with formal authority.[28] That distinction masks the fact that the framers believed that power comes in different types. Even as Madison expresses concern about the "encroaching nature" of power in general, he goes on to talk about "the several classes of power, as they may in their nature be legislative, executive, or judiciary." In talking about the danger of tyranny, Madison makes reference to the existence of legislative powers, executive powers, and judicial powers—and then warns against "a gradual concentration of the several powers in the same department."[29] Rather than thinking of these powers as general political influence or government authority, it is clearer to think of them as functions. Thus, the doctrine of separation of powers concerns itself with separating the various functions of government into different groups of officials.

Jeffrey Tulis summarizes this dynamic, explaining that the separation of powers provides for several different objectives of republican government.[30] Congressional supremacists have highlighted two of these objectives: responsiveness to the popular will and the protection of rights and liberties. In their zeal to subordinate the presidency to Congress they implicitly highlight a third: steady administration of the laws. What they ignore is the requirement for government to ensure the security and stability of the nation. All of these objectives were important matters of deliberation at the Constitutional Convention and the ratification debates. All are essential for effective republican government. They are also in tension with one another.

Congressional supremacists seem most concerned with how security claims by the executive could trump responsiveness or individual liberty. They ignore the possibility that democratic responsiveness itself can run roughshod over individual liberty, that a single-minded focus on liberty might sacrifice democratic responsiveness, and that an exaggerated concern for liberty or responsiveness might come at the expense of security. Security should not come at the total expense of democracy or liberty any more than liberty should come at the total expense of democracy or security or democracy at the total expense of liberty and security. The framers understood the importance of responsiveness and liberty, but, given their experience under the Articles of Confederation, they also understood the need for security and stability. The elevation of any one of these objectives over the others distorts the constitutional structure—a structure designed in part to regulate the natural tension that exists among these objectives. The framers did not privilege one function at the expense of others—all are necessary for effective republican government.[31]

The principal constitutional mechanism for promoting these different objectives of republican government is the structure of the different branches. Congress, for example, has as its primary concern representing the people and enacting policies in response to the popular will, as that will is refined and modified through the deliberative process. Congress is equipped to accomplish these goals through its plural structure and different levels of electoral accountability. That is to say, it is composed of many representatives who represent citizens in different ways through a complex system of frequent and staggered elections. Similarly, the federal judiciary has as its primary concern interpreting the law in cases and controversies, with a special mission to protect our rights and liberties from the tyranny of government or from the excesses of democratic majorities. Thus, the Court is a small body of learned experts who have job security that enables them to interpret the law dispassionately and indifferently.

According to Hamilton, the function of the executive consists of "the execution of the laws and the employment of the common strength, either for this purpose or for the common defense."[32] The presidency is designed to ensure the security and stability of the nation. The chief executive wears the dual hats of leader and clerk. In his leadership capacity, the president sets and clarifies goals and reacts to crises. In his clerkship capacity, the president pursues steady administration of the law.[33] As with the other two branches, the presidency is structured to provide these important objectives. The framers believed that the president had to possess the quality of energy to be able to act effectively in these areas and that the only way to give the office that energy was to make the institution a unitary office, composed of one person. The importance of energy in the constitutional system, often branded a Hamiltonian obsession, cannot be overstated. In the Federalist papers it was Madison who earlier underlined its importance to the system as a whole, writing in *Federalist* No. 37 that "energy in government is essential to that security against external and internal danger and to that prompt and salutary execution of the laws which enter into the very definition of good government." He follows that statement by making a similarly strong argument for the importance of "stability in government."[34] Hamilton provided the most famous statement of this principle, arguing in *Federalist* No. 70 that energy in the executive is "essential to the protection of the community against foreign attacks; it is not less essential to the steady administration of the laws; to the protection of property . . . to the security of liberty against the enterprises and assaults of ambition, of faction, and of anarchy."[35] Thus the presidency would not only ensure security and stability but also help to protect rights and liberties.

What, then, does the unitary executive branch provide to the republic that the other branches do not? Important qualities include "decision, activity, secrecy, and dispatch." "Promptitude of decision," "vigor," and "expedition" help constitute "the bulwark of the national security."[36] In the area of foreign affairs, specifically in negotiating treaties, John Jay favored the qualities of "secrecy and dispatch," found in the unitary presidency, not in the Senate (and even less in the House).[37] Hamilton's take on foreign affairs is quite similar. Rejecting the argument that the most democratic institution—the House—should share in the treaty-making process, he highlights the importance of an "accurate and comprehensive knowledge of foreign politics; a steady and systematic adherence to the same views; a nice and uniform sensibility to national character; decision, *secrecy*, and dispatch."[38] While some of these qualities may reside in the Senate, the focal point of the discussion is the structural qualities of the presidency that make it superior to the other branches in providing essential features to the constitutional system. Those features could be summarized as the ability to act swiftly, steadily, and even secretly. Plural institutions like legislatures are simply not structured to provide these qualities.

This argument should help put to rest the remaining propositions of the congressional supremacy camp. Common to Berger, Fisher, and Adler is their agreement with Roger Sherman that the presidency is "nothing more than an institution for carrying the will of the Legislature into effect." Sherman's remark was made quite early in the convention debate —June 1—before the argument over the nature of the executive branch had matured.[39] By contrast, it seems clear that the primary purpose of the executive is not simply to serve as the subordinate junior partner to Congress. Madison repudiates this notion in *Federalist* No. 51, when he describes the importance of separating the "distinct exercise of the different powers of government" in part by giving each branch "a will of its own"; and Hamilton insists that "it is certainly desirable that the executive should be in a situation to dare to act his own opinion with vigor and decision."[40] The framers intended each branch to be as independent of each other as practicable to allow them to perform their separate functions as effectively as possible. Thus, the presidency is not designed simply to carry out Congress's will but also to exercise appropriate authority in its own realm.

The concern for rights and liberties is a valid one but not at the expense or ignorance of security and stability. Indeed, the conflict presented by the choice between a republican model and an executive-centered model is a false dichotomy. There is nothing incompatible about an energetic executive operating in a republican system. One does not have to choose one or the other. One of the great accomplishments of the framers was to strengthen republican government with the addition of a properly structured and empowered presidency.[41] In a sense, the constitutional system represents the modern fulfillment of the ancient political form known as a mixed regime. Described most completely by such thinkers as Polybius and Cicero, this form of the state found a way to blend the virtues of monarchy described by Aristotle with the benefits of aristocracy and democracy. Adler properly notes that in republican government the "wisdom of the many was superior to the judgment of one," but that evaluation is best applied to the deliberative function of Congress, a plural entity, as it seeks to be responsive to the popular will. There remains in the American system a "wisdom of one" operable in other arenas that concern the presidency. Congress may have certain needs to be able to carry out its functions—but so does the president.

Thus, the congressional supremacists have a historically and philosophically inaccurate understanding of the framers' fear of tyranny, which was focused not solely on the executive branch but on all branches of government. They also have a deficient understanding of the separation of powers system, which creates independent branches of government that retain their own primary areas of concern and which arms each branch with the capability of fulfilling different and sometimes competing objectives of republican government. Included in those qualities specific to the presidency is "secrecy." It is now time to return to the question of executive privilege to see how it should be incorporated in this constitutional system.

Leadership, Clerkship, and Secrecy

In discussing the separation of powers system, I made reference to the president's dual roles as leader and clerk. Proponents of a strong presidency, such as Richard Neustadt, often emphasize the president's leadership role at the expense of his clerkship role. Proponents of congressional supremacy, as demonstrated above, emphasize the president's clerkship role at the expense of his leadership role. This phenomenon is understandable, for as Herbert Storing argued, the energetic executive and rule of law "are, in practice and in principle, in tension." Storing argues that this tension is inevitable and unavoidable—it is sewn into the very fabric of a constitutional system that tries to grant simultaneously all necessary power while also limiting it.[42] In his analysis of Charles Thach Jr.'s book *The Creation of the Presidency, 1775–1789*, Storing highlights the divergent views of the presidential functions represented by the terms "leadership" and "clerkship." Both functions require an energetic executive but also give rise to different visions of the president's relationship with Congress. On the one hand, the presidency's leadership function was designed in part to check a strong legislature, a role that implies true independence and equality. On the other hand, the presidency's clerkship function was designed to serve the nation through a more effective administration of the laws passed by Congress, a role that implies subordination. As Storing argues, "the beginning of wisdom about the American presidency is to see that it contains both principles and to reflect on their complex and subtle relation."[43]

Under his dual hats of leader and clerk, the president performs several tasks peculiar to his branch, empowered by the fact that he is a unitary institution endowed with energy, given specific powers and duties by Article II of the Constitution. As a leader, the president sets the national agenda. To pursue leadership through agenda-setting, the president gives information to Congress on the state of the union and recommends legislation for its consideration. We see a hint of this in Hamilton's discussion of a president undertaking "extensive and arduous enterprises for the public benefit."[44] As a leader, the president also responds to crises. To pursue leadership in such a scenario, the president is given the job of commander in chief of the armed services. His ability to make treaties with foreign countries and receive ambassadors expands this area of action to the larger arena of foreign policy. His oath of office makes explicit his duty to "preserve, protect and defend the Constitution of the United States," certainly a task of leadership. As a clerk, by contrast, the president pursues steady administration of the law. To pursue this clerkship function, the president has the power to staff and manage the executive branch and is charged to take care that the laws be faithfully executed. While there is no question that many aspects of the modern presidency appear quite different, even expanded, from its eighteenth-century counterpart, the structure of the Constitution seems to contain what Erwin Hargrove and Michael Nelson refer to as a "genetic code" for this development, making the question of secrecy in these roles time-less.[45]

This understanding of the president's function in the constitutional system helps clarify the place of secrecy in the executive branch, highlighting where it is most appropriate and where it is most questionable. When performing his leadership function, the president operates in a status of independence and equality with respect to Congress, and it is here that secrecy is a most critical quality. The obvious arena in which secrecy plays a part is when the president performs the role of crisis manager and chief diplomat. In modern parlance, this arena concerns national security. If secrecy and speed are qualities essential to effective national security, and one of the president's principal duties is ensuring the security of the nation, it stands to reason that secrecy and speed are integral features of a properly functioning executive branch. Indeed, as seen above, the framers designed the presidency as an institution with precisely these qualities in mind. Congress, as a plural institution designed to engage in lengthy and open deliberation about the merits of proposed legislation, is singularly unqualified in this area.

One does not have to go so far as to argue that the president's powers in this arena are "plenary and exclusive" to still acknowledge that he is the principal active agent when it comes to foreign policy and national security.[46] It would not take long to construct scenarios where speed and secrecy are essential to success in the military and diplomatic field, and where untimely public disclosure would greatly impair—perhaps even destroy—the goal of ensuring the security of the nation. Whether the issue is the precise timing of an impending military action, the implementation of a covert special operation, the protection of intelligence sources, or the negotiation of delicate diplomatic matters—all of these situations are tailor-made for executive branch action.[47] There have been any number of specific examples in American history, and certainly the rapidity and lethality of modern warfare make the wise employment of secrecy and speed that much more imperative.[48]

Secrecy also has a place when the president as leader performs the role of agenda-setter. Again, the president as leader is independent and equal in status to Congress. True, his role in the lawmaking process is carefully defined in the Constitution as primarily goal-setting and vetoing legislation. It is important to understand, however, that the different roles Congress and the presidency play in this process lead to different types of activities. Congress plays its part in the lawmaking process by deliberating in public, allowing citizens to see laws as they develop. This is wholly appropriate in a branch whose primary purpose is to make policy in response to the popular will. Often these policies originate in the executive branch. The president may outline a legislative agenda in his State of the Union address or recommend specific legislation to Congress, as per his Article II responsibilities.

While the president as leader may set a national agenda, Congress is not obligated to act on or fulfill that agenda. Congress may pursue the president's agenda, alter it, reorder it, or ignore it. As the function itself implies, the president's leadership role here is merely a starting point for the much longer deliberative process. What is important and relevant to Congress is the agenda itself. It is the actual finished product from the executive branch that Congress must wrestle with. The process by which the president constructed his agenda is a purely internal matter. The president may have come up with the policy in his own mind. He may have constructed it based on heavy input from his closest advisors. He may simply have signed off on a policy created in the bureaucracy. Whatever the precise procedure, the public part of it comes when he announces the agenda. The expectation in lawmaking is that Congress will act in public. The constitutionally sanctioned phase of the president's participation is his presentment of his policy to Congress, whether in a speech or a specific legislative recommendation. The preparation of that agenda is a purely executive matter.

Secrecy is important in this agenda-setting role because the president requires candid advice from his subordinates. Such qualities as the open exchange of ideas and the ability to brainstorm imaginatively would be greatly harmed, even eliminated, if executive branch officials knew that the substance of their conversations would be on the front page of the *New York Times* the next day. The framers themselves, of course, understood the importance of these qualities, which is why they conducted the Constitutional Convention in secret. That way, the delegates were free to explore fully all options without fear of political embarrassment or retribution. Similarly, presidents pondering the agenda they plan to submit to Congress ought to receive the full range of advice from aides and experts, however controversial or unpopular.

The need to ensure the confidentiality of internal White House deliberations extends beyond agenda-setting to crisis management, managing an ongoing war effort, and settling on a negotiation strategy with a foreign nation. For all of these activities the president needs frank and honest advice; and if that advice is not privileged, it may not be frank and honest. Secrecy, therefore, is an essential part of this dynamic.[49] Indeed, it would seem that secrecy is the defining quality of what we might call the deliberative and active part of leadership.

Secrecy in the deliberative role of Congress runs contrary to the constitutional design of open and public lawmaking. Secrecy in the deliberative process of a branch designed to perform a completely different role is wholly appropriate. Just as Supreme Court justices deliberate in secret in large part because they are not engaging in an essentially democratic process—the act of interpreting the Constitution is supposed to be sheltered from popular opinion—so the president deliberates in secret as he performs roles that either are not purely democratic (ensuring the security of the nation) or represent only the beginning of the democratic process (setting the national agenda).[50]

If secrecy is most important when it serves the president's leadership function, it would seem that it is most open to question when the president performs his clerkship function of administering the laws. The president as clerk operates in a role more subordinate to, rather than independent of, Congress. Although he has a tremendous amount of discretionary power due to the resources at his disposal, the essence of the president's administrative role is to take care that the laws are faithfully executed. Duly passed laws become his responsibility to execute. Roger Sherman was right that the presidency is "an institution for carrying the will of the Legislature into effect," but he was wrong to say that the presidency was "nothing more" than this. As leader, the president is more than a clerk, but as clerk, the president responds to the will of Congress. And that response should be an energetic one. It is important to recall that one of the impetuses for the Constitutional Convention was an ineffective administrative system under the Articles of Confederation. Hamilton argues in *Federalist* No. 70 that qualities like speed and energy are often negative characteristics in legislatures, but they are essential once legislation is complete and execution takes over. The qualities that give the presidency the capability of exercising effective leadership also serve to enable him to exercise effective clerkship.[51] Nevertheless, because Congress clearly has an interest in ensuring that its laws are, in fact, faithfully executed, it is in this arena that secrecy claims are more suspect.

Space does not permit a full history of executive privilege claims, and that history has been better told elsewhere. History makes clear, from authorities as divergent as Hamilton and Jefferson, that the president may withhold information from Congress when it is in the public interest or when it concerns primarily executive functions.[52] The analysis of leadership and clerkship functions, however, allows us to evaluate modern claims to secrecy in a more constitutionally grounded light.

Because a president's secrecy claim is strongest when he performs his leadership functions, here he should enjoy significant deference. Yet often Congress is far from deferential. During the investigation of the Iran-Contra scandal, for example, Congress sought access to President Reagan's personal diaries. After some resistance, the administration gave in to Congress's demand. It is difficult to imagine a case that involves a clearer example of purely internal deliberations than the president's own thoughts and personal assessments, but as Rozell points out, the typical pattern of the Reagan presidency was to claim privilege before eventually giving in. Similarly, in early 1991, House Democrats sought from the George H. W. Bush administration specific information connected with the build-up to the Persian Gulf War, including assessments of Iraqi and American strengths and weaknesses, diplomatic memoranda, and budgetary analyses. After initial refusal, President Bush backed down.

By contrast, in 1996 Congress tried to gain access to White House documents concerning American foreign policy in Haiti. President Clinton was willing to turn over a few of the documents but successfully invoked executive privilege for forty-seven others, arguing that disclosure "would inhibit the candid discussion that he must have with foreign leaders" and "interfere with the deliberative and analytic processes within the White House that are essential to the formulation of our foreign policy."[53] Also, in the wake of the devastating Hurricane Katrina in 2005, members of Congress sought and received from the George W. Bush administration hundreds of thousands of pages of documents and testimony from a variety of officials concerning the federal government's response to that disaster. Dissatisfied with that response, congressional Democrats wanted more, prompting the White House to state that it would deny requests for e-mail and other correspondence among top officials.[54] The administration prevailed. Finally, in June 2007 the Senate Judiciary Committee issued a subpoena for internal documents concerning the National Security Agency's warrantless wiretap program. Established in secret after 9/11 to monitor domestic-to-international communications, the program was regularly reauthorized by President Bush as part of the war on terror. Congress argued that it needed access to documents spelling out the legal justification of the controversial program in order to more effectively amend the pertinent statute. Although the administration provided Congress with volumes of records concerning the program, it set up a confrontation with Congress by claiming that a number of classified documents concerned issues of national security.[55] Thus, Congress's law-making role conflicted with the president's concern for national security.

All of these cases involved national security or crisis management in which secrecy might legitimately trump competing values. The controversy over the warrantless wiretap program is particularly difficult to resolve. An unconventional and open-ended war on terror requires the executive branch to take unusual measures to safeguard the security and stability of the nation, but it also requires both Congress and the president to consider carefully how to adjust laws concerning intelligence gathering for contemporary threats. The inaccessibility of certain documents does not prevent Congress from pursuing legislation altering a national security program to conform to its own vision of legality, but the president will understandably safeguard aspects of the formulation of this policy that he considers sensitive. As time moves on, the claim to secrecy may diminish, but the calculus for determining when documents should be open to public scrutiny involves questions of prudence best left to the political branches.

Presidential claims to secrecy when engaged in the agenda-setting function should also enjoy greater deference. Often these claims involve requests by Congress for documents written by nominees for high office when they worked in the White House, usually involving policy or legal analyses. For example, when President Reagan elevated Supreme Court Justice William Rehnquist to chief justice in 1986, the Senate Judiciary Committee sought documents Rehnquist had written as head of the Office of Legal Counsel under President Richard Nixon. Because those documents included confidential legal advice, Reagan chose to invoke executive privilege. When the Judiciary Committee insisted, Reagan backed down rather than force a fight.[56] A similar dynamic took place in 2005. First, President George W. Bush nominated Circuit Court Judge John Roberts to replace Sandra Day O'Connor on the Supreme Court. Senate Democrats wanted access to documents written by Roberts during his tenure on the attorney general's staff (1981–82), in the White House counsel's office (1982–86), and in the solicitor general's office (1989–93). The Bush White House chose to release seventy-five thousand pages of documents from the first two categories, while refusing to release documents from the third. Documents from Roberts's time in the attorney general's office had already been cleared for public release by the Clinton administration. Then, when Chief Justice Rehnquist died, Bush shifted Roberts to the chief justiceship and nominated White House counsel Harriet Miers for the O'Connor seat. Senators from both parties requested access to documents authored by Miers during her White House service. The White House refused and used the dispute to construct the pretext for her eventual withdrawal as nominee.[57] Despite Reagan's capitulation and the rather incongruous distinction in the Bush administration between Roberts's service in the White House counsel's office and the solicitor general's office, these are all examples of valid claims to candid advice.

One of the more controversial secrecy claims from the early Bush administration involved Vice President Richard Cheney's direction of a task force designed to develop the administration's energy policy. Following reports in the news media that industry groups had participated on the task force, two House Democrats requested information about the group's composition and activities. A complex tango ensued involving the GAO and an eventual court battle, which Cheney won. The central issues concerned that of Cheney's claim that the request interfered with the deliberative and policy development process in the executive branch and that of whether the vice president could claim a power normally employed by the president alone.[58] Based on the analysis above, however, the dispute does not seem so difficult to resolve. We should assume that the president granted the vice president authority to construct the administration's energy policy as part of the president's agenda-setting function. The most relevant aspect of that process for Congress is the final result—the actual energy policy proposed by the administration. As indicated above, nothing compels Congress to adopt the president's agenda, and it is entirely permissible for the administration to construct its agenda behind closed doors to protect the confidentiality of candid input. It may be that the administration "stacked the deck," so to speak, in one direction for its energy policy but presumably that would become clear to Congress once the policy was unveiled. Then Congress's deliberative process would begin and the various views about the merits of the policy would be aired. It is unclear what concern Congress should have about how the policy was developed. That is the business of the executive branch.

There are numerous examples of more problematic claims to executive privilege, which stem either from the president's clerkship function or from his desire to protect himself from investigation. Early in the Reagan administration, for example, Congress investigated the Mineral Lands Leasing Act and the enforcement of hazardous waste laws. Both cases involved attempts by Congress to acquire documents related to the implementation and enforcement of these laws, resistance by the administration based on the need to protect confidentiality and the national interest, and eventual capitulation by the administration in the face of mounting political pressure.[59] Although certain aspects of the initial privilege claims may have contained valid White House concerns, the fact that these efforts involved the administration of duly passed laws placed the president in a more subordinate position to Congress than he would be when exercising leadership functions. Just as problematic were early efforts by the George W. Bush administration to expand the scope of executive privilege. Late in 2001 the administration blocked access by Congress to Department of Justice records on closed criminal investigations, which seemingly had no significant connection to national security or agenda-setting concerns. Earlier that year, the Bush administration issued an executive order that allowed former presidents to assert executive privilege over their own papers, even if the sitting president disagrees, and allowing sitting presidents to claim executive privilege over former administration papers even if the former president disagrees.[60] Again, the connection to leadership functions was unclear. Finally, as the Nixon case ably demonstrates, presidents may resort to secrecy not to protect national security or agenda-setting but to protect themselves in a criminal investigation. President Clinton used executive privilege often in an attempt to hamper the independent counsel's investigation of various scandals in his presidency.[61] The attempt to protect himself from the consequences of a sex scandal was unconnected to larger national security and agenda-setting concerns. In fact, one could argue that Clinton's use of executive privilege involved his clerkship function to enforce the law, which is the arena least open to secrecy claims. The maneuvering over the CIA leak case raised similar suspicions during the Bush presidency.

Several of President George W. Bush's formal claims of executive privilege involved his clerkship function. Three times in the summer of 2007, following congressional subpoenas for documents and testimony concerning the 2006 firing of several federal prosecutors, White House resistance led to further subpoenas and votes of contempt of Congress. Allegations that the firings were politically motivated gave Congress solid reasons to investigate this incident, especially since it involved questions of the steady administration of the law. Because bureaucratic agencies are accountable both to Congress and the president, as well as the Constitution, Congress has a legitimate interest in how those agencies perform their tasks. That interest may include whether decisions made by the president run contrary to established norms or are unusually partisan by historical standards. The White House denied that President Bush was involved in the decision, so it was at first unclear why executive privilege should be invoked. Counterbalancing that argument, however, is the constitutional fact that the president can fire U.S. attorneys and many other federal officials (such as cabinet secretaries) for any reason he chooses. Although staffing the executive branch is in part a clerkship function, it happens to be one where the president enjoys wide discretion. The fact that the internal deliberations took place away from the president's purview does not diminish his constitutional role—and ultimate responsibility. Facing no charges of criminality, the administration admitted that it handled the case poorly and offered alternative settings for informal testimony. Legal maneuverings at the Bush White House pushed back a confrontation with Congress into the next administration.[62]

Limits to Executive Privilege

Having made the principled case for executive privilege and explained where it is most appropriate, we must acknowledge that presidents may be constitutionally unprincipled in their pursuit of their leadership and clerkship functions and may claim secrecy where it is constitutionally unwarranted. Both Rozell and Fisher warn that presidents have a tendency to withhold information more because it is embarrassing or politically damaging than because of a legitimate concern for the public interest.[63] If a president can construct a sound constitutional argument for a secrecy claim, his motive may be irrelevant. Unsound arguments, however, require other political actors to have a principled understanding of appropriate responses to this claim. Executive privilege is not an unlimited prerogative, even in the context of the president's leadership functions. In fact, there is an inherent tension in Hamilton's argument in *Federalist* No. 70 in favor of a unitary executive. On the one hand, Hamilton argues in favor of unity because it provides for an energetic executive who can employ a variety of qualities, including secrecy. On the other hand, he argues that the presidency's unitary quality allows the public and other political branches to hold the president responsible for his actions. Because the office is held by one person, it is more difficult for the president to shift blame and avoid accountability.[64] In Truman's words, "The buck stops here." Of course, one of the things people need to hold the president responsible is information, and the ability of the president to keep secrets can create problems for ensuring accountability.

Thus, it is quite possible that Congress will have a legitimate claim for information even when the president's privilege claim is strong. For example, it may be in the public interest for Congress to investigate executive branch failure in its crisis management capacity or executive branch malfeasance in its agenda-setting capacity. The inherent tension between liberty and security in the post-9/11 world is not always easily or obviously resolvable. A casual glance at modern privilege claims, covered exhaustively in

Rozell's book on the subject, demonstrates that such claims often fall into the weakest category outlined above; but even congressional claims that touch on the president's leadership function may express legitimate concerns.

The solution to this dilemma does not lie in judicial review. The notion that the Supreme Court can function as a neutral arbiter between Congress and the presidency is fraught with all sorts of problems both practical and political. Justices, for example, may promote their own preferred political outcomes in adjudicating such a dispute. Or they may respond to an energized public pushing one way or the other. In some cases they may refrain from ruling against the president out of fear that the executive may ignore its demands and that Congress will fail to back them up, perhaps through impeachment. Taking sides in such heated and often partisan controversies could very well undermine the Court's legitimacy in the public eye, thus jeopardizing the very neutrality that fans of judicial review prize.[65] But perhaps most fundamentally, in many executive privilege controversies both Congress and the presidency make legitimate claims, and there is no rule of law, but only political prudence and wise judgment, that can determine which claim better advances the public interest. The members of the U.S. Supreme Court, and federal judges more generally, have no particular claim on such prudence and judgment.

Instead, the healthiest way to resolve executive privilege disputes is through the very separation of powers system that created it. Madison states that none of the branches of government "can pretend to an exclusive or superior right of settling the boundaries between their respective powers," a judgment that includes the Court.[66] Then, in the climax to his argument against tyranny by any branch of government, Madison argues that the solution to such conflicts lies in "contriving the interior structure of the government" so that "its several constituent parts may, by their mutual relations, be the means to keeping each other in their proper places." Indeed, the "great security against a gradual concentration of the several powers in the same department consists in giving to those who administer each department the necessary constitutional means and personal motives to resist encroachments of the others . . . Ambition must be made to counteract ambition."[67] The framers believed that it would be natural for the branches to encroach upon each other's powers and prerogatives and that the mutual self-interest involved in protecting their rights and powers would compel them to resist such encroachment. In this case, the president's desire to withhold information will run up against Congress's desire to perform its tasks.

Congress has numerous checks on the president's powers that it can employ in its quest for information. It has the power to legislate, including funding or cutting off funds for government operations and programs. It has the power to block the president's agenda. Through its advice and consent role, the Senate can refuse to confirm presidential nominations in a timely manner.[68] Finally, if pushed too far, Congress can employ the ultimate check, impeachment.[69] Presumably, this interbranch dynamic will be driven by each branch's judgment of the importance of its position. If one of the branches wants something badly enough, it will use its political resources to full effect. Such disputes need not result in a destructive collision, however, if both branches retain a fuller understanding of the range of legitimate claims each branch may make.

Just as the president should not deny Congress information it needs to function properly, so should Congress not seek to use its powers to cripple the presidency. A healthier system of conflict resolution would involve the different branches recognizing each other's proper constitutional roles and tailoring their efforts accordingly. Absent this mutual respect for competing legitimate claims, congressional demands for information are likely to push the political system toward a doctrine of legislative supremacy, a situation as full of problems as that of the imperial presidency.

Ultimately, the most important check on presidential abuse of executive privilege may be found in the very structure of the office—its unitary character. As stated above, Hamilton argues that one sound reason for a unitary executive branch is the fact that it can be held responsible for its actions more readily than a plural executive. If, for example, Congress cannot get the information it wants and needs from a unitary executive, it can in the end threaten impeachment.[70] However, Hamilton also mentions "the restraints of public opinion that increase in efficacy when the executive is a single individual.[71] In the midst of a heated contest with Congress, this most visible of political actors will have to make its case for secrecy and that case will be evaluated by the people. Since the American people tend to be suspicious of secretive elites, the president's arguments, for the sake of his own reputation and legacy, as well as his political health, will have to prove convincing. John Locke understood this point long ago, for in his discussion of prerogative power he argued that the people would be the ultimate judge as to whether executive power was used for good or for ill.[72] These constitutional and political considerations should prove—and to date largely have proved—to be sufficient to moderate disputes over secrecy in the executive.

CHAPTER TEN

Impeachment in the Constitutional Order

JEFFREY K. TULIS

N O PRESIDENT OF THE United States has ever been convicted and removed from office as a result of an impeachment proceeding. Andrew Johnson was impeached by the House of Representatives but escaped conviction by one vote in the Senate. Richard Nixon resigned before he would have been impeached, and Bill Clinton beat House impeachment charges with substantial support in the Senate and in the country at large. What role does impeachment play and what role should impeachment play in a political system that has so rarely enacted, and has never completed, this process for punishing a president? Is impeachment an anachronism in a political order that has no real use for it? Or is the impeachment process a superfluous organ in the constitutional order, like an appendix in a human being, which may occasionally become inflamed but performs no important function for the health of the body? In this chapter, I show how and why the impeachment process, far from politically irrelevant, is a vital attribute of the theoretical architecture of a well-functioning separation of powers regime. The American pattern of disuse of the impeachment process may thus be a symptom of a serious problem in a constitutional order animated by separation of powers.

The Legalistic Interpretation

At least since the presidency of Andrew Johnson, political elites and the citizenry at large have generally understood the impeachment process to be a legal process, like a criminal prosecution. The constitutional structure and the norms and practices devised to enact it give considerable support to this conventional view. In the text of the Constitution, the House of Representatives is given the "sole power" to impeach a president, and the Senate is given the "sole power" to try the executive.[1] These separate but complementary functions mirror those of a grand jury (with the power to indict), on the one hand, and that of a criminal trial, on the other.

The Congress has developed norms and institutional practices that amplify the grand jury–criminal trial analogy.[2] A committee of the House investigates allegations, with the aid of its own lawyers, and in recent times, after a report from a special prosecutor or independent counsel. If grounds for impeachment are found, the committee recommends articles to the House, which votes on them one by one. This process corresponds to the generation of "counts" or "charges" in ordinary criminal proceedings. On the floor of the House, according to its rules, members can add, amend, or drop articles proposed by the committee, but in practice they have never added any, although they have dropped some. Again, there seems to be a close analogy to a typical grand jury proceeding. If articles of impeachment are approved by the whole House, "managers" are appointed to present the case to the Senate. Managers seem to serve a function analogous to prosecutors in a criminal trial.

If these articles are sent to the Senate, according to the Constitution itself, Senators are required to take a new oath, one additional to their oath of office.[3] Following this constitutional mandate the Senate has adopted the pledge "to do impartial justice according to the Constitution and the laws." By taking a new oath, the Senate attempts to recompose itself into a new body, a jury. The Senators signify that although they are the same individuals, they will act differently than they ordinarily do. Collectively, they are pledging to change the culture and function of the Senate as a whole. This institutional shift is reinforced by the presence of the chief justice of the United States, to whom the Constitution explicitly gives the task of presiding over the trial of a president (but not other officials). The Senate is recomposed as a trial jury and the normal leadership of the Senate (the vice president of the United States and other majority and minority leaders) lose their function and are replaced by a justice who serves as the trial's judge. The Senate is being asked to transform itself from a legislative body into a different entity, one with a judicial character.

In establishing the judiciary, the Constitution provides that "the trial of all Crimes, except in Cases of Impeachment, shall be by jury."[4] This seems to equate impeachable offenses with crimes. What sorts of crimes must these be? The offenses specified in the Constitution are these: "Treason, Bribery, or other High Crimes and Misdemeanors."[5] All of the offenses seem to be a subset of categories familiar to criminal law, crimes and misdemeanors. The history of the impeachment of presidents is largely a history of debate regarding the meaning of "other high crimes and misdemeanors." There was relatively little discussion of this phrase when the Constitution was drafted. George Mason had proposed to add "maladministration" to the offenses of treason and bribery. Reflecting hesitations and concerns expressed during the larger debate about assigning impeachment to the legislature, Madison objected that "maladministration" might suggest that the presidency served at the pleasure of the legislature rather than being an independent branch as the convention intended. Gouverneur Morris added that the electoral process is sufficient security against maladministration. Mason withdrew "maladministration" and replaced it with "other high crimes and misdemeanors." Although there is little discussion of the phrase in the convention notes, most commentators reasonably interpret this substitution as indicating that the president was not to be removed for mere partisan differences with the legislature. The rejection of the term "maladministration" is a central element of the legalist understanding of the impeachment process.[6]

Are "high crimes and misdemeanors" acts for which ordinary citizens might also be prosecuted, such as perjury, or murder, or tax evasion? Should the evaluation of evidence of these acts be similar to the evaluation of similar acts performed by ordinary citizens in ordinary criminal courts? The plain language of the text—language not technical but understandable on its face to ordinary citizens—seems to say yes. While the phrase appears to exclude some ordinary crimes in favor of "high crimes," legalists emphasize the idea that the offenses must be some subset of offenses comprehended by criminal codes. This legalistic view has prevailed in Senate debates regarding presidential misconduct since the time of Andrew Johnson.

It is a commonplace among historians that the motive for Andrew Johnson's impeachment was anger by the dominant political faction in Congress, the "Radical Republicans," over the president's refusal to support or to implement their domestic agenda for Reconstruction.[7] However, none of the ten articles of impeachment refers to the underlying policy debate that occasioned them. Johnson and his supporters convinced

Congress that the president could only be impeached for clear violations of law and that these violations needed to be definable as "treason, bribery, or other high crimes and misdemeanors." Conceding the president's premise, the Congress passed a law that secured the tenure of officers of the government until their replacements were confirmed by the Senate. This Tenure of Office Act thus had the effect of altering the president's removal power. Since the first Congress, the Constitution had been interpreted as granting the president sole power to fire his high-level executive branch subordinates without the consent of the Senate even though he shared the power of their appointment with them. The Reconstruction Congress thus sought to legally hamstring Andrew Johnson by reinterpreting and legalizing the removal power. When Johnson attempted to fire his secretary of war, Edwin Stanton, for advocating and executing policies at odds with the president's, Congressional Republicans charged that the president had broken the law. The key point here is that rather than respond to Andrew Johnson's uses of power, which had been repeatedly contested in the fight over Reconstruction, the Congress struggled to find a "legal" violation to express their political disillusionment.

In the course of the battle over Reconstruction, Andrew Johnson violated a nineteenth-century norm against presidents speaking directly to the people to campaign for legislation. Johnson not only made popular speeches but his speech was also accurately described as a series of "harangues." Johnson called his opponents in Congress "traitors" and likened himself to Jesus Christ. Because this speechmaking was so out of line with accepted standards for the conduct of his office, the House voted an article of impeachment for his inappropriate rhetoric.[8] Johnson's supporters succeeded in getting the Senate to drop that article, not because of lack of evidence for the allegation, but rather because it represented a political, rather than a strictly legal, charge. By establishing the principle that "high crimes and misdemeanors" must refer to violations of law, Johnson narrowed the debate to charges for which his guilt was very questionable. It was not clear that Edwin Stanton, appointed by Abraham Lincoln, was covered by the new Tenure of Office Act, for example; the act itself was arguably unconstitutional in light of the interpretation of the First Congress and the seemingly settled constitutional practice since the presidency of George Washington.

Although Johnson's supporters succeeded in deflecting attention from his obstruction of Congressional will regarding Reconstruction, the Tenure of Office Act, which was invented to impeach him, did not establish a criminal offense. Succeeding in legalizing the process, Johnson's opponents failed to actually criminalize his alleged misdeeds and that failure contributed to his acquittal.

Richard Nixon was investigated for his role in a burglary attempt of the offices of the opposition Democratic Party in the Washington, D.C., building complex known as the Watergate during the election campaign of 1972. Although it has not been demonstrated that Nixon had a role in the direct planning or execution of the Watergate break-in, he was deeply involved in efforts to cover up the illegal actions of some of his subordinates. When the president lost a court case regarding his executive privilege to withhold evidence from the courts, and congressional committees began to discuss incontrovertible evidence of crimes of obstruction of justice, the president decided to resign rather than face impeachment and conviction. Although the case for impeachment depended upon the discovery of legal violations, deeper sources of criticism and anger toward the president had developed over the course of his administration because of disputes regarding his conduct of the war in Vietnam and his use of executive power more generally. A few years after Nixon's resignation, constitutional scholar Philip Kurland wrote a book entitled *Watergate and the Constitution*, which said nothing about Watergate, the break-in, and very little about obstruction of justice but instead reviewed the political disputes regarding executive privilege, executive agreements, impoundment of funds, and other uses of executive power that challenged congressional prerogatives.[9]

It is important to note here that the actual processes of investigation for impeachment did not bring these political issues to the center, but rather, faithful to the Andrew Johnson precedent, confined the case to strictly legal violations. Democrats certainly pressed hard for a broader definition of impeachable offense than Republicans were willing to accept. This prolonged debate in Congress and in the country at large resulted in a compromise that gained widespread consensus: while executive privilege, impoundment, and the use of other unilateral powers went unmentioned, the language of the articles of impeachment encased the criminal charges in a broader rhetoric that asserted the president had abused his office.

A fascinating complication arose after Republicans were successful in confining impeachable offenses to strictly legal violations. As it became clear that a majority of the nation would be persuaded that the president was guilty of impeachable offenses, Republicans pressed for a political understanding of the punishment. "If impeachable conduct—that is, conduct for which Congress may impeach—is analogized to a statutory offense, the 'political' discretion of Congress is analogous to prosecutorial discretion or to a power of mitigation or pardon which is lodged in the executive which defined the offense or the court which tried it." They urged their colleagues to consider politically contextual mitigating circumstances and "whether the best interests of the country would be served by his removal or continuance in office."[10] In other words, Republicans argued, although the president should not be impeached for political crimes, his legal violations should be assessed from a political perspective.

President Bill Clinton was investigated for allegations that he had violated law in handling real estate investments prior to his election to the presidency. In the course of this investigation, the independent counsel discovered evidence that the president had a sexual affair with a young intern in the White House and subsequently attempted to cover up this fact by deceiving litigants in a sexual harassment suit regarding his actions as governor of Arkansas. The independent counsel also charged that Clinton deceived the grand jury impaneled during the investigation. The impeachment charges presented to the Senate were crafted as violations of ordinary criminal law, for example, "perjury." Clinton and his supporters successfully convinced the House to ignore claims that he had diminished his "office" by his relationship with a young intern but instead to focus on his cover-up.[11] In addition to the precedent that impeachment required a "crime," Clinton's supporters stressed a distinction between private and public conduct. Consensual sex was not a "crime" and, on this view, it was also a private matter that was not the Congress's or the public's business. Because President Clinton knew that the prevailing standards for impeachment were narrow, strictly legal, violations, he took care to lie in ways that probably would not constitute "perjury." Perjury is not just a matter of lies but is a matter of lies provable in very technical ways.[12] Appealing to archaic linguistic conventions, Clinton made the plausible claim that not all inappropriate intimate acts were "sex." Clinton's artful dodges and unusual distinctions provided much material for late night talk show hosts and other comedy routines, but the president was able to take advantage of the fact that, like Andrew Johnson, his defense was very strong on strictly legal questions, such as whether he had committed perjury, and very weak on the questions whether he had committed sex with a young intern in the Oval Office, whether he had deceived the public about his conduct, and whether by his conduct and his deceits he had diminished his office.

The arguments and actions of Presidents Andrew Johnson, Richard Nixon, and Bill Clinton all evidence the fact that the understanding of presidential impeachment as a predominantly legal process is now deeply ingrained in our political culture. Most students of impeachment would add that these three presidential episodes also show the superiority of a legal conceptualization over a political interpretation. On this reasoning, ours is a democratic polity where changes of partisan regimes should be a matter of election, not impeachment. It is good that coalitions should not attempt to repair their partisan political losses by short-circuiting the electoral process. On this view, Andrew Johnson should not have been thrown out of office because of his differences over policy with legislators. Had Nixon not violated the law, he should not have been forced from office because of political differences with the party opposite in Congress. And Republicans angry at Bill Clinton's "liberal" political views, or distressed by his governing style, should not have been able to accomplish in a "trial" what they could not accomplish in an election. Even if the motivation to impeach a president is political, the necessity to find a strictly legal ground for removal from office makes it more likely that the grounds for removal will be nonpartisan and that the coalition for removal will be bipartisan. Ours is not a parliamentary regime, with votes of no confidence. Ours is a separation of powers regime where the independence of the executive is a prized virtue of the system. On this view, presidents cannot be removed from office by Congress for acts that would be the usual basis for judgment in a democratic election.

The legalistic interpretation would not be so dominant if there were not some truth to its core claims about constitutional text, logic, structure, and the lessons of past impeachment proceedings. Some truth is not the whole truth, however. It is the burden of this chapter to show how and why the conventional wisdom is, nevertheless, wrong about the most important attributes of the impeachment process.

The Political Interpretation

Let me begin by returning to many of the same facts discussed from the legalistic point of view. The Constitution does offer a kind of template for an analogy between the processes for impeachment and conviction and those of indictment and trial. But the framers and subsequent institutional designers did not need to analogize this relation. They could have adopted the exact terms we use for criminal proceedings. Articles of impeachment could have been "counts;" impeachment clauses could have included the term "indictment"; the Senate "trial" could have referred to "criminal trial;" House managers could have been called prosecutors, and so on. If it was the intention to make the impeachment process a species of legal processes, the Constitution and the institutional practices that elaborate it could easily have said so. Instead, by making the impeachment process analogous to criminal trials, the Constitution signals that the two processes are alike in some respects and different in others. To say that the process of removal of a president is like a criminal proceeding is also to say that it is not a criminal proceeding.

In my review of the mechanics of the impeachment process, I did not mention that the Constitution mandates a punishment for conviction, removal from office,[13] and it also limits the punishment to removal from office "and disqualification to hold any Office of honor, Trust or Profit under the United States."[14] Should the president commit a crime for which, for example, an ordinary citizen might be executed, such as murder, all that Congress must do if they convict him is remove the president from office and all the Congress can do is fire the president and disqualify him from holding another governmental position. These constitutional stipulations have been interpreted to also mean that Congress, at its discretion, could deny the president his pension. But Congress could not hang him.

Indeed, the Constitution indicates that "the Party convicted shall nevertheless be liable to Indictment, Trial, Judgment and Punishment, according to Law."[15] The process of impeachment and conviction is thus distinguished and separated from the legal process in the text of the Constitution. Put another way, the Constitution indicates that the constitutional protection against "double jeopardy" does not prevent the president from being convicted by the Senate and later tried and convicted by ordinary legal processes for the same criminal acts. This can only be true if the first proceeding, the impeachment process, does not terminate in a legal decision but rather something different, a political conclusion.

As noted earlier, I mentioned that in a presidential impeachment the chief justice of the United States presides over the Senate trial. While the justice is expected to assist the Senate by ruling on the admissibility of evidence, procedural fairness, and like matters, no technical rules of evidence apply and the Senate is free to overrule the chief justice by simple majority vote. Indeed, in the trial of President Clinton, the Senate leadership developed a set of procedural rules that took away much of the influence from the chief justice. Finally, conviction for any article of impeachment requires a vote of two-thirds of the Senators present, rather than the unanimity of all jurors, which is always required in jury trials in federal criminal cases (and is typically required in state criminal cases as well).

Why does the Constitution analogize impeachment to a criminal prosecution if it intends a political process rather than a legal one? Why offer and induce an elaborate array of legalistic pretenses instead of a more straightforward signification of a political process? The Constitution requires impeachment as part of its political processes at the same time that it intends that such politics not be politics as usual. Independence of the executive and a commitment to a separation of powers regime does mean that presidents do not serve at the mere pleasure of the legislature. But presidents are also accountable to the legislature as well as to the people more generally. To preserve "independence" and "accountability" at the same time is the difficult puzzle that impeachment was designed to solve. The core idea is that the pretense of legality would structure an extraordinary political process—a process more elevated and less partisan than ordinary politics. And at the same time that the elaborate pretenses of the Constitution elevate ordinary politics, they domesticate subversive or revolutionary politics. Benjamin Franklin praised the impeachment process as an institutional surrogate for assassination.[16]

The difficult constitutional puzzle of creating a political process that was more elevated than ordinary partisan politics was the context in which drafters and ratifiers wrestled with the phrase "high crimes and misdemeanors." Maladministration seemed to make the process too political in the ordinary partisan senses, while restriction to crimes such as treason and bribery was not political enough. At the time of the Philadelphia Constitutional Convention, impeachment charges were being crafted in England against the British governor of India Warren Hastings for political failures. Although his trial had not yet begun, the plan for impeachment and the shape of the charges were well known to delegates in Philadelphia. Before Mason moved to add "maladministration" to treason and bribery as impeachable offenses, he indicated that Hastings had not committed treason or bribery. He appealed to his colleagues' sense that Hastings had failed to live up to his duties and that they needed to include that kind of "offense" in the Constitution.[17] Whether maladministration or high crimes and misdemeanors, the phrase should capture the kinds of political failures charged of Warren Hastings.

By contrast, legalists read the phrase through later understandings of crimes and misdemeanors despite the fact, as Raoul Berger argues, the phrase "high crimes and misdemeanors" actually preceded the invention of "misdemeanors" as a legal term, stating: "At the time when the phrase 'high crimes and misdemeanors' is first met in the proceedings against the Earl of Suffolk in 1386, there was in fact no such crime as a 'misdemeanor.' Lesser crimes were prosecuted as 'trespasses' well into the sixteenth century, and only then were 'trespasses' supplanted by 'misdemeanors' as a category of ordinary crimes."[18] Berger shows that impeachment was invented in England to punish actions beyond those comprehended by ordinary criminal law, and the phrase "high crimes and misdemeanors" was invented to capture such acts. "[Impeachment] was 'essentially a political weapon.'"[19]

Peter Charles Hoffer and N. E. H. Hull argue that the Constitution's impeachment processes were not modeled on English precedents, as Berger argues, but instead represent a new republican device originally invented for the state governments in America.[20] However one resolves their dispute with Berger, all agree that the variety of sources of the phrase construct impeachment as a political process. This is shown clearly in the most comprehensive account of the background of this phrase in the Constitution, a study by Joseph M. Bessette and Gary J. Schmitt, where English precedent, state governmental practices, constitutional convention debates, and the discussion in the ratifying conventions all depict a political understanding of this phrase. Indeed, Bessette and Schmitt note, for those interested in "original intention," that some delegates meeting in the ratifying conventions, discussing the phrase without knowledge of the deliberations at Philadelphia because the minutes and notes of that proceeding were still secret, assumed that the phrase meant what we now know it replaced—"maladministration." Others included "malconduct," "misconduct," "mal-practices," "deviation from duty," "violation of duty," "great offenses," "acts of great injury to the community."[21] Bessette and Schmitt make a compelling case that all these formulations reflect the distinction between the powers and duties of the office, which they have detailed in their chapter for the present volume.

"High crimes and misdemeanors" comprehends not only violations of duty, including ordinary crimes, but much more. These sorts of offenses are political crimes in two senses: First, executive duties are not requirements of a legal code but of a Constitution. Second, assessing the welter of presidential acts in light of the executive's many duties requires a political interpretation sensitive to the competing considerations and priorities that characterize everyday political life. Thus, the same act might or might not be a "crime" depending on the surrounding political circumstances.

Because it was written in the midst of the investigation of President Clinton, Bessette and Schmitt spend a great deal of their effort examining the question whether impeachable offenses include private acts or whether they are limited to failures of more explicit governmental responsibilities. They suggest that executing the "office" includes refraining from actions that might undermine one's authority as an enforcer of law and mention previous impeachments of judges and other governmental officials whose charges included such acts as drunkenness. I would add that one cannot separate the private from the public acts of the president, especially because the structure of his office effaces that distinction in a way unlike that of any other governmental office in the United States. Unlike the Congress, for example, which goes on recess, executive power is in being all the time and is vested in the president of the United States. One might say that while presidents sleep, executive power never does. Presidents thus have a greater obligation than other governmental officers to conduct their "private" life in a way consistent with their constitutional duties.

Perhaps the keenest insight into the political nature of "high crimes and misdemeanors" is offered by Charles Black, who reminds us that there are many actions an ordinary citizen could take that would clearly be impeachable offenses by a president. Black offers the hypothetical example of a president who publicly announces that he will not appoint any Catholics to his cabinet.[22] There is nothing "illegal" about that outrageous pledge and an ordinary citizen could not be punished by law for advocating that policy, but could anyone doubt that the president would violate his oath (to support a Constitution that includes "no religious tests") and should be removed from office were he to clearly advocate such a policy whether he carried it out or not?

Treason and bribery are violations of law that are directly connected to the functioning of the state. Ordinary crimes, like burglary or murder, are prosecuted by the state because they threaten social order even if they are directed at particular individuals. Impeachable crimes appear not to be crimes directed at individuals with indirect social effects but rather are crimes directed at the state itself. Treason, for example, is a betrayal of one's country and bribery is an attempt to subvert the political order for personal advantage. Presidential violations of duty, captured in the ambiguous phrase "high crimes and misdemeanors," are offenses that subvert the Constitution by neglecting the duties of governance in some way—perhaps diminishing the presidency itself by inappropriate conduct, perhaps by thwarting Congress by failing to execute a thoroughly deliberated legislative will, or perhaps by gross failures of political judgment as a president takes risks, though risks induced by his place in the constitutional order.

There may be no better illustration of these offenses than President Andrew Johnson. Johnson refused to enforce many properly enacted laws, indeed laws that had been passed over his vetoes; he refused to spend money appropriated for congressionally constructed institutions; he pardoned countless Confederates who would not pledge allegiance to the United States according to the law; he seized and returned land to former slave owners that had been legally confiscated and distributed to slaves who had worked the land; he used patronage power to bully politicians throughout the nation to support his version of reconstruction; and in a formal message to Congress he threatened to use military force against Congress to protect his understanding of the Constitution.[23] Yet despite the violation of the president's fundamental constitutional responsibilities evidenced by these acts, Congress limited its impeachment charges, as we have seen, to the fairly narrow issue of legal violations.

It is striking how often impeachment is mentioned in the Constitution. It appears in six clauses and in each of the three articles structuring the major branches of government. Impeachment is so woven into the fabric of the Constitution that clause-bound readings of its meaning are but the preface to the best way to understand this extraordinary process. Andrew Johnson's political actions were impeachable not because some clause explicitly listed them as offenses, but because they threatened the very functioning of a separation of powers Constitution. It is in that larger design of separation of powers that the political character of the impeachment process is best revealed.

The Constitutional Design

Legal academics generally discuss the development of a separation of powers doctrine, designed and elaborated to confine specified constitutional powers to assigned institutions. Political scientists usually understand separation of powers as a form of checks and balances, noting that it is hard to theoretically demarcate legislative and executive power. Attention to the place of impeachment in the logic of separation of powers allows us to recover an older more capacious understanding.[24] This older understanding, which I sketch below, may have become unfamiliar because the practice of politics in America has departed from it over time, much as the process of impeachment has become legalized over time. But elements of the theoretical view of the constitutional order persist despite this attenuation in practice.

Both the legalistic and political views of separation of powers are better understood as facets of a larger conception at the core of which is contestation between competing desiderata of democratic governance. In ordinary political discourse, the term *separation of powers* is used both to designate an aspect of the American system (such as the legal doctrine discussed by courts) and as a label for the system as a whole. How might it make sense to describe the whole American system of governance as separation of powers?

The president, Congress, and the Supreme Court are constituted not just by assigned power but rather by congeries of structures, powers, and duties. Plurality or unity of office holders, extent of the terms of office, modes of selection for office as well as specified powers and duties combine to create a set of institutions that behave and "think" quite differently from each other. In older "mixed" regimes these differences could be traced to different social orders. A crucial invention of the new American science of politics was to design institutions to represent different constitutive principles of democracy rather than social orders or alternative regimes.

Basic desiderata of all democratic regimes include provision for the expression of popular will in and about public policy, protection of individual rights, and (common to all regimes) provision for security or self-preservation. These desiderata exist in tension with each other. Separation of powers can be thought of as an attempt to productively resolve those tensions by representing them in and among competing institutions. To some degree Congress, the president, and the Court all concern themselves with all three desiderata—but the priority or institutional bias of their concern varies. Congress, generally, is more concerned than other branches with representing popular will; the Court with protecting individual rights; and the president with ensuring the nation's security. The structure of each institution, as well as the arrangement of legal powers, can be thought of as an institutional design to make productive the tension between popular will, rights, and security both within and among the major institutions of government.

Abraham Lincoln once remarked that the same political or constitutional issue may arise before the president and the Court and be resolved differently. Different branches might resolve the same issue differently because each branch brings a different perspective, a different set of priorities and considerations. Interbranch contestation is a way to insure that competing perspectives, competing arrays of reasons and considerations, are brought to bear on major issues of public policy.

In a separation of powers arrangement, the ambitions of political actors are tied to the duties of their institution such that they tend to press the case for that institution's power and perspective.[25] In the post-9/11 world, for example, the president has been aggressive in asserting executive prerogatives and in using executive power. The creation of military tribunals, the aggressive collection of intelligence without judicial warrant, and the expansive interpretation of his war powers are all manifestations of an institution intentionally biased in its design to emphasize security concerns and needs. Congress or the Court may have a very different perspective on the use of executive power given their own institutional biases and concerns, respectively, for constituent opinion and for individual rights. *The Federalist* stresses that the protection from potential abuses of executive power comes not from limiting the power, in principle, but rather from the exercise of competing powers by the coordinate institutions, Congress and the Court. If one has serious problems with executive overreaching, one should direct the complaint to Congress because, in a sense, the system is designed to incline each institution to overreach. Abuses of power in American national politics are much more the product of deference and abdication than they are the effect of power-wielding corruption. In principle, the president has any and all executive power necessary to carry out his duties. Rather than stint on power, including implied power, the Constitution creates a relationship between competing institutions that will ideally tailor the use of power to the contingencies of the moment. There is not a better word to capture the meaning of such a contest than the word "politics." This is politics not as craftiness or rule by the strongest or partisan selfishness but rather politics as the resolution of competing demands of democratic governance.

One can illustrate this process by reference to an earlier chapter in this volume, by David Crockett on executive privilege. Legalists worry whether the president has "executive privilege" because it is not explicitly mentioned in the Constitution. Crockett shows that the president has this power because he requires secrecy to faithfully perform the duties of his office. But it is also the case that Congress has competing powers and duties, to legislate new laws and evaluate old laws, for example. To carry out its duties, Congress sometimes needs information that the president seeks to deny. There is no legal principle or solution that will "balance" the needs of the president and Congress independent of the political circumstances that generate these competing claims. It is the separation of powers process itself that sorts out the relative importance of, for example, executive privilege and congressional oversight.

In a separation of powers system the three branches are said to be "equal and coordinate." While this suggests that they each represent equally important democratic principles, it does not mean that at any given moment all of the branches have equal power. Because of the president's institutional design and political biases, the executive has considerable advantages over the legislative at the outset of a policy process or political crisis. Because of the executive's place in the system, the unity of the office, and other attributes designed to give the government an ability to act quickly and decisively, presidents are in a position to push Congress and the nation into war or to focus attention on presidential priorities rather than a legislature's agenda. Presidents have prospective advantage in the constitutional order. In order for Congress to be effective it must have retrospective advantage.

Just as the president is designed to see problems before the polity as a whole understands them, to act quickly if necessary, to focus or force debate, and to set priorities, Congress as a deliberative body has its own structural advantages and virtues. Congress is better suited to retrospective evaluation and judgment. It has its own tools to force presidents to reconsider their actions, or to be accountable—that is, to politically pay for poor choices or failures of judgment. Congress can hold hearings, question executive officials, pass restrictive legislation, or deny appointments. What is a Congress to do if an executive persists in following a course disapproved by Congress despite the legislature's efforts to alter it? Suppose a Congress, for example, passes a resolution demanding that the president withdraw troops from a failed expedition, holds up funds for the president's pet projects, denies political appointments he seeks— all demonstrating legislative determination to reset the course of the nation's policy—and yet the president continues to ignore the legislature. It is necessary for the Congress to have the power of impeachment to make Congress's retrospective power an effective balance to the president's prospective advantage. Without impeachment, our political branches would not be "equal and coordinate."

The Constitution captures this idea of coordinate but asymmetrical power in the way it grants the pardoning power to the executive.[26] In his classic theory, John Locke had used the power to pardon as his sole example of the executive's awesome power to violate the law itself in an effort to advance the public good by meeting necessity in an emergency. Because true emergencies are by their nature unforeseen, a well-constructed executive has almost limitless power to meet such circumstances, and the ability to pardon is itself an example of a power usually interpreted as one without limits. In contrast, our Constitution limits the pardoning power. It precludes a president from pardoning one who has been impeached. Moreover, although no pardon (except for someone impeached) can be overturned by Congress or the Court, nothing prevents Congress from impeaching and convicting a president for misuse of his pardon power. The impeachment power trumps the pardoning power. In an effective Constitution founded on republican principles presidents are given extraordinary prospective powers, but Congress has the last word.

It is important to note that, in a theory of separation of powers, the utility of the impeachment process extends well beyond its deployment. To the extent that the culture embraces a robust political understanding of impeachment, the ordinary powers of Congress are enhanced and the likelihood of impeachment actually diminishes. If impeachment is a real political possibility, presidents will be much more likely to take seriously ordinary expressions of legislative will, such as resolutions, laws, budgets, appointments, and the like. These institutional actions gain in power and authority because executive opposition to them could itself become grounds for impeachment and conviction.

Impeachment is thus a constitutive feature in the theory of the constitutional separation of powers. Unfortunately, theory is not always reflected in practice. Since the mid-twentieth century it has increasingly become the case that Congress defers to the president over custody of its own constitutional powers (as is shown, for example, in the chapter in this volume by Jasmine Farrier on budget powers) or the president and Congress defer to the Court to resolve disputes between them (as is shown, for example, in some of the recent controversies regarding executive privilege). The political culture of Congress has changed in the twentieth century and its institutional self-confidence and self-understanding has waned. One of the deep sources of this development may be located in the constitutional design itself—in its reliance on pretense as a constitutional device.

Recall that the Constitution analogizes the impeachment process to a legal proceeding to elevate the kind of political process it actually intends. But for a pretense to be effective, it must be believed, and when believed, political actors will insist that the political process is a strictly legal one. Legalizing the impeachment process deprives the Congress of power necessary to the logic of separation of powers. However, unmasking the pretense, showing that the impeachment process is political in a broad sense risks "politicizing" impeachment the way James Madison feared if the constitutional standard was too loose, thereby potentially weakening the standards that ought to guide how leaders act and judge each other. Pretense as an attribute of constitutional design is an inherently unstable device of political architecture.

If there is a solution to this constitutional puzzle, it lies in replacing legal pretense with a more robust and self-conscious political understanding. Instead of elevating politics by indirect means, it might be necessary to forthrightly and directly construct an overtly political common law to guide the impeachment process and to fortify the Congress of the United States. Resources for this kind of political reformation are buried in our political tradition already and periodically resurface. The Andrew Johnson case did include, for a time, a political article. The case for a political understanding was pressed in the Watergate era, and Nixon's articles were framed in rhetoric that echoed the older political understanding. Impeachment trials of officials other than the president have sometimes articulated broad political standards for misconduct in office. I have argued that these counterexamples to a legalistic understanding actually prove the current legalistic norm governing presidential impeachments because they all were articulated by the losing side in presidential impeachment contests. Today these remnants of a more robust early nineteenth-century understanding of separation of powers can serve as models for broader political understanding of presidential accountability, much as dissenting opinions sometimes eventually surpass majority views on the Supreme Court. The trick will be not merely to revive these "dissenting precedents," though that may indeed be part of the solution to our present political pathology. It is more important to craft a new kind of civic education to replace the indirect mode meant to accompany our political architecture. Because "pretense" is an inherently unstable form of political design, we need to recognize ourselves as a democracy mature enough to rectify the imbalances of overlegalization in some eras and overpoliticization in others.

CHAPTER ELEVEN

Demagoguery, Statesmanship, and Presidential Politics

JAMES W. CEASER

PERHAPS THE MOST NOTABLE characteristic of the modern presidency is the direct and intimate connection that exists—or that many believe should exist—between the president and the public. Woodrow Wilson first described the ideal of this relationship more than a century ago in his classic work *Constitutional Government*: "The nation as a whole has chosen him, and is conscious that it has no other political spokesman . . . Let him once win the admiration and confidence of the country, and no other single force can withstand him."[1] Presidents and presidential candidates, according to this understanding, will regularly engage in grand efforts at mass persuasion seeking to elevate the public by their appeals to high principle.

To bring this all down to earth, presidents in the modern context need to rely extensively on the art or science known as "rhetoric" or "public relations." And this they all do. Presidents today employ teams of speechwriters and communications experts, many of whom become quite well known in their own right. No serious candidate would ever think of running a national campaign without hiring media consultants and pollsters.

These practices are fairly late developments in the history of the presidency. Although public support has always been important to presidents, the use of many techniques of public relations was greatly circumscribed in the nineteenth century. Presidents rarely took their case to the people in speeches treating matters of public policy, a practice that was regarded both as unpresidential and as an "unconstitutional" challenge to Congress' prerogatives.[2] Presidents had no staff to assist them with speech writing, and when they received help it was usually done discreetly. Presidential candidates likewise generally avoided openly canvassing for votes, discouraged from doing so by the norm that held that the office should seek the man, not the man the office. This view was of course widely known to be more fiction than fact, but it retained enough authority to command adherence to certain outward forms of behavior.

By the turn of the twentieth century, the reserve of both presidential candidates and presidents was being challenged. Powerful personalities such as William Jennings Bryan and Theodore Roosevelt refused to be contained by this model and sought direct links to the public. The traditional view, which regarded too much "popularity" in presidential leadership with suspicion, began to give way to a new conception that, in Wilson's words, held that "it is [only] natural that orators should be the leaders of a self-governing people."[3] Scholars of the presidency today refer to this new understanding of the presidential role by such labels as the "public presidency," the "personal presidency," and, most frequently, the "rhetorical presidency."[4]

The transformation from the reserved to the rhetorical presidency did not take place without objections. Some argued that the new conception would undermine constitutional restraints on the office and would greatly increase the risk of dangerous popular appeals, or what was once known as "demagoguery."[5] But these concerns were dismissed by the dominant thinkers of the Progressive movement who insisted that a more enlightened public had rendered such appeals all but obsolete. To succeed in modern politics, or so it was argued, leaders would have to reach the public by more rational and inspirational means.

Students of the presidency and of presidential campaigns since the Progressive Era who have studied public relations techniques up close have not been so optimistic. They have instead warned of the dangers of "merchandizing" and "packaging" presidents and candidates and decried the advent of the "permanent campaign" and "negative advertising." The titles of some of the books tell the story: *The Selling of the President* (Joe McGiniss), *Dirty Politics: Deception, Distraction, and Democracy* (Kathleen Jamison), and *Politics Lost: How American Democracy Was Trivialized by People Who Think You're Stupid* (Joe Klein). It seems that the dubious or sinister aspects of public relations techniques have developed hand in hand with the rise of the rhetorical presidency.

For all these worries, however, modern commentators have been reluctant to invoke the *d* word (demagoguery). As believers in the democratic ethos, they seem to find it difficult to attribute these problems to a popular source, which is what demagoguery implies. They have instead labored to show that the greatest dangers are connected to the oligarchic threats of "big money" and the "interests." Nor does the word "demagoguery" appear very often in leadership studies by contemporary political scientists. The dominant approaches in the discipline rely on theories of the principle-agent model and of entrepreneurship. Qualitative words like demagoguery, along with its frequent companion term (and antithesis) "statesmanship," seem too normative and too imprecise to allow for scientific analysis. After all, one woman's statesman is often another man's demagogue.[6]

No one can quarrel with the pursuit of rigor. But a science ultimately can only be as precise as its subject matter allows. Excluding qualitative concepts does more harm than good if it limits consideration of important issues, even when the meanings of these concepts are difficult to pin down.[7] This chapter accordingly revisits the concepts of demagoguery and, to a lesser extent, statesmanship. It begins from the top down, surveying how these terms have been defined and applied in the past. It then proceeds from the bottom-up analysis, investigating some of most noteworthy instances of presidential politics in which accusations of demagoguery were widespread. Just as the notion of "greatness" in the presidency cannot be examined without discussing specific cases of great presidents, so it is not possible to "appreciate" demagoguery without considering—and even ranking—some of our most effective demagogues. They merit no less.

The Founders and the Problem of Demagoguery

The office of the presidency that the founders created in 1787 represented a new kind of political institution. Its originality rested on two main features: a mix of powers and functions designed to supply republican government with the energy it had previously lacked, and (of greater interest here) the selection of the chief magistrate by a system that accorded great weight to popular preferences. If, as opponents to the Constitution charged, the president's powers resembled those of a king, they at least conceded that the new office was an "*elective* monarchy."[8] But while the founders took this bold democratic step, it is clear that they had serious reservations and welcomed restraints. Popular competition, they feared, could open the door to the "vicious arts by which elections are too often carried," enabling leaders adept at cultivating popular favor to win office and corrupt the entire system.[9]

The strongest term that the founders assigned to this danger was "demagoguery," a theme that frames *The Federalist*, figuring prominently in the first and the last of its eighty-five essays. Demagoguery for the founders thrived in the political space of direct leadership appeals to large popular audiences. The threat was potentially greatest during elections but might easily extend beyond this phase to affect sitting presidents, who, in their wish "to be continued," might show a "servile pliancy" to public passions or who might attempt to manipulate public opinion to gain an advantage.[10] The qualities of firmness and energy that the presidential office was intended to embody could be placed in jeopardy.

Following classical political science, the founders regarded demagoguery as a principal source of the instability of ancient republics. According to James Madison, the problem was already in evidence in some of the states following the American Revolution, where many representatives had become "the dupe to a favorite leader ... varnishing his sophistical arguments with the glowing colours of popular eloquence."[11] The founders thought, however, that they had discovered a new way to control the problem. By transforming popular government from democracy in a limited territory, where orators addressed the public in open assemblies, into representative government covering a large expanse, where direct communication of national leaders with the public was more limited, the opportunities for practicing demagoguery would be diminished.

The exclusion of the public from direct responsibility for making policy decisions was counted a great advantage, as it was in large meetings, where orators spoke on matters to be immediately decided, that demagoguery flourished. It is one of the "infirmities incident to collective meetings of the people," *The Federalist* contended, that "ignorance will be the dupe of cunning, and passion the slave of sophistry and declamation." The author (Madison in this case) continues: "the more numerous an assembly may be, of whatever characters composed, the greater is known to be the ascendancy of passion over reason. ... In the ancient republics, where the whole body of the people assembled in person, a single orator, or an artful statesman, was generally seen to rule with as complete a sway as if a scepter had been placed in his single hand."[12]

But even with these new safeguards, the founders remained wary.

Inventive demagogues might find novel ways to break through whatever barriers were erected to thwart them. Demagogues could arise not only in electoral contests but also inside political organizations or movements that provide a base for later political activity. Demagoguery was at its most dangerous, however, when found in the governing process where used to activate public opinion and transform it an immediate source of political influence. Rather than power deriving from the constituted authority of an office, it would rest on a noninstitutional claim to speak for the public. Formal constitutional government might then devolve into "informal," demagogic governance, a kind of shadow regime that threatened to undermine the new government from within. The founders' analysis here echoed that of Plutarch as seen in his treatment of the effects generated by one of Rome's "greatest" demagogues, Caius Gracchus. Caius subtly challenged the forms of existing constitutional practice. "Whereas other popular leaders had always hitherto, when speaking, turned their faces toward the senate house," Caius "was the first man that in his harangue to the people turned the other way." The effect of this seemingly "insignificant movement and change of posture" was to "mark no small revolution in state affairs, the conversion, in a manner of the whole government from an aristocracy to a democracy." Plutarch then expanded on this theme by detaching the practice of demagoguery from the person of the demagogue. To counter Caius's popular appeal, some of the leading senators persuaded the Senate to attempt to outbid him "by playing the demagogue in opposition to him and offering favors contrary to all good policy."[13] The founders similarly worried about the general practice of raising public opinion to assault the formal prerogatives of an office.

In view of the dangers of demagoguery, the founders took further steps to curb it by giving the new government a constitutional tone that would be enforced, if not by the political leaders themselves, then by enlightened parts of the public. *The Federalist* is filled with grave warnings against flattery and against the "artful misrepresentations of interested men" who encourage the people to indulge "the tyranny of their own passions."[14] But norms by themselves were insufficient. In the case of the presidency, the founders adopted a fairly lengthy term to allow presidents to pursue projects without the need to cater directly to public opinion. They also instituted formal mechanisms of public communication, obliging presidents to present to Congress "information on the state of the union" and to supply publicly the reasons for a veto. This system, according to Jeffrey Tulis, was meant to "constitutionalize" presidential communication by channeling it away from informal popular orations and toward more deliberative forms of rhetoric.[15]

For the presidential selection process, the founders counted heavily on the "automatic" effects that derived not just from the size of the national constituency but also from the multitude of interests that exist in a commercial republic. Candidates in this setting could not generally hope to win the presidency by playing to the intense passions of a single group. The same remedy the founders relied on to block majority faction would discourage demagoguery. These two problems were in fact tightly connected, as demagogues were the usual agents who activated factions. Once again, however, "auxiliary precautions" were introduced. The extended geographical sphere was not a foolproof solution and on occasion might make even matters worse, allowing the "misrepresentations of interested men," if they should manage to gain public support, to last "for a longer time."[16]

The presidential selection system accordingly provided for choice by specially chosen electors. Although this part of the plan was *not* adopted primarily to restrain democratic choice—indeed, in light of the nearly insuperable obstacles at the time to conducting a national popular vote, using electors was the only practical means available to provide for public influence—it allowed for the incorporation of certain features that afforded a degree of discretion for the electors.[17] Most important was the provision that gave each elector *two* votes for the presidency.[18] While public opinion might constrain the electors on one of their votes, they would have freer rein with the other and might use it to deny victory to a demagogic leader. Overall, the founders' selection system was designed to encourage a choice that focused on an assessment of the candidates' reputation and record of national service rather than on appeals candidates made during an election campaign.

Changes in Presidential Selection and in the Foundation of Presidential Power

The founders' complicated presidential selection system did not survive intact beyond the two elections of George Washington. By the third election (1796), political parties—the Federalists and the Democratic-

Republicans—had emerged and managed to have the electors selected on the basis of their pledge to support the party nominee. Parties also extended their instructions to the electors' "second" vote in an effort to control the choice of the vice president. In recognition of these changes and of the related mischief of the tie in electoral votes that occurred between Jefferson and Burr in 1800, the Constitution was amended in 1804 to end the two-vote system. Electors were now limited to a single vote for president and a separate single vote for vice-president. Much of the filtering effect that the electoral system had offered to prevent demagoguery was accordingly lost. This function was now assumed by the political parties, which took over the job of winnowing and selecting the candidates at the nominating stage.[19] The choice of the voters was now between two candidates who were already vetted by the parties to exclude potential demagogues.

This change meant, however, that if parties ceased to exist, the potential of demagoguery in the final election would loom much larger. Exactly this possibility presented itself during the "era of good feeling," when political party competition came to an end. In 1824 the one remaining party, the Democratic-Republicans, stopped functioning, and no national mechanism existed to nominate candidates and limit their number. Five candidates presented themselves for the final election, each making popular appeals to the electorate. With none of the candidates in this field appearing likely to attain an electoral majority, the strategies were aimed at winning a smaller segment of the electorate, enough to finish among the top three of the electoral vote recipients, which was the threshold for inclusion for the final election vote in the House of Representatives.

Led by Martin Van Buren, the junior senator from New York, the proponents of political parties argued that the system that developed in 1824 would be a disaster for the nation. The inability to produce a winner and majority at the electoral stage was destined to repeat itself. Just as important, the system served as an open invitation to demagoguery. In the words of one of Van Buren's followers, it inevitably resulted in candidates' "traveling through the country, courting support . . . and assiduously practicing all the low arts of popularity."[20] Appeals to sectional divisions proved to be especially effective as a demagogic tool. As Van Buren wrote: "If the old ones [party feelings] are suppressed, geographical divisions founded on local interest or, what is worse, prejudices between free and slaveholding states will inevitably take their place."[21]

With the presidential election being the focal point of national politics, Van Buren feared a descent into demagogic politics that would lead in short order to national disintegration.

Van Buren's remedy was the reestablishment of party competition as a permanent feature of the political system. Two moderate national parties, each having a long-term interest of its own, would nominate responsible candidates. Each party would try to build a coalition to win a national majority, with the result that the election would be decided at the stage of the voting by the electors; recourse to the undemocratic and problematic auxiliary system of selection by the House of Representatives, where each state has one vote, would be avoided. (In fact, no election has gone to the House since 1824.) Parties would serve as the gateways through which all the major aspirants to the presidency would have to pass, restoring a vital filtering mechanism to the selection process. Parties would stand "above" individual aspirants. Rather than advancing their own, temporary programs as the basis of their candidacies, which would be an invitation to demagoguery, candidates would have to embrace the long-term principles of a party.

Party nominations would also help to resolve another difficulty in American politics that emerged with the passing from the scene of the generation of the founders, which had supplied all of the nation's presidents through the presidency of James Monroe. All of these men possessed a commodity that now was short supply and that was difficult for the ordinary politician to acquire on his own: stature. Party nominations could supply responsible politicians, persons having no claim to being founders or military heroes, with the needed credibility. Then as now the investiture of an individual with a party nomination transforms him overnight into a new person, higher in rank than before.

The party system that was created in the 1830s assigned the task of nomination to the new institution of the party convention comprised of delegates who were generally strongly attached to the party organization and who now had a stake in the whole process, which they largely controlled. The parties generally ran the campaign, with the candidates remaining on the sidelines. As one scholar described the system: "The parties, trusting their professionals, deemed candidates exploitable and interchangeable. The party did not want a candidate to interfere: Parties were enduring; candidacies were fads."[22] However much these party builders differed from the founders in the means they employed, they shared with them the objective of discouraging individual demagogic appeals in presidential politics. The party system achieved this end in a new and arguably more democratic manner. The parties were not impermeable to popular movements of change or renewal from below. These movements had to achieve a fairly high threshold of support to become influential in the party, which meant generally that they needed to be something more than merely personal followings of a single individual.[23] Demagogic candidates were forced to the outer reaches of American politics in third parties.

Many of the fundamental elements of the nomination system that was created in the 1830s remain in place today. There has, however, been one critical change. In a long and drawn out process that began in 1912, but that was not completed until 1972, the nomination choice was removed from the party conventions (and the party-oriented delegates who controlled them) and given chiefly to the public in primary elections. The proponents of this change sought to reduce the corporate influence of the party in the nomination decision on the grounds that the parties were corrupt and controlled by big interests; the system, they alleged, stifled the emergence of genuine popular statesmen. The remedy was to reverse the presumption of the original system and place the individual candidate above the party, with the party forming around the successful nominee's program. As chief orator and leader of public opinion, the presidential candidate, and eventually the president, would enjoy expanded power and influence. The new system would supply the conditions in which individual popular appeals live and thrive. The consequences are evident in the modern selection process, where the long nomination phase is now open to a large number of aspirants making direct popular appeals. The appearance of demagogic campaigns has been evident. To date these candidates have been screened out before the final election phase, although not without having influenced the tone of presidential campaigns and perhaps the character of the presidency as well.

The Evolution of the Concept of Demagoguery

The term *demagogue*, deriving from the Greek roots of *demos* (people) and *agagos* (leading), emerged in the fifth century BCE. In Athens, and in many other Greek city-states of the time, the political situation was characterized by a division between two parties vying for control, one comprised chiefly of the nobles or oligarchs, the other of the common people. Initially, demagogue referred descriptively to a "leader of the people" or of the popular party and carried no special opprobrium. Themistocles, Pericles, and Cleon were all referred to as demagogues.[24] The qualitative dimension of the term appears to have developed from the contrasting portraits of Pericles and Cleon that were so vividly presented by Thucydides. Both were leaders of the popular party in Athens, but the difference between them was like day and night. Pericles appears as the great leader—educated, noble in vision, and accomplished as a memorable speaker (his funeral oration was one of the most famous addresses of antiquity). Pericles was so substantial a figure that, after a time, he was able to free himself from the passions and prejudices of the multitude. Under his leadership Athens was a democracy in name, but a "government by its first citizen" in fact.[25] His stature and independence enabled him to keep the public on an even keel: "Whenever he saw them [the people] unseasonably and insolently elated, he would with a word reduce them to alarm; and on the other hand, if they fell victims to a panic, he would at once restore them to confidence."[26]

Cleon, by contrast, lacked these attractive qualities and seemed to be concerned only with acquiring personal influence. This difference led to the distinction between the "demagogue," understood now in a pejorative sense, and the "statesman" (*politikos*), a term first used extensively by Plato.[27] The demagogue is now understood to be more than just a leader of the people; he is one who leads by inflammatory appeals or by flattery and proceeds without concern for the public good. The statesman, who may lead either the popular party or the party of the nobles, aims to serve the public good and has acquired knowledge of the art of doing so ("statesmanship"). Three hundred years later, Plutarch adopted and solidified this vocabulary in presenting his famous gallery of the leaders of Greece and Rome. Plutarch supplied the prototypes of demagogues and statesmen from which others drew, including, of course, William Shakespeare.

Political analysis since Plutarch has treated demagoguery and statesmanship as a dyad. But while the two terms clearly offer a contrast, they are not quite mirror opposites as they refer to different spheres of activities. Demagoguery always functions in the realm of appealing to a public, where it is a practice for boosting or enhancing popular standing. It tends to flourish in systems, or in parts of the systems, in which public approval or standing can generate power. It is thus not usually found in a senate, unless a senator is talking to the crowd, or in the internal councils of government, but in the mass assembly or on the street before a crowd, as in Marc Anthony's famous address following Caesar's assassination. The demagogue has accordingly been defined by the Oxford English Dictionary, in one of its main meanings, as "a popular leader or orator who espoused the cause of the people against any other party in the state."[28]

Demagoguery is not concerned with handling political affairs but with boosting popular support. Many classical demagogues preferred to limit their role to promoting positions in the assembly, which allowed them to avoid having to assume direct responsibility for their proposals. Demagoguery applies to decision-making or governing only incidentally, insofar as certain kinds of stock demagogic measures themselves, such as schemes for the redistribution of wealth, contribute to enhancing approval. Demagoguery in its pure sense is at best indifferent to the goodness of the policies it promotes, which is not to deny that some demagogues may sincerely believe in their programs. Yet because achieving the public good in politics is often difficult and frequently contrary to what wins immediate approval, demagoguery will usually, although not always, miss the mark. Walter Lippmann expressed this point well by observing that demagoguery "stops at relieving the tension by expressing the feeling. But the statesman knows that such relief is temporary, and if indulged too often, unsanitary. He therefore sees to it that he arouses no feeling which he cannot sluice into a program that deals with the facts to which the feelings give rise."[29]

Statesmanship, following Lippmann, is concerned chiefly with handling political affairs well. It is the art of directing matters to promote the public interest and, to add a "classical" touch, of educating or ennobling the public. Statesmanship often refers to activities where winning popular approval is not at issue, as in instances of managing a crisis or conducting diplomacy and negotiations. Statesmanship can therefore describe leadership in nondemocratic systems. In popular systems, however, statesmanship must deal with the democratic components of politics. The pursuit of good policies often involves securing popular support or winning sufficient votes to be elected to office. In these activities, the popular statesman, no less than the demagogue, must be expert in rhetoric. His rhetoric, however, will ordinarily be of a different kind than that of the demagogue. It will seek to calm rather excite, to conciliate rather than divide, and to instruct rather than flatter. The statesman is willing to speak sternly to the people, in the fashion of Pericles or especially of Publius; his characteristic posture is one of a willingness to say what the people *need* to hear rather than what they wish to hear. The statesman's way is not to "flatter [the people's] prejudice to betray their interests"; he is not an "adulator."[30] The demagogue's art, by contrast, is meant to satisfy the public's appetite; it is nicely compared by Socrates in the *Gorgias* to that of "the pastry chef."

The restrained and elevated tone characteristic of the statesman is not, however, always possible. As a system becomes more democratic in tone, with continual demands for communications between politicians and people, the kind of sternness just depicted may appear too forbidding or arrogant, if not simply boring. At some point in the democratization of a political system, greater familiarity—a dose of the "little arts of popularity"—is almost a requirement for a normal politician to survive. A far more important, and a different kind of consideration, applies to the extraordinary situation. To handle a great challenge, including the problem of trying to thwart an able and dangerous demagogue, the statesman might have no choice but have recourse to something like demagoguery; fire can sometimes only be fought with fire. These regrettable exceptions, constituting something like the exercise of "rhetorical prerogative" by the statesman, pose obvious complications for analysis. They require looking "behind" the external character of leadership appeals and making judgments about the intentions and the likely effects of actions. Insofar as definitions are helpful, it makes some sense to separate the demagogue from demagoguery. The demagogue is one who consistently practices demagoguery, doing so in a way that shows no restraint. The demagogue will not sacrifice his own interest for the public good.[31] The statesman will always wish to avoid demagoguery and will make use of it only where needed to avert greater harm to the city or nation.

Types of Demagogues

Classical political science distinguished between at least two different types of demagogues. The first, which we have been observing, was modeled after

Cleon, a person whose profile fits the likes of a George Wallace, a Jean-Marie Le Pen (a current demagogue in France), or a Patrick Buchanan. The demagogue in this case presents himself as not only for the people but also very conspicuously of the people. He has no family name or elite status, neither has he performed a notable service or heroic deed that has earned him great personal stature. (Cleon himself was the owner of a tannery[32]; neither Le Pen nor Buchanan has held important public office, while Wallace, as governor of Alabama, never obtained real distinction, as opposed to notoriety.) The demagogue wins political influence through oratory and position taking. He searches for a potential wave of opinion and then rides the swell as far as it will carry him. Where necessary, he produces his own swell by fomenting or exploiting latent divisions, finding a convenient target to assault, and introducing what are today called "wedges." The demagogue may pit the "people against the powerful," rural folk against city dwellers, or the "little guy" against the "pointy-headed intellectual." Because the appeal itself is the chief basis of his standing, the demagogue lacking any genuine personal stature, it is natural that he will often feel vulnerable to being outflanked or "out demagogued."[33] The demagogue's insecurity in relation to potential rivals pushes him to compete in the extremity of his appeals or in his sheer flamboyance. As Aristotle said of Cleon: "He was the first who shouted on the public platform, who used abusive language and who spoke with his cloak girt about him, while all the others used to speak in proper dress and manner."[34] Demagogues often attract attention to themselves by breaking existing norms or "forms" that protect propriety or the constitutional dimension of power.

The only way in which this kind of demagogue (referred to as "Type I" here) can obtain a measure of personal standing independent of his opinions is to show bravado in defying the elite. The demagogue will sometimes invite the contempt of the better sorts, which he then wears as a badge of honor. His barely concealed, or even openly avowed, appeals to envy fortify this image; he "stands up" for the "little guy." Yet because he lacks genuine stature, the public does not look up to or respect him. If he is not continually rising in his bid to win greater influence, the public is may drop or turn on him, as they did with Cleon. The demagogue pulls down the people in ways that many of them almost half sense. From this fact comes the famous backhanded compliment of democracy that the people are invariably better than their worst demagogues.

The Type I demagogue will also frequently appeal to the closed elements and prejudices of the community—the things that can be said to protect its traditions and way of life. The demagogue becomes the defender of the community's mores, orthodoxies, and creed against the persons or forces that they perceive as undermining them. This stance accounts for this type of demagogue's reliance on fear and anger, which are the passions most easily aroused among those who feel that their ancient way of life is being threatened. The demagogue in such instances often targets those who are different or alien or those said to be cosmopolitan (free thinkers and philosophers often fit in this group). Rhetoric of this kind enables the demagogue to expand his appeal well beyond the poor to a much broader audience, which can include portions of the elite class. Plato depicts a notable example in the *Apology*, where the demagogic accusers of Socrates win support by charging him with corrupting the youth by questioning conventional ideas about the gods.

Many in the upper classes treat Type I demagogues with contempt, disparaging them for being "mere" demagogues who stir things up but who lack the real ambition to rule, which is an aristocratic quality. The upper classes make the error of thinking that they can use these demagogues for their own purposes, allowing them to do some of their dirty work before disposing of them when the time is right. This strategy often works. According to V. O. Key, it was used with some success by elites in some of the Southern states in the early twentieth century, when they tolerated local demagogues to handle the "Negro problem." But the lower-class demagogues are not always compliant. Their crudeness and lack of breeding can hide a desire to rule and the ability and shrewdness to do so. Many German intellectuals and aristocrats in the 1930s believed that that they could control Adolf Hitler, a hope nicely captured by the German phrase, "den Führer führen," or "to lead the Leader"; it was too late before they realized their error.

While the likes of Cleon served as the initial model for the demagogue, classical thinkers identified a second type, one more dangerous for being less obvious. If flattery is most artful when it is least noticed, the "better" demagogue is the one who escapes ready labeling. This form of demagoguery (Type II) is usually exercised by a figure from the patrician class or one who has achieved stature from military exploits. Plato suggests this second type in his account of Pericles. Another example was the young and attractive Alcibiades, whom Plutarch labeled "the greatest of the demagogues."[35] Probably the most famous example, however, is Julius Caesar, who, according to Tim Duff, fit perfectly the model of "a popular leader who comes to power through demagogic means and uses that power to install himself as a tyrant."[36] "Caesarism" now serves as a label for absolutist rule established initially by popular means, and it applies to more modern figures like Napoleon. These leaders may appear initially easy-going or enlightened, at least until they secure their position; afterward, finding popular opinion too unstable a source on which to base authority, they subvert republican government. The *Federalist* Publius reminded Americans of this point when he observed that most of "those men who have overturned the liberties of republics . . . [began] their career by paying an obsequious court to the people, commencing demagogues and ending tyrants."[37]

The Appeals of Demagoguery

The "raw material" for demagoguery consists in the opinions and sentiments that can be exploited in a particular system at a particular time. Depending on circumstances, the "best" choice can range from the perennial standby of stimulating class hatred, to fomenting racial or religious prejudice, to manipulating a dislike of politicians or "insiders" (a technique brought to perfection by Ross Perot in 1992). The possibilities are almost limitless.

Two examples discussed in early American politics illustrate the uncanny variety of demagogic appeals. In *The Federalist*, Publius warned how the powerful sentiment of "jealousy" of authority (especially executive authority), which had served the nation well in the period leading up to the revolutionary struggle, might now become the basis of a demagogic campaign against the Constitution and be used to "stigmatize" the concern for "energy and efficiency in government" as "the offspring of a temper fond of despotic power and hostile to the principles of liberty."[38] This ploy was all the more effective (and demagogic) for posing as being friendly to the cause of liberty. Alexis de Tocqueville similarly identified "the *decentralizing* passions" as the great source of demagoguery in the 1830s, and he argued that the manipulation of these passions made up the core of Andrew Jackson's leadership as president. Even if, as many have argued, Tocqueville's charge was off the mark, his description of demagoguery can hardly be improved on: "He maintains himself and prospers by flattering these passions daily. General Jackson is the slave of the majority: he follows it in its wishes, its desires, its half-uncovered instincts, or rather he divines it and runs to place himself at its head."[39]

Despite the varied content of specific demagogic appeals, efforts have been made to generalize about demagoguery by identifying the root passions to which it appeals. Three passions stand out: envy, fear, and hope. Envy is the staple of class-based demagoguery, evoked usually in the case of those who lacking in some particular regard, such as wealth or position or honors. The demagogue calls attention to this lack, raising it to prominence and making it the chief object of a political appeal. He tells those in his audience that they are entitled to the object of their wishes — "every man a king," in the motto of Huey Long — and that those who do possess these things should be dispossessed of them. Envy, deliberately confounded with appeals to democratic justice, relies on some variant or other of the theme of "the people versus the powerful."

The cultivation of the other two general passions — fear and hope — allows the demagogue to appeal well beyond the confines of the poor. Plutarch referred to fear and hope as the chief "rudders" that govern men's political actions, and a number of philosophers have identified these passions as the natural psychological foundations of the religious impulse.[40] Demagogues often indulge or inflame these emotions as a way to build support. But much political rhetoric, and obviously not just that of the demagogue, is addressed to hope and fear. The statesman tries to make constructive use of these sentiments to promote the public good, sometimes moderating excessive appeals to hope or calming an unhelpful slide into fear. One of Franklin Roosevelt's most memorable phrases, that "the only thing to fear is fear itself," took place in the context of his effort to buoy Americans' spirit in the midst of the Depression and to offer hope.

Because demagoguery is a term of Greek origin, most discussions of it have drawn on persons from Greek and Roman history. A few analysts, however, have broadened the study to include another great source of antiquity, ancient Israel. Although kingship became the regime form in Israel after Saul's reign in the ninth century BCE, there remained a substantial role for popular speech, especially by those claiming to communicate with God through the "office" of prophecy. These persons generally took their message directly to public audiences, speaking to crowds of people in a highly vivid way. In his work *The Statesman's Manual*, Samuel Taylor Coleridge offered the Bible as the best source for understanding "the elements of *public* prudence, instructing us in causes, the surest preventatives, and the only cures, of public evils."[41] Coleridge focused much of his attention on demagoguery, which he highlighted by translating *mat'im* (Isaiah 9:16), usually rendered "those who lead the people astray," as "demagogues." The "demagogues" are found among the "false prophets" who "fill you with vain hopes," telling you "it shall be well with you," and that "no evil shall come upon you."[42] False prophets often managed to rise in influence — "the people love to have it so" — by fostering dangerous illusions.[43] By exposing these techniques, the biblical narrator (and Coleridge) sought to unmask the demagogue's art, enabling others to appreciate the danger.[44]

Coleridge's discussion serves as a bridge to a consideration of studies of demagoguery that have focused on modifications in different historical contexts of appeals to these three "natural" passions. One of the earliest overlays derived from the effects of revealed religion (Christianity), which provided new potential resource of public influence for the demagogue: a claim to speak for God and an opening to appeals either to sin and damnation (fear) or to redemption (hope). After the message of the Gospel won the day in the Roman Empire, the Church's place became partly that of as established institution, meaning that religious doctrine often supported authority. But there were also instances of religious appeals that were initiated from the bottom by popular leaders. A spectacular case occurred in the Florentine republic in the late fifteenth century. Amidst a people that was, in Machiavelli's account, "far from considering [itself] ignorant and benighted . . . Brother Girolamo Savonarola succeeded in persuading them that he held converse with God." Making use of rhetoric that spoke of damnation and that appealed mostly to the passion of fear, Savonarola managed to dominate the political life of the city for over a decade.[45]

The rise of Puritanism in England in the seventeenth century brought new challenges to established authority, with the religious dissenters' appeals to hopes and fears figuring prominently in creating the dissatisfaction that led to the English Civil War. Reflecting on these events, Thomas Hobbes condemned the recourse to religious sentiment in public life, decrying both the Church's appeals to superstitious beliefs and the

"Kingdom of Darkness," and the dissenters' new popular appeal to "conscience," which he believed served as a novel source of demagoguery.[46] David Hume later famously categorized these two forms of religious appeal into terms frequently used in early America: "superstition" and "enthusiasm." Superstition or "terrified credulity" referred (usually) to a defense of authority that played on "weakness, fear and melancholy." Enthusiasm was characterized by a "warm imagination," appealing sometimes to hope and sometimes to fear, that produced an unsettling political effect. The popular rhetoric of the Puritan republics of New England displayed elements of enthusiasm—of both damnation and messianic hope—as well as, occasionally, of superstition.

The Enlightenment created its own overlay on the basic human passions. It established a binary theoretical distinction between "prejudice," associated with a fear of the past (of "monkish ignorance and superstition"), and "enlightenment" with hope for the times to come.[47] In this account, any appeal to the past became a priori demagogic. This theoretical distinction was intended to immunize anyone in the Enlightenment inner circle from the charge of demagoguery, no matter how extreme their position. The Progressives adopted a variation on this theme by identifying any appeal to progress as being by definition nondemagogic. If a leader, Woodrow Wilson noted, reads correctly "the next move in the progress of politics [and] fairly hit the popular thought . . . are we to say that he is a demagogue?"[48] Evidently not. In reaction, conservatives in the aftermath of the French Revolution elaborated a mirror image distinction: any appeal to abstract principle or speculative reason was Jacobin or demagogic, intended to upset tradition and authority. Demagoguery now became a category of ideology. Both of these conceptions were applied in America during the party conflict of the 1790s. Federalists accused Jeffersonians of Jacobinism, while Jeffersonians charged Federalists with whipping up superstition and xenophobia to blind public opinion to a plot to institute monarchism.

Analysts of liberalism have often identified "comfortable self-preservation" as the dominant passion of modern society. Yet this passion, by its very ordinariness and sobriety, is an improbable source of support for a powerful demagogic appeal, although it has reinforced support of another sentiment—a fear of instability—that has provided fuel for demagogic appeals.[49] For the most part the sentiment of comfortable self-preservation has served as a resource for demagoguery by reason more for what it has provoked as a reaction than for what it has directly caused. Labeled by Romantic thinkers as "bourgeois" (or middle-class), this sentiment became the target of a powerful passion of contempt and disgust. Initially, in the nineteenth century, this passion was confined to disgruntled portions of the aristocratic classes and to a small "bohemian" element, but by the second half of the twentieth century it found a much larger audience among mainstream intellectuals and "alienated" youth. Numerous demagogues among the revolutionaries of the New Left in the 1960s regularly exploited this passion.

Probably the most pervasive sentiment of recent times, however, is a milder passion that has accompanied that of comfortable self-preservation among the middle classes: compassion or pity. This sentiment has an attractive, moralizing aspect to it, which is absent in the passion for comfortable self-preservation. Compassion is considered "good" and "hopeful" and is very much in tune with contemporary democratic instincts. It has been evoked in appeals not just to the middle class but also to large parts of the formerly "alienated" critics of the middle class, who have found in it a respectable public substitute for their former anger. It is a passion that can unite both the middle class and their critics into a common front. Demagoguery in this case consists of the artful cultivation of compassion that evokes sympathetic moral indignation against those who do not care. It undermines, where it does not outright reject, the appeal of some of the sterner virtues.[50]

The Rhetorical Situation

Popular political communication takes place inside of a "rhetorical situation." It consists of six formal components: (1) the source, (2) the medium of communication, (3) the prevailing "science" of public communication, (4) the audience, (5) the time horizon of the communication act, and (6) the objective. For example, applying this analysis to Periclean Athens, the six components might be characterized as: (1) an individual speaker (e.g., Cleon), (2) delivering a speech, (3) under theories of public relations derived from the sophists, (4) before the assembly, (5) to influence an imminent vote, (6) arguing for a specific policy or course of action.

A change in the rhetorical situation affects both the likelihood of the appearance of demagoguery and the form it assumes. Changes in the rhetorical situation are caused by shifts in the prevailing theory of communication, the size and legal character of political regimes, and the state of communication technology. A few comments can be made about each of these factors.

Popular oratory in Athens was influenced initially by a school known as sophistry, which specialized in the study of the art of mass persuasion or rhetoric. Teachers of sophistry traveled among different cities of Greece selling their services to clients interested in using mass persuasion to achieve a desired outcome. Sophistry per se was unconcerned with the well-being of the city. It was akin in this respect to the modern science of public relations. The sophists, not unlike many campaign consultants of the modern age—people like Pat Cawdell, Lee Atwater, Stanley Greenberger, Dick Morris, and Joe Trippe—were eager to win a reputation for cleverness, which served their financial interest while also feeding their often legendary egos. Leading sophists of the period were evidently quite well paid. As Plato reports, Evenus of Paros received a fee of 500 drachmae for a single job, which is competitive with the rates charged today by the best consultants.[51]

Beginning with Socrates, the philosophers sought to change the rhetorical situation by gaining control of the prevailing science of communication. This effort culminated in Aristotle's *Rhetoric*, the first and arguably still the best manual on persuasion ever written. Like the sophists, he discussed at great length the instrumental effectiveness of rhetoric and did so with a precision that in many ways went far beyond anything apparently found among the sophists. But unlike the sophists, Aristotle situated the science of rhetoric inside of political science. He thereby sought to connect communication studies to questions about the stability and quality of political regimes. Aristotle also stressed the deliberative component of rhetoric, contending that rational argument was a far more important element in persuasion than was acknowledged by the sophists, who stressed emotional appeals and various kinds of trickery. Aristotle's emphasis on rationality, according to Bryan Garsten, was meant "to respond to the dangers of demagogy" by "attempting to reform the rhetoricians' own understanding of what it takes to successfully master the art of rhetoric."[52] Aristotle sought to establish a new set of norms for the oratorical community—the teachers of oratory, the orators, and enlightened critics—that would make the science of rhetoric compatible with a decent political regime.

Turning to prevailing views of communication in America, it is no surprise to learn that Progressive era proponents of the rhetorical presidency had very high expectations for an elevated form of public rhetoric. These expectations both justified and sustained their call for institutional change, as in Woodrow Wilson's claim: "Thorough debate can unmask the plausible pretender . . . charlatans cannot long play statesmen successfully when the whole country is sitting as critic."[53] There was enormous belief in the salutary and democratic effect of "publicity." In Adam Sheingate's words, "progressive reformers at the turn of the century followed Kant in seeing publicity as a path to rational and enlightened deliberation."[54] Yet at the very moment the rhetorical presidency was being adopted, expert opinion on public persuasion had begun to arrive at the very opposite view. Reflecting the influence of the discovery of the subconscious in psychology and the spread of cinematic images, which penetrated the mind in new ways, social scientists argued that mass public opinion was governed mostly by irrational impulses and dominated by appeals to "symbols." Experience with the widespread use of mass propaganda techniques during World War I only served to confirm this view.[55]

A chasm now opened between the Progressives' erstwhile hopes and the dominant premises of social science. In this period, too, the modern profession of public relations, followed by political consultancy, was born. This profession adopted the understanding of public opinion that governed the social sciences, which stressed the irrationality of political persuasion. Both the science and the profession also preached that with an understanding of the processes of public opinion, it was possible to shape and control it. As Walter Lippmann wrote, "Persuasion has become a self-conscious art. . . . The knowledge of how to create consent will alter every political calculation and modify every political premise."[56] Like the sophists of antiquity, modern consultants sold their product (the art of mass persuasion) with no formal concern for the public good.

Since the 1960s, there has been a reaction to this understanding of public opinion and an attempt to alter the rhetorical situation by changing the prevailing theory of communication. The effort was inaugurated in a work by Herbert J. Storing entitled *Essays on the Scientific Studies of Politics*

(1962), which challenged the validity of the accepted "scientific" premises of political behavior and pointed out dangers posed by some of these premises for maintaining liberal democracy. It was necessary also, however, to demonstrate empirically that public opinion was not so beholden to image appeals that it could not respond in rational ways.

V. O. Key took up this argument in a book entitled *The Responsible Electorate*, which began with the simple but explosive contention that "voters are not fools." Key pointed out that prevailing academic theories of political communications not only sought to explain how persuasion took place but also bore partial responsibility for *influencing* the character of public discourse, which in his view now placed too great a stress on irrational appeals. In classical terms, social science itself helped to shape the character of the rhetorical situation. Social scientists therefore had an obligation, according to Key, to broaden their studies and to give consideration to the norms that support democratic government.

Two decades later, political scientist Joseph Bessette added breadth and depth to this argument in his book *The Mild Voice of Reason*. Bessette reintroduced the category of "deliberation" into political science and showed that, under suitable conditions, reasoning based on the merits exercised a genuine influence on aspects of democratic decision-making.[57] This position was one of the guiding premises of the Rhetoric Project in the 1970s at the University of Virginia with which Bessette was involved and from which Jeffrey Tulis's *The Rhetorical Presidency* also emerged. The Rhetoric Project was greatly indebted to the study of political communications in the thought of Aristotle and the founders. In this spirit, the Project considered the effects of prevailing ideas and current institutional arrangements on public discourse and urged inquiry into measures that might promote deliberation and statesmanship and reduce demagoguery, terms it did not flinch from using.

In the past two decades, a movement in normative political theory, based on premises drawing from the thought of Jürgen Habermas, has raised in a more abstract and idealistic fashion the question of how to promote what it calls "deliberative" or "discursive" democracy.[58] Taken together, these developments have had an influence on the modern oratorical community. While the public relations profession is as influential as ever, with successful political consultants still demanding and receiving the acclaim of those in the political classes, its practices have been subjected to greater scrutiny than before. The academic discipline that supports this profession now includes a component of thought that demands consideration of the impact of communications theories on the quality of public debate.

The greatest changes in the rhetorical situation over the ages, however, have usually owed more to shifts in the size and nature of regimes and to revolutions in communications technology than to deliberate efforts to redefine the science of rhetoric. Thus, by virtue of the great political transformation in antiquity from the city-state to the empire, speakers could no longer reach the relevant mass public through the medium of an ordinary address in an assembly. Indeed, with the demise of the republican form, the assembly as the sovereign ruling body ceased to exist. Oratory continued to be practiced in local venues, but the chief means of communication was by the circulation of written texts. The substance of these texts was sometimes disseminated by organizations to various local speakers, who aided in molding public opinion. The spread of the Gospel, as purveyed by the early Church, became the great model for capturing and influencing the public mind. Machiavelli later looked to it as the form by which he conceived that a new secular gospel might be disseminated. Given the mode of communication and the length of time it took to have an effect, the aim of the communication act was not usually to affect discrete policies of the day but to address a longer-term project or to undermine or support the character of the political order.

With the formation of the larger nations of Europe in early modern times, the most important source of rhetoric was no longer the individual speaker, but the writer. With the advent of the printing press, written tracts could be disseminated more quickly and easily. Although many works had a highly theoretical character meant to reach only a small group, some were designed for broader audiences, as was the case with John Locke's *Two Treatises*, David Hume's *Essays: Moral, Political, and Literary*, and Edmund Burke's *Reflections on the Revolution in France*. Where these works proved too difficult, second-tier writers or "publicists" would simplify and spread the messages.[59]

The rhetorical situation in America in the period leading up to the Revolution is highly instructive of the age. Because republican institutions existed from early on in the colonies, the forms of popular communication were more varied than elsewhere. There were highly influential popular speeches pronounced before live audiences, the most notable of which was James Otis's speech against the Writs of Assistance at the Old State House in Boston (1761), when, according to John Adams, "the child of the Revolution was born," and Patrick Henry's speech at St. John's Church in Richmond (1775), where he aroused all present with his plea to "Give me liberty or give me death."[60] Hundreds of sermons, many highly political in content, also stirred the public mind. Many of the addresses and sermons were also disseminated as written tracts, thus enjoying both a local and more widespread influence. Finally, there were the political writings of the period, never given as speeches. These included John Dickinson's "Letters from a Farmer in Pennsylvania," Thomas Jefferson's *A Summary View of the Rights of British America*, and Thomas Paine's extraordinary *Common Sense*. All "spoke" in a popular style that aimed to move a nation.

The medium of the written word altered the nature of popular appeals. It did so first by removing the physical presence of the person, and thus personal qualities, from the act of persuasion. Written communication also diminished the importance of certain kinds of pathetic or emotive appeals that depend on a live setting. Indeed, if the demagogue is defined as an orator, then, strictly speaking, demagoguery no longer operates; but if the meaning of demagoguery is allowed to be relaxed, one can speak not just of certain demagogic attributes of the written medium, but of its *distinctive* demagogic attributes. The written word gives more weight to rational and abstract argumentation, creating the possibility of theoretical or doctrinal demagoguery (or ideology).

The critique of theoretical demagoguery, developed by Hume, Burke, and Tocqueville, is also found in *The Federalist* in its attacks on "projectors," "visionary and designing men," and "utopian speculators" who favor theories that appealed without restraint or a sense of limits to hope. Unlike the traditional demagogue, these projectors were not usually looking to win popular approval for their own political careers. Either they were sincere devotees of their doctrines or they sought acclaim for their theoretical ideas, whether in their own day or for posterity. Whatever their personal motives, however, their writings could be used for demagogic purposes. In the late eighteenth century, as Tocqueville argued, the offerings of a group of men of letters endowed with a "literary spirit" and having no acquaintance with the realities of politics spun out theories that enflamed the intellectuals' mind and led to the catastrophic extremism of the French Revolution.[61] This property of ideological thinking became clearer in the late nineteenth and early twentieth centuries, when the supporters of socialism and fascism disseminated crude written tracts ("propaganda") designed to foment mass opinion.

Following the American founding, the speech continued to be an important part of American politics, both in political campaigns and popular meetings. There was also oratory in legislatures, although here speech was more deliberative in character. But when it came to reaching the nation at large, the speech itself could not be "heard" firsthand. For political leaders to contact the public, they needed the medium of writing, even if it was just to publish the text of a speech or message. The organization that developed an ongoing interest in disseminating public messages was the political party (or the clique within the party), and parties took on the responsibility in the early nineteenth century for establishing and subsidizing many of the nation's newspapers. Newspapers reflected the line of the party (or clique) and would sometimes directly publish messages of its leaders. Newspapers also became a source in the communications' system in their own right, as the editors developed some independence. Newspapers also gained influence by performing the function of selecting and reporting events. The independence of some newspapers grew by the mid-nineteenth century, as technological advances in printing and organizational innovations enabled them to survive on the revenues of their sales, dispensing with the need of party subsidies.[62] Then the editors and reporters, sometimes closely guided by the owners, became a central source in the communication system, far more important than most individual politicians. Newspapers engaged in something akin to demagoguery, in its crude and sensational efforts, known as "yellow journalism," to stir up public opinion.

By the middle of the twentieth century, these blatant attempts to indulge and manipulate public opinion fell into disrepute, at least in the upper echelons of the press. Journalism developed into a profession and adopted its own professional standards of objectivity in the interpretation of events. The claim to represent this higher standard, together with the increased status of major journalists in the leading newspapers, weeklies, and electronic media, led the top members of the national press to think of themselves as occupying a rank above the parties and politicians, who saw matters only in a partisan way. The press's assertion of both power and right was summed up in the pompous title: the Fourth Estate. Behind this façade, highbrow journalists often practiced a new and subtle kind of demagoguery that played up the importance of the immediate news events at the expense of developing a longer-term perspective and that allowed journalists to subtly promote their own values. Journalists were able to increase their influence relative to political institutions and political actors. Following the events of the 1960s, journalists also became adept at cultivating the sentiments of suspicion and distrust of political actors, again in ways that served to boost their authority.

Over the past two decades, as a result in part to legal and technological changes that have multiplied the points of access in the communications system, the power of the top journalists has waned. At the same time, by excesses in the actions of leading newspapers and networks, their claims of journalistic objectivity have been shattered. Few today accord any newspaper or network the full trust in objectivity that it once enjoyed. While the overall importance of the entire "system" of the media remains, the power of any single cadre within it is a mere shadow of what it had been. The system is now fragmented into hundreds of smaller pieces in which the practice of direct and petty demagoguery has now become far more common. It has coarser and more widespread than before, but also, because of both its variety and its lower status, less dangerous than the period of the Fourth Estate.

The other factor influencing the rhetorical situation in America has been changes in communications technology. The early twentieth century saw the rise of the cinema and newsreel, which downplayed the spoken word and reasoning in favor of the large pictorial image. The power of these new media probably contributed to the impression—and no doubt the reality, too—that public opinion was governed by deeply irrational forces. This great technological change was surpassed and overshadowed a few decades later by the advent of the electronic mass media, first radio and then television. The ultimate effect has been to allow the individual political leader to speak more or less directly and simultaneously to huge portions of the public. The contemporary period is characterized by a rhetorical situation that more closely resembles that of classical republics than anything that has existed in the past twenty-five centuries, although the differences between the two cases remains substantial in many respects.

Consider briefly the six components of the rhetorical situation explored earlier in the chapter in light of modern-day politics:

1. The main source in modern communication is the individual leader operating with a substantial degree of personal discretion. The leader is visible to the public and is judged in part on the basis of qualities and character, as seen in these public appearances. Displaying one's person is an important factor in modern persuasion.[63] Competing sources exist (newspapers, news networks, bloggers, parties, etc.), but they are less important today, relative to individual leaders, than they were a century ago.

2. The "speech," that is, the largely unmediated communication between the individual and public, which includes debates and personal interviews, has returned as a major medium of communication. Individuals have other ways of communicating with the public—ads, written messages, grassroots contacts—but these are less important than the speech. Two of the most important moments of the modern presidential campaign have revolved around the speech events of the nomination acceptance address and the presidential debates.

3. There is today, as there was in Periclean Athens, a profession of political consultants that claims expertise in techniques of persuasion. At the same time, the purely instrumental foundations of that profession have come under much greater scrutiny. Part of this comes from a much broader understanding of the role and effect of political communication. The study of rhetoric has made many aware of the dangers of a science unconnected to the public good.

4. The modern audience on important occasions consists of a substantial portion of the public viewing and assessing the speaker in "real time."[64] The mode of "assembling" the public differs, of course, from the classical situation. It is not a physical and collective gathering, but one in which people view an electronic image largely independently and privately. A television speech (even one seen being delivered to a live audience) limits the effectiveness of "speechification," in particular, it seems, the angrier and more fear-provoking "harangue." Television has been called a "cool"

medium, which seems to disadvantage pure Type I demagoguery, while opening new opportunities for demagoguery of a more familiar and insinuating kind.

5. The time horizon of the communication event in America depends on its institutional context. A presidential speech can be aimed at educating or persuading the public in preparation for a policy decision that could take place shortly. By contrast, in a presidential campaign the ultimate end envisioned is the election, which can be months or almost a year in advance. There are short-term points along the way (e.g., planning for a particular primary campaign or a debate), but the time horizon of the first part of the event is fixed by the nomination decision and the second part by the date of the final election. From the perspective of rhetorical theory, the campaign consists of one great speech act. The character of any demagogic appeal stretching over this length of time would undoubtedly have to be of a different kind than that which counted on an action taken by the public assembly immediately after hearing a speech.

6. The objective of the speech today again varies with the context. A president in many cases may aim his speech at trying to influence public opinion on an important policy matter, where the question at hand is deliberative in the ordinary sense, that is, deciding on the merits of a course of action. The presidential campaign has a different aim: to persuade people to support and vote for a candidate. Matters of "ordinary deliberation" may contribute to that objective—candidates give policy speeches—but they are only pieces of a larger whole, subordinate to the primary goal of winning support for the person.

Some Cases of Demagoguery

Demagoguery is (or was once) a concept of political science, but it has also become a highly charged political epithet, which threatens to destroy its worth as an analytic concept. Still, if the purely political aspects can be filtered out, a neutral core remains. It is noteworthy that demagoguery, while a term of derogation, is not treated as a synonym for ineffective or bad leadership. However poorly some judged the leadership of a Gerald

Ford or a Michael Dukakis, no one ever accused either of them of being demagogues. Demagoguery refers to certain kinds of alleged behavior consisting of using popular methods said to violate the letter or spirit of constitutional government and fomenting of great divisions by appeals to the passions. Based on these criteria, there are only a limited number of cases in American presidential politics where the accusations of demagoguery have been fairly widespread. These cases need to be examined critically to consider why the charges were made and then to determine if they were warranted. The inquiry should lead to a successive refinement of the general concept.

In the early republic, charges of demagoguery were leveled most frequently at Thomas Jefferson and Aaron Burr. Jefferson's case is the most important. The criticism was greatest during the 1790s, in the lead-up to the elections of 1796 and 1800. To many Federalists, Jefferson's support for the French Revolution after 1791 led them to think he fit squarely into the newly prescribed category of the radical ideological demagogue. In addition, as a self-proclaimed leader of the popular element against the few, Jefferson was accused of crossing the line and violating the forms of constitutional government by involving himself (secretly) with establishing a newspaper, where his message could reach the public, and by creating a political party, which was then regarded as an anticonstitutional instrument. Jefferson was most sensitive to this last charge, which he justified chiefly as an emergency measure to save the nation from a worse fate, the subversion of republican government. He also suggested that party competition was inevitable in a democracy and would become an accepted part of constitutional government. His foresight on this point attenuates retrospectively the main charge of demagoguery. Furthermore, once Jefferson was elected to the presidency the accusations of demagogic behavior diminished, even as opposition to many of his policies grew.[65] There was nothing demagogic in Jefferson's style of presidential leadership.

Andrew Jackson probably endured the most sustained onslaught of accusations for demagoguery of any sitting president. The charges began well before he assumed office, in the campaign of 1824, when it looked as if he might become the first popular leader of conspicuously popular origins and tastes to be elected president. A rough-cut Westerner known for his rashness and violence, Jackson was of a different "class" than the nation's first six presidents, lacking their education and refinement. His military background only added to the concerns about demagoguery, as many suspected him of trying to capitalize on the personal popularity deriving from his battlefield exploits to win a political office for which he, unlike Washington, bore no special fitness. The ferocious campaign waged on Jackson's behalf after the 1824 campaign, charging that the election had been stolen, further increased worries of lawlessness.

This controversy took place inside of a new electoral system that functioned without political parties and that was predicated on pure "personalism." Jackson's future ally and confidant, Martin Van Buren, expressed great concern on just this point: "His election as the result of his military services without reference to party, and so far as he alone is concerned, scarcely to principle, would be one thing."[66] When Jackson was elected on the basis of "personal faction" in 1828, the charges of demagoguery inevitably carried over; and when Jackson as president decided not merely to sit back and preside but to pursue a course of action contrary to a majority in Congress, his opponents upped the ante, accusing him of seeking to subvert the Constitution and to establish under the aegis of the executive power a kind of popular tyranny. Opponents despised Jackson's policies, but the crux of their public case against "King Andrew" was less these policies or Jackson's behavior than his use of presidential powers, which he employed in new and controversial ways, appealing to the public for vindication. The most serious charge of Jackson's demagoguery thus turns on an assessment of the actual character of presidential powers under the Constitution. On this count, Jackson's overall position not only had much support at the time, but also it has been largely vindicated by subsequent practice. The great paradox of Jackson's presidency is that the concern over his demagoguery helped to supply the political energy, under Martin Van Buren's artful maneuvering, for transforming the political system from one that focused on personalism to one that became more beholden to political parties.

The next serious allegations of demagoguery came not in reference to an individual, but to the Whig Party's presidential campaign of 1840. John Quincy Adams described it as marking "a revolution in the habits and manners of the people." The Whigs invented the campaign as a mass spectacle, mobilizing the people themselves as the medium to carry the message. The party organized its followers to hold rallies, sing songs, and enact skits, all to celebrate the down-home virtues of their candidate, William Henry Harrison ("Old Tip"), whose simple ways were captured in the campaign's symbols of the log cabin and hard cider. The Whigs, it appears, sought to out-Jackson Jacksonianism.

Harrison's popular qualities were set in stark contrast to the aristocratic and sybaritic tastes of President Van Buren, charged with having turned the White House into a palace of luxury. This campaign was all the more striking for coming from a party that had rejected the instrumentality of the party organization itself as being too popular and demagogic and that had prided itself on representing the more respectable elements of society that were too proud to truckle after votes. All this changed when, as a Whig observer remarked at the time, "men of the highest culture did not disdain at times to 'go down to the people.' "[67] The vulgarity of the campaign, which abandoned all pretence of high-mindedness and deliberation, astonished even some of its own architects.

The judgment of the day that this campaign was demagogic has partly dissipated in light of the subsequent acceptance of many of its elements as folkloric and as making up part of the fun and ritual of democracy. Americans have adjusted to a more "populist" tone, using this term not in its darker sense, but in a more benign sense that refers to the celebration (or flattery) of popular tastes against the slightest suspicion of pretense or snobbishness. The Whig campaign of 1840 confirmed for both parties, and thus on a bipartisan basis, the abstract idea of the sovereignty of public opinion as well as the concrete practice of the sovereignty of popular tastes. But while "populist" in this respect, the campaign avoided deeply divisive issues, perhaps even using the appeals to these milder popular passions as a sop to avoid recourse to more dangerous ones. Even though the campaign broke all precedent by bringing out the candidate to engage in open speechifying—a step accused of being demagogic—no one ever charged Harrison's inoffensive rhetoric with being in the least bit inflammatory. The contrary was true. Whig populism was so superficial that it was never intended to continue past the campaign. Once elected, Harrison, who died after little more than a month of service, showed no inclination to be a populist, much less a demagogic, president. And Tyler, too.

The next set of campaigns to face frequent charges of demagoguery came, predictably, with the breakup of the old parties, beginning with the

Whigs, in the 1850s. Into this void stepped first the American or Know-Nothing Party, which targeted foreigners and Catholics as the source of the nation's problems. The party's nativist message, which appealed openly to popular fears, fit one of the classic categories of demagoguery. All that it lacked was a real demagogue. The party's candidate in 1856, the former Whig President Millard Fillmore, was hardly a very compelling figure. The movement soon collapsed, in part because the more respectable conservative forces, which initially toyed with using the movement as a vehicle for riding to power, had second thoughts and abandoned the effort.[68]

Next to enter the fray was the Republican Party. Proponents of slavery in the south saw the new party as an extension of abolitionism and, in the case of its political leaders, an organization "gotten up" by ambitious demagogues seeking power. Similar complaints also came, however, from some opponents of slavery, including the leader of the rump of the New England Whigs, Rufus Choate, who charged the Republican Party with theoretical demagoguery (taking too seriously the "glittering generalities" of the Declaration of Independence) and religious inspired enthusiasm ("moralism"). Neither abstract ideas nor fervor had a place in democratic politics. Choate concluded by 1856 that only the Democrats, with their amorphous formulae, could hold the nation together and save it from the demagoguery of the "geographical party." In this way of viewing things, Abraham Lincoln was the demagogue, Stephen Douglas the statesman; and the divisiveness of the Republican appeal, epitomized in Lincoln's statement "A House divided against itself cannot stand," was certainly confirmed in the secession of southern states following Lincoln's election in 1860.[69]

This case obviously raises a basic issue about the concept of demagoguery. While the most serious instances of demagoguery involve dangerous and divisive popular appeals, does it follow that all appeals that are dangerous and divisive are necessarily demagogic? Lincoln's position shows that a public appeal to genuine principle, perhaps necessary for the public good, can also fall into the category of divisiveness. Statesmanship, which ordinarily aims to have a calming effect and seeks room for compromise, cannot at times avoid confronting, perhaps even provoking, division. Lincoln may have been "statesmanlike" (in the usual sense) in relation to his efforts to moderate the abolitionists, but he would not back down from a position that was judged to polarize the public. No simple, external criterion in such instances would thus seem to distinguish statesmanship from demagoguery. The nature of the appeal itself must be examined and judged in its political context.

Lincoln nevertheless sought to refine, as far as possible, the "objective" distinctions used to apply to the concept. First, he argued against the all too facile "conservative" conception of demagoguery, embraced by Rufus Choate, which alleged that the introduction of any abstract or theoretical principle into politics was demagogic. Lincoln insisted that a modern nation, if it were to remain unified and be capable of resolve, must possess a common "philosophical public opinion."[70] From the standpoint of practical statesmanship, the question is not whether there is a core theoretical proposition that underpins "public sentiment" but rather which one it is.

Second, on the issue of divisiveness, Lincoln responded that there are some great issues—slavery, of course, being the great example—that are of such a fundamental nature that they cannot, at least in an enlightened era, be ignored or finessed. Slavery had always been "an apple of discord and an element of division" in America, and it would never go away on its own until the question was resolved in one way or another.[71] The Republican Party was at once the expression of this truism and the instrument that highlighted (and promoted) the moral division. Finally, on the level of the rhetorical tactics employed, the Lincoln-Douglas debates make another point clear. Not only was Lincoln's message more principled but his rhetoric also relied far less on appeals to raw passion. Douglas pulled heavily and continually on the strings of fear, in the form of the prospect of contamination of the white race by amalgamation, and of hope, in the form of his appeals to progress through democratic expansion or manifest destiny. Lincoln on occasion, usually in response to Douglas, used appeals that spoke to the emotions. (He certainly appealed frequently to the moral sense.) But the distinguishing characteristic of his rhetoric in this period was its reliance on "logic" and rational argument. Lincoln's speeches also displayed a remarkable sobriety, which often contrasted sharply with the enthusiasm of many spokesmen from his own party.

Lincoln's conduct as president was scrupulous in its reserve, which ended all talk of demagoguery. His stature steadily grew, and by the time of his assassination he had earned the reputation of being a statesman of the highest rank. His rhetoric alternated between speeches of almost clinical rationality (like his First Inaugural) and addresses unequaled in their poetic grandeur (like the Gettysburg Address and the Second Inaugural). The Second Inaugural stands out as the greatest of all American speeches. It is also one of the most unique in its mysterious tone, with no speech before being in any way a model. It is notable not only in expressing a firm and unbending resolve to complete the harsh task at hand but also in seeking to lay a foundation for reconciliation between the North and South.

By the time of his re-election in 1864, Lincoln emerged as a new "model" of the great democratic leader: a man of the people in origin and appearance, without any hint of elitism or outward aristocratic pretence (surpassing in this respect even "Old Tip" or "Old Hickory"), but yet one who possessed the highest personal virtues and had gone as far as any leader in mastering the art of democratic statesmanship. This model has intrigued yet bedeviled American politics ever since. It represents an ideal that is always looked and hoped for, but that has not yet again been realized.

The next significant charge of demagoguery appeared in the case of William Jennings Bryan, who burst onto the national scene in 1896. Bryan's fit with some of the main features associated with the demagogue makes the appearance of these charges seem in retrospect to be almost inevitable. Bryan was a self-proclaimed champion of the "people," who early on earned the title of "the Great Commoner"; he was a leader of the Populist movement inside the Democratic Party; he was a religious advocate, an evangelical, who brought all the fervor of "enthusiasm" into political life; and last, but certainly not least, he was widely known in 1896 for being an "orator." At just thirty-six years of age, and with scant national political experience, Bryan seized on his opportunity to address the Democratic Convention managing to catapult himself from a mere convention delegate to the nominee of his party. His remarkable Cross of Gold Speech, delivered on July 9, 1896, left his audience spellbound, and the delegates rallied to him the next day to select him as their new leader. Probably no single speech in American political history has had a greater immediate impact. It derived much of its power from its sheer divisiveness, pitting a virtuous agrarian and democratic vision against a wicked capitalist conspiracy to destroy the people: "Burn down your cities and leave our farms, and your cities will spring up again as if by magic. But destroy our farms and the grass will grow in the streets of every city in the country."

Following the convention, Bryan campaigned openly for the presidency, following in the footsteps of Harrison, Douglas, and Greeley, traveling across the country and delivering hundreds of speeches. More than anyone else, he can be credited with establishing the modern role for the presidential candidate as a campaigner and speech giver. At the time, Bryan was taken to task in many quarters for demeaning the election by engaging so extensively in the practice of personally soliciting support. His response was classic: "I would rather have it said that I lacked dignity than that I lacked backbone to meet the enemies of the government who work against its welfare from Wall Street."

The presidential campaign of 1912 led to many of the most conspicuous charges of demagoguery in American history. The campaign was the first in which the new system of selecting convention delegates by primary elections was in effect, and the first therefore in which candidates openly campaigned for their party's nominations. They did so on the basis of their "personal" programs, thus replicating at an earlier stage (nomination) the kind of candidate-centered politics that prevailed in 1824 at the final election stage. By the terms of the analysis of Woodrow Wilson, the new system opened a space for popular statesmanship; by Martin Van Buren's analysis, it opened a space for demagogic appeals.

Teddy Roosevelt's candidacy immediately put this question to the test. For Roosevelt and his followers, the nomination race was a great opportunity both to overthrow a sitting president who had veered from a progressive line and to renew the Republican Party. Others viewed Roosevelt's return to politics as motivated by personal opportunism. His appeals to the working class against the business interests and his attacks on the courts led President Taft to take the extraordinary step of publicly branding him "a dangerous demagogue."[72] The Socialist candidate Eugene Debs, who was trying to maintain control of the Left in the general election, followed up later on this theme, calling Roosevelt "a charlatan, mountebank, and an . . . utterly unprincipled self seeker and demagogue."

The new nomination system, which concentrated so much on the individual leader, also contributed to the "personalist" kind of "third party" presidential candidacy that came to characterize such efforts in the twentieth century, most notably in the candidacies of George Wallace (in 1968) and Ross Perot (in 1992 and 1996). Roosevelt initiated the model for this development as well, bolting from the Republican Party after being denied the nomination to head the Progressive ticket, which very much relied on Roosevelt's personal appeal.

Of the twentieth-century presidents, Franklin Roosevelt was probably the one most frequently accused of practicing demagoguery. The charges surfaced after he was elected, as his campaign in 1932 proceeded in a fairly low-keyed manner. The accusations fit FDR into a new pattern, at least by American standards, that had been pioneered by his cousin Theodore: a "patrician" by birth who sided conspicuously with the popular party and claiming to represent the "common people" and the "little man." FDR's rhetorical skills were legendary and included the ability of being able to create a feeling of personal closeness between himself and his audience. Roosevelt exploited a new medium of communication (radio), using it to develop a more familiar kind of rapport with the American people than had been tried by his two predecessors. The talks became known as "fireside chats," with the word "chat" bespeaking this new informality. Roosevelt often began by addressing his audience as "my friends," seeking to reduce distance between the president and the public and to establish a direct psychological link. Many found this intimate approach to be a threat to the tone of a constitutional office. It established a "personal" presidency.

These issues of tone only set the stage for the more substantive charges of demagoguery, which concerned the content of FDR's message. He was accused of fomenting class division, typified by his rhetoric castigating of the "tyranny" of "economic royalists," and then for attacking the Supreme Court. Controversy about Roosevelt's leadership appeals raged not just at the time, but it has continued ever since among his biographers. Many have lauded him for being the supreme popular leader, a piece of praise that seems to concede that he at least flirted with the demagogic arts. His defenders, however, insist he stopped short of ever crossing the line.

Roosevelt's success as president, though it cannot completely exonerate him of these charges, has shifted historical judgments in his favor. He has profited in this regard most from his role as war leader, which enabled him to rise above heated internal divisions and become a unifying national figure. On the specific charges, the following responses have been offered on FDR's behalf.

First, regarding his close personal relation to the public, the Depression was a period of such acute distress that the public needed someone to minister to the mood of despair and to provide reassurance and hope. As Saul Bellow remarked of his performance during the first one hundred days of his administration, "The secret of his political genius was that he knew exactly what people needed to hear, a personal declaration by the president that took account of the feelings of the people."[73] According to this view, FDR's informality was justified for helping the American people to get through a supreme crisis.

Second, on the question of class division, FDR's defenders argue that his rhetoric, however extreme, served to undercut similar, but more radical appeals, by Father Charles Coughlin and Huey Long, whom Roosevelt considered to be the real demagogues. By giving vent to the existing anger against the wealthy, but not ultimately threatening the capitalist system, FDR saved it. According to Morton Frisch, "the rhetoric of the class struggle was one of the facts of political life that had to be accepted or approved or stolen in order to be moderated."[74] Defenders add that many of Roosevelt's most provocative appeals to class division occurred during the presidential campaign of 1936. Although a campaign does not free a president from all restraints, it has generally come to be understood as granting a president more leeway than usual, allowing him to "step down" and assume the role of a candidate. FDR played no small part in promoting this role for the president when he surprised the nation in 1932 by becoming the first party nominee (and thus the first president) to deliver a convention acceptance address. In another indication of the personalism of modern leadership, this address has now replaced the party platform as the central statement of the "party's" position.

Two charges of presidential demagoguery stand out in modern times, one involving Richard Nixon, the other Bill Clinton. The accusations consist of taking advantage of the prestige of the presidency to foment a division to pursue a political aim, unrelated to any pending policy matter. In Nixon's case, the president sought to avoid direct, personal involvement in his venture by making use of his vice president, Spiro Agnew. Agnew was unleashed in 1970 to engage in a series of attacks that targeted what

Nixon and Agnew saw as the media elite and intellectuals undermining America. The speeches castigated an "effete corps of impudent snobs," the "nattering nabobs of negativism," and the "radiclibs."

No one, of course, had the slightest doubt that this "campaign," which used White House speechwriters, was orchestrated by President Nixon. This demagogic tactic was consistent with a certain "history" by Richard Nixon, who had been well known for running tough and polarizing campaigns in the past. These had earned him a reputation, at least among his foes, for red-baiting and McCarthyism. Furthermore, even the most casual observer had no difficultly detecting in Nixon a personality who was consciously struggling to prevent himself from giving vent to emotional appeals based on anger and fears. He employed the mask of a practiced and inflated "statesmanlike" demeanor to assist him, but on occasion the mask would fall and what observers called the "Old Nixon," always lurking just beneath the surface, would reappear. That Nixon was often severely provoked was certainly true—even paranoids have real enemies—but this excuse changes nothing for judging the use of demagoguery for the office of the presidency.

In Bill Clinton's case, there is a strong temptation when thinking of his unusual uses of popular rhetoric, following his acquittal in the Senate impeachment trial, where he spoke of his "journey," of his "spirit [having been] broken" and of "the rock bottom truth of where I am," before making known that he had repented and was asking forgiveness. But his pleading here was of a "personal" kind, involving the use of a "forensic" rhetoric reminiscent of the pleas made in popular judicial settings and stands outside the category of political demagoguery under consideration. The germane charges of demagoguery involve the instances where Clinton engaged in veiled or direct attacks against strong conservatives. These occurred in the aftermath of the Oklahoma City bombing, when he decried certain "loud and angry voices . . . spread[ing] hate . . . over the airwaves," which seemed clearly directed at hosts of talk radio; in his oblique charge, by way of not being able to affirm the contrary, that there was a "national conspiracy" based on "racial hostility" in the burnings of black churches; and in the declaration of his wife, Hillary Clinton, of the existence of a "vast right wing conspiracy" devoted to bringing down her husband. (Like Nixon, Bill Clinton was constantly maligned and provoked by a group of inveterate Clinton-haters.)

With Clinton, as with Nixon, there was a prehistory in his rhetoric that almost guaranteed that charges of demagoguery would be forthcoming, although in his case with matters touching more on tone than substance. Bill Clinton relished the experience of giving speeches before live audience, a task at which he excelled. He had a famed capacity, and evidently a felt urge as well, to "connect" with people in an empathetic mode, a trait that was often satirized in his supposed wish to "feel your pain." Clinton was also in tune with modern sensibilities in his appeal to compassion, which he could also quickly turn into an effective polarizing theme by striking at the target group of the "haters" and the uncompassionate. Finally, Clinton had few reservations in breaking with forms. As a candidate, he appeared on a youth entertainment network (MTV), which some considered undignified; and he subsequently appeared on a late-night TV show playing the saxophone — "jamming" — while wearing sunglasses. His legendary ability to connect with people spread to his mastery of the medium of television, where he was especially adept at technique of creating a feeling of intimacy. He famously brought this familiarity to a new level during the first ever "town hall" style presidential debate in 1992, when he stepped out from behind the podium, literally reducing the distance between himself and the audience, and directly engaged in a personal dialogue with a citizen who was asking him a question. President George H. W. Bush remained glued behind his podium.

An Assessment

Surveying American history, it is fair to conclude that no president merits the dubious honor of being called a clear demagogue, although a few have engaged in acts of demagoguery. Even on this score, however, the charges have been rare, especially if one grants, for the modern period, a modest license for presidents to go a bit further than usual during the campaign season. One reason for this relative immunity is that the presidential office has had built into it, almost like a genetic code, a tone of "dignity," or, if this term sounds too stuffy or Victorian to the modern ear, a strong norm demanding that occupants of the office act "presidentially." This norm has served as a powerful restraint on demagoguery, at least where it can be plausibly recognized as such. The origin of this norm lay, as has been suggested, in the understanding of constitutional forms as articulated in *The Federalist*; but this abstract idea was given flesh and life by George Washington, who viewed one of the primary tasks of his presidency to be the establishment of sound precedents. Finding the right tone of democratic dignity, somewhere between formality and openness, was one of his great concerns and one of his greatest accomplishments. Steps to alter the tone and popularize the office have been attempted, and a number have had success, in the sense either of contributing to the popularity of a particular innovator or of being subsequently embraced as behavior consistent with being presidential. The office is more popular or familiar than before, although not by very much. But it is also the case that many actions have run afoul of concerns for the dignity of the office, from Andrew Jackson's rowdy inaugural party at the White House in 1828 to Jimmy Carter's calculated populist gesture of carrying his own luggage. It was Bill Clinton's lackadaisical attitude toward the dignity of the presidency—which was not limited to the Monica Lewinsky affair—that brought on him much of the obloquy that he received.

Turning from the presidency to presidential campaigns, the story is different. Incidents of demagoguery have been frequent, and they have not abated in modern times. They are found especially in the personalist candidacies of some of the nomination campaigns and of the third party candidacies. Personalist politics is not the same thing as demagoguery, but it is a form of politics that opens the door to demagogic appeals. One of the better known demagogues was George Wallace. His quest for the presidency began within the primary process in the Democratic Party in 1964, where he tested with some success some of the backlash themes that he subsequently employed in his 1968 personalist third party campaign, in which he captured more than 13 percent of the popular vote.

Wallace was back inside the Democratic Party in 1972, showing more appeal than before from voters outside the South, before he was crippled by an assassination attempt during the primary campaign in Maryland. How far Wallace might have gotten in this race is unknown, although nomination by his party, or election to the presidency, seem to have been well beyond his reach. Looking back, it is tempting, though perhaps too hopeful, to consider Wallace as the last of a breed, a traditional (Type I) demagogue, who appears out of place in the softer-style politics of the TV age.

A very different sort of demagogic candidacy appeared in 1992, in the singular person of Ross Perot. Unlike Wallace, Perot seemed positioned for a time not just to make a decent showing but to offer a real prospect for capturing the presidency. The mild division he fomented was not between different parts of the populace but rather between the whole body of the citizenry untainted by involvement in a corrupted system ("outsiders") and the class of politicians and influence peddlers currently operating it ("insiders").

In one sense this division only echoed the typical cleansing and purging reform appeal of the type seen in the past, with Ross Perot serving as the outsider in chief and promising, in a slightly updated mechanical metaphor, to "open up the hood and fix it." It was the tone of flattery and total nominal subjugation of the leader to the public that marked its special demagogic character, all summed up in the pithy five-word populist slogan, "I'm Ross, you're the boss." The anticonstitutional overtones of this appeal became more evident, as Perot spoke vaguely of forms of consultation between the leader and public by means of polls. (This idea was reminiscent of the "Caesarist" acts of European leaders to hold plebiscites to support their positions.) The technique of "official" consultation by an Internet vote did not end with Ross Perot but was picked up later by Howard Dean in the 2004 nomination campaign, when he sought—and received—an endorsement from his supporters to break a pledge to accept public funding for his campaign and instead raise money from private contributions only.

It is the nomination process, however, that has served as the true nursery for candidacies by modern-day "orators." Among the more significant have been Jesse Jackson, Pat Robertson, Patrick Buchanan, Alan Keyes, Al Sharpton, and Howard Dean. These candidates sought to raise an issue or cause within their party by spirited and sometimes provocatively divisive appeals. Reversing the previous notion that candidates should be judged in large part on the basis of a reputation for significant service in a public career, these candidates sought to win their reputation during the campaign, even using in some cases the presidential selection system process to help boost or restart a career. The most extraordinary recent case of the orator, however, has been the successful 2008 Democratic Party campaign of Senator Barack Obama. A candidate with little experience in national politics when he launched his presidential bid, Obama gained favor with the American people during his run for the presidency, relying in substantial degree on eloquence and oratory. Unlike some of the others cited, Obama eschewed divisiveness and aimed the most "rhetorical" aspects of his appeal at evoking a general sentiment for "change." His candidacy could only have emerged under the institutional arrangements that opened the door to the rhetorical politics envisaged by Woodrow Wilson.

From the time of the founding, the defenders of constitutionalism have sought to build and maintain a series of concentric walls around the presidency to protect it from demagoguery. The innermost wall consists of structural features designed to fortify a president against the immediate pressures of public opinion; next are attendant norms that prescribe a code of "presidential" conduct and encourage a certain dignity in comportment; beyond this are the moderating effects of election in a large territory with a multiplicity of interests, which diminish the ultimate success of classic demagogic appeals; finally, occupying the outer ring, are the restraining institutional devices of the electoral system, which for a long time rested on the mighty bulwark of traditional political parties.

This last barrier has been breached by a new party nomination process that allows a point of entrance for demagoguery and that therefore adds stress to the other parts of the network of defense. Some argue that whatever happens to this outer wall, the inner walls provide more than an adequate defense. This view is too hopeful. The office of the presidency is probably more "friendly" to the use of demagoguery today than it was in the past, and currently available means of communication facilitate its exercise. In facing a danger of this magnitude, there can be no such thing as too much vigilance. Given the lower institutional barriers to demagoguery today, greater responsibility for checking it must fall to other means. A better understanding of demagoguery is an essential element in erecting new lines of defense against it.

Chapter One: On the Constitution, Politics, and the Presidency

1. Edward Corwin, *The President: Office and* Powers, 4th ed. (1940; repr. New York: New York University Press, 1957), vii, 307. For a full understanding of Corwin's theory of the presidency, one should not overlook the excellent collection of his essays in *Presidential Power and the Constitution*, ed. Richard Loss (Ithaca, NY: Cornell University Press, 1976).

2. Randall W. Bland, Theodore T. Hindson, and Jack W. Peltason updated the work in 1984 as *The President: Office and Powers, 1787–1984*, 5th rev. ed. (New York: New York University Press, 1984).

3. Emphasis in the original; Richard Neustadt, *Presidential Power: The Politics of Leadership* (New York: John Wiley & Sons, 1960), preface, 43, 179, 35, 183. See also the preface to the 1976 edition, "Reflections on Johnson and Nixon."

4. James MacGregor Burns, *The Deadlock of Democracy* (Englewood Cliffs, NJ: Prentice-Hall, 1963), 6.

5. See, for example, Burns, *Deadlock of Democracy*, 327–32, and Louis Koenig, "More Power to the President," in *The Power of the Presidency*, ed. Robert Hirshfield, 2nd ed. (Chicago: Aldine, 1973), 362. The call for reforms like these has been recently revived by Sanford Levinson in *Our Undemocratic Constitution: Where the Constitution Goes Wrong (And How We the People Can Correct It)* (New York: Oxford University Press, 2006).

6. The following are among the most important: Raoul Berger, *Executive Privilege: A Constitutional Myth* (Cambridge, MA: Harvard University Press, 1974); Raoul Berger, *Impeachment* (Cambridge, MA: Harvard University Press, 1973); Louis Fisher, *President and Congress* (New York: Free Press, 1972); Louis Fisher, *The Constitution between Friends: Congress, the President, and the Law* (New York: St. Martin's Press, 1978); Louis Henkin, *Foreign Affairs and the Constitution* (New York: Norton, 1972); Phillip Kurland, *Watergate and the Constitution* (Chicago: University of Chicago Press, 1978); Abraham D. Sofaer, *War, Foreign Affairs, and the Constitution: The Origins* (Cambridge, MA: Ballinger Publishers, 1976).

7. The principal exception is Louis Fisher.

8. See particularly Thomas Cronin, *The State of the Presidency* (Boston: Little, Brown, 1975); Thomas Cronin and Rexford Tugwell, *The Presidency Reappraised* (New York: Praeger, 1977); Erwin Hargrove, *The Power of the Modern Presidency* (Philadelphia: Temple University Press, 1974); and the third edition of Louis Koenig's *The Chief Executive* (New York: Harcourt Brace Jovanovich, 1975).

9. Louis Fisher, *Constitutional Dialogues: Interpretation as Political Process* (Princeton, NJ: Princeton University Press, 1988); Louis Fisher, *The Politics of Shared Power: Congress and the Executive* (College Station: Texas A & M Press, 1998); Louis Fisher, *Constitutional Conflicts between Congress and the President*, 5th rev. ed. (Lawrence: University Press of Kansas, 2007).

10. Louis Fisher, *Military Tribunals and Presidential Power: American Revolution to the War on Terrorism* (Lawrence: University Press of Kansas, 2005); Louis Fisher, *Presidential War Power*, 2nd rev. ed. (Lawrence: University Press of Kansas, 2004); Louis Fisher, *In the Name of National Security: Unchecked Presidential Power and the Reynolds Case* (Lawrence: University Press of Kansas, 2006); Louis Fisher, *The Politics of Executive Privilege* (Durham: Carolina Academic Press, 2004); Louis Fisher, *Nazi Saboteurs on Trial: A Military Tribunal and American Law* (Lawrence: University Press of Kansas, 2005); Louis Fisher, *Congressional Abdication on War and Spending* (College Station: Texas A & M Press, 2000).

11. See especially William G. Howell, *Power without Persuasion: The Politics of Direct Presidential Action* (Princeton, NJ: Princeton University Press, 2003) and Charles M. Cameron, *Veto Bargaining: Presidents and the Politics of Negative Power* (Cambridge: Cambridge University Press, 2000).

12. Stephen Skowronek, *The Politics Presidents Make* (Cambridge, MA: Belknap, Harvard University Press, 1993).

13. For more detail on this point, see Jeffrey K. Tulis, "The President in the Political System—In Neustadt's Shadow," in *Presidential Power*, ed. Martha Kumar, Robert Shapiro, and Lawrence Jacobs (New York: Columbia University Press, 2000), 265–73. Two other studies critical of Neustadt that, nevertheless, rely on and extend his fundamental perspective are Samuel Kernell, *Going Public: New Strategies of Presidential Leadership*, 4th ed. (Washington, DC: CQ Press, 2006) and Fred I. Greenstein, *The Hidden Hand Presidency*, rev. ed. (Baltimore: Johns Hopkins University Press, 1994).

14. The "rational choice" institutionalists are also institutional partisans. Some, like William Howell, continue to view the polity from the perspective of the presidency, while others, like David Epstein and Sharyn O'Halloran, adopt a Congress-centered perspective. See Howell, *Power without Persuasion*; David Epstein and Sharyn O'Halloran, *Delegating Powers: A Transaction Cost Politics Approach to Policy Making Under Separate Powers* (Cambridge: Cambridge University Press, 1999).

15. Joseph M. Bessette and Jeffrey Tulis, eds., *The Presidency in the Constitutional Order* (Baton Rouge: Louisiana State University Press, 1981); Jeffrey K. Tulis, *The Rhetorical Presidency* (Princeton, NJ: Princeton University Press, 1987); Joseph M. Bessette, *The Mild Voice of Reason: Deliberative Democracy and American National Government* (Chicago: University of Chicago Press, 1994). See also, David Nichols, *The Myth of the Modern Presidency* (State College: Pennsylvania State University Press, 1994): James Ceaser, *Presidential Selection: Theory and Development* (Princeton, NJ: Princeton University Press, 1982); Sidney Milkis, *The President and the Parties: The Transformation of the American Party System since the New Deal* (New York: Oxford University Press, 1993); Jeffrey K. Tulis, "The Interpretable Presidency," in *The Presidency in the Political System*, ed. Michael Nelson, 3rd ed. (Washington, DC: CQ Press, 1985).

16. Arthur S. Miller, *Presidential Power in a Nutshell* (St. Paul, MN: West Publishing, 1977), 323. The same view is "rediscovered" in Levinson, *Our Undemocratic Constitution* (2006).

17. Alexander Hamilton, James Madison, and John Jay, *The Federalist Papers*, ed. Clinton Rossiter, with a new introduction and notes by Charles R. Kesler (New York: New American Library, Mentor Books, 2003), No. 51, 319.

18. James D. Richardson, ed., *A Compilation of the Messages and Papers of the Presidents, 1789–1897*, 10 vols. (Washington, DC: Government Printing Office, 1896–1899), 5:615.

19. Theodore Roosevelt, *An Autobiography* (New York: Macmillan, 1913), 395. For a brief discussion of other examples of forcefulness on the part of "weak" presidents, see Joseph M. Bessette, "The Presidency," in *Founding Principles of American Government*, ed. George J. Graham and Scarlett G. Graham (Bloomington: Indiana University Press, 1977), 205–7.

20. President Ronald Reagan, "Statement on Signing the Independent Counsel Reauthorization Act of 1987," December 15, 1987, at www.presidency.ucsb .edu/ ws/index.php?pid=33827.

21. Richardson, ed., *Messages and Papers of the Presidents*, 2:582. Also found at www.presidency.ucsb.edu/ws/index.php?pid=67043&st=veto&st1=bank.

22. *Federalist* No. 72, 435; No. 71, 433; and No. 72, 436. Instructive on this last point was President Nixon's dramatic effort to improve relations with China and the Soviet Union. Arthur Burns, chairman of the Federal Reserve Board during the Nixon administration, assessed Nixon's actions this way: "He's a president now. . . . He has a noble motive in foreign affairs to reshape the world, or at least his motive is to earn the fame that comes from nobly reshaping the world. Who can say what his motive is? But it's moving him in the right direction." Quoted in William Safire, *Before the Fall* (New York: Belmont Tower Books, 1975), 524.

23. *Federalist* No. 70.

24. *Federalist* No. 51, 319.

25. See Charles C. Thach Jr., *The Creation of the Presidency, 1775–1789* (1923; repr. Baltimore: Johns Hopkins Press, 1969), 25–54.

26. *Federalist* No. 23, 149, 152; No. 25, 163; and No. 26, 165–66.

27. *Federalist* No. 74, 446.

28. *Ex parte Milligan*, 71 U.S. 2 (1866), 119, 121, 118–19, 120–21.

29. Ibid., 127.

30. Ibid., 127.

31. This account of *Milligan* ignores the fascinating debate between the five justices who signed on to the opinion of the Court, written by Justice David Davis, and the four others who, through the opinion of Chief Justice Salmon P. Chase, agreed with the holding but took strong issue with the majority's assertion that not even Congress had the power to establish military tribunals if the civil courts were open. Both sides agreed that necessity could justify acts not otherwise allowed, but the four concurring justices faulted the majority for not explicitly rooting such necessary actions in specific constitutional provisions: "Congress has the power not only to raise and support and govern armies but to declare war. It has, therefore, the power to provide for carrying on war. This power necessarily extends to all legislation essential to the prosecution of war with vigor and success" (ibid., 139). It could well happen, Chase wrote, that even if the civilian courts were open, they might be "wholly incompetent to avert threatened danger, or to punish, with adequate promptitude and certainty, the guilty conspirators. If this were the case, Congress could properly establish military tribunals under its powers to declare war and to provide the means to win it" (ibid., 141).

32. Letter from Lincoln to Albert G. Hodges, April 4, 1864, in *The Collected Works of Abraham Lincoln*, ed. Roy P. Basler, 9 vols. (New Brunswick, NJ: Rutgers University Press, 1953), 7:281.

33. Letter from Lincoln to Matthew Birchard and others, June 29, 1863, ibid., 6: 302.

34. See, for example, Lincoln's letter to James C. Conkling, August 26, 1863, ibid., 6: 408; Message to Congress in Special Session, July 4, 1861, ibid., 4: 430, 440; First Inaugural Address, March 4, 1861, ibid., 4: 265, 270; and Emancipation Proclamation, ibid.

35. References here are to the 2004 edition of the book, Arthur M. Schlesinger Jr., *The Imperial Presidency*, with a new introduction (Boston: Mariner Books, 2004), which includes the text from the original 1973 work, a lengthy epilogue originally published in 1989, and a new introduction written in 2004.

36. Schlesinger, *Imperial Presidency*, 323, 459.

37. John Locke, *The Two Treatises of Government*, ed. Peter Laslett, rev. ed. (New York: New American Library, 1960). All references are to the standard

paragraph numbers of the *Second Treatise*. The quotations are at No. 159 and No. 160.

38. Schlesinger, *Imperial Presidency*, 9 (emphasis in the original), 322.

39. Ibid., 323, 459.

40. Ibid., xiii, 112. Although Schlesinger defends FDR's use of emergency powers as legitimate, it is hard to see how, given his own account of FDR's actions, they meet his "stringent" criteria governing prerogative.

41. Ibid., 459.

42. Locke, *Second Treatise*, No. 168.

Chapter Two: The Powers and Duties of the President

1. Edward S. Corwin, *The President: Office and Powers, 1787–1957*, 4th rev. ed. (New York: New York University Press, 1957), 3.

2. Forrest McDonald, *The American Presidency: An Intellectual History* (Lawrence: University Press of Kansas, 1994), 2.

3. Justice Robert Jackson, concurring opinion in *Youngstown Sheet and Tube Co. v. Sawyer*, 343 U.S. 579 (1952), 634.

4. For a contrary view, see Richard Neustadt's *Presidential Power: The Politics of Leadership* (New York: John Wiley & Sons, 1960). Neustadt particularly criticizes Presidents Truman and Eisenhower, in contrast to President Franklin Roosevelt, for their love of and devotion to duty, rather than power. See especially 165, 173, 175–78.

5. Hamilton made this argument as "Pacificus" in defending President George Washington's constitutional authority to issue the Proclamation of Neutrality in 1793. See chap. 3 by Gary J. Schmitt in this volume: "President Washington's Proclamation of Neutrality."

6. Madison (June 16, 1789), in *Documentary History of the First Federal Congress of the United States of America, March 4, 1789–March 3, 1791: Debates in the House of Representatives, First Session: June–September 1789*, ed. Charlene Bangs Bickford, Kenneth R. Bowling, and Helen E. Veit (Baltimore: Johns Hopkins University Press, 1992), 10:868.

7. Edward S. Corwin, *Presidential Power and the Constitution*, ed. Richard Loss (Ithaca, NY: Cornell University Press, 1976), 72.

8. Note that when William Blackstone turned to a discussion of the king in his *Commentaries on the Laws of England*, he addressed the "King's Duties" in chap. 6 of book 1 before detailing the "King's Prerogatives" in chap. 7. The duties, which required but four pages to describe, were "all . . . that a monarch can owe to his people; viz. to govern according to law: to execute judgment in mercy: and to maintain the established religion" (William Blackstone, *Commentaries on the*

Laws of England [Chicago: University of Chicago Press, 1979], 229). The prerogatives of the king respecting "his royal authority," which "constitute the executive power of the government" (covering twenty-one pages) included such varied items as sending and receiving ambassadors, making treaties and alliances, determining on war and peace, issuing letters of marque and reprisal, granting safe-conducts, vetoing parliamentary enactments, commanding the armed forces of the state, raising and regulating armies and navies, conserving the peace of the kingdom, prosecuting crimes, pardoning offenses, issuing proclamations, erecting and disposing of offices, establishing public markets, regulating weights and measures, coining money, and governing the national church (ibid., 233, 271, and 245–70).

Note also that, when Blackstone treated "Subordinate Magistrates" in chap. 9 of book 1, he used the language of "powers and duties"—or, equivalently, "rights and duties" throughout: for example, "the powers and duties of his majesty's great officers of state" (ibid., 327); "the magistrates and officers, whose rights and duties it will be proper in this chapter to consider" (ibid., 328); "I shall inquire into . . . lastly, their rights and duties" (ibid.); "We shall find it is of the utmost importance to have the sheriff appointed according to law, when we consider his power and duty" (ibid., 331); "The power, office, and duty of a justice of the peace depend on his commission, and on the several statutes, which have created objects of his jurisdiction" (ibid., 342).

9. These data are drawn from the biographies in M.E. Bradford's *Founding Fathers: Brief Lives of the Framers of the United States Constitution*, 2nd rev. ed. (Lawrence: University Press of Kansas, 1994).

10. Max Farrand, ed., *The Records of the Federal Convention of 1787*, rev. ed., 4 vols. (New Haven, CT: Yale University Press, 1966), 1:62–67 (June 1) and 1:98–104 (June 4).

11. Although Alexander Hamilton had outlined a plan of government, with detailed provisions on the "authorities & functions" to be vested in the national executive, in his five to six hour speech on June 18, he did not formally submit these to the Convention. Nor did the delegates submit Hamilton's plan to the Committee of Detail.

12. Farrand, *Records*, 1:244–45 (June 15).

13. Farrand, *Records*, 3:606, Appendix D. The original version of the Pinckney Plan has not been found. This version was reconstructed by Max Farrand based largely on the work of J. Franklin Jameson, who relied on documents found among James Wilson's papers related to the work of the Committee of Detail. Farrand described his version as "a fairly good idea of the Pinckney Plan" (ibid., 604). Farrand's reconstruction uses italics, quotation marks, and parentheses to identify the various sources. For ease of reading, these have been eliminated here.

14. On June 6, Pinckney announced that he had changed his mind and no longer saw the value of giving the heads of the principal departments a constitutional role in the veto power: "These could be called on by the Executive Magistrate whenever he pleased to consult them." Farrand, *Records*, 1:139.

15. The draft constitution of the Committee of Detail can be found at Farrand, *Records*, 2: 177–89. Article X on the executive is at 185–86. The committee placed the president's qualified veto power not in Article X but in Article VI, Section 13, among the provisions on the legislature (ibid., 181).

16. Farrand, *Records*, 2:405, emphasis in the original.

17. Farrand, *Records*, 2:419.

18. Farrand, *Records*, 2:553.

19. The Committee of Style's constitution is at Farrand, *Records*, 2: 590–603.

20. Clinton Rossiter, *1787: The Grand Convention* (New York: New American Library, Mentor Books, 1966), 196.

21. Farrand, *Records*, 3:170, 420, 499, emphasis in the original. It is Ezra Stiles who reported in his diary Baldwin's claim of Morris's role. In one respect, however, the diary entry is wrong; for it also accords equal credit to James Wilson, who did not serve on the Committee of Style.

22. See Charles Z. Lincoln, *The Constitutional History of New York*, 5 vols. (Rochester, NY: Lawyers Co-operative Publishing Co., 1906), 1:471–558, especially 471 and 496.

23. See, for example, Charles C. Thach Jr., *The Creation of the Presidency, 1775–1789* (1923; repr. Baltimore: Johns Hopkins Press, 1969), 52–54 and 176.

24. Following common practice, President James Buchanan, Lincoln's predecessor, had called the Senate alone into special session beginning the first day of the next presidential term. This enabled the Senate to confirm presidential appointments. The Senate was in session from March 4 through March 28, 1861.

25. Accounts of Washington's actions during the Whiskey Rebellion may be found in Bennett M. Rich, "Washington and the Whiskey Insurrection," *Pennsylvania Magazine of History and Biography* 65 (1941): 334–52; Bennett M. Rich, *The Presidents and Civil Disorder* (Washington: Brookings Institution, 1941), 2–20; and John Alexander Carroll and Mary Wells Ashworth, *George Washington: First in Peace* (New York: Charles Scribner's Sons, 1957), 180–213.

26. Washington to the Secretary of the Treasury, September 7, 1792, in John C. Fitzpatrick, ed., *The Writings of George Washington* (Washington, DC: Government Printing Office, 1939), 32: 144.

27. Proclamation of September 15, 1792, in James D. Richardson, ed., *A Compilation of the Messages and Papers of the Presidents, 1789–1897*, 10 vols. (Washington, DC: Government Printing Office, 1896–99), 1:124–25.

28. Hamilton's major opinion of August 2, 1794, suggesting the use of armed

force is in Henry Cabot Lodge, ed., *The Works of Alexander Hamilton* (New York: G.P. Putnam's Sons, 1904), 6: 353–58. It begins, "In compliance with your requisitions . . ." Later it notes, "The case upon which an opinion is required, is summarily as follows."

29. I Stat. 264.

30. See Washington's Sixth Annual Address to Congress, November 19, 1794, in Richardson, *Messages and Papers of the Presidents*, 1:164, and his Proclamation of Amnesty of July 10, 1795, 1:181.

31. Ibid., 1:161.

32. Rich, *Presidents and Civil Disorder*, 12–14.

33. "Letters from a Federal Farmer, VII" in *The Complete Anti-Federalist*, ed. Herbert J. Storing, 7 vols. (Chicago: University of Chicago Press, 1981), 2:264.

34. The 1807 statute has sometimes been interpreted as evidence that the president was not understood to have independent constitutional authority to use the nation's armed forces to enforce domestic law. But note the following: First, neither the Militia Bill of 1792 nor that of 1795, both of which authorized calling out the state militia to enforce domestic law, mentioned the regular armed forces. The presumption here seems to be that the president did not need legislative authorization to use federal forces, although he did need such authorization to use the state militia for this purpose. The Constitution implies as much when it gives Congress the power "to provide for calling forth the Militia to execute the Laws of the Union" (Article I, Section 8) and makes the president the commander in chief "of the Militia of the several states, when called into the actual Service of the United States" (Article II, Section 2).

Second, prior to 1807 there were at least two instances where presidents used at least some regular armed forces to help enforce domestic law. The first, in fact, was the Whiskey Rebellion itself. Although the state militia from four states had the major responsibility for putting down the resistance, Washington did assign a small force of regular troops from the fort at Pittsburgh to accompany excise inspector John Neville on the night of the attack on his Bower Hill home, the most violent disturbance of the insurrection. And one month later, in conjunction with the planned march of the twelve-thousand-man militia force, Washington ordered the garrison at Pittsburgh reinforced from Fort Franklin.

Third, in 1799 President John Adams met a less serious resistance to federal tax laws in eastern Pennsylvania—which came to be known as the Fries Rebellion—with both a contingent of the Pennsylvania militia and five hundred federal troops. Apparently, no constitutional objections were raised to this use of federal troops, and both the House and Senate warmly and formally approved the President's actions. (See W.W.H. Davis, *The Fries Rebellion, 1798–1799* [Doylestown, PA: Doylestown Publishing Co., 1899]; Rich, *Presidents and Civil Disor-*

der, 21–30; and Richardson, *Messages and Papers of the Presidents*, 1:286–87, 289, 292, and 294.)

Fourth, although the 1807 act had been submitted by the Jefferson administration because of uncertainties as to the president's authority to employ the regular troops to thwart Aaron Burr's treasonous activities on the western frontier in the fall and winter of 1806–7, Jefferson himself did not await congressional authorization to use the army. As early as November 25, 1806, Jefferson issued orders to the regular troops stationed on the Ohio and Mississippi rivers to intercept Burr's flotilla. Provision was also made to defend New Orleans against the expected attack. And in February of 1807, after Burr's expedition has collapsed, federal troops arrested him near the Spanish frontier. All this was done before the authorization of 1807.

Finally, it must be noted that the 1807 act reached not just to violations of federal law but also of state law. Some in Congress may have accepted the president's independent constitutional authority to use federal troops to enforce federal law but have also believed that Congress must authorize use of federal troops when no federal law was in jeopardy. (See Dumas Malone, *Jefferson the President: Second Term, 1805–1809* [Boston: Little, Brown and Co., 1974], 252–53; Richardson, *Messages and Papers of the Presidents*, 1: 407; Henry Adams, *History of the United States during the Administrations of Jefferson and Madison* [New York: Charles Scribner's Sons, 1890], 3:283–85 and 327; and Paul Leicester Ford, ed., *The Works of Thomas Jefferson* [New York: G.P. Putnam's Sons, 1905], 10: 334.

35. Farrand, *Records*, 2:64–69 (July 20), 132, and 186 (August 6).

36. Ibid., 2:499 (September 4).

37. Ibid., 2:550–52 (September 8).

38. Although there is no record of an extended debate about the meaning of "high crimes and misdemeanors," Mason's reference to the impeachment of Warren Hastings is especially interesting in light of the larger argument we are making about the president's powers and duties. In April 1786, after several years of debate and inquiries into the East India Company's policies while Hastings was governor of India, the House of Commons impeached Hastings for "sundry high crimes and misdemeanors." According to the formal "Articles of Charge of High Crimes and Misdemeanors," Hastings was impeached because he had employed his discretionary authorities as governor in a manner contrary to British principles of sound and just rule and not for violations of the law. In the subsequent opening speech before the House of Lords (then sitting as the final court of impeachment), Edmund Burke argued that the "high crimes and misdemeanors" with which Hastings had been charged rested "not upon the niceties of a narrow jurisprudence, but on the enlarged and solid principles of state morality."

Impeachment in this instance, he suggested, was to ensure that those "who by the abuse of power have violated the spirit of the law can never hope for protection from any of its forms." In short, Hastings had been impeached for "high crimes and misdemeanors" for using legitimate authorities in a fashion that undermined his larger official duties. (Although Burke's speech—February 2, 1788—came after the Constitutional Convention had adjourned, the particulars of Hastings' impeachment had been reported in U.S. newspapers, such as the *Pennsylvania Gazette*.) See *The Writings and Speeches of Edmund Burke*, vol. 6 of *India: The Launching of the Hastings Impeachment 1786–1788*, ed. P. J. Marshall and Paul Langford (New York: Oxford University Press, 1991). On Burke's intent behind leading the effort to impeach Hastings, see Harvey C. Mansfield Jr., *Statesmanship and Party Government: A Study of Burke and Bolingbroke* (Chicago: University of Chicago Press, 1965), 147–54.

Chapter Three: President Washington's Proclamation of Neutrality

1. The treaties can be conveniently found through the Avalon Project at www.yale.edu/lawweb/avalon/diplomacy/france/fr1788–1.htm and www.yale .edu/lawweb/avalon/diplomacy/france/fr1788–2.htm.

2. Jefferson to Washington (April 7, 1793), in *Papers of Thomas Jefferson*, ed. John Catanzariti, 26 vols. to date (Princeton, NJ: Princeton University Press, 1992), 25:518, and Washington to Jefferson and Washington to Hamilton (April 12, 1793), in *Papers of George Washington: Presidential Series*, ed. Philander D. Chase, 12 vols. to date (Charlottesville: University of Virginia Press, 2005), 12:447–48.

3. Ibid., "To the Cabinet" (April 18, 1793), 452–53; "Minutes of Cabinet Meeting" (April 19, 1793), 459; "Neutrality Proclamation" (April 22, 1793), 472–73.

4. Madison to Jefferson (June 13, 1793) in *Papers of Thomas Jefferson*, 26:272–73; see also, Madison to Jefferson (June 19, 1793) and James Monroe to Jefferson (June 27, 1793), ibid., 324 and 382. Early in the crisis, Jefferson echoed Madison's sentiment that—faced with a potential naval blockade of France by Britain and its allied powers—the prospect of hostilities were such that he "suppose[d] Congress would be called, because it is a justifiable cause of war, and as the Executive cannot decide the questions of war on the affirmative side, neither ought it to do so on the negative side, by preventing the competent body from deliberating on the question," Jefferson to Madison (March 25, 1793), ibid., 25:442–43.

5. See, for example, "An Old Soldier" (May 22, 1793), "Veritas" (June 1, 5, 8, and 12, 1793) and "Brutus" (June 6, 1793) in the *National Gazette*. See also, the unsigned essay in the *National Gazette* (May 15, 1793), written in all probability

by Pennsylvanian Hugh Brackenridge, which, in addition to criticizing the proclamation, raised the question of whether it was "constitutional" for Washington to
"declare the disposition of the people with regard to war" when the power to
declare such resides "in the Congress" under the Constitution. *Life and Writings
of Hugh Henry Brackenridge*, ed. Claude Milton Newlin (Princeton, NJ: Princeton University Press, 1931), note 16, 131–32. For an overview of the opposition's
reaction to Washington's decision, see Donald H. Stewart, *The Opposition Press
of the Federalist Period* (Albany, NY: State University of New York Press, 1969),
147–49, and Stanley Elkins and Eric McKitrick, *The Age of Federalism* (New York:
Oxford University Press, 1993), 342 and 356.

    6. *Papers of Alexander Hamilton*, ed. Harold Coffin Syrett, Jacon E. Cooke,
and Barbara Chernow, 27 vols. (Columbia University Press, 1961–87), 15: 33–43,
55–63, 65–69, 82–86, 90–95, 100–6, 130–35. The essays were published in
Philadelphia's *Gazette of the United States* between June 29 and July 27, 1793.
Long out of print, the Pacificus-Helvidius debates are now available in a new
edition, *The Pacificus-Helvidius Debates of 1793–1794: Toward the Completion
of the American Founding*, edited with an introduction by Morton J. Frisch (Indi-
anapolis, IN: Liberty Fund, 2007).

    7. Ibid., 38–39. Pacificus eases his readers into this broad reading of "the exec-
utive power" by arguing initially that the authority to issue a proclamation of this
sort cannot be said to belong to either the legislative or judicial branch since its
substance is "foreign" to their normal activities: enacting laws and deciding cases.
By default, then, the power must be the executive's. In support of this view, Pacificus points to the fact that specific, widely accepted presidential tasks (such as
acting as the organ of intercourse with other states or functioning as commander
in chief) reflect this broader view of executive power, one consistent with the "general theory and practice" of separation of powers. Only after preparing his read-
ers in this way does Pacificus then conclude with his bolder argument about the
extent of "the executive power" being vested with the president by the Constitution's Article II.

    8. Ibid., 39–41. Pacificus admits that the judgment being exercised in this
instance is "similar" to the one Congress would make in determining "whether the
Nation be under the obligation to make war or not" as it exercises its own power
to "declare war" or not. And because each branch is "free to perform its own duties"
as it sees fit, the potential exists, Pacificus argues, for the president's administration of the country's foreign affairs to overlap and potentially conflict with Congress' power to declare war. In certain instances, then, this "division of [the]
Executive Power" between the president and Congress will give rise to a system
of "*concurrent* authority" in matters relative to war and peace (ibid., 40–42).

    9. Ibid., 36. Pacificus's first argument rested on his contention that the 1778

treaty was wholly defensive in nature and that France, by declaring war on Great Britain and announcing its intent to help overthrow existing royal governments, had forfeited its right to call on the United States to help defend its island possessions. The focus of the remaining essays is on disputing the opposition's claim that it was either in the United States' interest to join France in an active alliance or the country's duty to do so given the assistance Paris had provided the United States in its war of independence. For the actual terms of the accord, see Treaty of Amity and Commerce (1778), *Treaties and Other International Acts of the United States of America*, ed. David Hunter Miller, 8 vols. (Washington, DC: Government Printing Office, 1931), 2:3–29.

Although Pacificus became the most famous defender of the president's proclamation, his was not first. In late April and early May, John Quincy Adams (writing as "Marcellus") authored a series of essays for Boston's *Columbian Sentinel*. Marcellus argued that the U.S. guarantee to protect the islands was no longer binding given the treaty had been signed with a government that no longer existed and given the behavior of the new government. Marcellus also suggested that the United States was not bound by the treaty's terms, because to fulfill the guarantee would result in the country's exposing itself to possible destruction by the combined arms of France's enemies, violating a "law of nature," which takes precedence over any prior "human legislation, or compact." *The Writings of John Quincy Adams*, ed. Worthington C. Ford, 7 vols. (New York: Macmillan, 1913), 1:135–46.

10. Jefferson to Gouverneur Morris (April 20, 1793) and James Monroe (June 28, 1793), *Papers of Thomas Jefferson*, 25:575–76, and 26:392. See also Edward Carrington to Alexander Hamilton (April 26, 1793) about the "public mind of Virginia," *Papers of Alexander Hamilton*, 14:347. Although these letters reflect nothing more than reasonable guesses about the state of public opinion at the time, the fact that Jefferson and others believed them to be generally accurate helps explain their behavior.

11. See, for example, the following essays published in the spring of 1793 in the *National Gazette*: "A Democrat" (May 22), "An Old Soldier" (May 22), and "An American" (June 12). Although the desire to avoid involvement in the war was prevalent among Republican writers, it was not universal. Hugh Brackenridge, for example, suggested in an unsigned essay (May 15), also run by the *National Gazette*, that the United States "assist" France by attacking Britain's North American possessions. *Life and Writings of Hugh Henry Brackenridge*, 131–32.

12. In addition, both the French government and many Americans argued that it was not in France's immediate interest to have the United States enter the war on its side. By remaining a friendly "neutral," the United States could serve as a

reliable source of supplies to France during the war and a possible base of operations for French privateering against British shipping. On these and related points, see the essays published in the *National Gazette* cited above; Jefferson to Morris (April 20, 1793) in *Papers of Thomas Jefferson*, 15:576; Elkins and McKitrick, *Age of Federalism*, 332–35; and Charles Marion Thomas, *American Neutrality in 1793: A Study in Cabinet Government* (New York: AMS Press, 1967), 63–64.

13. See "Jefferson's Opinion on the Treaties with France," in *Papers of Thomas Jefferson*, 15:597–618, and Jefferson to Madison (June 23), Jefferson to Monroe (July 14), and Jefferson to Madison (August 11), ibid., 346, 501, and 649.

Both supporters and critics of the proclamation complained that its language lacked precision. In a letter to Hamilton, Rufus King, a New York Federalist senator, wondered whether the absence of the "word 'Neutrality'" might not confuse the public and lessen the "force" of the proclamation. For the critic "Veritas," however, that the proclamation made no mention of the treaties with France at all left open the possibility that Washington no longer considered the treaties in force. Jefferson wrote Madison that he thought the proclamation was "badly drawn" and, as a result, opened itself up to being read more broadly than was intended. See *Life and Correspondence of Rufus King*, ed. Charles King, 6 vols. (New York: G. P. Putnam's Sons, 1894), 1:439; "Veritas" (June 1, 1793), *National Gazette*; and Jefferson to Madison (August 11, 1793) in *Papers of Thomas Jefferson*, 15:649.

14. Jefferson to Madison (July 7, 1793) in *Papers of Thomas Jefferson*, 26:443–44. Jefferson asked Madison to "take up your pen, select the most striking heresies, and cut him to pieces in the face of the public." However, Jefferson doesn't specify what "heresies" he had in mind.

15. "Letters of Helvidius," in *Papers of James Madison*, ed. Thomas A. Mason, Robert A. Rutland, and Jeanne K. Sisson, 17 vols. (Charlottesville: University Press of Virginia, 1985), 15: 66–73, 80–87, 95–103, and 106–11. The Helvidius essays were published, like those of Pacificus, in Philadelphia's *Gazette of the United States*. They appeared in the *Gazette*'s August 24 and 31 and September 7–11 and September 14 editions.

Madison never offered an explanation of why he chose the pseudonym "Helvidius." Marvin Meyers, in *The Mind of the Founder: Sources of Political Thought of James Madison* (Hanover, NH: University Press of New England for Brandeis University Press, 1981), suggests that Madison was probably drawing on the "admiring portrait of [the Roman noble] Helvidius Priscus" by Tacitus (200). Helvidius was exiled by Nero and, on returning to Rome, fought to resurrect some of the Senate's lost authority, including the authority to regulate the affairs of the treasury.

16. *Papers of James Madison*, 15:69. Although Pacificus and Helvidius differ on the nature of "the executive power," they agree that the vesting provision that begins Article II is a substantive grant of power.

After summarizing the argument of Pacificus on executive power, Helvidius asks, rhetorically, what possible sources Pacificus could have drawn on to support his views. In response to his own question, Helvidius suggests the "writers, of authority, on public law," meaning Locke, Montesquieu, and Blackstone. But then Helvidius rejects their authority in this instance by claiming that their views of executive power had been "warped" by their attachment to the English model and only Pacificus's own attachment to that model could explain his willingness to equate, as the "British commentators" do, "royal prerogatives" with "Executive prerogatives" (ibid., 68 and 72). Instead, Madison argues that the "best guides" in these matters are "our own reason" and the text of "our own constitution." And, under "our own reason," he includes the work of those Americans who had some "influence in conciliating the public assent to the government in the form proposed." Madison then concludes by quoting passages from *The Federalist* (No. 69 and No. 75, each authored by Hamilton) to support the case that the specific foreign affairs powers given the president (such as, the power to receive ambassadors and make treaties) do not reflect the broader notion of executive power put forward by Pacificus (ibid., 72–73, 97, and 109).

17. Ibid., 69. However, once the decision has been made to go to war, its execution resides with "the competent authority." Just as the legislature enacts laws and the executive administers them, Congress may declare war and the president, as commander in chief, is responsible for its conduct (ibid., 69–71).

18. Since Helvidius does not consider the powers to declare war and make treaties to be executive in nature (and, hence, exceptions to the general grant of "the executive power" found in Article II), he rejects the idea of "concurrent" authorities put forward by Pacificus. To the contrary, "executive pretensions" "must narrow" once it is understood "that the powers of making war and treaty" are "substantially of a legislative, not an executive nature." And because the power to declare war is different in nature and distributed to a distinct branch of government, this power and the judgments associated with its exercise reside *"fully and exclusively"* with the Congress (emphasis in the original). In matters of war and peace, then, it appears "the executive has no other discretion than to convene and give information to the legislature on occasions that may demand it" (ibid., 69, 86, and 108). See, however, note 36 below.

In rejecting the idea of concurrent authorities, Helvidius adopts a relatively rigid view of the doctrine of separation of powers and promotes, as a principal element in maintaining that separation, a presidential deportment that is defined by its overt deference to Congress (ibid., 80–87, 106–7). If Pacificus had chosen to respond to Helvidius, he might well have quoted passages from those Madison-authored essays of *The Federalist* (No. 47–No. 51) that suggest that a strict adherence to the doctrine is unlikely and which, in turn, stress the head-butting between the branches as the key means for maintaining the Constitution's own adoption of the doctrine.

19. Of course Helvidius's constitutional argument had substantive policy implications. By crafting the argument as he had, Helvidius left open the status of the alliance between France and the United States. With expectations that the new Congress—scheduled to meet in December—would be more sympathetic to Republican concerns, it was important that its say in these matters be kept open. See Jefferson to Thomas Pinckney (December 3, 1793), *Papers of Thomas Jefferson*, 25:696; see also, Forrest McDonald, *The Presidency of George Washington* (Lawrence: University Press of Kansas, 1974), 106–7.

20. Washington never repudiated Hamilton's defense of his actions. Jefferson, however, claimed that the president was "uneasy" with Pacificus's arguments. But about precisely what Washington was uneasy is not known. *Papers of Thomas Jefferson*, 26:606, and *The Complete Jefferson*, ed. Saul K. Padover (New York: Duell, Sloan, and Pearce, 1943), 1268. For other accounts by Jefferson of Washington's intent with respect to the proclamation, see *Papers of Thomas Jefferson*, 26:649–50, and *Complete Jefferson*, 1266–67.

Much of what we know about Washington's views on the proclamation is found in letters or memoranda drafted by Jefferson, especially in his notes (*The Anas*) of the cabinet meetings. But *The Anas* was not published until 1818, a quarter century after the proclamation had been issued. And, as Jefferson makes clear in his introduction, the decision to publish his notes was taken with a specific purpose in mind, correcting the inaccuracies of John Marshall's *The Life of Washington*. Jefferson was especially concerned with correcting the chief justice's account "of the period immediately following the establishment of the present constitution." In his judgment, Marshall's Federalist "party feelings" had led him to misinterpret the official papers he had been given access to. By publishing his notes of the cabinet meetings, Jefferson hoped to rectify the record and provide the American public with a better understanding of the Republican Party's origins and, in particular, the party's effort "to preserve the legislature pure and independent of the executive . . . and not permit the constitution to be construed into a monarchy." Before publishing *The Anas*, Jefferson admitted that he had edited them and given them "a calm revisal." See *The Complete Jefferson*, 1204–5, 1211.

Jefferson's own views about the proclamation were not free of ambiguity. At the cabinet meeting in which it was decided to issue the proclamation, Jefferson only recorded that it was agreed to unanimously. Unlike at other cabinet sessions in which serious disputes arose and were recorded by Jefferson, in this instance, his record made no mention of a debate. The only evidence that a debate took place is found in letters Jefferson wrote to Madison and Monroe late in June and mid-July—two months after the proclamation had been issued and following letters from them complaining about Washington's decision. In fact, prior to receiving Monroe's letter, Jefferson had written Monroe a note that downplayed any notion that there was a serious split within the cabinet on policy. In addition, prior to receiving Madison's letter, Jefferson had twice written him and described the administration's policy as one of "neutrality." Only after Jefferson had received Madison's letter did he suggest that there had been a debate in the cabinet and that he, Jefferson, had fought to keep the word "neutrality" out of the proclamation. See Elkins and McKitrick, *Age of Federalism*, 338; Dumas Malone, *Jefferson and the Ordeal of Liberty* (Boston: Little, Brown, 1962), 72; *Papers of Thomas Jefferson*, 25: 619, 26: 25–26, 272–73, 323–24, 346, 381–82, 510, and 651–52. Compare Jefferson's letter to Madison (March 24, 1793), 25: 442.

21. See Dorothy Twohig, ed., *The Journal of the Proceedings of the President, 1793–1797* (Charlottesville: University Press of Virginia, 1981), 117, 118, and 120. See also the letters Washington sent out to various cities and counties that had passed resolutions in support of his policies, in particular, letters to New Castle County, Delaware (August 24, 1793), and Chester County, Pennsylvania (September 9, 1793), which can be found in John C. Fitzpatrick, ed., *Writings of George Washington*, 39 vols. (Washington, DC: Government Printing Office, 1931–44), 33:60, 85–86. See also Washington's letter (May 6, 1793) to Governor Henry Lee of Virginia in which the president describes the proclamation as "announcing the disposition of this Country towards the Belligerent Powers" (ibid., 32:449). However, compare the above letters with the one sent by Washington to Frederick County, Virginia (November 23, 1793), in response to its resolution of support (ibid., 33:155–56).

22. *Annals of Congress* (December 6, 1793) 4:138.

23. Irving Brant, *James Madison: Father of the Constitution, 1787–1800* (New York: Bobbs-Merrill, 1950), 386.

24. Ibid.

25. *Annals of Congress* (December 9, 1793), 4:17–18.

26. See *Papers of Alexander Hamilton*, 15: 42–43 and series of essays by John Marshall—writing as "Aristides" and "Grachus" in response to Monroe's "Agricola" essays—that appeared in the fall of 1793 in the *Virginia Gazette*. See, especially, the October 16, 1793, edition of the *Virginia Gazette*.

27. For the political background to Washington's decisions, see Elkins and McKitrick, *Age of Federalism*, 341–52, 354–65, and Harry Amon, "The Genet Mission and the Development of American Political Parties," in *Journal of American History* 52 (March 1966): 725–41; and see also Abraham D. Sofaer, *War,*

Foreign Affairs, and Constitutional Power: The Origins (Cambridge, MA: Ballinger, 1976), 116.

28. Thomas, *American Neutrality*, 91–117.

29. The proclamation had warned U.S. citizens "to avoid all acts and proceedings whatsoever, which might in any manner tend to contravene" the government's intention to pursue a policy "friendly and impartial towards the belligerent powers." The proclamation then concluded by stating that the president had "given instructions" to the appropriate officials "to cause prosecutions to be instituted against all persons, who shall, within the cognizance of the Courts of the United States, violate the laws of nations, with respect to the powers at war, or any of them." *Writings of George Washington*, 32:430–31.

30. Edmond Charles Genet, France's ambassador to the United States, complained that the prohibition was unjustified in light of the fact that there was no law or treaty that specifically prohibited individuals from enlisting in the service of France or its ships. But the administration's position was that the United States was, by treaty, at peace with several of the nations at war with France. Hence, it was a violation of U.S. law for its citizens to engage in activities contrary to those accords. Chief Justice John Jay and Justice James Wilson endorsed the administration's position in their charges to local grand juries who were reviewing cases in which individual citizens had accepted commissions aboard French privateers.

In one widely reported case (Gideon Henfield) the local jury ignored these instructions. It appears they did so out of general sympathy for the French cause and because they were not inclined to see Henfield go to jail for violating something that was, in their mind, less a law than an executive dictate. Despite this setback, the administration continued its efforts to enforce the prohibition on U.S. citizens enlisting in the service of any of the belligerents. See Thomas, *American Neutrality*, 165–88; Francis Wharton, ed., *State Trials of the United States during the Administrations of Washington and Adams* (1849; repr. New York: Burt Franklin, 1970), 49–77, 83–88; and "Brutus" (June 8, 1793) in the *National Gazette* and *National Gazette* (August 31, 1793).

31. Thomas, *American Neutrality*, 119–37.

32. See Charles S. Hyneman, *The First American Neutrality*, 20 vols. (Urbana: University of Illinois, Illinois Studies in the Social Sciences, 1934), 20:77–82, and John Alexander Carroll and Mary Wells Ashworth, *George Washington: First in Peace* (New York: Charles Scribner's Sons, 1957), 111.

33. For an overview of these affairs, see Elkins and McKitrick, *Age of Federalism*, 330, 334, 341–54, and 366–67, and Thomas, *American Neutrality*, 125, 134–42, 167–70, 174, and 207–33.

34. Although Helvidius concentrates on distinguishing between "the execu-

tive power" and the power of Congress "to declare war" and the Senate "to make treaties," he does not address the full range of authorities that lie between them. As Robert Scigliano has pointed out, after Helvidius presents his minimalist account of the president's executive power, he "does not," as one might expect, turn and "claim the powers of war and management of foreign affairs to be legislative in nature." Helvidius only claims that the authorities to declare war and make treaties are "substantially" (which is, to say, not simply) legislative in character. And, from this, Scigliano argues, Helvidius "infers" only a moderate amount of additional power for Congress to wield: specifically, the "rights to judge the causes of war and to unmake or suspend treaties." What Helvidius leaves open is the allocation of the remaining national security authorities and the day-to-day management of the country's foreign affairs. Robert Scigliano, "The War Powers Resolution and the War Powers," in *The Presidency in the Constitutional Order*, ed. Joseph M. Bessette and Jeffrey Tulis (Baton Rouge: Louisiana State University Press, 1981), 129–30.

35. As Ruth and Stephen Grant have written, "Madison did not fear the strength of the president within his sphere as long as that sphere was properly contained." However, as they also point out: "The executive function of administration has the potential for a dangerous expansion under certain circumstances. The executive function is circumscribed by law, but it also supplies the defects of law within those bounds by applying a general rule to particular circumstances. Its discretionary character in the ordinary conduct of executive business is not easily distinguishable in kind from expanded discretion under conditions where the variety, number, irregularity, or pressing character of the particulars render them ungovernable by a general rule." Ruth Weissbourd Grant and Stephen Grant, "The Madisonian Presidency," in *Presidency in the Constitutional Order*, 53.

36. For an overview of the French government's sometimes unrealistic and somewhat contradictory expectations about what role the United States might take during this conflict, as evidenced by its instructions to Genet, see Elkins and McKitrick, *Age of Federalism*, 330–35. According to Jefferson, Genet held the view that America's guarantee to defend France's island possessions was not tied to a determination of whether the war was defensive or not. "His doctrine is that . . . the moment France was engaged in war, it was our duty to fly to arms as a nation." *Papers of Thomas Jefferson*, 26:653.

37. A principal complaint by Helvidius about the broad claim of executive authority made by Pacificus is that it opened the way for a president in practice to interfere with, and perhaps even undermine, Congress' authority to fully exercise its judgment about war and peace. Yet, as Helvidius notes, the president's duty to maintain the status quo—in this case, peace—until Congress decides oth-

erwise may also lead him to take actions that result in offending some other state. Avoiding war from one quarter, he admits, may "in some cases . . . incur war" from another. *Papers of James Madison*, 15:86.

38. Quoted in Thomas, *American Neutrality*, 229.

39. See *Papers of Thomas Jefferson*, 25:569 and 607, and 26:615 and 627.

40. Ibid., 26:463–65. Genet's belief that Congress was "the sovereign" was connected to his and the French government's failure to understand how large a break the new American constitution was from the Articles of Confederation, a form of government that had no separate executive and only a governing congress. Hence, Genet was formally designated by Paris as minister to "Congrès des Etats Unis de l'Amerique" and instructed to negotiate a new commercial accord with the "Ministres du Congress" (ibid., 686).

Jefferson probably reinforced this view when, in order to delay discussions about a new treaty, he told Genet negotiations would have to wait until the new Senate could meet. From this, Genet apparently gained the impression that Senate was ultimately in charge of foreign affairs and that the president was a subordinate minister. In addition, Jefferson was perhaps too open with Genet about cabinet politics and Republican hopes to control the new Congress. As a result, when Genet first read "Veritas's" attack on the proclamation and Washington in the *National Gazette*, he was convinced it had been authored by the secretary of state himself. See Elkins and McKitrick, *Age of Federalism*, 343–44, and *Papers of Thomas Jefferson*, 26:749–50.

41. Ibid., 465. Jefferson's response to Genet about the president's authority is not as sweeping as it first appears. According to Jefferson's account of the exchange, he does not claim that the president retains a general authority over foreign affairs by virtue of his being vested with "the executive power." A president's preeminence in this instance rests on his constitutional duty to ensure the execution of all U.S. laws. According to Jefferson, regarding "all the questions which had arisen" over how the treaties between the two states were to be interpreted, Washington's judgment was final since it was his responsibility to carry out the laws of the land, which under the Constitution includes treaties.

But, as the secretary of state knew, not every question related to the treaties had arisen. Still outstanding was the question of America's guarantee to France to protect its West Indian possessions. It is possible that Jefferson had this issue in mind when he admitted to Genet that, despite the president's normal supremacy in these matters, there may be some points in a treaty's execution—albeit "very few"—about which Congress "could take notice of."

See also Jefferson's draft letter to Genet of mid-July, which attempts to instruct him on the president's place in the constitutional order. The letter was never sent. Genet's increasingly impolitic behavior forced the administration to turn from deliberating about how to educate him on the appropriate protocol for dealing with the U.S. government to requesting, instead, his recall to Paris (ibid., 514).

42. See *Papers of Thomas Jefferson*, 26:484–85, 520, and 524–31.

43. See Hamilton's opinion to Washington (May 15, 1793) in *Papers of Alexander Hamilton*, 14:459. Given the small circle of government officials that characterized the early years of the new government, it's no surprise that the administration knew in advance that the Court's answer would likely be no. *Papers of Thomas Jefferson*, 26:537 and 607.

44. In Jefferson's initial draft of the questions to be submitted to the Court, his last was this: "Which of the above prohibitable things are within the competence of the President to prohibit?" When the cabinet met to review Jefferson's list, along with one drafted by Hamilton, it cut a number of Jefferson's questions, including the last (ibid., 525–26 and 531). In addition, in the memorandum he prepared on the cabinet's decision (July 12) to seek the Court's counsel, his initial draft stated that the administration was asking the Court to "take into consideration certain matters of public concern." In editing the memorandum, Jefferson cut the first three words ("take into consideration") and replaced them with a new phrase ("give advice on"). The edit suggests a desire to maintain the view that the cabinet, in seeking the Court's assistance, was not conceding any of its own authority (ibid., 484–85).

45. The Court formally responded to Washington's request for advice on August 8. It argued that the "lines of Separation drawn by the Constitution between the three Departments of Government—their being in certain respects checks on each other—and our being a Court of last Resort" precluded it from responding favorably to the president's request. The Court also suggested that the provision in Article II allowing the president to demand opinions from his department heads evidenced a desire on the part of the Constitution's architects to "*purposely*" limit such requests "to *executive* departments" (emphasis in the original), *Papers of Thomas Jefferson*, 26:526.

46. As Donald Stewart has suggested: "Genet's most lasting influence was to be found in the rise of the Democratic Societies, so suggestive to Federalists of those in Paris. These were by no means entirely the creation of the French minister, but it is significant that they sprung up almost simultaneously with his arrival and that they uniformly and enthusiastically supported him. They appeared suddenly, and Federalists who had been inclined to smile at popular manifestations of Francophile frenzy began to frown in worry or to protest harshly. Jacobin societies, not unlike these organizations had come into being just prior to the uprising in France. . . . Clearly, [the societies] constituted a political threat of no mean

import, and they talked of coordinating their efforts through correspondence committees as had American revolutionaries two decades earlier" (*The Opposition Press*, 169).

47. On this issue, see Forrest McDonald, *Alexander Hamilton: A Biography* (New York: Norton, 1979), 282; Stewart, *The Opposition Press*, 151; *Papers of Thomas Jefferson*, 26:601–3; and Harry Ammon, "The Genet Mission and the Development of American Political Parties," in *Journal of American History* 52 (March 1966), 726–27.

Elkins and McKitrick argue in *The Age of Federalism* that the "Proclamation was by and large favorably received, for two fairly obvious reasons. One was the desire for peace was all but universal . . . [and] the other reason was the tremendous prestige of Washington." (356). But this assessment was not widely understood to be the case by the president's supporters in the days immediately following the proclamation's issuance, as evidenced by the materials Elkins and McKitrick themselves provide in their account of this period.

48. See *Papers of Thomas Jefferson*, 26:448 and 687–88. For an overview of the partisan debate associated with this incident, see Stewart, *The Opposition Press*, 162–64.

49. As Madison wrote to Jefferson (August 27, 1793), the plan of the Federalist "cabal" in was "to drag before the public the indiscretions of Genet; and turn them & the popularity of the P[resident] to the purposes driven at." See *Papers of James Madison*, 15: 75.

50. *Papers of Thomas Jefferson*, 26:598 and 652; *Papers of Alexander Hamilton*, 15:145. See also, Elkins and McKitrick, *Age of Federalism*, 361–62; McDonald, *Alexander Hamilton*, 280–81; Stewart, *The Opposition Press*, 162; and Ammon, "The Genet Mission," 728–29.

51. A typical resolution made three points: first, it condemned any effort on the part of a foreign state's representative to involve himself in internal U.S. affairs; second, it expressed confidence in the president; and, third, it endorsed the policy of neutrality. See Ammon, "The Genet Mission," 729–30, and McDonald, *Alexander Hamilton*, 281.

52. *Papers of Thomas Jefferson*, 26:651. See also, Ammon, "The Genet Mission," 730–32.

53. *Papers of James Madison*, 15: 79. Madison's goal, he told Jefferson in an August 27, 1793, letter, was to generate "an authentic specimen of the *Country* temper" (ibid., 75; emphasis in the original). Most of the resolutions up to that point had come from northern cities. Madison was concerned that they would be taken to represent public opinion in general. He thought the task at hand was "calling out the real sense of the people" by having additional resolutions passed along the lines drafted by him and Monroe. See also, the editor's note, "Resolutions on

Franco-American Relations," ibid., 76–79; McDonald, *Alexander Hamilton*, 281; and Ammon, "The Genet Mission," 732.

54. *Papers of Thomas Jefferson*, 26:651–52, and Elkins and McKitrick, *Age of Federalism*, 364–65.

55. See Sofaer, *War, Foreign Affairs, and Constitutional Power*, 116.

56. Monroe to John Breckinridge (August 23, 1793), quoted in Ammon, "The Genet Mission," 733–34.

57. King to Hamilton (August 3, 1793) in *Life and Correspondence of Rufus King*, 493.

58. It is interesting to speculate whether the Hamiltonian view of presidential power would have been better off if Hamilton had not set about to defend so boldly the decisions taken by Washington, generating Madison's own strong response in turn. In the absence of their debate, might not the precedent of Washington's own deeds have been the "controlling" element here? Although Washington's decision to issue the proclamation was criticized in some quarters—and certainly more so than the president was accustomed to—a majority was ultimately satisfied with the decision itself. But letting "sleeping dogs lie" is something founders have a difficult time doing, believing, naturally enough, that early precedents will have such a lasting impact on the country's direction that they must be publicly defended or challenged, as the case may be.

59. See Charles Thach Jr., *The Creation of the American Presidency, 1775–1789* (1923; repr. Baltimore: Johns Hopkins Press, 1969), 55–75, and James Madison to Thomas Jefferson (October 24, 1787), in *Records of the Federal Convention of 1787*, ed. Max Farrand, 4 vols. (New Haven, CT: Yale University Press, 1937), 3:131–32.

Chapter Four: Theodore Roosevelt and William Howard Taft

Epigraphs. Theodore Roosevelt, *An Autobiography*, in *The Works of Theodore Roosevelt*, national edition, 20 vols. (New York: Charles Scribner's Sons, 1926), 20:347; William Howard Taft, *Our Chief Magistrate and His Powers*, with a foreword, introduction, and notes by H. Jefferson Powell (Durham, NC: Carolina Academic Press, 2002), 139–40.

1. David H. Burton, "The Learned Presidency: Roosevelt, Taft, Wilson," *Presidential Studies Quarterly* (Spring 1985): 486–499.

2. The common reliance on these passages from Roosevelt and Taft is illustrated in the following selection of volumes on the presidency. Jeffrey Cohen and David Nice, eds., *The Presidency: Classic and Contemporary Readings* (Boston: McGraw-Hill, 2003), 12–16; Christopher H. Pyle and Richard M. Pious, eds., *The President, Congress, and the Constitution: Power and Legitimacy in American Politics* (New York: Free Press, 1984), 68–71; Robert S. Hirschfield, ed., *The Power*

of the Presidency: Concepts and Controversy, 3rd ed. (New York: Aldine De Gruyter, 1982), 49. In each of these volumes the two presidents are contrasted sharply with each another, representing diametrically opposed views of the character of executive power.

3. Roosevelt argues that for both historical and scientific writing to be useful it must be readable: "for writings are useless unless they are read, and they cannot be read unless they are readable." Roosevelt, "History as Literature," 12:11. See also "Biological Analogies in History," 12:27. Roosevelt's best biographer, Edmund Morris, says in regard to TR's writings: "Ninety-nine percent of the millions of words he thus poured out are sterile, banal, and so droningly repetitive as to defeat the most dedicated researcher." Edmund Morris, *The Rise of Theodore Roosevelt* (New York: Coward, McCann & Geoghegan, 1979), 467. On Taft's writing, see Paolo E. Coletta, *The Presidency of William Howard Taft* (Lawrence: University Press of Kansas, 1973), 2.

4. See note 2 above.

5. Roosevelt, "The Presidency," in *Works of Theodore Roosevelt*, 13:306–15. "Perhaps the two most striking things in the Presidency," Roosevelt writes, "are the immense power of the President, in the first place; and in the second place, the fact that as soon as he has ceased being President he goes right back into the body of the people and becomes just like any other American citizen" (313–14).

6. Some of the words used to illuminate the meaning of steward are the following: superintendent, agent, manager, administrator, seneschal, overseer, landreeve, supervise, proctor, and execute. Each of these conveys the sense of subordination to a superior will.

7. Alexander Hamilton, James Madison, and John Jay, *The Federalist Papers*, introduction by Clinton Rossiter (New York: New American Library, 1961), 317.

8. Roosevelt, *Autobiography*, *Works of Theodore Roosevelt*, 20:352.

9. *Federalist* No. 71, 432.

10. Harvey Mansfield Jr., *America's Constitutional Soul* (Baltimore: Johns Hopkins University Press, 1991), 16.

11. Ibid., 210. See also William Kristol, "The Problem of the Separation of Powers: *Federalist* 47–51," in *Saving The Revolution: The Federalist Papers and the American Founding*, ed. Charles R. Kesler (New York: The Free Press, 1987), 116–17, on how the judiciary and separation of powers allow the reason of the people to rule the government and the government to rule the passions of the people, thus separating the people from actually governing themselves.

12. This principle is illuminated by James Ceaser, who has described the American system of government "as operating on three basic levels, each successive level being influenced, but not fully determined, by the levels that precede it. These levels are (1) fundamental sovereignty (2) the exercise of primary powers,

and (3) the policy-making process," Ceaser, "In Defense of Separation of Powers," in *Separation of Powers—Does It Still Work?*, ed. Robert A. Goldwin and Art Kaufman (Washington, DC: American Enterprise Institute, 1986), 174.

13. Mansfield notes in *America's Constitutional Soul*, 124, that "*The Federalist* is careful not to identify the result [the Constitution] in terms of a regime." Elsewhere, Mansfield has written that the Constitution was thought by its authors to represent "a true solution for the partisan ills that put a term to regimes," Mansfield, "Returning to the Founders: the Debate on the Constitution," *The New Criterion* 12, no. 1 (September 1993): 51–52. Michael Allen Gillespie makes a similar point in an analysis of party and *Federalist* No. 10. Gillespie argues that the Constitution was intended to eliminate the contention over regime fundamentals by great parties by channeling competition through lesser interest-based parties that did not upset or challenge the system as a whole. "Political Parties and the American Founding," in *American Political Parties and Constitutional Politics*, ed. Peter W. Schramm and Bradford P. Wilson (Lanham, MD: Rowman and Littlefield, 1993), 17–43.

14. Roosevelt's understanding of the working out of historical progress left him with the perception that the great pursuit of liberty by political means was concluded, at least for the United States, at the end of the Civil War. From that time the great questions for politics in the United States became human welfare, which could only be achieved by government intervention. See Theodore Roosevelt, "Social Evolution," in *Works of Theodore Roosevelt*, 13: 223; *Autobiography*, *Works of Theodore Roosevelt*, 20:414.

15. Roosevelt, *Autobiography*, *Works of Theodore Roosevelt*, 20:347, 348.

16. Joseph M. Bessette argues, in *The Mild Voice of Reason* (Chicago: University of Chicago Press, 1994), 46–55, that deliberation includes three ingredients: information, argument, and persuasion. Each of these ingredients is fostered in an institutional setting such as the House of Representatives, the Senate, or the presidency in a way that is absent from common public opinion, which all too often demonstrates the tendency to be persuaded not by arguments based on accurate information, but by base rhetorical appeals to ideology, passion, or interest.

17. Roosevelt, "The Winning of the West," in *Works of Theodore Roosevelt*, 8:3.

18. Roosevelt, "Manhood and Statehood" (Address at the Quarter-centennial Celebration of Statehood in Colorado, at Colorado Springs, August 2, 1901), in *Works of Theodore Roosevelt*, 13:453.

19. Roosevelt, "The Winning of the West," in *Works of Theodore Roosevelt*, 9:11. See also *Works of Theodore Roosevelt*, 8:7, 11, 12, 13, 18, 19, and 22; Roosevelt, *Thomas Hart Benton*, *Works of Theodore Roosevelt*, 7:4, 6, 8, 10, 12, 14, 15, 23–24, 26, and 33.

20. Taft, *Our Chief Magistrate*, vii. The six minor powers are these: consult-

ing heads of departments, informing Congress of the State of the Union, recommending measures, issuing commissions to officers, convening Congress, and adjourning Congress. Of the major powers, the veto is considered in the first chapter with the distribution of powers because of its legislative nature (Taft, *Our Chief Magistrate,* 29). The remaining five major powers are the following: having the power of appointment, taking care that the laws are executed, being commander in chief, handling foreign relations, and using the pardon, each of which offer extraordinary opportunity to the president in the unhindered exercise of extraordinary power, according to Taft.

21. Taft, *Our Chief Magistrate,* 2.

22. Ibid., 1–2.

23. Ibid.

24. Ibid., 44.

25. Ibid., 45.

26. Ibid., 4–6, 8–9. The particular issue through which Taft frames this discussion of the corrosive power of influence is the budget process. He argues for reform in order to achieve efficiency. And in typical progressive fashion, Taft argues for the addition of administrative mechanisms under executive control and therefore for the inhibition of political mechanisms that operate between the primary political branches.

27. Ibid., 78.

28. Ibid., 88–89.

29. Ibid., 88–89.

30. Louis Fisher, *President and Congress: Power and Policy* (New York: Free Press, 1972), 35.

31. Alexander Hamilton, "Pacificus No. 1," in *Selected Writings and Speeches of Alexander Hamilton,* ed. Morton J. Frisch (Washington, DC: American Enterprise Institute, 1985), 402.

32. Taft, *Our Chief Magistrate,* 92.

33. Ibid., 93, 95–96.

34. Ibid., 94.

35. Alexander Hamilton, "Pacificus No. 1," in *Selected Writings and Speeches of Alexander Hamilton,* 398–400.

36. Roy P. Basler, ed., *The Collected Works of Abraham Lincoln,* 9 vols. (New Brunswick, NJ: Rutgers University Press, 1953), 4:429.

37. Taft, *Our Chief Magistrate,* 14, 78.

38. *Myers v. United States,* 272 U.S. 52, 117–18, 128.

39. Roosevelt, *Autobiography, Works of Theodore Roosevelt,* 20:347–48.

40. Ibid., 20:360, 347.

41. For the difficulties involved in attempting to claim prerogative power for

the executive, see *Federalist* No. 25, 167, and No. 41, 257. See also Robert Scigliano, "The President's 'Prerogative Power,'" in *Inventing the American Presidency*, ed. Thomas E. Cronin (Lawrence: University Press of Kansas, 1989), 236–256, and Gary J. Schmitt, "Thomas Jefferson and the Presidency," in ibid., 335–43.

42. "The report of the Country Life Commission was transmitted to Congress by me on February 9, 1909. In the accompanying message I asked for $25,000 to print and circulate the report and to prepare for publication the immense amount of valuable material collected by the Commission but still unpublished. The reply made by Congress was not only a refusal to appropriate the money, but a positive prohibition against continuing the work. The Tawney amendment to the Sundry Civil bill forbade the President to appoint any further Commissions unless specifically authorized by Congress to do so. Had this prohibition been enacted earlier *and complied with*, it would have prevented the appointment of the six Roosevelt Commissions. But I would not have complied with it," Roosevelt, *Autobiography*, *Works of Theodore Roosevelt*, 20:407 (emphasis in the original). Roosevelt here clearly states an intent to violate an enacted statute, but he had in fact already diverted personnel to these commissions from other administration duties for which funding had been appropriated.

43. Roosevelt, *Gouverneur Morris*, *Works of Theodore Roosevelt*, 7:329; Roosevelt, "The College Graduate and Public Life," in *Works of Theodore Roosevelt*, 13:77.

44. See the first chapter of Roosevelt, "The Winning of the West," in *Works of Theodore Roosevelt*, vol. 8, and the first three chapters of Roosevelt, *Thomas Hart Benton*, vol. 7, *Works of Theodore Roosevelt*.

45. Roosevelt, *Autobiography*, *Works of Theodore Roosevelt*, 20:352–53.

46. Ibid., 20:354.

47. Coletta, *The Presidency of William Howard Taft*, 95.

48. Taft, *Our Chief Magistrate*, 144.

49. Ibid., 147–48.

50. Ibid., 148. See also note 2.

51. Ibid., 139–40.

52. Coletta, *The Presidency of William Howard Taft*, 11.

53. Ibid., 16.

54. Ibid., 19.

Chapter Five: Constitutional Controversy and Presidential Election

1. 531 U.S. 98 (2000). When the vote count was completed on November 8, Bush led Gore by 1,784 votes. This did not include overseas ballots, which were not due until November 18. This lead was less than 0.5% and, under Florida law,

triggered an automatic machine recount, unless Gore refused it. Gore did not. Bush's lead shrank to 327 votes. On November 9, Gore called for a hand recount of the votes in Broward, Miami-Dade, Palm Beach, and Volusia counties, all counties in which Gore had a substantial lead. Florida statute required final vote counts to be submitted by November 14, but only Volusia County had completed its hand recount by that date. Florida Secretary of State Katherine Harris was prepared to certify the election results on November 18, after receiving the overseas vote and the Volusia County recount. At this point Bush's lead had increased to 930 votes. A Florida trial court rejected a call by Broward, Miami-Dade, and Palm Beach counties to extend the deadline for a recount but stayed certification until the case was reviewed by the Florida Supreme Court. On November 21 the Florida Supreme Court overruled the trial court and extended the deadline until November 26. Bush asked the U.S. Supreme Court to review the Florida Supreme Court's decision, and on December 4 it vacated the decision of the Florida Court, and asked it to clarify the grounds of its decision.

In the meantime the recounts had continued. Only Broward County completed its recount by the November 26 deadline, however Palm Beach County completed its recount a few hours later, only to have Secretary Harris refuse to include it in the final tally. Miami-Dade County had abandoned its recount because officials did not believe they could complete it by the deadline. On November 26 Harris certified Bush the winner by 537 votes. Had the Palm Beach recounts been included Bush's lead would have been down to 300 votes. On November 27 Gore brought suit in Florida state court to contest the certification. The trial judge ruled against Gore. He appealed to the Florida Supreme Court, which reversed the trial judge and ordered that the late results from Palm Beach be included as well as the partial totals from the abandoned recount in Miami-Dade County. Bush still maintained a 154-vote lead, but the Court also ordered a recount of approximately 60,000 ballots statewide that had not registered a vote for president in the machine counts. Bush then appealed to the U.S. Supreme Court, which voted 5–4 to stay the recount pending its review. On December 12, by another 5–4 vote, the Supreme Court called for an end of the recounts with Gore's concession following the next day.

2. Alan M. Dershowitz, *Supreme Injustice: How the High Court Hijacked Election 2000* (New York: Oxford University Press, 2001), 52.

3. For the purposes of this chapter, I accept the conventional wisdom regarding the partisan preferences of the justices. Thus, although Justices Souter and Stevens were appointed by Republican presidents, they are generally considered to be on the more liberal wing of the Court and therefore supportive of the Democratic Party. Whereas the remaining five Republican appointees and the two Democratic appointees are associated with the parties that appointed them.

4. Dershowitz has an entire chapter on the inconsistencies among the majority justices but does not give similar scrutiny to the dissenters. Dershowitz, *Supreme Injustice*, 121–72.

5. *Bush v. Gore*, 531 U.S. 98 (2000), at 128.

6. An unsigned editorial in the *New Republic* insisted that it was a 5–4 and not a 7–2 decision. Only "Republican spinners" would claim otherwise; "Unsafe Harbor" in *New Republic*, December 25, 2000, 9. Although the *New Republic* may not deserve all the credit, public opinion has generally accepted the belief that it was a 5–4 decision. The fact that two justices who thought the recounts failed to meet constitutional standards did not want to hear the case in the first place is subject to different interpretations. On the one hand, it could be argued that these two justices thought the constitutional problems with the recount were so insignificant that they did not warrant intervention by the Court. On the other hand, one might question how two justices could justify voting against certiorari in a case involving what they later admitted to be fourteenth amendment violations that might alter the outcome of a presidential election.

7. 531 U.S., at 111.

8. Michael McConnell makes this argument in "A Muddled Ruling," *Wall Street Journal*, December 14, 2000, A26.

9. 531 U.S., at 134.

10. 531 U.S., at 146.

11. 531 U.S., at 146

12. 531 U.S. 70 (2000).

13. 531 U.S., at 76.

14. 531 U.S., at 78.

15. Dershowitz, *Supreme Injustice*, 41, and Linda Greenhouse, *New York Times*, February 20, 2001, A18.

16. Dershowitz, *Supreme Injustice*, 41.

17. Dershowitz, *Supreme Injustice*, 41–42.

18. John Yoo, "In Defense of the Court's Legitimacy," in *The Vote: Bush, Gore, and the Supreme Court*, ed. Cass R. Sunstein and Richard Epstein (Chicago: University of Chicago Press, 2001), 240.

19. Harvey J. Mansfield, "What We'll Remember in 2050," *Chronicle of Higher Education*, January 5, 2001, B15–16. Noemie Emery makes a similar, but more partisan, version of this argument claiming that "Democrats are the party of malleable standards, in the interest of what they think of as just. Republicans are the party of bright lines and hard and fast rules, in the interests of what they think is just" (Noemie Emery, "First Principles in Florida: Conservatives Believe in Rules, Liberals Want to Be 'Fair,'" *Weekly Standard*, December 11, 2000, 24).

20. Richard H. Pildes, "Democracy and Disorder," in Sunstein and Epstein, *The Vote,* 160–61.

21. Ibid., 162–63.

22. The Democrats might claim that they were only following the rules in pursuing every available legal mechanism to challenge the results, just as the Republicans might say that they were only trying to protect the democratic choice of the people from being thwarted by a corrupt recount process. But the Democrats ultimate justification for pursuing every legal mechanism was to guarantee that the intention of the voters was determined, and the Republicans' view of democratic choice was defined by their belief in a process that established clear rules and procedure for identifying democratic preferences.

23. See Akhil Reed Amar, "The Electoral College Unfair from Day One," *New York Times,* November 9, 2000, A23.

24. Dershowitz, *Supreme Injustice,* 25.

25. The ballot was designed by the Supervisor of Elections who was a Democrat and approved by a Board of Elections dominated by Democrats.

26. See John J. DiIulio Jr., "Equal Protection Run Amok: Conservatives Will Come to Regret the Court's Rationale in *Bush v. Gore,*" reprinted in *Bush v. Gore: The Court Cases and Commentary,* ed. E.J. Dionne Jr. and William Kristol (Washington, DC: Brookings Institution Press, 2001), 321–23.

27. See for example Jesse L. Jackson and John J. Sweeney, "Let the Count Continue," *Washington Post,* December 12, 2000, A47.

28. Richard A. Epstein, "'In Such Manner as the Legislature Thereof May Direct': The Outcome of *Bush v. Gore* Defended," in Sunstein and Epstein, *The Vote,* 16.

29. Cass R. Sunstein, "Order without Law," in Sunstein and Epstein, *The Vote,* 213.

30. Ibid., 215.

31. Bruce A. Ackerman, "Off Balance," in *Bush v. Gore: The Question of Legitimacy,* ed. Bruce A. Ackerman (New Haven, CT: Yale University Press, 2002), 195. Even Sunstein admits that "the principle behind the equal protection ruling has considerable appeal. In a statewide recount, it is not easy to explain why votes should count in one area when they would not count elsewhere" (Sunstein, "Order without Law," in Sunstein and Epstein, *The Vote,* 221).

Michael McConnell also points out that, "It may be true that the Equal Protection Clause typically protects against discrimination against identifiable groups, but as recently as last year, the Court summarily affirmed the principle that it also protects against 'irrational and wholly arbitrary' state action, even where the plaintiff does not allege that unequal treatment was on account of 'membership in a class or group.'" (*Village of Willowbrook v. Olech,* 528 U.S. 562,

563–66 (2000)); Michael McConnell, "Two-and-a-Half Cheers for *Bush v. Gore*," in Sunstein and Epstein, *The Vote*, 115.

32. Mark Tushnet, "The Conservatism in *Bush v. Gore*," in Ackerman, *Bush v. Gore*, 169.

33. Cass R. Sunstein, "Order without Law," in Sunstein and Epstein, *The Vote*, 215.

34. Pamela S. Karlan, "The Newest Equal Protection: Regressive Doctrine on a Changeable Court," in Sunstein and Epstein, *The Vote*, 77–78.

35. Ibid., 78.

36. 509 U.S. 630 (1993); 515 U.S. 900 (1995); 517 U.S. 952 (1996); 526 U.S. 541 (1999); 528 U.S. 62 (2000); 531 U.S. 356 (2001).

37. Ibid., 78.

38. Tushnet, "Conservatism," 174.

39. 514 U.S. 779 (1995).

40. 514 U.S., at 849.

41. 514 U.S., at 850.

42. 514 U.S., at 859.

43. 514 U.S., at 802.

44. 531 U.S., at 123.

45. 514 U.S., at 840.

46. Bruce Ackerman provides a good explanation of this phenomenon. "The idea of 'judicial activism' is an unusually vexed one, above all because any claim that judges are 'activists' seems to depend on accepting a certain theory of legitimate interpretation. If originalism is the right approach to constitutional law, then Justice Scalia is no activist. If democracy reinforcement is the right approach to interpretation, then Earl Warren is hardly an activist. Here is the problem: if we need to agree on a theory of interpretation in order to know whether judges are activists, discussion of the topic of activism will become extremely difficult and in a way pointless. A disagreement about whether judges are activists will really be a disagreement about how judges should be approaching the Constitution; the notion of activism and restraint will have added nothing" (Ackerman, *Bush v. Gore*, 189). Ackerman proposes to avoid this problem by using a "neutral" definition of activism, but I would argue that any such definition is unsatisfactory. Activism is not mere activity, but activity that goes beyond the normal constitutional powers of the office. We cannot determine who is an activist, without first determining the legitimate role of a judge under the Constitution.

47. 531 U.S., at 144.

48. 531 U.S., at 148–49.

49. 531 U.S., at 144.

50. Michael W. McConnell makes a similar argument in "A Muddled Ruling," *Wall Street Journal*, December 14, 2000, A26; 531 U.S., at 144.

51. 531 U.S., at 144.

52. Ford Fessenden and John M. Broder, "Study of Disputed Florida Ballots Finds Justices Did Not Cast the Deciding Vote," New York Times, November 12, 2001, A1. The study conducted by the National Opinion Research Center (NORC) showed that Bush would have won any recount based on either the standards set by the Florida Supreme Court or the standards requested by Gore. Kirk Wolter, Diana Jergovic, Whitney Moore, Joe Murphy, and Colm O'Muirchertaigh, "Reliability of the Uncertified Ballots in the 2000 Presidential Election," *The American Statistician* 57, no. 1 (February 2003), 1–13. According to this study, Gore would have won in a statewide recount of undervotes and overvotes. But as Michael McConnell points out, Gore's "only hope of winning, it now turns out, was to recount the overvotes in predominantly Republican parts of the state — just what they were trying to avoid" (McConnell, "Muddled Ruling," 121). But no one had asked for, nor had any Court ordered, such a recount. Even if they had, such a recount would have fallen short of "counting all the votes." Like the NORC study, it would have recounted only those votes that had been determined on the basis of the machine counts to have registered an overvote or undervote, a relatively small portion, 175,000 of the 6,138,000 ballots cast in Florida and far from a complete recount.

53. When the Federalists dominated the Court at the beginning of the nineteenth century, they supported judicial activism and the Jeffersonians opposed it. By the late 1850s, Democrats were defending the activism of the Taney Court and the Republicans were opposing it. From the end of the nineteenth century through the New Deal years, the conservatives supported the activism of the Court, and the liberals opposed it. And when liberals came to dominate the Court in the 1960s, liberals defended judicial activism and conservatives opposed it. The pattern is the same with partisan attitudes toward executive power. Activist Democratic presidents such as Jackson and Polk gave rise to a Whig Party that came together largely in opposition to the expansion of executive power. Lincoln's presidency, however, turned the Democrats into opponents of executive discretion. By the late 1960s, however, Republicans began to win the White House with some regularity, and of course their attitudes toward executive power, as well as those of their opponents, changed again.

54. See for example Mark Tushnet, *Taking the Constitution Away from the Courts* (Princeton, NJ: Princeton University Press, 1999). See also Sunstein's claim that "the Rehnquist Court has reinvigorated the commerce clause . . . has sharply limited congressional authority under Section 5, of the Fourteenth Amendment, in the process striking down key provisions of the Americans With

Disabilities Act, the Religious Freedom Restoration Act, and the Violence Against Women Act . . . has imposed serious barriers to campaign finance legislation, has thrown affirmative action programs into extremely serious question . . . and has interpreted regulatory statutes extremely narrowly," Cass R. Sunstein, "Does the Constitution Enact the Republican Party Platform? Beyond *Bush v. Gore*," in Ackerman, *Bush v. Gore*, 182–83.

55. 514 U.S. 549 (1995) and 521 U.S. 898.

56. See, for example, *Nollan v. California Coastal Commission* (483 U.S. 825 [1987]), *Lucas v. South Carolina Coastal Council* (505 U.S. 1003 [1992]), and *Dolan v. City of Tigard* (512 U.S. 374 [1994]). See also the series of cases cited by Sunstein in note 58 above as examples of Republican activism.

57. Sunstein, in Ackerman, *Bush v. Gore*, 189. For the classic defense of judicial intervention in the name of democratic principles, see John Hart Ealy, *Democracy and Distrust: A Theory of Judicial Review* (Cambridge, MA: Harvard University Press, 1980).

58. Edward Corwin, *The President: Office and* Powers, 4th ed. (1940: repr. New York: New York University Press, 1957); Richard Neustadt, *Presidential Power: The Politics of Leadership* (New York: John Wiley & Sons, 1960).

59. Tushnet, in Ackerman, *Bush v. Gore*, 175.

Chapter Six: Military Tribunals, Prerogative Power, and the War on Terrorism

I thank Joseph Bessette, Jeffrey Tulis, Christopher Pyle, and Louis Fisher for their comments, corrections, and editorial suggestions.

1. Quoted in *60 Minutes II*, CBS, September 11, 2002.

2. Quoted in Charles Lane, "Fighting Terror vs. Defending Liberties," *Washington Post National Weekly Edition*, September 9–15, 2002, 30.

3. "Military Order on Detention, Treatment and Trial of Certain Non-Citizens in the War Against Terrorism," *Federal Register* 66 (2001): 57831. Pentagon rules are in *Procedures for Trials by Military Commissions of Certain Non-United States Citizens in the War Against Terrorism*, Department of Defense Military Commission Order No. 1, March 21, 2002.

4. Military Commission Order No. 1, Sec. 4(c).

5. *ABA Recommendations on Trial Tribunal Procedures*. The American Bar Association's Annual Convention in 2002 recommended that military tribunals guarantee due process of law to defendants by a vote of 286–147.

6. Federal courts overturned laws making membership in the Communist party a crime when *Dennis v. United States*, 341 U.S. 494 (1951) was overturned by *Noto v. United States*, 367 U.S. 290 (1961), *Scales v. United States* 367 U.S. 203 (1961), and *Yates v. United States* 354 U.S. 298 (1957).

7. Clearance requirement for counsel in the *Classified Information Procedures Act*, Public Law 96-456, 94 Stat. 2025 (1980), upheld in *U.S. v. Osama bin Laden*, 58 F.Supp. 2d 113 (1999).

8. Sec. 4(C)(8)

9. Katharine Q. Seelye, "Pentagon Says Acquittals May Not Free Detainees," *New York Times*, March 22, 2002, A13.

10. Sec. 7(B)(2). For the argument that presidential war powers should not be subject to judicial review, see John Yoo, "Judicial Review and the War on Terrorism," *George Washington Law Review* 72 (December 2003), 427 and passim.

11. See, for example, the World War II cases: *Ex parte Quirin*, 317 U.S. 1 (1942); *In re Yamashita*, 327 U.S. 1 (1946).

12. "Means of Attack," in *National Strategy for Homeland Security* (Washington, DC: The White House, 2002).

13. International Committee of the Red Cross, "States Party to the Geneva Conventions and their Additional Protocols" (Geneva, 2005).

14. Patrick Philbin, unpublished memorandum to Alberto Gonzales, Office of White House Counsel, Washington, DC, November 6, 2006.

15. These apply to "those who, at a given moment and in any manner whatsoever find themselves, in case of conflict or occupation, in the hands of a Party to the conflict . . . of which they are not nationals." *Convention (IV) Relative to the Protection of Civilian Personnel at a Time of War* (Fourth Geneva Convention), www.unhchr.ch/html/menu3/b/91.htm.

16. Common Article 3 of *Convention (III) Relative to the Treatment of Prisoners of War* (Third Geneva Convention), www.unhchr.ch/html/menu3/b/91.htm.

17. Article 102, www.yale.edu/lawweb/avalon/lawofwar/geneva03.htm.

18. Article 105, www.yale.edu/lawweb/avalon/lawofwar/geneva03.htm.

19. Common Article 3, Fourth Geneva Convention, www.unhchr.ch/html/menu3/b/92.htm.

20. Jean-Marie Henckaerts and Louise Doswald-Beck, eds. *Customary International Humanitarian Law*, 2 vols. (Cambridge: Cambridge University Press, 2005).

21. 11 Op. Att'y Gen. 297 (1865).

22. www.oas.org/juridico/english/Treaties/a-60.html.

23. www.unhchr.ch/html/menu3/b/a_ccpr.htm.

24. *Chahal v. United Kingdom*, Eur. Ct. H.R. (1996).

25. "Military Order on Detention, Treatment and Trial of Certain Non-Citizens in the War against Terrorism," *Federal Register* 66 (2001): 57831.

26. Article 3 of the Fourth Geneva Convention, www.unhchr.ch/html/menu3/b/92.htm.

27. Article 17, www.unhchr.ch/html/menu3/b/91.htm.

28. Office of the Assistant Attorney General, Washington, DC, August 1, 2002, "Memorandum for Alberto R. Gonzales, Counsel to the President Re: Standards of Conduct for Interrogation under 18 U.S.C. Secs. 2340–2340A."

29. *The Detainee Treatment Act, Title X—Matters Related to Detainees, Department of Defense Appropriations Act of 2006,* Public Law 109-148, Sec. 105(b)(1)(a), provides that any Combatant Status Review Board or similar or successor tribunal or board may assess the probative value of evidence obtained as a result of the coercion of a detainee.

30. *Youngstown Sheet and Tube v. Sawyer,* 343 U.S. 579 (1952) at 636.

31. "The provisions of this chapter conferring jurisdiction upon courts-martial do not deprive military commissions, provost courts, or other military tribunals of concurrent jurisdiction with respect to offenders or offenses that by statute or by the law of war may be tried by military commissions, provost courts, or other military tribunals." 10 U.S.C. Sec. 821 (1994).

32. H.J. Res. 64 (2001), "Authorizing Use of United States Armed Forces Against Those Responsible for Recent Attacks Against the United States."

33. *Hearings before the Committee on Military Affairs,* U.S. Senate, 62nd Cong., 2nd Sess. 1912, 35. See the analysis by Ruth Wedgewood, "Al Qaeda, Military Commissions, and U.S. Self Defense," *Political Science Quarterly* 117, no. 3 (2002): 13–15.

34. Alexander Hamilton, James Madison, and John Jay, *The Federalist Papers,* ed. Clinton Rossiter, with a new introduction and notes by Charles R. Kesler (New York: New American Library, Mentor Books, 2003), No. 48, 306.

35. Thomas Langston and Michael Lind, "John Locke and the Limits of Presidential Prerogative," *Polity* 24, no. 1 (Fall 1991), 49–68.

36. Harold Koh, *The National Security Constitution* (New Haven, CT: Yale University Press, 1990), 135–149; Michael Glennon, *Constitutional Diplomacy* (Princeton, NJ: Princeton University Press, 1990), 111–18, 314–21.

37. *Hamdi v. Rumsfeld,* 542 U.S. 507 (2004); *Rumsfeld v. Padilla,* 542 U.S. 426 (2004).

38. *Ex parte Quirin* 317 U.S. 1 (1942), at 27.

39. Ibid., at 29.

40. *In re Yamashita,* 327 U.S. 1 (1946)

41. "Military Order on Detention, Treatment and Trial of Certain Non-Citizens in the War against Terrorism," *Federal Register* 66 (2001): 57831.

42. Franklin D. Roosevelt, Proclamation 2561, "Denying Certain Enemies Access to the Courts," July 2, 1942, *Federal Register* 7 (1942): 5101.

43. 28 U.S.C. Sec. 2241 Para. (3); Peter Raven-Hansen, "Detaining Combatants by Law or by Order? The Rule of Lawmaking in the War on Terrorists," *Louisiana Law Review* 64 (2004), 831–50.

44. *Rasul v. Bush*, 542 U.S. 466 (2004).

45. The cases are discussed in Erwin Chemerinsky, "Enemy Combatants and Separation of Powers," *Journal of National Security Law and Policy* 1 (Spring 2005), 73–89.

46. 128 S. Ct. 2229 (2008).

47. Ibid., at 2271.

48. *Anti-Torture Act*, 18 U.S.C. Sec. 2340A.

49. Article 36, *Uniform Code of Military Justice*, 10 U.S.C. Sec. 836.

50. Salim Ahmed Hamdan signed an affidavit admitting he was Osama Bin Laden's driver between 1996 and 2001, but he denied participating in terrorist activities. He was captured in Afghanistan in November 2001 and taken to Guantánamo Bay detention camp. In *Hamdan v. Rumsfeld*, 415 F. 3d 33 (2005), the Court of Appeals ruled that it had habeas corpus jurisdiction, but it held that the 1949 Third Geneva Convention did not give Hamdan a right to enforce international treaty obligations in federal court, and that a noncitizen detainee had no right to seek enforcement of any rights claimed under the Geneva Convention in a federal court. On all issues of treaty interpretation, the Court sided with the president, on the grounds that it is "the sort of political-military decision constitutionally committed to him," ibid., 23.

51. *Hamdan v. Rumsfeld*, 126 S. Ct. 2749 (2006).

52. For an analysis of *Hamdan* that emphasizes its limited reach, see Jeremy Rabkin, "Not as Bad as You Think: The Court Hasn't Crippled the War on Terror," *The Weekly Standard* 11, no. 41 (July 17, 2006).

53. *Hamdan v. Rumsfeld*, 126 S. Ct. 2749 (2006), at 2848.

54. Sheryl Gay Stolberg, "Justices Tacitly Backed Use of Guantanamo, Bush Says," *New York Times*, July 9, 2006.

55. "A Bill, To Facilitate Bringing Terrorist Enemy Combatants to Justice through Full and Fair Trial by Military Commissions and for Other Purposes," For Discussion Purposes Only, Deliberative Draft—Close Hold, Department of Defense, undated.

56. R. Jeffrey Smith, "Detainee Abuse Charges Feared," *Washington Post*, July 29, 2006.

57. Washington Post/ABC Poll, July 1, 2006.

58. Mary Cheh, "Should Lawyers Participate in Rigged Systems? The Case of the Military Commissions," *Journal of National Security Law and Policy* 1 (2005), 374–408.

59. Neil H. Lewis, "Two Prosecutors Faulted Trials for Detainees," *New York Times*, August 1, 2005.

60. National Defense Authorization Act for Fiscal Year 2006, Public Law 109-163, Div. A, Title XIV, Sec. 1401–1406; 119 Stat. 3136 (2006), at 3474–80.

61. This amendment contradicts the flat prohibition on the use of testimony secured through torture or extreme coercion in the *Uniform Code of Military Justice*, 10 U.S.C. Sec. 863.

62. The Graham amendment was designed to nullify the Supreme Court decision in *Rasul v. Bush*, 124 S. Ct. 2686 (2004). The Court held that detainees at Guantanamo could file habeas petitions to contest their detentions. The amendment limits such review to the validity of decisions of the Combatant Status Review Tribunals, a preliminary proceeding. It would mean that federal courts could not determine if the McCain antitorture amendment had been violated.

63. White House Signing Statement, December 30, 2005.

64. Richard M. Pious, *The Presidency* (New York: Allyn and Bacon, 1996), 465–66.

65. Richard M. Pious, *The American Presidency* (New York: Basic Books, 1979), 47–84; "Public Opinion Turns against the President in a Backlash Situation: Polls Show That 63 Percent of Americans Believe the US Should End Violations of International Conventions in Dealing with Prisoners at Guantanamo Bay," Knowledge Networks Poll, sponsored by the Center on International Cooperation—Project on International Courts and Tribunals, New York University, May 11, 2006.

66. *Federalist* Nos. 47 and 51.

67. Erwin Chemerinsky, "Enemy Combatants and Separation of Powers," *Journal of National Security Law and Policy* 1 (Spring 2005): 82.

68. *Sosa v. Alvarez-Machain* 124 S. Ct. 2739 (2004); *Alien Tort Claim Act*, 28 U.S.C. Sec. 1350.

69. The 9/11 Commission Report: Final Report of the National Commission on Terrorist Attacks on the United States (Washington, DC: Government Printing Office, 2004), 390.

70. Gene Johnson, "Judge Chides Anti-Terror Tactics while Sentencing Would-Be Millennium Bomber," *Associated Press*, July 29, 2005; Mike Siegel, "Ressam Judge Decries U.S. Tactics," *Seattle Times*, July 29, 2005.

Chapter Seven: Executive Orders

1. Richard E. Neustadt, *Presidential Power and the Modern Presidents: The Politics of Leadership from Roosevelt to Reagan* (New York: Free Press, 1990), 4.

2. The language leading up to this maxim is cited less frequently but gives weight to the argument that Neustadt was unenamored of authority: "The President of the United States has an extraordinary range of formal powers, of authority in statute, law, and in the Constitution. Here is testimony that despite his

'powers' he does not obtain results by giving orders—or not, at any rate, merely by giving orders," *Presidential Power*, 11.

3. Neustadt, *Presidential Power*, 24.

4. Neustadt, *Presidential Power*, 10.

5. Kenneth R. Mayer, *With the Stroke of a Pen: Executive Orders and Presidential Power* (Princeton, NJ: Princeton University Press, 2001); William G. Howell, *Power without Persuasion: The Politics of Direct Presidential Action* (Princeton, NJ: Princeton University Press, 2003); Phillip J. Cooper, *By Order of the President: The Use and Abuse of Executive Direct Action* (Lawrence: University Press of Kansas, 2002); Adam L. Warber, *Executive Orders and the Modern Presidency: Legislating From the Oval Office* (Boulder, CO: Lynne Rienner Publishers, 2006); William G. Howell and Kenneth R. Mayer, "The Last 100 Days," *Presidential Studies Quarterly* 35, no. 3 (September 2005): 533–53; Terry Moe and Scott Wilson, "Presidents and the Politics of Structure," *Law and Contemporary Problems* 57 (1994): 1–44; Terry Moe, "Presidents, Institutions, and Theory," in *Researching the Presidency: Vital Questions, New Approaches*, ed. George C. Edwards, John H. Kessel, and Bert A. Rockman (Pittsburgh: University of Pittsburgh Press, 1993); Brian W. Marshall and Richard L. Pacelle Jr., "Revisiting the Two Presidencies: The Strategic Use of Executive Orders," *American Politics Research* 33, no. 1 (January 2005): 81–105; Kenneth R. Mayer and Kevin Price, "Unilateral Presidential Powers: Significant Executive Orders, 1949–1999," *Presidential Studies Quarterly* 32, no. 2 (June 2002): 367–86; William G. Howell, "Unilateral Powers: A Brief Overview," *Presidential Studies Quarterly* 35, no. 3 (September 2005): 417–39; Christopher J. Deering and Forrest Maltzman, "The Politics of Executive Orders: Legislative Constraints on Presidential Power," *Political Research Quarterly* 52, no. 4 (December 1999): 767–83; George Krause and David Cohen, "Presidential Use of Executive Orders, 1953–1994," *American Politics Quarterly* 25, no. 4 (October 1997): 458–81; Phillip J. Cooper, "Presidential Memoranda and Executive Orders: Of Patchwork Quilts, Trump Cards, and Shell Games," *Presidential Studies Quarterly* 31, no. 1 (March 2001): 126–41; Graham G. Dodds, "Executive Orders from Nixon to Now," in *Executing the Constitution: Putting the President Back into the Constitution*, ed. Christopher S. Kelley (Albany: State University of New York Press, 2006). George Krause and Jeffrey Cohen, "Opportunity, Constraints, and the Development of the Institutional Presidency: The Case of Executive Order Issuance, 1939–1996," *Journal of Politics* 62, no.1 (February 2000): 88–114.

6. Justice Robert H. Jackson's concurrence in *Youngstown* argued that the authorities on executive power "largely cancel each other," noting "A Hamilton may be matched against a Madison. Professor Taft is counterbalanced by Theodore Roosevelt. It even seems that President Taft cancels out Professor Taft";

Youngstown Sheet and Tube v. Sawyer 343 U.S. 579, 635 (1952), note 1 (citations omitted).

7. Mayer, *With the Stroke of a Pen*, 34–35.

8. Executive orders are also distinct, observable, and frequent, enhancing their value in empirical research.

9. Executive Order no. 10,744, *Federal Register* 22 (December 13, 1957): 10001; Executive Order no. 11,943, *Federal Register* 41 (October 28, 1976): 47213; Executive Order no. 13,043, *Federal Register* 62 (April 18, 1997): 19217.

10. Keith E. Whittington and Daniel P. Carpenter, "Executive Power in American Institutional Development," *Perspectives on Politics* 1, no. 3 (September 2003): 496.

11. Mayer, *With the Stroke of a Pen*, chap. 2

12. Jennifer K. Elsea and Richard F. Grimmett, *Declarations of War and Authorizations for the Use of Military Force: Historical Background and Legal Implications*, Report RL31133 (Washington, DC: Congressional Research Service, 2006). World Wars I and II are counted as single acts, though each involved multiple declarations against separate countries. In addition, Congress has in a few instances specifically approved prior military deployments, under the War Powers Resolution.

13. The former number is from William G. Howell and Jon C. Pevehouse, "Presidents, Congress, and the Use of Force," *International Organization* 59 (Winter 2005): 217; the latter is from Richard F. Grimmett, *War Powers Resolution: Presidential Compliance*, RL 33532 (Washington, DC: Congressional Research Service, 2006), 12.

14. Gary J. Schmitt, "Thomas Jefferson and the Presidency," in *Inventing the American Presidency*, ed. Thomas E. Cronin (Lawrence: University Press of Kansas, 1989), 337–38.

15. Joseph Ellis, *American Sphinx: The Character of Thomas Jefferson* (New York: Vintage Books, 1998), 243.

16. Robert Knowles, "The Balance of Forces and the Empire of Liberty: States' Rights and the Louisiana Purchase," *Iowa Law Review* 88 (2003): 343–419.

17. See James D. Richardson, ed., *A Compilation of the Messages and Papers of the Presidents, 1789–1897*, 10 vols. (Washington, DC: Government Printing Office, 1896–99), 6:15–19.

18. Clinton Rossiter, *The American Presidency*, rev. ed. (New York: New American Library, 1960), 129.

19. Louis Fisher, for example, concludes that Truman's legal authority was "nonexistent." See Louis Fisher, *Presidential War Power*, 2nd rev. ed. (Lawrence: University Press of Kansas, 2004), 85.

20. Executive Order 10,340, 17 *Federal Register* 3139 (April 10, 1952).

21. Eric Schmitt, "New Power to Down Jets Is Last Resort, Rumsfeld Says," *New York Times*, September 28 2001, B7; Executive Order 13,228, *Federal Register 66* (October 10, 2001): 51812. Congress later established the Department of Homeland Security as a cabinet-level agency (Public Law 107-296, November 25, 2002); Military Order of November 13, 2001, "Detention, Treatment, and Trial of Certain Non-Citizens in the War against Terrorism," *Federal Register 66* (November 16, 2001): 57833–836; see U.S. Department of Justice, Office of Legislative Affairs, letter to James F. Sensenbrenner Jr., March 24, 2006. Available on the House Committee on the Judiciary Web site, http://judiciary.house.gov/media/pdfs/responses032406.pdf; See the discussion below of George W. Bush's statement on signing the 2006 Defense Appropriations Act, below.

22. Mayer, *With the Stroke of a Pen*, 85; Howell, *Power without Persuasion*, 83.

23. *Federalist* No. 70

24. Harvey C. Mansfield Jr., *Taming the Prince: The Ambivalence of Modern Executive Power* (Baltimore: Johns Hopkins University Press, 1993), xx.

25. For example, much is made of the fact that Article II's vesting clause does not include the "herein granted" qualifier used in the vesting clause of Article I. For some, the lack of the qualifying clause means that "the President is to have *all* of the executive power;" Steven G. Calabresi and Kevin H. Rhodes, "The Structural Constitution: Unitary Executive, Plural Judiciary," *Harvard Law Review* 105, no. 6 (April 1992): 1176. But other sources attribute the difference to unimportant drafting changes, not any substantive agreement about the meaning of the vesting clause; Henry P. Monaghan, "The Protective Power of the Presidency," *Columbia Law Review* 93, no. 1 (January 1993): 1–74. This tie cannot realistically be broken. Charles Thach argues that Governour Morris, who prepared the Constitution's final draft, purposely omitted the "herein granted" language but concedes he has no evidence to support his position; Charles C. Thach Jr., *Creation of the Presidency, 1775–1789: A Study in Constitutional History* (Baltimore: Johns Hopkins Press, 1923), 139.

26. *Youngstown Sheet and Tube v. Sawyer* 343 U.S. 579, 634–35 (1952) (Jackson, J., concurring).

27. Peter M. Shane and Harold H. Bruff, *Separation of Powers Law: Cases and Materials* (Durham, NC: Carolina Academic Press, 1996), 14.

28. Mayer, *With the Stroke of a Pen*; Howell, *Power without Persuasion*; Howell and Mayer, "The Last 100 Days."

29. Not even Nixon, who had asserted executive privilege in refusing to give up White House Office tapes to a district court, could defy a unanimous Supreme Court, which ruled that he had to turn them over. *United States v. Nixon*, 418 U.S. 683 (1974).

30. Terry M. Moe and William G. Howell, "The Presidential Power of

Unilateral Action," *Journal of Law, Economics, and Organization* 15, no. 1 (March 1999): 138.

31. Moe, "Presidents, Institutions, and Theory," in *Researching the Presidency*. See note 5 above for the complete citation.

32. Mayer, *With the Stroke of a Pen*, chap. 4.

33. Public Law 95-511.

34. Almost all of the legal restrictions on the intelligence community involve activities inside the United States or targeting U.S. citizens or "persons" (a term with a distinct legal meaning, encompassing more than simply U.S. citizenship). Whether Congress *could* regulate the president's authority to conduct intelligence collection abroad against foreign powers is a different question.

35. Elizabeth B. Bazan and Jennifer K. Elsea, "Presidential Authority to Conduct Warrantless Electronic Surveillance to Gather Foreign Intelligence Information," unpublished memorandum, Congressional Research Service, Washington, DC, January 5, 2006; James Risen and Eric Lichtblau, "Bush Lets U.S. Spy on Callers without Courts," *New York Times*, December 16, 2005, A1.

36. See, for example, Bruce Fein, "Presidential Authority to Gather Foreign Intelligence," *Presidential Studies Quarterly* 37, no. 1 (March 2007): 23–36.

37. U.S. Department of Justice, Office of Legislative Affairs, unpublished letter to James F. Sensenbrenner, Chair of the House Committee on the Judiciary, March 24, 2006.

38. See the account in Louis Fisher, "Invoking Inherent Powers: A Primer," *Presidential Studies Quarterly* 37, no. 1 (March 2007): 1–22, especially 17–19.

39. Eric A. Posner and Adrian Vermeule, *Terror in the Balance: Security, Liberty and the Courts* (New York: Oxford University Press, 2007), 80–82. While the weight of academic legal scholarship was critical, Neal Katyal and Richard Caplan argued that there was clear precedent that established the legality of the program. See Neal Katyal and Richard Caplan, "The Surprisingly Stronger Case for the Legality of the NSA Surveillance Program: The FDR Precedent." *Stanford Law Review* 60, no. 4 (February 2008): 1023–77, and Richard A. Posner, *Not a Suicide Pact: The Constitution in a Time of National Emergency* (New York: Oxford University Press, 2006).

40. See Jack Goldsmith, *The Terror Presidency: Law and Judgment inside the Bush Administration* (New York: Norton, 2007); Eric Licthblau, *Bush's Law: The Remaking of American Justice* (New York: Pantheon Press, 2008).

41. *Myers v. United States* 272 U.S. 52 (1926), holding that the president has an unlimited authority to remove appointed officials (later limited to officials with policy duties) that Congress cannot curtail; *Youngstown Sheet and Tube v. Sawyer*, 343 U.S. 579 (1952), holding that the president does not have unlimited emergency powers to act contrary to a statutory requirement.

42. Legal challenges to the Terrorist Surveillance Program have proven unsuccessful and the immunity granted to the telecom companies will discourage additional litigation. A federal district court judge did issue an injunction against the National Security Agency after declaring the program unconstitutional, but her ruling was overturned on appeal (*ACLU v. National Security Agency*, case 06-2095/2140, July 6, 2007). The Sixth Circuit did not reach the constitutional issues, holding instead that the plaintiffs lacked standing. In February 2008 the Supreme Court denied certoriari, allowing the Sixth Circuit's decision to stand. A different challenge involved plaintiffs who claimed they can show direct injury from the program (*Al-Haramain Islamic Foundation et al. v Bush et al.* (C-07-0109 VRW)). In July 2008, a district court judge dismissed this case on standing grounds as well, holding that the plaintiffs had not shown they had been targeted and that the suit could not proceed unless they did. Eric Lichtblau, "Judge Rejects Bush's View of Wiretaps," *New York* Times, July 3, 2008, A17.

43. Not all of the response was negative. In the spring of 2006, the House Judiciary Committee rejected a minority attempt to require the Justice Department to turn over all documents and records relating to the program. U.S. Congress, House Committee on the Judiciary, *Directing the Attorney General to Submit to the House of Representatives All Documents in the Possession of the Attorney General Relating to Warrantless Electronic Surveillance of Telephone Conversations and Electronic Communications of Persons in the United States Conducted by the National Security Agency: Adverse Report*. H. Report 109-382. 109th Cong., 2nd sess., March 2, 2006.

44. Walter Pincus and Charles Babington, "Specter Wants More Debate on Spying: Senator to Try to Block Program's Funding," *Washington Post*, April 28, 2006, A4.

45. HR 5825, *The Electronic Surveillance Modernization Act*, passed on a largely partisan 232–191 margin in September 2006.

46. Keith Perine and Seth Stern, "White House Gets Secret Court's Backing for Surveillance Program," *CQ Weekly Report*, January 22, 2007, 258. In a background briefing on January 17, an unnamed Justice Department official told reporters that the decision to work with the Foreign Intelligence Surveillance Court "should remove or take away the heat for such a debate or the need for such a debate" on imposing additional statutory limits on electronic surveillance. Federal News Service, "Background Briefing with Senior Department of Justice Officials on the Terrorist Surveillance Program via Teleconference," January 17, 2007. Obtained from Lexis-Nexis.

47. Dan Eggen, "Court Will Oversee Wiretap Program," *Washington Post*, January 18, 2007, A1; Mark Mazzetti, "White House to Release Details on Eavesdropping," *New York Times*, January 31, 2007, A1.

48. One key contention was that Foreign Intelligence Surveillance Act required a warrant even when both parties to a communication were outside the United States, as long as the data or the transmission were routed through a U.S. communications node.

49. *The Protect America Act of 2007*, Public Law 110-55, August 5, 2007.

50. The specific surveillance provisions sunset on January 31, but the House and Senate agreed on one fifteen-day extension to iron out disagreements on the permanent legislative framework. See Elizabeth B. Bazan, *The Foreign Intelligence Surveillance Act: An Overview of Selected Issues* (Washington, DC: Congressional Research Service, 2008).

51. David M. Herszenhorn, "Sharp Exchanges Over Surveillance Law," *New York Times*, February 16, 2007, 16.

52. Elizabeth B. Bazan, Gina Marie Stevens, and Brian T. Yeh, *Government Access to Phone Calling Activity and Related Records: Legal Authorities* (Washington, DC: Congressional Research Service, 2007), 1–2.

53. After the Protect America Act lapsed in February 2008, the White House claimed that the government lost important intelligence information because companies were unwilling to grant access. Dan Eggen and Ellen Nakashima, "Spy Law Lapse Blamed for Lost Information: Some Telecom Firms Not Cooperating for Fear of Liability," *Washington Post*, February 23, 2008, A3.

54. *Foreign Intelligence Surveillance Act of 1978 Amendments Act of 2008*, Public Law 110-261, Sec. 201 ("Protections for Electronic Communication Service Providers").

55. Barbara Sinclair, "Leading the New Majorities," *PS: Political Science and Politics* 41, no. 1 (January 2008), 3.

56. Executive Order 12,800, "Notification of Employee Rights Concerning Payment of Union Dues or Fees," *Federal Register* 57 (April 14, 1992): 12985.

57. Ann Devroy, "Bush Moves to Enforce Union Curb," *Washington Post*, April 14, 2002, A1.

58. Executive Order 12,836, "Revocation of Certain Executive Orders Concerning Federal Contracting," *Federal Register* 57 (February 1, 1993): 7045.

59. Executive Order 13,201, "Notification of Employee Rights Concerning Payment of Union Dues or Fees," *Federal Register* 66 (February 17, 2001): 11221. The United Auto Workers sued, arguing that the president did not have the authority to issue this rule. An appeals court rejected the challenge (*UAW-Labor Employment and Training Corporation et al. v. Chao*, 325 F. 3d 360 (D.C. Cir., 2003)). On the abortion policy, see Ceci Connelly and R. Jeffrey Smith, "Obama Positioned to Quickly Reverse Both Actions," *Washington Post*, November 2, 2008, A16.

60. In his last few weeks, Clinton issued hundreds of pardons, created mil-

lions of acres of new national monuments, and issued new limits on arsenic in drinking water; see Howell and Mayer, "The Last 100 Days." On last-minute regulatory activity during the waning days of the Bush administration, see Robert Pear, "Bush Aides Rush to Enact a Rule Obama Opposes," *New York Times*, November 28, 2008. Pear identified "about 20 highly contentious rules the Bush administration is planning to issue in its final weeks." The rules deal with issues as diverse as abortion, auto safety, and the environment.

61. Howell and Mayer, "The Last 100 Days," 551.

62. Mayer, *With the Stroke of a Pen*, 27–28; Moe and Howell, "The Presidential Power of Unilateral Action," 166.

63. Howell, *Power without Persuasion*, Appendix 4.

64. *Hamdan v. Rumsfeld*, 548 U.S. 557 (2006); *Rasul v. Bush*, 542 U.S. 466 (2004); *Hamdi v. Rumsfeld* 542 U.S. 507 (2004). The sharpest judicial rebuke was *Boumediene v.Bush* 553 U.S. (2008), which held that the enemy combatants at Guantánamo Bay have the right of *habeas corpus*, and that the language in the Military Commissions Act (P.L. 109-366) suspending that right is unconstitutional.

65. *Department of Defense Appropriations Act for 2006*, section 1003 (a), Public Law 109-148.

66. This approach was reflected in a memo to White House Counsel Alberto Gonzalez, in which Assistant Attorney General Jay S. Bybee, argued that the definition of torture was limited to the intentional infliction of pain equivalent to "serious physical injury, such as organ failure, impairment of bodily function, or even death." Memorandum for Alberto R. Gonzales, Counsel to the President, "Re: Standards of Conduct for Interrogation under 18 U.S.C.§§2340–2340A" (Washington, DC: U.S. Department of Justice, 2002).

67. *Weekly Compilation of Presidential Documents* 41 (December 27, 2005–January 2, 2006), 1918.

68. Cooper, *By Order of the President*, chap. 7; Christopher S. Kelley and Bryan W. Marshall, "The Last Mover Advantage: Presidential Power and the Role of Signing Statements" (paper presented at the 2006 annual meeting of the Midwest Political Science Association, Chicago, IL, April 20–23). One journalistic account estimated that Bush has used the strategy more than 750 times; Charlie Savage, "Bush Challenges Hundreds of Laws," *Boston Globe*, April 30, 2006.

69. American Bar Association, "Task Force on Presidential Signing Statements and the Separation of Powers Doctrine: Recommendation" (Chicago: American Bar Association, 2006), 5.

70. Curtis A. Bradley and Eric A. Posner. "Presidential Signing Statements and Executive Power." *Constitutional Commentary* 23, no. 3 (Winter 2006): 307–64. Defenders of Bush's use of signing statements point to a 1993 Office of

Legal Counsel opinion, in which Assistant Attorney General Walter Dellinger advised President Clinton that signing statements are a "useful and legally significant" tool that presidents can use to, among other things, declare that a provision in a bill "is unconstitutional on its face, and . . . will not be given effect by the executive branch." *The Legal Significance of Presidential Signing Statements*, Department of Justice, Office of Legal Counsel, Memorandum Opinion for the Counsel to the President, November 3, 1993. See www.usdoj.gov/olc/signing.htm.

71. House Committee on the Judiciary. *Presidential Signing Statements under the Bush Administration: A Threat to Checks and Balances and the Rule of Law?* 110th Cong., 1st sess., 2007. Serial No. 110-6.

72. Mayer, *With the Stroke of a Pen*, chap. 3; Mayer, "Executive Orders and Presidential Power"; Deering and Maltzmann, "The Politics of Executive Orders."

73. George A. Krause and David B. Cohen, "Presidential Use of Executive Orders, 1953–1994," *American Politics Quarterly* 25, no. 4 (October 1997): 458–81.

74. The spike in orders in December 2001 is not directly related to September 11. In that month, Bush issued separate orders specifying the order of succession for nine cabinet agencies. While there is a continuity-of-government purpose to these orders, they are otherwise routine.

75. On this point, David Mayhew, *Divided We Govern: Party Control, Lawmaking, and Investigations, 1946–2002*, 2nd ed. (New Haven, CT: Yale University Press, 2005) remains the benchmark.

76. Joel Fleishman and Arthur Aufses, "Law and Orders: The Problem of Presidential Legislation," *Law and Contemporary Problems* 40, no. 3 (Summer 1976): 1–46.

77. James Bennett, "True to Form, Clinton Shifts Energies Back to U.S. Focus," *New York Times*, July 5, 1995.

78. Krause and Cohen, "Opportunity, Constraints, and the Development of the Institutional Presidency" (see note 5 above for full citation).

79. Mayer, *With the Stroke of a Pen*; Dennis W. Gleiber and Steven A. Shull, "Presidential Influence in the Policy Making Process," *Western Political Quarterly* 45, no. 2 (June 1992): 441–68; Marshall and Pacelle, "Revisiting the Two Presidencies" (see note 5 above for full citation).

80. Deering and Maltzman, "The Politics of Executive Orders" (see note 5 above for full citation).

81. Pat Towell, "Campaign Promise, Social Debate Collide on Military," *Congressional Quarterly*, January 30, 1993.

82. Howell, *Power without Persuasion*, 99.

83. William G. Howell and Jon C. Pevehouse, *While Dangers Gather: Congressional Checks on Presidential War Powers* (Princeton, NJ: Princeton University Press, 2007).

84. David Gray Adler, "*The Law:* Textbooks and the President's Constitutional Powers," *Presidential Studies Quarterly* 35, no. 2 (June 2005): 379.

85. Louis Fisher, "A Dose of Law and Realism for Presidential Studies," *Presidential Studies Quarterly* 32, no. 4 (2004), 673.

86. John Yoo, who served in the Office of Legal Counsel, was the most forceful advocate of this position, particularly with respect to foreign affairs and war powers. See John C. Yoo, "War and the Constitutional Text," *University of Chicago Law Review* 69, no. 4 (2002): 1639–84; John C. Yoo, *The Powers of War and Peace: The Constitution and Foreign Affairs After 9/11* (Chicago: University of Chicago Press, 2005).

87. Harvey C. Mansfield Jr., *Taming the Prince: The Ambivalence of Modern Executive Power* (Baltimore: Johns Hopkins University Press, 1989).

88. *Federalist* No. 70.

89. This is a prediction rather than an observation, because Obama, as of this writing, has not yet taken office. Bruce Fein, a former Justice Department official who has argued forcefully against President Bush's view of executive power (see note 36), predicted that Obama would "take everything that Bush has given him and wield it with even greater confidence, because Congress has given him a safe harbor to do so with impunity." Jonathan Mahler, "After the Imperial Presidency," *New York Times Magazine*, November 9, 2008, 61. Note that Fein is also arguing that congressional majorities will prompt more unilateral action, rather than less.

Chapter Eight: Budget Power, Constitutional Conflicts, and the National Interest

1. See Louis Fisher, *Constitutional Abdication on War and Spending* (College Station: Texas A&M University Press, 2000).

2. See Jasmine Farrier, *Passing the Buck: Congress, the Budget, and Deficits* (Lexington: University Press of Kentucky, 2004).

3. See Daniel J. Palazzolo, *Done Deal? The Politics of the 1997 Budget Agreement* (New York: Chatham House / Seven Bridges Press, 1999).

4. For more details about the legislative management of President Bush's agenda during the Republican Congress, see Thomas E. Mann and Norman J. Ornstein, *The Broken Branch: How Congress Is Failing America and How to Get It Back on Track* (New York: Oxford University Press, 2006).

5. David D. Kirkpatrick, "Question of Timing on Bush's Push on Earmarks," *New York Times*, January 29, 2008, www.nytimes.com/2008/01/29/washington/29earmark.html.

6. Debate on the *Emergency Economic Stabilization Act of 2008*, HR 1424, 100th Congress, 2nd sess., *Congressional Record* 154: H10756, October 3, 2008.

7. Carl Hulse, "Congress Unites, Briefly, to Welcome New Members," *New York Times,* November 18, 2008.

8. See Samuel P. Huntington, "Congressional Responses to the Twentieth Century," in *The Congress and America's Future,* ed. David B. Truman (Englewood Cliffs, NJ: Prentice-Hall, 1965); Lawrence C. Dodd, "Congress, the Constitution, and the Crisis of Legitimation," in *Congress Reconsidered,* ed. Lawrence C. Dodd and Bruce I. Oppenheimer, 2nd ed. (Washington, DC: CQ Press, 1981); James L. Sundquist, *The Decline and Resurgence of Congress* (Washington, DC: Brookings Institution, 1981); Bruce I. Oppenheimer, "The Paradox of Republican Control," in *Congress Reconsidered,* ed. Lawrence C. Dodd and Bruce I. Oppenheimer, 6th ed. (Washington, DC: CQ Press, 1997); Kenneth R. Mayer and David T. Canon, *The Dysfunctional Congress? The Individual Root of an Institutional Dilemma* (Boulder, CO: Westview Press, 1999); and Joseph Cooper, "From Congressional to Presidential Preeminence," in *Congress Reconsidered,* ed. Lawrence C. Dodd and Bruce I. Oppenheimer, 8th ed. (Washington, DC: CQ Press, 2005).

9. For a multi-institutional view of historical executive expansion, see Andrew Rudalevige, *The New Imperial Presidency: Renewing Presidential Power after Watergate* (Ann Arbor: University of Michigan Press, 2005).

10. James Madison, Alexander Hamilton, and John Jay, *The Federalist Papers,* ed. Clinton Rossiter (New York: Mentor/Penguin, 1961), 346.

11. *Federalist* No. 58, 359.

12. *Federalist* No. 78, 465.

13. *Federalist* No. 71, 432.

14. *Federalist* No. 72, 435–56.

15. Herbert J. Storing, "The Creation of the Presidency," in *Toward a More Perfect Union: Writings of Herbert J. Storing,* ed. Joseph M. Bessette (Washington, DC: AEI Press, 1995), 376. See also Harvey C. Mansfield Jr., "The Ambivalence of Executive Power," in *The Presidency in the Constitutional Order,* ed. Joseph M. Bessette and Jeffrey Tulis (Baton Rouge: Louisiana State University Press, 1981).

16. *Federalist* No. 42, 268.

17. Hanna F. Pitkin, *The Concept of Representation* (Berkeley and Los Angeles: University of California Press, 1967) and Joseph M. Bessette, *The Mild Voice of Reason: Deliberative Democracy and American National Government* (Chicago: University of Chicago Press, 1994).

18. Lawrence C. Dodd, "Congress, the Constitution, and the Crisis of Legitimation," in *Congress Reconsidered,* ed. Lawrence C. Dodd and Bruce I. Oppenheimer, 2nd ed. (Washington, DC: CQ Press, 1981) and Sarah Binder, "Congress, the Executive, and the Production of Public Policy: United We Govern?" in *Con-*

gress Reconsidered, ed. Lawrence C. Dodd and Bruce I. Oppenheimer, 7th ed. (Washington, DC: CQ Press, 2001).

19. Allen Schick, *Congress and Money: Budgeting, Spending, and Taxing* (Washington, DC: Urban Institute Press, 1980), chap. 2. See also James P. Pfiffner, *The President, the Budget, and Congress: Impoundment and the 1974 Budget Act* (Boulder, CO: Westview Press, 1979). This section of the essay is derived from a much longer treatment of the 1974 budget act in Farrier, *Passing the Buck,* chap. 3.

20. *Weekly Compilation of Presidential Documents,* vol. 8. (Washington, DC: Government Printing Office, 1972), 1498, cited in Schick, *Congress and Money,* 44.

21. House Rules Committee, *Budget and Impoundment Control Act of 1973,* 93rd Cong., 1st sess., 1973, H. Rept. 93-658, 31.

22. Joint Study Committee on Budget Control, *Hearing on Improving Congressional Budget Control,* 93rd Cong., 1st sess., March 6, 1973, 25.

23. Ibid., March 9, 168.

24. Joint Study Committee on Budget Control, *Improving Congressional Control over Budgeting Outlay and Receipt Totals, Interim Report,* 93rd Cong., 1st sess., 1973, H. Rept. 93-13, 2.

25. Joint Study Committee on Budget Control, *Hearing on Improving Congressional Budget Control,* 93rd Cong., 1st sess., March 7, 1973, 108.

26. House Rules Committee, *Budget and Impoundment Control Act of 1974, Public Law* 93-344, 88 *Stat.* 297, 30.

27. See Fisher, *Congressional Abdication,* chap. 5, and Farrier, *Passing the Buck,* chap. 6, for more on the background and aftermath of the Line-Item Veto Act.

28. For more on the history of Office of Management and Budget, the confirmation controversy, and the results of Senate appointment involvement, see Fisher, *Presidential Spending Power,* 47–55; Larry Berman, *The Office of Management and Budget and the Presidency, 1921–1979* (Princeton, NJ: Princeton University Press, 1979); and Shelley Lynne Tomkin, *Inside OMB: Politics and Process in the President's Budget Office* (Armonk, NY: M.E. Sharpe, 1998).

29. Reprinted in James P. Pfiffner, ed., *The Managerial Presidency,* 2nd ed. (College Station: Texas A&M University Press, 1999), 135, 137–78.

30. Through today, the Congressional Budget Office has retained a strong reputation for more accurate forecasts of the state of the economy and the long-run cost of policy proposals than OMB. See Samuel Kernell and Erik J. Engstrom, "Serving Competing Principals: The Budget Estimates of OMB and CBO in an Era of Divided Government," *Presidential Studies Quarterly* 29 (December 1999): 820–29.

31. See Committee for a Responsible Federal Budget, fiscal 2009 deficit estimate, www.crfb.org/documents/trilliondollardeficit.doc.

32. See Farrier, *Passing the Buck,* chap. 4 (Gramm-Rudman-Hollings, 1985

and 1987), chap. 5 (Budget Enforcement Act of 1990), and chap. 6 (Line-Item Veto Act of 1996).

33. Ceci Connolly and Mike Allen, "Medicare Drug Benefit May Cost 1.2 Trillion: Estimate Dwarfs Bush's Original Price Tag," *Washington Post*, February 9, 2005, A01 (this estimate was based on the White House's own figures); Linda Bilmes and Joseph E. Stiglitz, "The Economic Cost of the Iraq War: An Appraisal Three Years After the Beginning of the Conflict" (paper prepared for presentation at the Allied Social Science Association meeting, Boston, January 2006); David M. Herszenhorn, "Estimates of Iraq War Cost Were Not Close to Ballpark," *New York Times*, March 19, 2008; "Analysis of the Growth in Funding for Operations in Iraq, Afghanistan, and Elsewhere in the War on Terrorism," Congressional Budget Office, February 11, 2008, Table 1, www.cbo.gov/ftpdocs/89xx /doc8971/02–11–WarCosts_Letter.pdf.

34. House Committee on the Budget, Congressional Budget Office Testimony, *Hearing on Extending the Budget Enforcement Act*, 107th Congress, 1st sess., June 27, 2001, 5. See *www.cbo.gov/showdoc.cfm?index=2896&sequence=0*.

35. See Robert Pear, "House Approves $94.5 Billion for Military Operations and Hurricane Recovery," *New York Times*, June 14, 2006, and "Bush Signs Spending Bill for Wars and Hurricanes," June 16, 2006.

36. www.washingtonpost.com/wp-dyn/content/article/2006/01/31/AR 200601311468.html.

37. Donald B. Marron, testimony of the Congressional Budget Office before the House Subcommittee on the Legislative and Budget Process, Committee on Rules, "CBO's Comments on H.R. 4890, the Legislative Line Item Veto Act of 2006," 109th Cong., 2nd sess., March 15, 2006, 8. See www.cbo.gov for full document, as well as deficit projections and historic tables.

38. House Committee on Rules, H. Rep. 109-505, Part 2, *Legislative Line Item Veto Act*, 109th Cong., 2nd sess., June 19, 2006, Sec. 4.

39. Extension of Remarks on HR 4890, *Legislative Line Item Veto Act*, 109th Cong., 2nd sess., *Congressional Record* 152 (June 21, 2006): E1349.

40. Ibid., E1246.

41. Andrew Taylor, "Line-Item Veto Draws Sen. Byrd's Scorn," *Associated Press*, May 2, 2006, and "Congress Likely to Resist Giving President Line-Item Veto Power," Associated Press, July 23, 2006.

42. See www.whitehouse.gov/omb/budget/fy2008/message.html.

43. See "Up to Their Earmarks," a graphic of annual earmarks based on a Congressional Research Service Report, as interpreted by the Washington Post, January 27, 2006, www.washingtonpost.com/wp-dyn/content/graphic/2006/01/27/ GR2006012700168.html.

44. Said by Stephen Slivinski, director of budget studies at the Cato Insti-

tute, as quoted in David Jackson, "Bush Makes More Veto Threats in 2007," *USA Today*, August 5, 2007, www.usatoday.com/news/washington/2007-08-05-vetoes_N.htm.

45. Ibid.

46. "Rescission Time in Congress," *New York Times*, March, 11, 2005.

47. For more on this rescission and data summarizing previous presidents' use of the power, see Brian M. Riedl, "The President's Proposed Line-Item Veto Could Help Control Spending," Web Memo 1021, Heritage Foundation, March 30, 2006, www.heritage.org/research/budget/upload/wm_1021.pdf; Farrier, *Passing the Buck*, 174 .

48. "The Budget Message of the President," February 6, 2006, www.white house.gov/omb/.

49. House floor remarks on HR 2642, *Supplemental Appropriations Act of 2008*, 110th Cong., 2nd sess. *Congressional Record* 154 (June 19, 2008): H 5702.

50. Ibid., H 5703.

51. White House, Office of the Press Secretary, "President Bush Signs HR 2642, the Supplemental Appropriations Act of 2008," June 30, 2008, www.white house.gov/news/releases/2008/06/20080630.html.

52. Tabassum Zakaria, "Bush Proposes Steps to Deal with Mortgage Crisis," *Reuters*, August 31, 2007.

53. Statement by the President on Homeownership Financing, August 31, 2007, White House, Office of Press Secretary, www.hud.gov/content/releases/pr07-123statement.cfm.

54. Senator Charles E. Schumer, Opening Statement of Chairman before Joint Economic Committee, *What Should the Federal Government do to Avoid a Recession?* 110th Cong., 2nd sess., January 16, 2008, 1–2.

55. Prepared remarks, Opening Statement of Chairman Christopher J. Dodd, Senate Committee on Banking, Housing, and Urban Affairs, "Turmoil in U.S. Credit Markets: Recent Actions Regarding Government Sponsored Entities, Investment Banks and Other Financial Institutions," 110th Cong., 2nd sess., September 23, 2008, 2, http://banking.senate.gov/public/_files/DoddOpening Statement7.pdf.

56. Prepared remarks, Secretary Henry M. Paulson Jr. before the Senate Banking Committee, "Turmoil in US Credit Markets: Recent Actions Regarding Government Sponsored Entities, Investment Banks and Other Financial Institutions," 110th Cong., 2nd sess., September 23, 2008, www.ustreas.gov/press/releases/hp1153.htm.

57. Committee on Financial Services (Republican minority page), press release of opening statement of Rep. Bachus, http://republicans.financialservices.house .gov/news/PRArticle.aspx?NewsID=266.

58. See Government Accountability Office Report to Congressional Committees, "Troubled Asset Relief Program: Additional Actions Needed to Better Ensure Integrity, Accountability, and Transparency," December 2008, www.gao.gov/new.items/d09161.pdf.

59. See www.cbo.gov/budget/budproj.shtml.

60. Sotirios A. Barber, *The Constitution and the Delegation of Congressional Power* (Chicago: University of Chicago Press, 1975).

61. Theodore J. Lowi, *The End of Liberalism: Ideology, Policy, and the Crisis of Public Authority*, 2nd ed. (New York: Norton, 1975) and David Schoenbrod, *Power without Responsibility: How Congress Abuses the People through Delegation* (New Haven, CT: Yale University Press, 1993).

62. Jeffrey K. Tulis, *The Rhetorical Presidency* (Princeton, NJ: Princeton University Press, 1987) and Joseph M. Bessette and Jeffrey Tulis, "The Constitution, Politics, and the Presidency," in *The Presidency in the Constitutional Order.*

Chapter Nine: Executive Privilege

1. Arthur M. Schlesinger Jr., *The Imperial Presidency* (Boston: Houghton Mifflin, 1973).

2. For a discussion of how contemporary congressional deference leads to the "imperial presidency," see especially Andrew Rudalevige, *The New Imperial Presidency: Renewing Presidential Power after Watergate* (Ann Arbor: University of Michigan Press, 2005), who borrows explicitly from Schlesinger's model. Michael A. Genovese and Robert J. Spitzer also make use of the "imperial presidency" metaphor in "Re-examining the War Power," *PRG Newsletter* XXX (Fall 2005).

3. The use of the term *executive privilege* in this chapter is intentionally elastic. Presidents do not always formally invoke executive privilege when they seek to withhold information, sometimes justifying their actions on legal or other constitutional grounds, perhaps in an effort to expand their ability to keep secrets without resorting to a tool sometimes seen as illegitimate in the wake of Watergate. Their arguments, however, are identical to those found in formal claims of privilege.

4. See especially the extended argument in Robert M. Pallitto and William G. Weaver, *Presidential Secrecy and the Law* (Baltimore: Johns Hopkins University Press, 2007).

5. For full discussions of these examples, see Mark J. Rozell, *Executive Privilege: Presidential Power, Secrecy, and Accountability*, 2nd ed. (Lawrence: University Press of Kansas, 2002).

6. Richard W. Stevenson, Sheryl Gay Stolberg, and John M. Broder, "Some Documents of Court Choice Will Be Released," *New York Times*, July 26, 2005, A1.

7. Robin Toner, David D. Kirkpatrick, and Anne E. Kornblut, "Steady Erosion of Support Undercut[s] Nomination," *New York Times*, October 28, 2005, A16.

8. Neil A. Lewis, "Former Aide to Cheney Gains Access to His Notes," *New York Times*, February 25, 2006, A11.

9. Eric Lipton, "A Mountain of Documents on Hurricane Response, but Democrats Seek More," *New York Times*, January 26, 2006, A16; Eric Lichtblau, "Bush Defends Spy Program and Denies Misleading Public," *New York Times*, January 2, 2006, A11.

10. For a detailed account of this sequence of events, see Mark J. Rozell and Mitchel A. Sollenberger, "Executive Privilege and the U.S. Attorneys Firings," in *Presidential Studies Quarterly* 38 (June 2008): 315–28.

11. Dan Eggen, "White House Blocks Release of FBI Files; Privilege is Cited in CIA Leak Case," *Washington Post,* July 17, 2008, A4.

12. Raoul Berger, *Executive Privilege: A Constitutional Myth* (Cambridge, MA: Harvard University Press, 1974), 3, 13, 52; Alexander Hamilton, James Madison, and John Jay, *The Federalist Papers*, ed. Clinton Rossiter (New York: Mentor, 1999), 290; James Madison, *Notes of Debates in the Federal Constitution of 1787* (New York: Norton, 1969), 46.

13. See especially Gary J. Schmitt, "Executive Privilege: Presidential Power to Withhold Information from Congress," in *The Presidency in the Constitutional Order*, ed. Joseph M. Bessette and Jeffrey Tulis (Baton Rouge: Louisiana State University Press, 1981), 154–94; and Rozell, *Executive Privilege*.

14. Louis Fisher, *The Politics of Executive Privilege* (Durham, NC: Carolina Academic Press, 2004), 3–5.

15. Ibid., xvi, 255–59.

16. David Gray Adler, "Con: A Broad Executive Privilege Is Essential to the Successful Functioning of the Presidency," in *Debating the Presidency: Conflicting Perspectives on the American Executive*, eds. Richard J. Ellis and Michael Nelson (Washington, DC: CQ Press, 2006), 132–40. Pallitto and Weaver also appear to support Sherman's statement. See Pallitto and Weaver, *Presidential Secrecy*, 197.

17. Fisher, *Politics of Executive Privilege*, 229, 258; Adler, "Con," 135; *United States v. Nixon*, 418 U.S. 683 (1974).

18. See especially chaps. 2–3 of Charles C. Thach Jr., *The Creation of the Presidency 1775–1789* (1923; repr. Baltimore: Johns Hopkins Press, 1969).

19. *Federalist* No. 48, 276–77.

20. *Federalist* No. 47, 269.

21. Aristotle, *Politics*, III.7, trans. Ernest Barker, rev. R. F. Stalley (Oxford: Oxford University Press, 1995).

22. *Federalist* No. 48, 278–79.

23. In fact, at the constitutional convention James Wilson repudiated the notion that "the parliament was the palladium of liberty," explicitly linking the legislature to tyranny in political systems marked by a weak executive. See Madison, *Notes of Debates*, 464.

24. *Federalist* No. 51, 290.

25. *Federalist* No. 52, 294–95, and No. 63, 353.

26. *Federalist* No. 71, 400.

27. For a full discussion of this goal, see Louis Fisher, "The Efficiency Side of Separated Powers," in *Journal of American Studies* 5 (August 1971): 113–31.

28. Richard E. Neustadt, *Presidential Power and the Modern Presidents: The Politics of Leadership from Roosevelt to Reagan* (New York: Free Press, 1990), 29.

29. *Federalist* No. 47, 269; No. 48, 276; No. 51, 289.

30. Jeffrey K. Tulis, *The Rhetorical Presidency* (Princeton, NJ: Princeton University Press, 1987), 41–45.

31. Discussion of the threat secrecy poses to democracy comes up several times in Pallitto and Weaver, but the authors make no mention of the natural tension that exists between security concerns and democracy, implying instead that the threat to democracy should end the discussion. Their casual dismissal of the constitutional and systemic approach to studying the presidency may be responsible for this oversight. See Pallitto and Weaver, *Presidential Secrecy*, 4–5, 125, 217.

32. *Federalist* No. 75, 418.

33. On the juxtaposition of leader and clerk, see Neustadt, *Presidential Power*, chap. 1.

34. *Federalist* No. 37, 194.

35. *Federalist* No. 70, 391.

36. Ibid., 392–95.

37. *Federalist* No. 64, 360–61.

38. *Federalist* No. 75, 420, emphasis in the original.

39. One of the problems with citing the framers at the constitutional convention is that often the debates are incomplete and do not reflect later final decisions. It is very easy to extract isolated quotes to make any point. While congressional supremacists prefer Roger Sherman on the proper role of the executive, Gouverneur Morris, who has a far stronger claim as one of the architects of the presidency, argued on July 17 *against* the president's being "the mere creature of the Legislative" branch, expressing fear of "usurpation and tyranny on the part of the Legislature" should Congress select the president. See Madison, *Notes of Debates*, 306–8.

40. *Federalist* No. 51, 289; *Federalist* No. 71, 401.

41. See Harvey C. Mansfield Jr., *Taming the Prince: The Ambivalence of Modern Executive Power* (Baltimore: Johns Hopkins University Press, 1993).

42. Herbert J. Storing, "A Plan for Studying the Presidency," in *Toward a More Perfect Union: Writings of Herbert J. Storing*, ed. Joseph M. Bessette (Washington, DC: AEI Press, 1995), 393–94.

43. Herbert J. Storing, "The Creation of the Presidency," in *Toward a More Perfect Union: Writings of Herbert J. Storing*, ed. Joseph M. Bessette (Washington, DC: AEI Press, 1995), 370–72.

44. *Federalist* No. 72, 405.

45. Erwin C. Hargrove and Michael Nelson, *Presidents, Politics, and Policy* (Baltimore: Johns Hopkins University Press, 1984), 12; see also David K. Nichols, *The Myth of the Modern Presidency* (University Park: Pennsylvania State University Press, 1994).

46. See *U.S. v. Curtiss-Wright Export Corporation*, 229 U.S. 304 (1936).

47. The first Congress recognized these branch-specific strengths and established a secret discretionary contingency fund for the president. Washington did not have to specify how he spent the money—he simply had to tell Congress that he had spent it. See Stephen F. Knott, *Secret and Sanctioned: Covert Operations and the American Presidency* (New York: Oxford University Press, 1996), 49–60.

48. See Rozell, *Executive Privilege*, 43–46, 50–51.

49. Ibid., 46–48.

50. For that matter, even members of Congress deliberate in secret, both officially and unofficially, and they are not required to reveal the content of their conversations.

51. *Federalist* No. 70, 393–95.

52. See especially Rozell, *Executive Privilege*, 28–33.

53. Ibid., 103–5, 112–13, 135–38.

54. Lipton, "Mountain of Documents," A16.

55. Eric Lichtblau, "Senator Threatens to Charge White House with Contempt," *New York Times*, August 21, 2007, A16.

56. See Rozell, *Executive Privilege*, 103, and Fisher, *Politics of Executive Privilege*, 76–77.

57. Stevenson, Stolberg, and Broder, "Documents of Court Choice," A1; Toner, Kirkpatrick, and Kornblut, "Steady Erosion of Support," A16. About four thousand pages of documents from Roberts's tenure in the White House Counsel's office had already been made public, and the administration argued that the Presidential Records Act covered the rest. The context with respect to Miers—serving a sitting president rather than one twenty years past—was obviously quite different.

58. See Fisher, *Politics of Executive Privilege*, 183–98, for a complete account.

The pretext for the original congressional inquiry was the concern that private meetings had been held at federal facilities, possibly violating the Federal Advisory Committee Act). The administration argued that the statute did not apply to task forces composed solely of federal employees and that the task force had simply met with a variety of groups to gather information.

59. See Rozell, *Executive Privilege*, 98–102, and Fisher, *Politics of Executive Privilege*, 124–30.

60. Rozell, *Executive Privilege*, 147–49, 151–54.

61. Ibid., 125–28, 138–44.

62. Michael Abramowitz and Dan Eggen, "Administration Again Rebuffs Senators," *Washington Post*, August 2, 2007, A6; Carrie Johnson, "Court Won't Force Testimonies on Firings of U.S. Attorneys; Issues Left to Next Congress in Victory for White House," *Washington Post*, October 7, 2008, A19.

63. Ibid., 30; Fisher, *Politics of Executive Privilege*, 11.

64. *Federalist* No. 70, 395–97.

65. See Schmitt, "Executive Privilege," 178–82, for a fuller discussion of this problem.

66. *Federalist* No. 49, 282.

67. *Federalist* No. 51, 288–90.

68. See Fisher, *Politics of Executive Privilege*, for an exhaustive account of the many ways Congress can make life difficult for the president.

69. For different views on the place of executive privilege in impeachment proceedings, see Charles L. Black Jr., *Impeachment: A Handbook* (New Haven, CT: Yale University Press, 1974), 20–23; and Michael J. Gerhardt, *The Federal Impeachment Process: A Constitutional and Historical Analysis*, 2nd ed. (Chicago: University of Chicago Press, 2000), 113–15.

70. For example, see the third article of impeachment against Richard Nixon.

71. *Federalist* No. 70, 397.

72. John Locke, *The Two Treatises of Government*, ed. Peter Laslett (Cambridge: Cambridge University Press, 1988), *Second Treatise*, para. 164 through 168.

Chapter Ten: Impeachment in the Constitutional Order

1. Art. I, Sec. 2 of the Constitution; Art. I, Sec. 3

2. For a more detailed summary of the formal procedures, see Charles L. Black Jr., *Impeachment: A Handbook* (New Haven, CT: Yale University Press, 1974), chap. 2.

3. Art. I, Sec. 3.

4. Art. III, Sec. 3.

5. Art II, Sec. 4.

6. Another proposal that was rejected was impeachment on application of a majority of the governors of the states. This provision would have mixed the parliamentary and federal ideas.

7. See for example, Michael Les Benedict, *The Impeachment and Trial of Andrew Johnson* (New York: Norton, 1973).

8. Jeffrey K. Tulis, *The Rhetorical Presidency* (Princeton, NJ: Princeton University Press, 1987), 87–93.

9. Philip B. Kurland, *Watergate and the Constitution* (Chicago: University of Chicago Press, 1978).

10. "Minority Memorandum on Facts and Law," *Hearings before the Committee on the Judiciary, House of Representatives*, 93rd Cong., 2d sess. (July 22, 1974), 44–45.

11. The House Judiciary Committee passed a broad "abuse of power" article, similar to two of the Nixon charges, but this was decisively rejected by the House.

12. Standards for perjury differ between the various federal court circuits. Clinton had given his deposition in Washington, D.C., where it was not perjury to omit information.

13. Art. II, Sec. 4.

14. Art. I, Sec. 3. And the question of "disqualification" would be decided by a separate vote and, presumably, an additional discussion of political considerations.

15. Art. I, Sec. 3.

16. See John R. Labowitz, *Presidential Impeachment* (New Haven, CT: Yale University Press, 1978), 8–9.

17. Raoul Berger, *Impeachment: The Constitutional Problems* (Cambridge, MA: Harvard University Press, 1973), 86. The term *high misdemeanor* has been used to refer to crimes such as misappropriation of funds and corruption.

18. Ibid., 61.

19. M. V. Clarke, "The Origin of Impeachment," in *Oxford Essays in Medieval History* (Oxford: Oxford University Press, 1934), 164, 185, quoted in Berger, *Impeachment*, 59.

20. Peter Charles Hoffer and N. E. H. Hull, *Impeachment in America 1635–1805* (New Haven, CT: Yale University Press, 1984), 266–70.

21. Joseph M. Bessette and Gary J. Schmitt, "What Does 'High Crimes and Misdemeanors' Mean?" Report from the Henry Salvatori Center, Claremont McKenna College, Claremont, CA, December 15, 1998.

22. Black, *Impeachment*, 33.

23. Nicole Mellow and Jeffrey K. Tulis, "Andrew Johnson and the Politics of Failure," in *Formative Acts: American Politics in the Making*, ed. Stephen Skowronek and Matthew Glassman (Philadelphia: University of Pennsylvania

Press, 2007), 153–70; Benedict, *Impeachment and Trial of Andrew Johnson*; Albert Castel, *The Presidency of Andrew Johnson* (Lawrence: University Press of Kansas, 1979).

24. For a more detailed discussion of this logic of separation of powers, see Jeffrey K. Tulis, "Deliberation between Institutions," in *Debating Deliberative Democracy*, ed. James S. Fishkin and Peter Laslett (Oxford: Blackwell, 2003), 207–9.

25. *Federalist* No. 51.

26. Art. II, Sec. 2, the president "shall have Power to grant Reprieves and Pardons for Offenses against the United States, *except in cases of Impeachment*" (emphasis added). It follows that the president may have the power to pardon in all other instances, and those pardons would stand, but I would argue that he may be impeached for his poor judgment after the fact.

Chapter Eleven: Demagoguery, Statesmanship, and Presidential Politics

1. Woodrow Wilson, *Constitutional Government in the United States* (1908; repr. New York: Columbia University Press, 1961), 68.

2. Although presidents did not generally give policy speeches, many pre–Civil War presidents did go on tours and deliver speeches of greeting. See Jeffery Tulis, *The Rhetorical Presidency* (Princeton, NJ: Princeton University Press, 1987), 64.

3. Woodrow Wilson, *Congressional Government: A Study in American Politics* (Boston: Houghton Mifflin, 1885), 85.

4. The most important work in this field is Jeffrey Tulis's *The Rhetorical Presidency*. See also James Ceaser, Glenn Thurow, Jeffrey Tulis, and Joseph Bessette, "The Rise of the Rhetorical Presidency," *Presidential Studies Quarterly* 11 (1981): 158–71: Theodore Lowi, *The Personal Presidency* (Ithaca, NY: Cornell University Press, 1985); and George Edwards, *The Public Presidency* (New York: St. Martins Press, 1983).

5. *Populism* is another term that was once used—and still is—to characterize dangerous popular leadership appeals. For example, the current Venezuelan president, Hugo Chavez, is often referred to, usually in derogatory sense, as politician who uses populist methods. But in American politics the term has recently been sanitized, and it often carries today, for both the Left and the Right, a favorable connotation. Thus, the 2004 Democratic vice-presidential candidate, John Edwards, was regularly described as having a positive "populist" message, while many conservative Republicans have proudly sought office on populist themes.

6. A few political scientists who use these models have introduced some normative elements under the names of "shirking," "pandering," and "manipulation."

The terms *pandering* and *manipulation* have parallels to certain elements of demagoguery. For discussion of these issues from different viewpoints, see in particular Brandice Canes-Wrone, *Who Leads Whom? Presidents, Policy, and the Public* (Chicago: University of Chicago Press) 2005; Brandice Canes-Wrone and Kenneth W. Shotts, "The Conditional Nature of Presidential Responsiveness to Public Opinion," *American Journal of Political Science* 48, no. 4 (2004): 690–706; and Lawrence Jacobs and Robert Shapiro, *Politicians Don't Pander* (Chicago: University of Chicago Press, 2000). Some of the limitations of the modern approaches to leadership are discussed by Randall Strahan, "Personal Motives, Constitutional Forms, and the Public Good: Madison on Political Leadership," in *James Madison: The Theory and Politics of Republican Government*, ed. Samuel Kernell (Palo Alto, CA: Stanford University Press, 2003).

7. Aristotle, *Nichomachean Ethics*, 1094 b 11–13.

8. George Mason, from his speech at the ratification debate in Virginia, June 17, 1788. It can be found at http://press-pubs.uchicago.edu/founders/documents /a2_1_1s16.html.

9. *Federalist* No. 10.

10. *Federalist* No. 71.

11. From James Madison, "Vices of the Political System of the United States" as cited in Bryan Garsten, *Saving Persuasion* (Cambridge, MA: Harvard University Press, 2006), 202. According to Garsten, Madison arrived at the Convention holding the view that "the demagogy of ambitious men was a major cause of disorder and civil strife in his own day" (202).

12. *Federalist* No. 58.

13. Plutarch, "Life of Caius Gracchus," in *The Lives of the Noble Grecians and Romans*, trans. John Dryden (New York: Modern Library, 1957), 1011.

14. *Federalist* No. 63.

15. Tulis, *The Rhetorical Presidency*, 45–47.

16. *Federalist* No. 63.

17. David Nichols, *The Myth of the Modern Presidency* (University Park: Pennsylvania State University Press, 1994).

18. In the original plan of the Constitution, there was no separate vote for the vice president. The vice president was selected as the runner-up in the presidential vote.

19. This change also raised the threshold for being elected at the electoral stage, increasing it from a number equal to a quarter of the electors to a number equal to a half of the electors.

20. Thomas Ritchie, *The Virginia Enquirer*, January 1, 1824. See also *The Virginian Enquirer*, December 23, 1823. Cited in James Ceaser, *Presidential Selection* (Princeton, NJ: Princeton University Press, 1979), 137.

21. Letter from Martin Van Buren to Thomas Ritchie, January 13, 1827. Cited in Ceaser, *Presidential Selection*, 138.

22. Gill Troy, *See How They Ran* (New York: Free Press, 1991), 45.

23. See Andrew Busch, *Outsiders and Openness in the Presidential Nominating System* (Pittsburgh: University of Pittsburgh Press, 1997).

24. To avoid the negative implications we attach to the term, Carnes Lord in his translation of Aristotle's *Politics* renders *demagogos* as "popular leaders." See *The Politics* (Chicago: University of Chicago Press, 1984), 278.

25. I rely here on Melissa Lane's "The Evolution of the 'Demagogue' and the Invention of the 'Statesman' in (Reflections on) Ancient Athens" (paper delivered at a conference at Yale University, "Statesmen and Demagogues: Democratic Leadership in Political Thought" March 31–April 1, 2006).

26. Thucydides, *History of the Peloponnesian War* (Loeb translation), 2.65.9.

27. It was part of Plato's divine genius that he challenged the judgment that Pericles was a statesman. He concluded instead that Pericles had in fact artfully corrupted the Athenians during his tenure, making them more unjust and less virtuous (see the *Gorgias*, 515c–516d). Aristotle, staying slightly closer to the surface, argued that Pericles managed to enjoy "good repute with the better sorts" and that Athens remained in "fairly good condition" as long as he was on the scene; but Aristotle concurred with Plato that Athens became worse afterward, due largely to Pericles' policy of introducing wages for the people. Aristotle praises Pericles as a leader, but suggests he descended at times into demagogy, perhaps inevitably or necessarily so. No leader of the popular party, perhaps no leader of any kind in a thoroughly democratic system, can eschew all aspects of demagoguery and survive or thrive. See *The Constitution of Athens*, 97–98; Aristotle, *The Politics*, 1274a 6–10.

28. Online version, 1989, http://dictionary.oed.com/cgi/entry/50060328?query_type=word&queryword=demagogue&first=1&max_to_show=10&sort_type=alpha&result_place=1&search_id=BHDy-fJY4gF-11374&hilite=50060328.

29. Walter Lippmann, *Public Opinion* (New York: Free Press, 1955), 157.

30. *Federalist* No. 71

31. If one wished to include the more difficult and problematic criterion of intention, the demagogue is one who employs his demagoguery with pure malice aforethought, that is, with the chief aim or end of boosting his power, without regard for the public good.

32. Victor Ehrenberg, *From Solon to Socrates* (New York: Methuen, 1973), 266.

33. After being defeated in the governor's race in Alabama in 1958, George Wallace is reliably reported to have told one of his campaign aides, "I was out-niggered, and I will never be out-niggered again," www.pbs.org/wgbh/amex/wallace/sfeature/quotes.html.

34. Aristotle, *Constitution of Athens*, trans. Kurt Von Fritz (New York: Hafner, 1950), 99.

35. Plutarch, *Moralia: Quomodo Adult*, 52E.

36. Tim Duff, *Plutarch's Lives: Exploring Virtue and Vice* (Oxford: Clarendon Press, 1999), 303.

37. *Federalist* No. 1.

38. *Federalist* No. 1.

39. Alexis de Tocqueville, *Democracy in America*, trans. Harvey Mansfield and Delba Winthrop (Chicago: University of Chicago Press, 2000), 377.

40. Plutarch, "Life of Pericles," in *Lives*, 195.

41. Samuel Taylor Coleridge, "A Lay Sermon" in *Coleridge's Writings on Politics and Society*, ed. John Beer, 4 vols. (Princeton: Princeton University Press, 1991) 1:101–2.

42. See also Jeremiah 23:16. The "demagogues" in this case refer not just to "false prophets" but also include certain priests and political figures.

43. Jeremiah 23 and 5:31.

44. The study of false prophets is not the only the place where one encounters the theme of demagoguery in the Bible. It is a subject of inquiry throughout the "historical" narratives, nowhere more explicitly than in the accounts of Absalom, David's son and would-be usurper. A clear Type II demagogue, Absalom appealed with his good looks, flowing hair, and loose lifestyle. He would hang around the gates of Jerusalem, familiarizing himself with the people and making generous promises: "Every man with a suit or cause might come to me, and I would give him justice" (2 Samuel 15:4).

45. Machiavelli, *Discourses* I: 11. According to historian Guicciardini, "If he was good, we have seen a great prophet in our time; if he was bad, we have seen a great man. For, apart from his erudition, we must admit that if he was able to fool the public for so many years on so important a matter without ever being caught in a lie, he must have had great judgment, talent and power of invention" (Guicciardini, *History of Florence*, chap. 16).

46. Hobbes's warnings duplicate the biblical criticism of false prophecy, although without allowing for the idea of true prophecy. See Thomas Hobbes, *Leviathan*, ed. Richard Tuck (Cambridge: Cambridge University Press, 1996), 297. I am following here the arguments of Garsten, *Saving Persuasion*, 43.

47. This well-worn phrase, which Blackstone used in his *Commentaries*, was picked up by Jefferson and used in his letter to Roger Weightman, June 24, 1826.

48. Woodrow Wilson, *Leaders of Men* (1890; repr. Princeton: Princeton University Press, 1952), 42.

49. This kind of demagogic appeal has been associated with the politician Pierre Poujade in France, who played on the fears of shopkeepers and small busi-

ness owners on the issue of social change. The phenomenon now has its own term, *poujadisme*.

50. I rely here on the analysis of Clifford Orwin, found in his Bradley Lecture, "Moist Eyes: Political Tears from Rousseau to Clinton," delivered on April 14, 1997, at the American Enterprise Institute, at www.aei.org/publications/pubID.18967,filter.all/pub_detail.asp.

51. See Larry Sabato, *The Rise of Political Consultants* (New York: Basic Books, 1981); Joe Klein, *Politics Lost* (New York: Doubleday, 2006); and Dennis Johnson, *No Place for Amateurs* (London: Routledge, 2001).

52. Garsten, *Saving Persuasion*, 13.

53. Woodrow Wilson, "Cabinet Government in the United States," in *College and State*, ed. Ray Stannard Baker and William E. Dodd, 2 vols. (New York: Harper Brothers, 1925) 1:37.

54. Adam Sheingate, "'Publicity' and the Progressive-Era Origins of Modern Politics," *Critical Review* 19, nos. 2–3 (2007): 465, 466.

55. See the works of Harold Lasswell, Walter Lippmann, and, much later, the authors of the *American Voter*.

56. Lippmann, *Public Opinion*, 158. For a discussion of the rise of consultancy, see Sheingate, "'Publicity' and the Progressive-Era Origins of Modern Politics."

57. Joseph Bessette, "Deliberative Democracy: The Majority Principle in Republican Government," in *How Democratic Is the Constitution?*, ed. Robert A. Goldman and William A. Schambra (Washington, DC: AEI Press, 1980) and *The Mild Voice of Reason* (Chicago: University of Chicago Press, 1994).

58. Besides Jürgen Habermas, some of the others who have contributed to the theme of discursive democracy include John Rawls, Joshua Cohen, Amy Gutmann, Dennis Thompson, and Seyla Benhabib.

59. Tocqueville devoted a famous chapter in his volume on the *Old Regime and the French Revolution* to showing how this process operated in eighteenth-century France, with the spread of ideas from the theorists, to the "men of letters," to many of those who made the Revolution: "When we closely study the French Revolution we find that it was conducted in precisely the same spirit as that which gave rise to so many books expounding theories of government in the abstract," author's translation, part 3, chap. 1.

60. John Adams claimed: "Every man of a crowded audience appeared to me to go away as I did ready to up arms against the writs of assistance. Then and there was the first scene of the first act of the opposition to the arbitrary claims of Great Britain. Then and there the child of Independence was born." Available at www.mass.gov/courts/stc/john-adams-b.html.

61. Alexis de Tocqueville, *The Old Regime and the French Revolution*, part 3,

chap. 1, which is titled, "How Towards the Middle of the Eighteenth Century Men of Letters Took the Lead in Politics and the Consequences of this New Development."

62. See especially Michael Schudson, *Discovering the News* (New York: Basic Books, 1978).

63. For Aristotle, persuasion by showing one's character and credibility (*ethos*) is one of the three basic types of proof in rhetoric. The other two are *pathos* (emotional appeals) and *logos* (rational argumentation). A notable example of a decisive failure of ethos was Al Gore's performance during his first debate with George Bush in 2000, when he exaggerated a story and was observed to sigh and smirk, thereby displaying an unmerited arrogance. This performance was widely regarded as turning the campaign against him.

64. Almost as direct are the replays of large sections of the speeches on news programs in subsequent days and throughout the campaign.

65. John Marshall put it this way, "By weakening the office of President he [Jefferson] will increase his personal power," quoted in Raymond Tatalovich and Thomas S. Engeman, *The Presidential Political Science: Two Hundred Years of Constitutional Debate* (Baltimore: Johns Hopkins University Press, 2003), 38.

66. Martin Van Buren to Thomas Ritchie, January 13, 1827. Cited in Ceaser, *Presidential Selection*, 160.

67. Robert Gunderson, *The Log Cabin Campaign* (Lexington: University of Kentucky Press, 1957), 7.

68. Seymour Martin Lipset and Earl Raab, *The Politics of Unreason* (New York: Harper & Row, 1970), 50–55.

69. Harry Jaffa notes that Douglas's supposed indifference to slavery, not caring whether it was voted up or down, "may then in fact have been an act of prudence of the highest kind . . . From this point of view, Douglas's suppression of the morality concerning slavery would be a higher act of virtue than Lincoln's gratification of his feelings on the subject." Harry Jaffa, "Abraham Lincoln" in *American Political Thought*, ed. Morton Frisch and Richard Stevens (Dubuque, IA: Kendall Hunt, 1971), 130.

70. Lincoln made two comments that shed light on his view of the role of abstract principles. First, from his Speech at New Haven (1860): "Whenever the question of [slavery] shall be settled, it must be settled on some philosophical basis. No policy that does not rest on some philosophical public opinion can be permanently maintained." Second, from his Letter to Henry L. Pierce, & Others (1859): "All honor to Jefferson—to the man who . . . had the coolness, forecast, and capacity to introduce into a merely revolutionary document, an abstract truth, applicable to all men and all times." Abraham Lincoln, *Selected Speeches and Writings* (New York: Library of America, 1992), 216, 257.

71. From the Lincoln-Douglas Debates, 1858 (first debate at Otttawa, Illinois).

Lincoln went on: "I ask you to consider whether, so long as the moral constitution of men's minds shall continue to be the same, after this generation and assemblage shall sink into the grave, and another race shall arise with the same moral and intellectual development we have—whether, if that institution is standing in the same irritating position in which it now is, it will not continue an element of division?" The debates are online at: www.nps.gov/archive/liho/debates.htm.

72. Taft's speech at Cambridge, Ohio, is available at http://ehistory.osu.edu/osu/mmh/1912/content/TRSeeksGOPNomination.cfm

73. As cited in Jonathan Alter, *The Defining Moment: FDR's Hundred Days and the Triumph of Hope* (New York: Simon and Schuster, 2006), 220–21.

74. Morton Frisch, "Franklin Roosevelt," in Frisch and Stevens, *American Political Thought*, 236.

JOSEPH M. BESSETTE is the Alice Tweed Tuohy Professor of Government and Ethics at Claremont McKenna College. He is the author of *The Mild Voice of Reason* (University of Chicago Press), and coeditor of *The Presidency in the Constitutional Order* (Louisiana State University Press).

JAMES W. CEASER is a distinguished visiting fellow at the Hoover Institution and professor of politics at the University of Virginia. His publications include *Presidential Selection* (Princeton University Press).

DAVID A. CROCKETT is an associate professor of political science at Trinity University, San Antonio. He is the author of *The Opposition Presidency* (Texas A&M University Press) and other publications.

JASMINE FARRIER is an associate professor of political science at University of Louisville and the author of *Passing the Buck* (University of Kentucky Press).

KENNETH R. MAYER is a professor of political science at the University of Wisconsin, Madison. His publications include *With the Stroke of a Pen* (Princeton University Press).

DAVID K. NICHOLS is an associate professor of political science at Baylor University and a senior fellow at the Alexander Hamilton Institute. He is the author of *The Myth of the Modern Presidency* (Pennsylvania State University Press).

RICHARD M. PIOUS is the Adolf S. and Effie E. Ochs Professor of American Studies at Barnard College. He is the author of *Why Presidents Fail* (Rowman and Littlefield), *The Way of Terrorism and the Rule of Law* (Oxford University Press).

LANCE ROBINSON is a lieutenant colonel, retired, in the United States Air Force. Material for his chapter was drawn from his Ph.D. dissertation, Claremont Graduate University.

GARY J. SCHMITT is a resident scholar and the director of the Program on Advanced Strategic Studies at the American Enterprise Institute, Washington, D.C. His writings include *Silent Warfare* (Brassey's), with Abram N. Shuley.

JEFFREY K. TULIS teaches political science at the University of Texas at Austin and is coeditor of the Johns Hopkins Series in Constitutional Thought. His publications include *The Rhetorical Presidency* (Princeton University Press) and *The Presidency and the Constitutional Order* (coeditor; Louisiana State University Press).

Black, Charles L., Jr., 239, 342n69, 342n2
Black, Scott C., 142
Blackstone, William, 59, 293–94n8, 302n16, 347n47
Board of Trustees v. Garrett, 110
BOB. *See* Bureau of the Budget
Boehner, John, 143
Boies, David, 111
Boumediene v. Bush, 137
Brackenridge, Hugh. *See* "Brutus"
Bradbury, Steven G., 141
Bradley, Curtis A., 331n70
Brahms, David M., 142
Breyer, Stephen, 97–103, 111, 115–18, 140
Broder, John M., 319n52, 338n6
"Brutus," 298n5, 305n30
Bryan, William Jennings, 248; as campaigner and speech giver, 281; as demagogue, 280
Buchanan, James, 11, 14, 91–95, 295n24
Buchanan, Patrick, 105, 287; as demagogue, 259
Budget and Accounting Act, 186
budget deficits, 9, 177
Budget Enforcement Act, 174, 186, 190
Bureau of the Budget (BOB), 187, 188
Burke, Edmund 269, 270, 297n38; *Reflections on the Revolution in France,* 269
Burns, Arthur, 185
Burns, James MacGregor, 3, 4, 185, 289n4, 289n5, 291n22
Burr, Aaron, 297n34; as demagogue, 275
Bush, George H. W., 162, 174, 189, 220, 285
Bush, George W.: and the budget, 189–99; and the economy, 174–75; executive orders, 154, 166, 171–72, 331n74; and executive power, 1, 171; and federal prosecutors, 224; as high water mark for presidential power, 189; and imperial presidency, 178, 203; military tribunals, 123–24, 127–41, 144–47, 157, 329n42; perceived rights of, 164, 203, 204, 224; ratings, vii; and secrecy, 221–23; signing statements,

331n70; and 2000 election, 96–121, 314–15n1, 319n52; and unified government, 174, 190. See also *Bush v. Gore*
Bush v. Gore, x, 96–122, 316n5, 317n26, 317n28, 317n31, 318nn31–32, 318n46, 320n54, 320n57, 320n59; Democrats' view of, 104; majority and republicanism, 115; minority and democratic values, 117; uncertified Florida ballots, 319n52
Bush v. Palm Beach County Canvassing Board, 99, 101, 102, 103, 116
Bush v. Vera, 110
Byrd, Robert, 193

Caesar, Julius, 257; as demagogue, 261
campaign: candidates' behavior, 247; as mass spectacle, 276
Canada, 56
Carpenter, Daniel P., 151, 326n10
Carroll, John Alexander, 295n25, 305n32
Carter, Jimmy, viii, 203, 286
Cato Institute, 194
Ceaser, James, 247, 291n15, 312n12, 344n4, 345n20, 346n21, 349n66; levels of Constitutional operation, 311n12
Central Intelligence Agency (CIA), 132, 142, 144, 204, 224, 339n11
Chavez, Hugo, as populist, 344n5
checks and balances, 3, 15, 26, 132, 146, 148, 156, 173, 178, 203, 207–11, 241. *See also* separation of powers
Chemerinsky, Erwin, 323n45, 324n67
Cheney, Richard B., xi, 124, 204, 222
Chertoff, Michael, 124
Choate, Rufus, 278
CIA. *See* Central Intelligence Agency
Cicero, 215
civic education, 246
Civil War, English, 263
Civil War, U.S., 17–20, 46, 92, 129, 135, 312n14
Cleon, 256, 259, 260, 265; as demagogue, 256
Clinton, William J.: and abortion, 162, 163; actions at end of presidency,

dent, 153; George W. Bush's use of, 166, 204; and interrogating prisoners, 143; Korean War and, 154; and laws and treaties, 138; Lincoln in 1861, 152; and the Louisiana purchase, 151; and public popularity, 166, 167

executive privilege, xi, 12, 204–7, 215, 220–27, 233, 243, 245; definition of, 203, 338n3

Ex parte Milligan, 17, 19, 23, 134, 135, 292n28

Ex parte Quirin, 134, 321n11, 322n38

"Farmer in Pennsylvania, A," 270

Farrand, Max, 294n10, 294nn12–13, 295nn14–19, 295n21, 297n35, 310n59

Farrier, Jasmine, x, 173, 245, 333n2, 351

FBI. *See* Federal Bureau of Investigation

Federal Bureau of Investigation (FBI), 135, 205, 339n11

federalism, x, 108, 110, 112, 114, 115

Federalist, The (general): and the budget, 173, 179; and popular government, 110, 250–51, 261, 270; and the presidency, 10, 13–16, 55, 155, 180–81, 286; and separation of powers, 133, 146, 200, 209–13, 243. See also *Federalist, The* (individual papers)

Federalist, The (individual papers): No. 1, 347nn37–38; No. 10, 180, 312n13, 345n9; No. 23, 292n26; No. 25, 314n41; No. 37, 213, 340n34; No. 41, 314n41; No. 42, 182, 334n16; No. 47, 182, 209, 210, 303n18, 324n66, 339n20, 340n29; No. 48, 322n34, 339n19, 340n22; No. 49, 183, 342n66; No. 51, 178, 206, 209, 214, 291n17, 292n24, 303n18, 311n11, 324n66, 340n24, 340n29, 340n40, 342n67, 344n25; No. 52, 340n25; No. 55, 179; No. 58, 179, 334n11, 345n12; No. 62, 180; No. 63, 180, 340n25, 345n14; No. 64, 340n37; No. 69, 49, 302n16; No. 70, 55, 180, 214, 220, 225, 291n23, 327n23, 333n88, 340n35, 341n51, 342n64, 342n71; No. 71, 180, 291n22, 311n9,

334n13, 340n26, 340n40, 345n10, 346n30; No. 72, 181, 291n22, 334n14, 341n44; No. 74, 50, 292n27; No. 75, 302, 340n32, 340n38; No. 78, 180, 334n12

Federalists (political party), 56, 63, 70–75, 252, 264, 275, 308n46, 319n53

Fein, Bruce, 328n36, 333n89

Fillmore, Millard, 278

FISA. *See* Foreign Intelligence Surveillance Act

Fisher, Louis, 6, 289nn6–7, 290nn9–10, 341–42n58, 342n68; executive privilege, 206–8, 225; and Harry S Truman, 326n19; separation of powers, 5, 170, 211, 214; and William Howard Taft, 85

Fitzpatrick, John, C., 295n26, 304n21

Florida recount (2000), 96–122; butterfly ballot, 105, 106; Florida secretary of state and, 118; National Opinion Research Center at the University of Chicago and, 118, 319n52; voting machines and, 105–7. *See also* election, of 2000; Florida Supreme Court; Harris, Katherine; *New York Times*

Florida Supreme Court, 98–101, 115–18, 315nn25–26, 319n52

Ford, Gerald, 275

Foreign Intelligence Surveillance Act (FISA), 159

France, 56–67, 70, 73, 152, 259, 269; Revolution of, 56, 264, 271, 275; use of American ports, 65

Fratto, Tony, 194

Frisch, Morton J., 283, 299n6, 313n31, 349n69, 350n74

frontlash, x, 146; definition of, 123

fundamental law, 4, 10, 16, 25, 27

Gallatin, Albert, 152

GAO. See General Accounting Office

Garsten, Bryan, 266, 345n11

General Accounting Office (GAO), 204, 222

Genet, Edmond Charles, 64–67, 70–72, 305n30, 306n36, 307–8nn40–41, 308n46

Congress, 237, 245; as criminal trial, 230; impeachable offenses, 8, 50, 51, 231, 238, 240; interpretations of, 229, 232–36, 245; managers as prosecutors, 230; other than president, 246, 297–98n38; and political common law, 246; public vs. private behavior, 239; punishment for conviction, 236; substitution for assassination, 237

Imperial Presidency, The (Schlesinger), 20, 203, 227, 292n35–36, 293n38, 338n1

impoundment, 186, 193, 194, 195
independent counsel, 12, 230, 234
Inhofe, James, 176
"institutionally partisan," 7
In re Neagle, 85
In re Yamashita, 135, 321n11, 322n40
Iran-Contra, 12, 146, 220
Iraq, 157, 175, 190, 191, 336n33; budget process and war, 195

Jackson, Andrew, 12, 28, 45, 78, 86, 91, 92, 261, 276, 277, 286; as demagogue, 275
Jackson, Jesse, 287, 317n27
Jackson, Robert H., 133, 156, 293n3, 325n6
Jacobin(s), 70, 264, 308; as demagoguery, 264
Jacobs, Lawrence, 290n13, 345n6
Jay, John, 42, 70, 214, 291n17, 311n7, 322n34, 334n10, 339n12; as chief justice, 305n30
Jefferson, Thomas: and Aaron Burr, 253, 275, 297n34; concept of presidency, 1, 12, 69, 200, 308nn42–45; as demagogue, 275; on despotism, 210; letter to Roger Weightman, 347n47; Louisiana Purchase, 152, 154; notes of early cabinet meetings, 303n20; and perogative power, 121; and Proclamation of Neutrality (1793), 57–62, 298n4, 301nn13–14, 303nn19–20; relationship with Genet, 65–71, 306n36, 307–8nn40–41
Johnson, Andrew, 229–35, 240, 246, 343n7; actions and Constitution, 241; similarity to Bill Clinton, 235

Johnson, Lyndon B., 5, 38
Johnson v. Eisentrager, 136
Johnson, William, 32
Jones, John Paul, 65
judiciary, 80, 221, 222; activism and, 115, 119, 120, 146, 318n46, 319n53; and individual rights, 242; review, 125, 126, 154, 160, 226
jus in bello, 127

Kant, Immanuel, 267
Kelley, Christopher S., 325n5, 331n68
Kennedy, Anthony, 98–118, 137
Kennedy, John F., 5
Kernell, Samuel, 290n13, 335n28, 345n6
Kerry, John, 193
Key, V.O. 260, 268
Keyes, Alan, 287
Kimel v. Board of Regents, 110
King, Rufus, 32, 70, 72, 301n13, 310n57
Kirkpatrick, David D., 333n5, 339n7
Klein, Joe, 248, 348n51
Know-Nothing Party, 278
Koenig, Louis, 289n5, 290n8
Korea, 14
Korean War, 28, 153
Krause, George A., 325n5, 332n73
Kristol, William, 311n11, 317n26
Kurland, Philip B., 289n6, 343n9

leadership: demagogue as leader, 256–58, 261, 274–75, 281–83; and the national budget 173–77; popular, 81, 82; and the president, 2, 166, 182, 213, 216–26; problems of, 6; rudders of political action, 262
Lee, Richard Henry, 48
Le Pen, Jean-Marie, as demagogue, 259
Levinson, Sanford, 289n5, 291n16
Libby, Lewis "Scooter," 204
Lichtblau, Eric, 328n35, 329n42, 339n9, 341n55
Lieber, Francis, 139
Lieberman, Joe, 105
Lincoln, Abraham, 171, 319n53; Civil War actions of, 19, 20, 46, 135, 152–53; and interbranch conflict, 242; as leader, 280; Lincoln-Douglas debates

Nixon, Richard, 5, 20, 157, 183–88, 205, 222–24, 246, 289n3, 291n22, 325n5, 327n29, 342n70, 343n11; and the budget, 183–188; as demagogue, 283; executive privilege, 222; impeachment of, 8, 9, 229, 233, 235, 283; as imperial president, 178, 203
"No Jacobin," 70, 71
Northwest Territory, 56

Obama, Barack, 162–63, 172, 199, 333n89
O'Connor, Sandra Day, 98, 102, 111–18, 204, 222
Office of Emergency Management, 153
Office of Homeland Security, 154, 166, 321n12, 327n21
Office of Management and Budget (OMB), 158, 187, 188, 335n28, 335n30
"Old Soldier, An," 298n5, 300n11
Olson, Theodore, 111
Oppenheimer, Bruce I., 334n8, 334n18
Otis, James, 270
overshooting, x, 146; and collapse, 124
oversight: after-the-fact, 176; and Florida recount, 160; and take care clause, 48, 49. *See also* Congress (U.S.)

Pacelle, Richard L., Jr, 325
"Pacificus," 55, 59, 60, 61, 62, 63, 66, 73, 74, 86, 87, 94, 293n5, 299–300nn7–9, 301n15, 302n18, 303n20, 306n37, 313n31; debate with "Helvidius," ix, 229n6, 302n16. *See also* Hamilton, Alexander; Madison, James
Paine, Thomas, 270. See also *Common Sense*
Panama Canal Zone, 86
parchment barriers, 16
pardon, 34–43, 47–52, 86, 163, 234, 294n8, 313n20, 330n60, 344n26; John Locke's conception of, 244
partisan/political regime, 6, 81, 266
Paterson, William, 32
Patriot Act. *See* USA Patriot Act
Paulson, Henry M. "Hank," 175, 197–99
"pay-as-you-go" rules, 190

Pear, Robert, 330n60, 336n35
Pelosi, Nancy, 143, 194
Pepper, Claude, 185
Pericles, 256, 258, 346n27, 347n40; as Type II demagogue, 260
perjury, 231; definition of, 234
Perot, Ross, 261, 282, 286, 287
Pevehouse, Jon C., 326n13, 332n83
Pickering, Timothy, 42
Pildes, Richard H., 104, 317n20
Pinckney, Charles, 32
Pinckney Plan, 32, 294n13
Pious, Richard, 310n2, 324nn64–65, 351
Planned Parenthood v. Casey, 103
Plato, 256, 260, 266, 346n27; *Apology,* 260; *Gorgias,* 258
Plutarch, 251, 256, 260, 262, 345n13, 347nn35–36, 347n40
political parties, 5, 69, 90, 104, 119, 168, 175, 176, 183, 187, 201, 222, 252–73, 276, 277; and demagogues, 253, 288; as gateways to presidency, 254. *See also individual parties*
politics: behavior, ix, 2, 4, 5, 10, 122, 268; systemic view of x, 7, 13
Polk, James, 319n53
Polybius, 215
populism, 72, 95, 122, 171, 286, 287, 344n5
Posner, Eric A., 331n70
Posner, Richard A., 328n39
prerogative, 59–61, 130–33, 137, 142, 148, 154, 185, 187, 225, 228, 258; criteria for the exercise of, 21; in Florida recount, 106, 117, 118; Jefferson's view, 121; John Locke and, 23; and military tribunals, 132; power and, 146, 293n8, 302n18, 313n41, 320n59, 322n35; and terrorism, 124. *See also* discretion
president/presidency: as clerkship, 213–25; connection with the people, 247; fame as motivator, 14; as lame duck, 163; ministerial party government theory, 77; modern, 2, 77, 121, 217; and national security, 242; oath of office, 10, 50, 80, 217; persuasion, 149; reliance on rhetoric, 247; rhetorical,

president/presidency (*cont.*)
248, 267; secrecy and dispatch, 214;
as steward, 26; suppressing insurrections and repelling invasions, 47;
weak vs. strong, 11–13. *See also*
Neustadt, Richard; stewardship;
and individual presidents
presidential power(s), 1–5, 14–16, 20,
24, 26, 55, 63, 73, 78, 126, 132, 149–
56, 164, 170, 200, 203, 289n3;
appointment(s), 42, 86; commander-
in-chief, 19, 33–44, 49, 124, 126, 134–
140, 151, 158, 216; as discretion, 7, 20,
23, 43–46; and duties compared, ix,
29–36, 39, 43, 49–53, 79, 83–91, 94,
180, 216, 239, 241, 243, 297n38; and
military tribunals, 129, 133; necessity
of, 16, 19; recalling Congress, 46; suspension of habeas corpus, 152; vesting
clause, 29; power to pursuade, 149.
See also executive order(s); executive
privilege; separation of powers
presidental prerogative(s), x, 10, 20–
24, 59–61, 121–124, 130, 133, 137,
142, 146, 148, 154, 185, 187, 225, 228,
258; ability to move first, 156; does
not speak directly to the people, 232;
gets last word, 165. *See also* discretion; prerogative
*Presidency in the Constitutional Order,
The* (Bessette), vii, xi, 7, 291n15, 306n,
334n15, 338n62, 339n13
primary elections. *See* election (presidential)
Printz v. United States, 120
prisoner(s) of war (POW), 126, 127, 128,
129, 131, 136, 143
Proclamation of Neutrality (1793), ix,
54, 55, 59, 60, 61, 74, 293n5
Prosper, Pierre-Richard, 124
public law, viii, 2, 4, 5, 123, 149, 170
public opinion, 29, 56, 69–75, 81, 82,
87, 148, 169, 170, 227, 288; and deliberation, 201; and demagoguery, 250–
255, 264, 267–79; and discretion,
74; and executive orders, 166, 167;
public relations, 247, 248, 265–68;
responsiveness to popular will, 212
"Publius," 258, 261

Puritanism, 263
Pyle, Christopher H., 310

Randolph, Edmund, 32, 58
Rangel, Charles, 175
Rasul v. Bush, 136, 323n44, 324n62,
331n64
Rawls, John, 348n58
Reagan, Ronald, 11, 12, 20, 132, 158,
189, 203, 204, 220–23, 291n20
Reconstruction, 231–33
Red Cross, 129, 321n13
Reform Party, 105
Rehnquist, William, 98–103, 108, 111,
115, 118, 222, 319n54
Religious Freedom Restoration Act,
320n54
Reorganization Act of 1939, 187
republican/republicanism (ideal), 1, 4,
48, 55, 68, 74, 90, 91, 97, 115–22,
206–15, 238, 244, 249, 261, 269, 275;
characteristics of, 212; and competing
demands, 243; and Florida recount
(2000), 115; as rule of law, 107; type
of government, 107
Republican (political party): as demagogic to Southerners, 278; Radical
Republicans, 231; view of *Bush v.
Gore*, 104
rescission, 191. *See also* impoundment
Ressam, Ahmed, 148
Revolutionary War (U.S.), 56, 65
rhetoric, 10, 94, 106, 107, 183, 194, 195,
201, 233, 246, 247, 252, 257, 273; as
connected to the good, 266; "count all
the votes," 105; and demagoguery,
262–269, 277–285; and principles, 9;
and stewardship, 88; working for the
good of the polity, 188
Rhetorical Presidency, The (Tulis), 7,
268
rhetorical situation, 265–73
Richardson, James D., 291n18, 291n21,
295n27, 296n30, 297n34, 326n17
Ritchie, Thomas, 345n20, 346n21,
349n66
Roberts, John, 139, 143, 204, 222,
341n57
Robertson, Pat, 287

Souter, David, 97–103, 111, 115–18, 315n3
Spain, 55, 57
Specter, Arlen, 160
Spratt, John, 193
Stanton, Edwin, 232
State of the Union, 40, 86, 180, 191, 216, 252
statesmanship, 90, 247, 249, 256, 257, 268, 278–81, 298n38; as dyad with demagoguery, 256; as leadership, 257
Stevens, John Paul, 97, 100–102, 111–18, 139–41, 315n3
stewardship, 51, 76–95, 121; definition of, 79; origin of word, 78
Stewart, Donald H., 299n46, 308n46, 309nn47–50
Stolberg, Sheryl Gay, 323n54, 338n6
Storing, Herbert J., viii, 181–83, 216, 267, 296n33, 334n15, 341nn42–43; *Essays on the Scientific Studies of Politics*, 267
Story, Joeseph, 112
Sunstein, Cass R., 108, 316n18, 317n20, 317nn28–31, 318n31, 318nn33–34, 319n54, 320nn56–57
Supreme Court (U.S.), 68, 85, 88, 164, 194, 207, 246, 282; and constitutional meaning, 5, 12, 13; and Florida recount (2000), 96–101, 106–11, 115–26, 315n1; and impeachment, 9; nominations to, 36, 44, 204; and partisanship, 97; secret deliberation, 219; separation of powers, 222, 226, 241; and terrorism, 134–48, 154, 324n62, 329n42. *See also individual court cases and justices*

Tacitus, 301n15
Taft, William Howard, 14, 158, 281, 312–13n20, 313n26, 325n6, 350n72; author of *Our Chief Magistrate and His Powers*, 84; as chief justice, 88; on executive function, 93; on foundations of the modern presidency, 76; on Jefferson's presidency, 93; on Lincoln's presidency, 92; and powers of the executive, 83, 84, 86; on presidential authority, 94
Taliban, 127, 128

Taney, Roger B., 45, 319n53
TARP. *See* Troubled Asset Relief Program
tax cuts, 175, 191
Tenure of Office Act, 232, 233
Terrorist Surveillance Program, 159
Thach, Charles C., Jr., 73, 216, 292n25, 295n23, 310n59, 327n25, 339n18
Themistocles, 256
Thomas, Clarence, 98, 102, 108, 111, 115, 118
Thucydides, 256, 346n26
Tocqueville, Alexis de, 261, 270, 347n39, 348n59, 348n61
torture, 128, 132, 142–45, 164. *See also* Guantánamo, Cuba
town meetings, 71
Treaty of Amity and Commerce, 57, 65
Troubled Asset Relief Program (TARP) 198, 199. *See also* economic crisis (2008)
Truman, Harry S, vii, 14, 20, 149, 153, 154, 170, 225, 293n4, 326n19. See also *Youngstown Sheet and Tube Co. v. Sawyer*
Tulis, Jeffrey K., 1, 149, 212, 229, 252, 268; on presidential rhetoric, 252, 268; on separation of powers, 212. See also *Rhetorical Presidency, The*
Tushnet, Mark, 109, 110, 121
two-party system, 3
Tyler, John, 277
Tyranny of the Majority, 83

UCMJ. *See* Uniform Code of Military Justice
Uniform Code of Military Justice (UCMJ), 124, 132, 133, 140, 323n49, 324n61
United States Term Limits v. Thornton, 111
United States v. Lopez, 120
United States v. Nixon, 207, 327n29, 339n21
unlawful combatants, 28, 127–31, 154, 158, 166
USA Patriot Act, 125, 126

Van Buren, Martin, 253, 254, 276–81, 341n21, 349n66